Mascha K. Brichta
»Love it or Loathe it«

**Cultural Studies** | The series is edited by Rainer Winter | Volume 39

**Mascha K. Brichta** (Dr.) is a professional media researcher and photographer. She took her Ph.D. at the University of Westminster in London, UK, and now lives in Hamburg, Germany. Her research interests include audiences, the press, and the popular media.

Mascha K. Brichta
# »Love it or Loathe it«
Audience Responses to Tabloids in the UK and Germany

[transcript]

With a foreword by Peter Dahlgren, Lund University, Sweden

**Bibliographic information published by the Deutsche Nationalbibliothek**
The Deutsche Nationalbibliothek lists this publication in the Deutsche Nationalbibliografie; detailed bibliographic data are available in the Internet at http://dnb.d-nb.de

© 2011 transcript Verlag, Bielefeld

All rights reserved. No part of this book may be reprinted or reproduced or utilized in any form or by any electronic, mechanical, or other means, now known or hereafter invented, including photocopying and recording, or in any information storage or retrieval system, without permission in writing from the publisher.

Cover concept: Kordula Röckenhaus, Bielefeld
Cover illustration & layout: Mascha Brichta
Proofread by Heather Sutherland
Typeset by Mascha K. Brichta
Printed by Majuskel Medienproduktion GmbH, Wetzlar
ISBN 978-3-8376-1885-3

Global distribution outside Germany, Austria and Switzerland:

**Transaction Publishers**
**New Brunswick (U.S.A.) and London (U.K.)**

| Transaction Publishers | Tel.: (732) 445-2280 |
| Rutgers University | Fax: (732) 445-3138 |
| 35 Berrue Circle | for orders (U.S. only): |
| Piscataway, NJ 08854 | toll free 888-999-6778 |

# Contents

**Acknowledgements** | 7

**Foreword**
by Peter Dahlgren, Lund University, Sweden | 9

**Chapter 1: Introduction**
Studying Tabloid Reading Cross-Nationally | 11
    Background Contexts | 13
    Book Outline | 17

## PART I: TABLOIDS FROM A CROSS-NATIONAL PERSPECTIVE

**Chapter 2: Similar Phenomena**
Aspects of the British *The Sun* and the German *Bild* | 21
    Profitable: *The Sun* & *Bild* as Commercial Enterprises | 21
    Controversial: Historical Events involving *The Sun* and *Bild* | 29
    Distinguishable: Editorial Characteristics of the Tabloid Press | 42
    Conclusions | 51

**Chapter 3: Differing Contexts**
Media Systems & Journalistic Traditions in Britain & Germany | 53
    Press History | 53
    Press Laws | 61
    Press Markets | 64
    Professional Traditions | 67
    Conclusions | 72

## PART II: TABLOIDS IN THE ACADEMIC DEBATE

**Chapter 4: Theorising Tabloids**
Approaches to Popular Newspapers | 77
    Implying Detrimental Effects: Traditional Approaches | 77
    Turning to 'The Other': Alternative Approaches | 87
    Conclusions | 95

**Chapter 5: Milestones Revisited**
Building on Previous Audience Studies | 97
    Providing the Ground | 97
    Newspaper Audiences in the Spotlight | 105
    Tabloid Newspaper Reception | 108
    Conclusions | 121

## PART III: TABLOIDS FROM AN AUDIENCE POINT OF VIEW

### Chapter 6: Methodology
Planning, Devising and Carrying out the Research | 125
    Comparing Nations: Conceptual Framework | 126
    Devising the Tools: the Research Design | 129
    Linking Principles and Practice: the Research Experience | 136
    Reaching Conclusions: the Data Analysis | 154
    Conclusions | 157

### Chapter 7: Balancing Tensions
The Politics of Reading Tabloids | 159
    Trivialising Tabloids: the "Light Entertainment" View | 159
    Scrutinising Tabloids: the "Flawed Journalism" View | 166
    Endorsing Tabloids: the "Social Value" View | 174
    Dismissing Tabloids: the "Ideological Imposition" View | 179
    Conclusions | 187

### Chapter 8: Fostering Engagement
The Participatory Potential of Tabloids | 191
    Access to News | 192
    A Currency of Communication | 195
    Spaces of Negotiation | 200
    Conclusions | 208

### Chapter 9: Managing Identity
Tabloids as Tools for Social Belonging | 211
    Rehearsing Nationhood: 'the Trouble with this Country' | 212
    Flagging Nationhood: Socially Accepted Contexts of Patriotism | 224
    Belonging and Distinction: Notions of Status and Class | 232
    Conclusions | 238

### Chapter 10: Tabloid Modes of Engagement | 241
    Reading Popular News | 243
    The Tabloids' "Negotiative Space" | 247
    Subtle Distinctions: Cross-National Differences | 255
    Looking Ahead: Future Perspectives | 261

### Bibliography | 265

### Appendix: Focus Group Guide (English version) | 291

# Acknowledgements

This book is an edited version of my Ph.D. dissertation in Communication, which was written at the Communication and Media Research Institute at the University of Westminster in London, UK. The study has greatly benefited from the support and inspiration of many brilliant friends and colleagues. I am enormously grateful to all of them. It would be a tremendous task to name all the names of those who deserve thanks for accompanying me on the journey to complete the Ph.D. and the writing of this book, for which there is not adequate space here. I would, however, like to express my gratitude to a few particular individuals, but I am by no means less thankful to those not explicitly named here.

This book would not have been possible without the contribution of the 104 readers of *The Sun* (in the UK) and *Bild* (in Germany), who took part in the focus groups for this research. I am indebted to them in many ways, and I would especially like to thank each and every one of them for their interest, and for educating me about their views and opinions.

My appreciation also goes to my supervisors at the University of Westminster, UK, Professor Annette Hill and Dr. Peter Goodwin, as well as Professor Jutta Röser at the Leuphana University of Lüneburg, Germany, all of whom have guided, motivated and supported me in every step of the way, at times having more confidence in me than I had in myself. I would also like to express my deepest gratitude to the two distinguished scholars who kindly examined my Ph.D. thesis. For being prepared to read through and discuss the work, and for making the VIVA such a pleasant experience, I thank Professor Peter Dahlgren from the University of Lund, Sweden and Professor Colin Sparks from the University of Westminster, UK.

I was fortunate to have received much encouragement and intellectual stimulation from colleagues and students at the University of Westminster, the Leuphana University of Lüneburg and the University of Hamburg. The thriving academic community at the University of Westminster has provided an excellent institutional home for this research, and I owe special thanks to the staff at the School of Media, Arts and Design, for awarding me a three-year doctoral scholarship and stipend. I would also like to express my gratitude to my fellow Ph.D. researchers in Germany and the UK, for their company and peer support, motivation and sympathy, comfort and congeniality.

Finally, I am hugely grateful to my parents and to Mr Smith, whom I would like to thank for their patience, for offering their unconditional love and support, and for sustaining me emotionally, spiritually and financially during the writing of this book.

# Foreword

PETER DAHLGREN, LUND UNIVERSITY, SWEDEN

The field of media and communication studies is a rather heterogeneous domain of academic endeavour; its profile is rather sprawling, and its disciplinary origins are plural. In practice today researchers will often make use of several of the many areas that the field encompasses, as well as cross established field boundaries, borrowing from and engaging with other intellectual currents. Observers have rightly noted that this "lack of discipline" yields both strengths and weaknesses: on the negative side, it courts all the usual dangers associated with eclectic efforts. On the plus side, it offers the intellectual excitement of prismatic perspectives and a broad theoretical and methodological toolkit for dealing with complex phenomena that are often difficult to adequately grasp within a single, narrow analytic framework.

This book by Mascha K. Brichta happily belongs to the admirable category that is both robustly broad in its efforts to address a multifaceted research question, and eminently successful in mastering the various intellectual building blocks necessary to do so. The result is a comparative study of excellent quality, an entirely thorough analysis of British readers of *The Sun* and German readers of *Bild*. Conceptually well-formulated and adroitly carried out, this innovative cross-national comparison of tabloid reading experiences also addresses the socio-political contexts of the two countries, their respective media landscapes, as well as the character of the two tabloids themselves. In exploring the similarities and differences between the two cases, the author illuminates how readers make sense of and evaluate the two papers – and in the process she highlights many interesting facets of the complex layers of context in which such reading takes place.

The study is founded on a fine command of the previous research on tabloids, as well as on a deep emersion in the theoretical literature and the history of debates that centre on the themes of journalism, democracy, the public sphere, political participation, popular culture and nationhood. In mobilising this broad array of literature, the author never sacrifices depth and precision. Methodologically, the study is self-aware and well-equipped. With an anchoring in the general horizons of Cultural Studies, which underscores the processes of sense-making in socio-cultural contexts, the author opts for a series of focus group interviews in each country. All methodological choices have their limitations (as she acknowledges), but the strength of this approach is that it allows for meaning to emerge collectively in live talk: it injects a dynamic dimension into the process of how the respondents talk about the respective tabloids.

Moreover – and I think it is really important to underscore this – the book is operating in several theoretical domains where there is considerable controversy: theoretical orientations are contested, conceptual definitions lack consensus, and one finds clashes over competing research approaches. Not least the author straddles what is often a very deep divide within media and communication studies – on the one hand the traditions associated with Cultural Studies, which emphasise such concerns as subjectivity, identity, and meaning-making; on the other hand, the tradition of political science and political communication. The strength of these latter currents is that they deal with politics, obviously enough, and can offer much insight regarding how its structures and dynamics function. They tend, however, not to address the kinds of themes that the Cultural Studies trajectory highlights, often leaving many unanswered questions about the deeper, subjective processes that come into play with regard to the political. Thus, with so many diverse views in circulation, it is to Brichta's credit that she is not only well-versed in these theoretical domains, understanding the issues at stake, but she can also in an elegant and convincing manner synthesise them, navigate her own course through them, and bring the reader along in her arguments and reasoning. The reader feels – and rightly so – that he or she is in good hands.

Studies that go against the grain – or the torrents – of established common sense are generally speaking the more interesting kinds to read. Here we have a prime example; this research shows that the prevailing impressions about tabloids – and their readers – are not accurate, and the author challenges her readers to rethink these matters. Tabloid newspapers, for all the issues associated with them, do in fact play a significant role in the life of democracies. This book demonstrates this in part by underscoring that a viable democracy is not just a formal system, an abstract entity of structures and processes – it also has cultural and subjective pre-conditions.

It may sound as if this is a work that will be difficult to read – that it will be a "heavy" text to deal with. I am delighted to report that Brichta writes in an accessible and engaging style. The discussion is clear and nuanced; she navigates neatly between the various theoretical positions as well as between the analytic horizons and her empirical data. In particular, the citations from the interviews and her analyses of them make for a most animated text. This is a fine piece of academic workmanship and a welcome contribution to the international research in our field.

# Chapter 1: Introduction
Studying Tabloid Reading Cross-Nationally

> Tickle the public, make 'em grin,
> The more you tickle, the more you'll win.
> Teach the public, you'll never get rich,
> You'll live like a beggar and die in a ditch.

Fleet Street journalists are said to have coined the anonymously-attributed verse above in the nineteenth century (cf. Engel 1996). Emerging at a crucial time in the development of British popular journalism, the rhyme continues to convey a central element of the controversy characterising contemporary debates and discussions about the tabloid press. Today, popular newspapers with a national reach are, indeed, often immensely profitable; they enjoy a very high circulation and wide audience shares. The papers chosen as case studies for this research, the British tabloid *The Sun* and the German popular daily *Bild* (lit: picture)[1], occupy the two top positions amongst Europe's best-selling newspapers. Outnumbering all other papers in their respective countries, they are prominent features in the daily lives of more than 7.8 million readers in Britain, and 12.5 million people in Germany (National Readership Surveys Ltd 2010; Media-Micro-Census GmbH 2010).

The tabloids' evidently huge appeal for a mass audience, consisting, in large parts, of people from social groups of lower incomes and educational levels, ignites and fuels a controversy that surrounds the popular media in both Germany and the UK. *The Sun* and *Bild* regularly exasperate and infuriate the public in both countries, attracting criticism from the academy, the journalistic profession, and other public realms such as politics, finance and law. The papers are frequently attacked

---

[1] The German tabloid is also commonly referred to as *Bild-Zeitung*; also spelled *Bildzeitung* or *BILD-Zeitung* (lit: picture newspaper). However, I will confine myself to using the term *Bild* throughout this book, for such is the name displayed on the paper's front page.

for their legal and ethical flaws of reporting, their potential impact on readers' political opinion formation, and their general "lack" of democratic functions, amongst other reasons. In line with perceptions of a trend towards a 'tabloidization' of the media, the most notable drift of thinking in the field is channelled towards devaluing popular newspapers in the context of democratic theory. Revolving around a dismissal of tabloid news values and narrative strategies, such approaches regard popular papers and 'tabloidized' content as a threat to the rational public sphere. The wishful thinking implied in this interpretation of the genre may be exemplified by early arguments aired by Klaus Weber(1978: 282), who demanded that society needs to work towards making tabloid newspapers appear 'unnecessary and unwanted throughout' [author's translation][2].

Why, then, study tabloid newspapers? And why study their audiences? To begin with, there is a mismatch between the traditionally prominent position of the press in media theory, and the fact that it still represents an under-researched field in comparison to that of television, which has attracted many scholars. Moreover, the wealth of theories and textual analyses of the genre of popular news and journalism exist in inverse proportion to the rather few academic studies foregrounding an audience point of view – albeit a recently more pronounced academic interest in the popular media and its audience can be noted. Yet, while the phenomenon of 'tabloidization' seems to spread, there is a continuous decline in newspaper readership around the world. Empirical evidence regarding what it is that people want from newspapers, therefore, seems imperative, particularly in light of debates about whether or not printed news have a future at all (cf., for instance, the special issue of *Journalism Studies* (2008) on *The Future of Newspapers*). Two classics in the newspaper genre, *The Sun* and *Bild*, shall be recognised as important cultural products, worthy of academic attention by this study. Examining the perspective of the audience appears truly fascinating; such an approach can provide valuable and timely empirical evidence for the social, cultural and personal significance of popular papers in two contemporary Western societies, shedding a little light on some of the reasons for the success, or failure, of modern newspapers.

Hence, this study focuses on exploring, understanding and comparing audience responses and reading experiences of tabloid newspapers in two different countries. In investigating the reception of the *The Sun* and *Bild* cross-nationally, the research builds on findings from a previous small-scale reception study of *Bild* (Brichta 2002), which drew attention to the crucial relationship between the German tabloid's largely unfavourable social reputation and readers' interpretations of the paper. While acknowledging audiences as 'active' producers of meaning, this more recent study has been carried out assuming that public discourses about popular

---

2  I am translating all German quotes used in this book into English, but will refrain from signalling my authorship of the translation each time, in the interest of readability.

newspapers have some impact on the way they are read. However, as public opinion about tabloids presumably exists in relation to a nation's specific media system, journalistic and, indeed, academic tradition, the diverse social, cultural and historical backgrounds of Britain and Germany provide a tantalising contextual framework for the cross-national comparison of tabloid reading experiences.

## BACKGROUND CONTEXTS

### Cross-National Framework

The objects of comparison, the two national tabloids *The Sun* and *Bild*, can be regarded as similar phenomena in differing contexts, thus creating a potentially fruitful setting for a cross-national comparative study. Both newspapers share a number of formal characteristics typical of the genre, relating to their style features, content preferences and narrative strategies. The papers each enjoy a comfortable market position, serving a huge readership and claiming large shares of the less-educated lower-income audience sections. Moreover, *The Sun* and *Bild* both look back on a turbulent history, and are equally controversial in their respective countries.

While these aspects establish the 'conceptual equivalence' (Edelstein 1982: 15) of the research objects, the two tabloids exist in diverse social and cultural settings, which determine key dimensions of national variance. Britain and Germany, despite sharing a number of similarities, differ in key aspects relating to their historical development, their media systems and journalistic traditions, and their contemporary tabloid marketplace. For instance, the diverse histories of the press in Britain and Germany are notable, particularly the various developments of popular journalism and tabloid newspapers. Such formats had long been established in the UK before they emerged in Germany for the first time. As a result of these diverse developments, the two contemporary tabloid marketplaces also differ considerably. The British newspaper market overall is dominated by *national* tabloids, with a particular feature being strong competition and concentration in the London area. In contrast, *Bild* is the only national tabloid in Germany and there is far less competition among the national titles, as a result of the country's long-standing tradition favouring local newspapers and home delivery. Adding to these structural differences, the legal conditions of journalism differ in Britain and Germany. UK journalists enjoy more freedom in terms of what, whom and when to publish; German journalists have to abide by stricter legal protections regarding their subjects' privacy. At the same time, journalists in the UK are at a disadvantage compared to their German colleagues when it comes to professional privileges. As a result, the British press has been described as being more 'ruthless' than its German counterpart (Esser

1999: 303). It would seem that such differences are of significance to the way readers in both countries understand and evaluate tabloids. Yet, the similarities between *The Sun* and *Bild*, conversely, suggest that some aspects of the reading experience may, indeed, be comparable. This research therefore aims to generate insights concerning the impact of different social and cultural backgrounds on the way readers interpret popular newspapers.

## Theoretical Approach

Studying tabloid newspapers and their audiences involves facing the challenging task of situating the research within a rather polarised debate. Essentially, there are two major interpretations of popular newspapers that scholars have employed in recent years. The first deals with tabloids as a threat to society and democracy, reflecting dominant intellectual and political concerns entailed in classic Frankfurt School positions relating to popular culture. Within this well-rehearsed canon of criticism, the discussions amongst British and German scholars and practitioners show similar agendas. The debate in the US and the UK, in particular, has branched out towards a lament relating to perceived changes in reporting considered to be heading in the direction of a 'tabloidization' of media content. Scholars particularly foreground concerns about a 'dumbing-down' of journalistic standards (cf., for instance, Blumler 1999; Brants 1998; Esser 1999; Marlow 2002, Bromley 1998). Similar issues have been addressed in Germany; however, the tabloid *Bild*, as the country's only national tabloid, is predominantly placed as the centre of attention in these discussions. A wide range of textual analyses, both ancient and more recent, have pronounced *Bild*'s reporting unsatisfactory in the context of journalistic quality (cf., for instance, Droege 1968; Link 1986; Jäger 1993; Büscher 1996; Schirmer 2001; Jogschies 2001; Virchow 2008). Other works have lamented reporters' and editors' ruthless behaviour, claiming they disregard ethical principles and practices, and arguing for a greater responsibility in the making of *Bild* and its treatment of people (cf., for instance, Küchenhoff and Keppler 1972; Wallraff 1977, 1979, 1981; Wende 1990; Ionescu 1996; Minzberg 1999). Further strands of argumentation, in both the UK and Germany, consider the popular press as an instrument for swaying mass opinions. Scholars taking this view have raised serious concerns about the papers' impact on audiences' political opinion-formation, and express massive discomfort with the papers' ideologies (cf., for instance, Bechmann et al. 1979; Albrecht 1982; Rust 1984; Bebber 1997; Gehrs 2006; *The Sun*'s political influence is covered by Linton 1995; Curtice 1999; Black 2002; and Douglas 2004, 2005).

Some of these notions clearly need to be considered carefully when thinking about the relationship between tabloid newspapers and their readers, and about the papers' role in society. Concerns about perceived changes in and to the media, such as those addressed in the 'tabloidization' argument for instance, highlight crucial issues relating to the structure of media industries along capitalist lines of production and consumption. Likewise, the debate raises valid questions about the power and responsibility of popular red-tops and huge media enterprises, such as the publishing houses *News Corp* and *Axel Springer AG*. Still, common to most of these works are rather pessimistic conclusions about the potentially harmful effects of tabloid reporting on readers and democracy. A strong devaluation of the popular media is implied in these views, showing distinct parallels to Adorno and Horkheimer's early perspective that condemned the popular media as socially, politically and culturally worthless (1972). In the context of binary oppositions of "high" and "low" culture, a rather passive view of the audience emerges from this approach. Drawing on certain beliefs regarding how information and learning works, and on whom it works, these approaches, indeed, entail a rather 'disabling perspective' of the popular media and their audience (Corner and Pels 2003: 4; cf. also Storey 1993; Gauntlett 2008: 22 pp.) However, these conceptions do not account for the potential functions, uses and enjoyments readers may derive from the genre.

Challenging such uniformly depreciative theories about the role of the popular media in society, the polar opposite of these views can be traced back to an intellectual tradition that has come to be called 'Cultural Studies'. There is some convergence of British media studies and Cultural Studies, as many of the theoretical and methodological approaches within media studies tend to be drawn from, and shared with, Cultural Studies and vice versa. This book is firmly set in an overlap between these two disciplines. Yet, as the study is also situated within the domain of media consumption and media audiences, the readership research primarily draws on the paradigms emerging from the form of qualitative audience studies stemming from the Cultural Studies tradition (cf. Jensen 1991). One of the most important principles worth noting here includes, above all, the notion of the 'active audience'. This view of audiences as active with regards to their meaning-construction from media texts provides an essential intellectual framework for the research. Likewise, informing my approach is the re-evaluation of popular culture as a form of lived, everyday 'way of life', for entertainment and 'the trivial' are self-evident elements of culture from a Cultural Studies point of view (cf. Jäckel and Peter 1997; Turner 2003; Storey 1993). These ideas have been drawn on and developed extensively over the past 20 years or so, particularly by British and US-American scholars; they contribute to a considerable body of works on the study of popular culture. In comparison, Cultural Studies' drifts of thinking have long been neglected by German media researchers, and have only recently been placed on the academic agenda. Yet, as indicated, this book subscribes to the view that the popular media should be granted some social and cultural value, adding to traditional functions of the media (such as informing citizens and providing for participation within the rational public sphere), rather than impeding these purposes. Some of these issues seem particularly worth investigating from the point of view of audiences in Germany and the UK; in particular notions concerning the role of the popular media in the construction of belonging and community, as expressed in citizenship, social participation and collective identity formations.

## Questions

This study is guided by the desire to examine the specificities and idiosyncrasies of experiences and understandings of tabloid newspapers in two different countries, taking as case studies the two national tabloids *The Sun* and *Bild*. The research aims to contribute to the on-going debate about tabloid news values; to fill the knowledge gap regarding the reception of tabloid newspapers; to provide an account of different and shared characteristics in the UK and Germany, and to offer explanations for the similarities and differences identified by the study. Hence, the research enquiries comprise two sets of key questions:

### I. Exploring the tabloid reading experience
- How do tabloid readers make sense of reading *The Sun* and *Bild*?
- How do audience members evaluate the papers?

### II. Comparing tabloid reading cross-nationally
- How do tabloid readers in the UK and Germany differ in the way they make sense of tabloids and evaluate them? How can such differences be explained in relation to the specific social and cultural contexts in either country?
- What aspects of the British and German tabloid reading experience are similar, and how can such similarities be explained?

Issues to consider in relation to the first broad field of enquiry concern various questions relating to how readers approach and make sense of the tabloids and their texts. For instance, then, this text explores how audiences assess tabloid reporting in relation to the journalistic ideal in each country, and what they make of the contradictions embedded in the genre. I was also intrigued to investigate if reading tabloids is ultimately translated into the expression of civic, cultural or other forms of citizenship; and I examine here in what ways the papers fit in with notions of belonging and identity. Moreover, I was guided by the desire to explore if the papers' social reputation "rubs off" on readers' attitudes, and if so, what that means to the reading experience; comments on this also feature in this book.

The second field of enquiry relates to the cross-national comparison. I explore what similarities and differences can be observed between British and German readers' modes of engagement with tabloids, asking if these relate back to individual traditions in either country. The study seeks to examine the impact of *The Sun* and *Bild*'s similarities on the reading experience, while finding out in what ways the varying media systems and journalistic cultures in Germany and the UK influence readers' views. For instance, I asked if tabloids are more accepted socially in the UK, due to their longer tradition and dominance on the market. Likewise, can stronger ethical judgements be observed among German readers, as a result of the country's detailed press laws and journalists' generally less aggressive approach to researching and reporting? And, what are the implications of the fact that the papers state their political opinions rather differently (explicitly in the UK, implicitly in Germany)?

## Method

This book is concerned with examining collective processes of meaning creation, whilst paying particular attention to the way in which this is negotiated in a larger group setting. Aiming to reproduce social reality, focus group discussions were chosen as the method of data collection. In total, 104 adults drawn from diverse backgrounds participated in 18 focus groups spread across the two countries, of which 12 groups were selected for detailed analysis. Participants were asked about their likes and dislikes regarding the chosen papers, and were invited to discuss particular aspects of *The Sun* or *Bild*. Three distinct front pages from the tabloids were introduced to the respondents in either country, in order to direct the discussion towards specific themes, such as notions of nationhood, politics, and scandal. The extensive qualitative data collected allowed a detailed investigation of the research questions, and provided a wealth of fascinating material to draw on in the analysis and interpretation of the results.

## BOOK OUTLINE

The book consists of ten chapters, which are divided into three principal sections. I begin by setting the scene for the cross-national comparison in the first section, unfolding the conceptual comparative framework for the research and explaining my argument about *The Sun* and *Bild* as similar phenomena in differing contexts. Chapter 2 establishes the 'conceptual equivalence' of my research objects. Reviewing key facts relating to *The Sun* and *Bild*'s commercial, historic, social and editorial contexts, a range of commonalities between the two papers are highlighted. Chapter 3, then, brings to light key dimensions of variance through the comparison of Britain and Germany, with regard to their historic, legal and economic contexts.

The second section of the book investigates the academic debate relating to tabloids by reviewing dominant approaches to popular newspapers and related media formats in Britain and Germany. Chapter 4 represents the first half of the literature review. It maps existing theoretical approaches to the genre and establishes the epistemological and theoretical beliefs that underpin my investigation of readership responses; traditional and alternative perspectives on popular journalism in Germany and the UK are discussed. The subsequent Chapter 5 represents a detailed résumé of previous studies in the field of qualitative audience research and tabloid newspaper reception, highlighting what has been done and, indeed, what needs to be done.

Section three of this book contains the primary readership research. It considers tabloids from an audience point of view. The first chapter in this section, Chapter 6, marks a detailed explanation of my research methodology; an explanation of the choices made to meet the twin criteria of validity and reliability is offered, as is justification for the value and logic of the study's approach. I discuss the premises, and describe the steps leading to the realisation of the project. The following three chapters deal with a discussion of the research findings. The results have been grouped around key questions and aspects identified in the analysis of the data. Chapter 7 is concerned with the tensions and contradictions surrounding the reception. It maps generic and nationally-variant audience responses to *The Sun* and *Bild*, unfolding four principal modes of engagement with popular newspapers and highlighting similarities and differences surrounding the tabloid reading experience in Germany and the UK. The central theme of the following two chapters is to explore the role of popular newspapers in contemporary Western society. Examining the potential of tabloids to facilitate significant notions of inclusion, sharing, belonging and identification, my arguments are divided into two parts. Chapter 8 attends to important ways in which popular newspapers foster communicative, social, and cultural participation by activating and stimulating their readers. Chapter 9 takes a closer look at tabloids as tools for social belonging, discussing the papers' ability to contribute to notions of community and identity. Finally, the concluding Chapter 10 reflects on the study's key findings and discusses the role of the popular press in contemporary Western society. I consider the papers' potential to stimulate readers through their idiosyncratic style features and narrative strategies; draw attention to the "negotiative space" generated by tabloids; explain the "vision of the good and bad" that readers' develop in response to the papers' reporting, and emphasise popular papers' significance to readers' social and cultural identity formations.

# Part I

# Tabloids from a Cross-National Perspective

# Chapter 2: Similar Phenomena
Aspects of the British *The Sun* and the German *Bild*

Setting the scene for the cross-national comparison, this chapter establishes the 'conceptual equivalence' (Edelstein 1982: 15) of the research objects of this study, the two national daily tabloids *The Sun* and *Bild*. The papers are distributed in different countries, drawing on and contributing to diverse national and cultural contexts. However, although they hardly resemble each other entirely, they can be regarded as similar phenomena. Reviewing key facts relating to the tabloids' commercial, historic, social and editorial contexts, this chapter highlights a range of commonalities between the papers, and points out some aspects of variation. Important commonalities include, for instance, the dominant market position, readership composition, controversial histories and social reputation, as well as a set of typical tabloid style features, which both papers share.

A wider aim of this chapter is to provide for a profound understanding of the characteristics of the genre of popular newspapers in general, and the two tabloids *The Sun* and *Bild*, in particular. Examining the papers from various perspectives, this chapter considers major controversies and reviews important elements of tabloid journalism that frame the discussion of audience responses in the third section of this book.

## PROFITABLE:
## *THE SUN* & *BILD* AS COMMERCIAL ENTERPRISES

Both *The Sun* and *Bild* are commercial commodities existing in market-driven societies. As such, their primary aim is to sell and to make profit. This section examines a range of formal aspects relating to the tabloids' market positions and appearances, their publishers, their production and distribution schemes, their editorial staff, as well as their readership composition. Thus, important commercial and economic similarities between the two print outlets are pointed out.

## Circulation & Share

An obvious commonality between *The Sun* and *Bild* relates to the papers' comfortable market positions. Despite declining sales in the entire daily sector, the two tabloids remain Germany's and the UK's circulation pace-setters. They occupy top positions in the line-up of Europe's highest-selling daily national newspapers (World Association of Newspapers and News Publishers 2009). At the time of writing, 3.1 million copies of *Bild* and 3.0 million copies of *The Sun* are sold daily Monday to Saturday. Their Sunday sisters (each with a slightly different style and separate editors) are similarly profitable. *Bild am Sonntag* (lit: picture on Sunday) has a circulation of 1.7 million, and *The Sun*'s Sunday equivalent, *News of the World*, sells 2.9 million copies (cf. ABC 2010; IVW 2010). What is more, *Bild* and *The Sun* outnumber all other print outlets in Germany and the UK, in terms of their audience shares. *Bild* apparently reaches 12.5 million people every day, Monday to Saturday (Media-Micro-Census GmbH 2010), and *The Sun* is read by 7.8 million people (National Readership Surveys Ltd 2010).

## Market Appearance

In Germany, tabloids are commonly referred to as 'boulevard' newspapers, indicating their primary selling technique on the street. Most of *The Sun* and *Bild*'s circulations are, indeed, sold at newsagents, news-stands and in shops. Stefan Schirmer (2001: 27) remarks that popular papers are subject to what he terms the 'economic imperative of maximum saleability'. However, in Germany the selling technique "on the boulevard" is exclusive to tabloids (cf. Bruck and Stocker 1996: 16), in contrast to most other German dailies – particularly broadsheets – to which people can take out subscriptions in order to have them delivered to their home every morning (cf. Chapter 3). In 2004, *Bild* introduced an optional subscription and home delivery offer; readers, however, did not seem to take to this very well. In 2010, only about one percent of the daily circulation was distributed via home delivery (IVW 2010).

With regard to matters of formal appearance, Colin Sparks observes that 'there is an obvious and commonsense meaning to the term 'tabloid': it refers to a particular size and shape of a newspaper' (2000: 10). Yet, an apparent distinction between *The Sun* and its German counterpart springs to mind in relation to this statement: *Bild* may be tabloid in style, but it is published in a rather large shape, the so-called 'nordic format' (57 x 40 cm/22.4 x 15.7 inches), still the original size introduced by Axel Springer when he first published the paper in 1952. A few years ago, the *Axel Springer AG* introduced plans to publish an additional "tabloid-sized" version of *Bild* (cf. www.bild.de/BILD/regional/muenchen/dpa/2009/06/12/bild-macht-in-muenchen-den-tabloidversuch.html), which has, however, not been hugely successful. Unlike the German red-top, *The Sun*'s smaller size is considerably easier to handle. Published in the 'half broadsheet' format (30 x 37.5 cm/1.18 x 1.2 inches), it is truly tabloid in shape.

Both *The Sun* and *Bild* are relatively inexpensive in comparison to other British and German newspapers. In 2007, *The Sun* lowered its price to 20 pence in London, remaining at 30p elsewhere in the UK. This cut made it the cheapest national newspaper in the capital, alongside the *Daily Star*. Meanwhile, however, the cover price has been raised again to 25p in London, and 35p elsewhere in the UK. A copy of *Bild* currently costs between 50 and 70 Euro cents (about 45-60p), depending on the region of Germany in which it is sold. Despite a rise in price as of May 2011, *Bild* is still the cheapest national daily in Germany; only a few regional tabloids, such as the *Hamburger Morgenpost*, match its price. A key difference between the two papers is indicated here. *Bild* is Germany's only national tabloid, while *The Sun* has many rivals. This aspect is resumed in Chapter 3, which considers characteristics of the British and German press markets.

## Publishing Houses

*The Sun* and *Bild* are each part of the portfolio of huge publishing houses. In Britain, *The Sun* is published by *News International Ltd.*, a subsidiary company of the media conglomerate *News Corporation*, which ranks among the world's ten largest media enterprises. The company's major titles include the daily broadsheet *The Times*, the weekly *Sunday Times*, the tabloid *The Sun* and its Sunday sister *News of the World*. Aside from this, Australian-born Rupert Murdoch, the company's chairman, chief executive officer and founder, owns a large range of media companies, including magazine and book publishers, movie production businesses, television channels plus many more. Murdoch is generally regarded a highly controversial media mogul who maintains a strong grip on the market, and who aspires to make significant impact through his news publications (cf. Grimberg 2002; Esser 1998; also cf. my discussion of *The Sun*'s history, page 33).

*Bild* is published in Germany by the *Axel Springer AG*. Not as huge as *News Corporation Ltd.*, but still ranking among the world's 50 largest media companies (cf. Hachmeister and Rager 2005), the *Axel Springer AG* can clearly be considered a "big player" within the German media landscape. Certainly, the company has powerful agenda-setting potential, as it publishes two of the five national German newspapers: the tabloid *Bild* and the mid-market broadsheet *Welt*. Like Rupert Murdoch, the late German company founder Axel Cäsar Springer used to be the country's dominant newspaper owner. He was also a highly controversial figure until his death in September 1985. Springer tried, and partly succeeded, to interfere with party politics by using *Bild*'s powerful voice (cf. the section on the history of

*Bild*, p. 34). Today, the tabloid and its various mono-themed sisters, such as *Auto Bild, Computer Bild, Computer Bild Spiele, Sport Bild* and *Bild der Frau, Tier Bild, Reise Bild, Bildwoche* and *Gesundheitsbild*, constitute a highly successful brand, and represent the publisher's 'financial cart horse' (Minzberg 1999: 36). Both, *News International Ltd.* and the *Axel Springer AG*, along with their chief executives, continuously polarise public opinion in both countries and regularly ignite debates over the concentration of ownership, agenda-setting powers, political influence, and editorial and ethical responsibilities.

## Production & Distribution

Two national tabloids, *The Sun* and *Bild* are distributed to selling points across the country. *Bild*'s makers even claim that, geographically speaking, the tabloid is the most easily accessible newspaper in Germany. As a result of a cleverly devised distribution scheme, *Axel Springer AG* maintains that anyone in Germany can get hold of a copy of *Bild* within no more than, allegedly, seven walking minutes of their home, at one of the paper's 110,000 points of sale. A special edition of *Bild* is also printed and distributed in several favoured German holiday destinations, such as Spain, Italy, Greece and Turkey (cf. Axel Springer AG (2000); Höke 2004). *The Sun* is produced in Wapping (London) and Knowsley (Liverpool), and is likewise distributed across most parts of Great Britain (Höke 2004: 139).

The headquarters of *Bild* have long been based in Hamburg, until 2008 when the paper relocated to Germany's capital, Berlin. However, a large number of local editorial offices are spread across the entire country. These offices work on the local content of the paper. According to *Axel Springer AG*'s sales promotion, *Bild* is currently published in 25 different regional versions (http://www.axelspringer-mediapilot.de/portrait/*Bild*-Regional-BILD-REGIONAL_723232.html). The number apparently varies depending on who is asked; Susanne Höke (2004: 145), for example, basing much of her argumentation on interviews with editors, speaks of 36 regional editions. However many, all of *Bild*'s editions contain a number of identical set pages, plus an individual regional section (cf. also p. 46).

Such a strongly regionalised structure is not echoed by *The Sun*. Indeed, it is rather uncommon in the British newspaper landscape, which can more clearly be separated into national and local titles (Tunstall 1996; also cf. Chapter 3). A copy of *The Sun* bought in London, therefore, matches a copy bought in Liverpool on the same day. However, there is some geographic variation in the UK; while an identical version of *The Sun* is available in England, Wales and Northern Ireland, a Scottish edition based in Glasgow is published in Scotland. Known as *The Scottish Sun*, it has an average circulation of 344,000 (cf. www.abc.org.uk, August 2010). Likewise, an Irish edition based in Dublin is published in the Republic of Ireland. *The*

*Irish Sun* sells about 87,000 copies daily. Both, *The Scottish* and *Irish Sun* carry much of the content of the English edition, but they include additional regional coverage.

### Editorial Staff

The current chief editor of *Bild*, Kai Diekmann, has been in office since 2001. Ulrike Dulinski (2003: 295 pp.) emphasises the traditionally strong impact of *Bild*'s chief editors, who have always been associated with specific events in the history of the tabloid and the paper's editorial stance. According to Dulinski (ibid) and Höke (2004), approximately 800 to 1,000 people work in the editorial production, administration and layout of *Bild*. Their working routines exemplify the German model of the journalist as an "all-rounder"; individual journalists write as well as edit reports, and occasionally they even lay-out the paper (cf. Höke 2004: 35; Dulinski 2003: 201; Esser 1998: 351; also cf. Chapter 3).

Jeremy Tunstall claims that in Britain, tabloid editors are, likewise, involved in a wide range of activities within the process of newspaper-making. Emphasising the significance of editors today, he asserts that they 'can be compared to prima donnas, or orchestra conductors, or film directors' (ibid 1996: 118). Since September 2009, the editor of *The Sun* has been Dominic Mohan. Höke (2004: 139) asserts that about 320 salaried journalists work for the British tabloid, alongside several freelancers and trainees. Their tasks are strictly divided by the 'copy flow' principle (Esser 1998: 408 pp.); a reporter is merely responsible for researching and writing up facts, while reports focussing on opinion are written by leader-writers, commentators or columnists.

### Readership Composition

The overall composition of the *The Sun* and *Bild*'s readership is rather similar, particularly with regard to the categories of sex, occupation and age (leaving aside some national variation concerning a somewhat younger core readership of *The Sun*). Both papers are frequently identified as working-class papers (cf. for instance, Seymour-Ure 2001), reflecting the fact that the largest proportion of readers can be allocated to the socio-economic categories C2, D and E.

However, it is important to note that there is not *one* typical tabloid reader. The data suggests that the tabloids' readerships include a wide range of audience members with highly varied socio-economic characteristics (cf. also Bird 1992; Höke 2004; Brichta 2002). For instance, although less than 10 per cent of all readers stem from categories A and B, their total number is significant. If we consider *Bild*'s readership, in the region of 900,000 well-educated, and presumably affluent, Germans read the paper. This may represent a small percentage of the overall readership, but if we compare the total number to that of the readership of the German broadsheet *Süddeutsche Zeitung (SZ)*, the figure appears impressive. With a circulation of 439,000, *SZ* is Germany's best-selling broadsheet (Media-Micro-Census GmbH 2010). It reaches 1.2 million readers every day. Of these 1.2 million, roughly 276,000 belong to Germany's "top-class" target group, characterised by high educational qualifications, upper-managerial positions and incomes that are considerably higher than average (cf. LAE – Leseranalyse Entscheidungsträger e.V. 2009). Yet, the total number of affluent *Bild* readers is still higher than the total number of *SZ* readers in that category. Although it needs to be acknowledged that the various readership analyses available in each country are difficult to compare (cf. Chapter 6, p. 136), it is noteworthy that the audiences of both *The Sun* and *Bild* are spread across the entire British and German population. The two tables that follow exemplify this, by comparing the basic demographic categories of the two newspapers' readerships.

Table 1: Readership Composition of The Sun and Bild: Sex & Age

|   |   | The Sun | | Bild | |
|---|---|---|---|---|---|
|   |   | Share (in %) | Total (in mil) | Share (in %) | Total (in mil) |
| Total readership | | 15.5 | 7.8 | 17.8 | 12.5 |
| **Sex** | Male | 21.8 | 5.0 | 23.0 | 7.9 |
|   | Female | 15.7 | 3.8 | 12.7 | 4.6 |
| **Age** | 15-19 (UK) 14-19 (Ger) | 22.4 | 0.8 | 10.3 | 0.5 |
|   | 20-29 | 22.8 | 1.7 | 18.0 | 1.8 |
|   | 30-39 | 24.4 | 2.0 | 19.7 | 2.0 |
|   | 40-49 | 18.0 | 1.5 | 19.9 | 2.7 |
|   | 50-59 | 16.3 | 1.2 | 19.5 | 2.2 |
|   | 60-69 | 14.2 | 0.8 | 18.5 | 1.7 |
|   | 70+ | 12.4 | 0.8 | 14.4 | 1.6 |

*Table 2: Readership Composition of* The Sun *and* Bild: *Occupational Groups*

|  |  | The Sun | | Bild | |
|---|---|---|---|---|---|
|  |  | Share (in %) | Total (in mil) | Share (in %) | Total (in mil) |
| **British occupational categories (used by the *NRS*)** | **German occupational categories (used by the *ma*)** | | | | |
| **Social grade A** 'upper middle class'; higher managerial, administrative or professional | | 7.0 | 0.1 | | |
| | Company owners, freelancers, self-employed farmers | | | 12.9 | 0.9 |
| **Social grade B** 'middle class'; intermediate managerial, administrative or professional | | 8.1 | 0.8 | | |
| | Employees and clerks in managerial positions | | | 10.8 | 0.7 |
| **Social grade C1** 'lower middle class'; supervisory or clerical and junior managerial, administrative or professional | 'Other' (non-managerial) employees and clerks | 16.6 | 2.3 | 14.7 | 4.5 |

*Table 2: Readership Composition of* The Sun *and* Bild: *Occupational Groups (continued)*

|  |  | The Sun | | Bild | |
| --- | --- | --- | --- | --- | --- |
|  |  | Share (in %) | Total (in mil) | Share (in %) | Total (in mil) |
| **British occupational categories (used by the *NRS*)** | **German occupational categories (used by the *ma*)** |  |  |  |  |
| **Social grade C2** 'skilled working class'; skilled manual workers | Skilled workers | 26.1 | 2.6 | 25.5 | 4.4 |
| **Social grade D** 'working class'; semi and unskilled manual workers | 'Other' workers | 24.1 | 2.1 | 24.8 | 2.0 |
| **Social grade E** 'those at the lowest level of subsistence'; state pensioners or widows (no other earner), casual or lowest grade workers |  | 21.2 | 0.9 |  |  |
|  | Unemployed, pupils, students, trainees, n/a |  |  | 22.6 | 1.5 |

The data used in the two tables above relate to the *ma 2010 Presse II* (cf. Media-Micro-Census GmbH 2010), and the *NRS Readership Estimates* from June 2010 (cf. National Readership Surveys Ltd 2010). All figures are based on the 14+ population in Germany (70.5 million), and the 15+ population in the UK (49.8 million).

# Controversial:
# Historical Events Involving *The Sun* and *Bild*

Both *The Sun* and *Bild* can be said to have intensified popular journalism in both countries (cf. Chapter 3, p. 57). In the following section, a review of important events relating to the specific histories of *The Sun* and *Bild* is offered, demonstrating that comparable development routes can be identified. Moreover, part of the controversy surrounding the two tabloids stems from some of the events described here, events that continue to impact upon the way the papers are viewed today.

## The British *Sun*

### *The Sun*'s Early Years: Murdoch's Takeover

In its current appearance, *The Sun* was first published on 17 November 1969. The date marked the second re-launch of the paper within five years, for the paper was initially launched as a 'mid-market daily aimed at young educated readers' (Rooney 2000: 92)on 15 September 1964. Replacing the *Daily Herald*, a trade union broadsheet that had lost many readers over the years, *The Sun* that existed prior to 1969 more or less continued the position of the then market leader and established Labour tabloid, the *Daily Mirror* (cf. Douglas 2004). Matthew Engel (1996: 250) notes that is 'usually remembered as a terrible paper'; as a result, circulation and advertising revenues fell quickly away.

*The Sun* that we know today, having celebrated its 40$^{th}$ anniversary in November 2009, is closely connected to Rupert Murdoch's purchase of the paper in 1969. The new Australian owner had already acquired the weekly *News of the World*, which today is recognised as the Sunday sister of *The Sun*. Murdoch had a vision for the then 48-page *Sun*. He re-launched it as a tabloid, as 'The paper that cares about people. About the kind of world we live in.' (Griffiths 2006: 361). Torin Douglas (2004) remarks on the BBC News website that *The Sun* 'rewrote the tabloid rulebook'. Now a direct competitor to the *Daily Mirror*, Murdoch turned *The Sun* into an entirely new newspaper. Although a number of *Mirror* features were utilised, (such as the general layout, the title's red appearance, as well as some of the regular columns), *The Sun* is seen to have greatly intensified the British tabloid's trend towards 'sex, sport and sensation' (ibid), thereby having 'invented or reinvented contemporary tabloid journalism' (Tunstall 1996: 13).

The first two long-serving editors of *The Sun*, Larry Lamb (serving – with some interruption – from 1969-1980) and Kelvin MacKenzie (1981-1994), helped to establish the tabloid's lucrative 'unique, jocular, venomous style' (Tunstall 1996: 13). Highly profitable, the first edition of Murdoch's paper sold more than one million copies. After twelve months, circulation figures had doubled; after four years, *The*

*Sun* sold more than three million copies (Höke 2004: 138). In 1978, with sales of four million, it overtook the *Daily Mirror* and became the UK's top-selling daily newspaper (cf. Douglas 2004) – a position it has maintained for more than 30 years now. A year after it was first published, a picture of a topless girl appeared in the paper for the first time. A more flippant version of the bikini-clad girls frequently appearing on its rivals' pages, *The Sun*'s page three soon became a 'social institution' (Douglas 2004).

## *The Sun* in the Eighties: Thatcherism, 'Death' of Fleet Street, 'Hamster-Eating' & Hillsborough

Roy Greenslade (2009) of *The Guardian* describes the 1980s as 'something of a 'wild west' period' for the tabloid. In terms of political direction, Engel (1996: 263) identifies many 'twists and turns' in *The Sun*'s editorial stance. Although *The Sun* has earned a reputation for proclaiming the political position of its owner, Engel maintains that the tabloid's endorsement of whatever political direction has always been a sales-driven consequence relating to whichever party was most likely to win a general election. In its early years, *The Sun* continued on its inherited path and supported Labour Prime Minister Harold Wilson. However, it switched allegiances when he lost to support his Conservative (Tory) successor, later intensely endorsing Margaret Thatcher (Douglas 2004). A famous *Sun* headline passing into language was 'Crisis? What Crisis?', on 11 January 1979, during the 1978-1979 'Winter of Discontent' – a Shakespearean phrase likewise made popular by *Sun* editor Larry Lamb in an editorial. The paper's 'Crisis? What Crisis?' line was not new, for it also referred to the title of the rock band Supertramp's fourth album released in 1975, but it was, nevertheless, met with some public enthusiasm. The phrase scornfully ridiculed Labour Prime Minister Jim Callaghan's reaction to several trade union strikes over the government's attempt to control inflation by freezing pay rises in the public sector, which had lead (amongst other things) to mounting rubbish in the streets (BBC News 2000). A rather unambiguous stance, *The Sun*'s headline on 3 May 1979, then, read 'Vote Tory this time'. In fact, the tabloid is seen to have helped bring down the Labour government in 1979 (cf. ibid).

Tory Prime Minister Margaret Thatcher (who served 1979-1990) is, in particular, commonly regarded as 'Mr. Murdoch's political friend' (Tunstall 1996: 13). Indeed, Thatcher enjoyed strong support from *The Sun*. In 1982, during the Falklands War between Argentina and the UK, editor Kelvin MacKenzie (1981-1994) and his team became 'cheerleader[s] for Mrs Thatcher' (Douglas 2004; also cf. Engel 1996: 266 pp.) *The Sun* ran some of its most famous and most controversial headlines during this period. When the Thatcher government rejected Argentina's peace move, the front page on 20 April 1982 read 'Stick it up your Junta'. Then, on 4 May 1982, the gloating 'Gotcha – our Lads sink Gunboat and hole Cruiser' appeared to mark Britain's opening attack. There was quite some public dispute over the headlines' controversial stances. Some were concerned that *The Sun* was inciting readers; others believed that 'Gotcha' had captured, not created, the nation's mood. However, hardly anyone saw the original page as it only appeared on the first Northern editions. Peter Chippindale and Chris Horrie, in their account of *The Sun*'s history entitled *Stick it up your Punter. The uncut Story of the Sun Newspaper* (1999), remark that a modified version of the tabloid appeared later that day, for the headline became intolerable in view of the Argentine losses. Despite this, 'Gotcha' remains legendary in front page history.

By the mid-1980s, Murdoch's prominent role in what became known as the 'Death of Fleet Street' (Tunstall 1996: 18) attracted many of the negative emotions of a conflict. Murdoch was the first to relocate the entire production of his titles to a newly built printing plant in the East London docklands' district of Wapping in 1986. Employing new technologies that involved significantly less money and workforce, this move dramatically transformed production and distribution practices in the industry. Spearheading a true newspaper revolution, Murdoch's move resulted in nearly all national papers and publishing companies transforming their printing practices, and leaving their former central London home in Fleet Street. The process was only recently completed when the last big news organization, Reuters, left their quarters in Fleet Street on 15 June 2005 (cf. ibid).

Murdoch's move to Wapping in 1986 was accompanied by substantial job cuts, evoking nearly a year of print union strikes. Amplified by demonstrations outside Murdoch's plant, the call for a public boycott of his two national dailies and two Sundays grew. Still, *The Sun*'s sales remained steady. Murdoch's company was able to produce its newspapers despite the strike impediments, partly due to the new labour-saving equipment. When the strikes subsided in February 1987, power had shifted away from the print unions in favour of owners and editors. Moreover, the considerable changes to the political economy of the British press after the move to Wapping have been linked to concerns about a 'dumbing down' of the press (cf., for instance, Blumler and Gurevitch 1995). An important point in the recent history of the UK press, the Wapping dispute was also of wider social significance. Recognised as a decisive moment in the UK's trade union history, it embodied the Thatcher government's political victory over the union movement (Tunstall 1996: 18-30).

A further significant theme of the 1980s is the fact that *The Sun* was increasingly recognised for failing journalistic standards throughout the decade. For instance, the paper's front page on 13 March 1986 sported the headline 'Freddie Starr ate my Hamster', alleging the British comedian had eaten his girlfriend's hamster following a row. An almost legendary headline, it was certainly a laugh to many; however, it also brought to the wider public's attention the paper's debatable truthfulness, earning *The Sun* a reputation for publishing made-up stories and lies (cf. Chippindale et al. 1999). However, it was another, more serious controversy in 1989 that considerably enraged the public, having a long-lasting negative effect on the paper's sales and reputation. On 15 April 1989, one of the worst international football incidents occurred at the Hillsborough football stadium in Sheffield. The online edition of *The Telegraph* (2009) reports that as a result of a human crush, 96 people died, 766 were injured and around 300 were hospitalized. On 19 April 1989, *The Sun* lead with a story headlined 'The Truth', blaming hooliganism of Liverpool F.C. fans for the tragedy. Greenslade (2009) recalls, in *The Guardian,* that following the tragedy some journalists were, allegedly briefed "off the record" by police sources who said that drunken Liverpool fans had caused the crush. While *The Sun* was not the only newspaper to mention these accusations, it was the only one that 'gave them credence' by publishing them 'as if they were fact' (ibid). The story claimed that Liverpool fans had 'attacked rescue workers as they tried to revive victims' and that 'police officers, firemen and ambulance crew were punched, kicked and urinated upon' (ibid). In August 1989, the interim report by the Lord Justice Taylor principally held 'failure of police control' as responsible for the disaster, as highlighted in the online edition of *The Telegraph* dated 14 April 2009. However, *The Sun* and its editor Kelvin MacKenzie had already been under tremendous attack by then. The paper has regretted its Hillsborough coverage ever since, and issued many apologies (a recent one appearing in '*The Sun* Says' editorial on 7 July 2004). Nevertheless, sales in the metropolitan county of Merseyside in North West England remain low to this day, for many Liverpudlians still refuse to buy the paper to which they refer as 'The Scum' (*The Guardian on Saturday*, 18 April 2009: 10).

### *The Sun* in the Nineties: Circulation Peak & 'The Sun Wot Won It'

The tabloid's circulation ascended in the 1990s, sales peaking at more than 4 million copies per day between 1994 and 1996. The decade also saw a succession of editors; Kelvin MacKenzie handed over to Stuart Higgins in 1994, with David Yelland inheriting the post in 1998.

Marc Pursehouse (1991) claims public mood towards *The Sun* changed in the 1990s, a mood characterised by more of a relaxed attitude. Still, growing concern surfaced with regard to the tabloid's 'significant political influence, thanks to its penetration of the all-important C2 voters' (Douglas 2004). Although it is not quite clear exactly what influence the paper has on voters, *The Sun* enjoys portraying itself in a powerful light. During the 1992 election campaign, the paper supported Thatcher's successor, John Major. Claiming that it had swung the election for Major, *The Sun* triumphed on 11 April 1992: 'It's *The Sun* Wot Won It'. The newspaper had ridiculed Labour Party leader Neil Kinnock, exclaiming on the day of the election: 'If Kinnock wins Today will the last Person to leave Britain please turn out the Lights'. McKenzie later claimed in *The Sun* that the line was 'an average gag'; however, neither politicians nor the general public subscribed to this view (cf. Douglas 2005 on the BBC News website). Five years later, *The Sun* switched allegiances and backed Labour leader Tony Blair in the 1997 general election, despite fundamentally opposing some of the New Labour politics, particularly relating to the EU (cf. Black in *The Guardian*, 8 January 2002: 5). Illustrating the presumed significance of the paper's political support, Douglas (2004) reports that Blair and his Director of Communications and Strategy, Alastair Campbell, had decided that 'if Labour were ever to win, they must at least neutralise the paper'. Intensive discussions about *The Sun*'s actual influence on the outcome of an election frequently re-emerge and remain a topical controversy within both the industry and academia to this day (cf., for instance, Linton 1995; Curtice 1999; Douglas 2004, 2005). Beliefs about the British tabloid's political impact have even found their way into Germany publications (cf., for instance, Gehrs in the *Frankfurter Rundschau* from 15 August 2006: 13; Bebber 1997).

## The 21st Century *Sun*

*The Sun*'s circulation has declined continuously since its peak in the 1990s. In fact, the entire daily newspaper sector has decreased in the UK, Germany and many other countries. A debate about the 'crisis' of the newsprint industry therefore arose in the early 2000s, attracting much concern from academics and journalists alike, all of whom have pondered the future of newspapers ever since (cf., for instance, Journalism Studies on *The Future of Newspapers* (2008); Pasquay 2010). Despite falling circulations, however, *The Sun* remains highly profitable. The current editor of the paper, Dominic Mohan, succeeded Rebekah Brooks (née Wade) in September 2009; Wade made history as the first and, to this day, only female editor of the tabloid.

Politically, *The Sun* supported Tony Blair in his three successive general election victories in 1997, 2001 and 2005. Adapting the traditional Vatican white smoke signal, a puff of red smoke was issued from the *News International Ltd.*'s Wapping premises in April 2005, to signal the paper's election intent. The front page of April 21 then read *'Sun smoke goes RED for Blair. One Last Chance'*. After the election, *The Sun*'s political influence was discussed and disputed. Stephen Glover (2005) of *The Independent* argues that the paper cannot swing a general election 'unless a majority of its readers do'. Yet, Douglas (2004) remarks that the tabloid's political position has seemed somewhat obscure in recent years: 'It backed Blair on Iraq but remains fervently anti-Europe, and can't bring itself to love the new Tory leadership.' *The Sun* switched allegiances back to Tory in 2009, claiming on its front page on September 30 that 'Labour's Lost It'. Thus, in announcing its support for the Conservatives the paper caused yet another media stir (cf. Waugh in the *Evening*

Standard 2009; Steel in *The Independent* 2009; Sparrow & Stratton in the *Guardian* 2009).

In general, *The Sun* today appears rather well behaved in comparison to its rambunctious past. Former editor Rebekah Brooks is quoted in a report issued on the BBC News website (2003) as saying that there has been 'constant improvement' in the tabloid's standards. Nevertheless, the tabloid and its editors frequently attract both admiration and controversy by landing "scoops", issuing campaigns or making blunders. A recent example is the paper's long-standing 'naming and shaming' campaign against paedophiles, which started in 2000. Other events include *Sun* reporter Anthony France smuggling a fake bomb into the House of Commons in 2004 (cf. BBC News 2004); *The Sun*'s photos of Saddam Hussein in his cell (*The Sun*, 22 May 2005), and the publishing of a picture of Prince Harry wearing a Nazi uniform to a fancy dress party, beneath the front page headline 'Harry the Nazi' (*The Sun*, 13 January 2005).

## The German *Bild*

### *Bild*'s Early Years: Easily Digestible 'Picture' News to Politicization

*Bild* is some years older than *The Sun*. It was founded by the late newspaper publisher Axel Springer, and was launched on 24 June 1952, as the first (and to this day only) national daily tabloid in Germany, with a circulation of 250,000. The literal meaning of its name (picture) suggests that the publisher placed much emphasis on the visual character of the tabloid from its outset. The initial idea was to publish a printed response to the anticipated development of television in Germany (Lohmeyer 1992: 150). Originally, *Bild* was modelled on popular dailies from the UK and Scandinavia; however, owner Springer was of the opinion that after World War II, 'German readers did not wish to ponder much anymore' (Brumm 1980: 137), thus the early *Bild* consisted of only four pages, two of which were covered almost entirely with pictures and captions. Aside from that, the paper carried short human-interest stories, an editorial, horoscopes and several jokes – but no political content whatsoever. Michael Sontheimer has termed this mix the 'edifying restorative treacle' of the tabloid's first year (ibid 1995: 39).

This early version of *Bild* was not cost-efficient and the paper soon matured into a more "conventional" tabloid. Henno Lohmeyer (1992: 156) remarks that the first editor-in-chief, Rudolf Michael (who served 1952-1957), created a newspaper that was 'rude and reckless, sizzling and unscrupulous, cheeky and occasionally flippant – a paper with an instinct but without taste; valuing a good tear jerker more than the stock quotes.' The period under his directorship, is widely recognised as *Bild*'s true hour of birth (cf. Sontheimer 1995). The editor's intent was to produce 'a cherry-picked newspaper' (Müller 1968: 79). Yet, the paper was still devoid of any serious political coverage. Michael's strategy paid off as circulation soared and the paper soon became Germany's bestselling daily. 300,000 copies of *Bild* were sold in March 1953; 500,000 in April; 600,000 in May, and 700,000 in June. By December 1953, *Bild* had a circulation of approximately 1.2 million (Brumm 1980: 18). Sales hit the two million mark in 1955, and continued rising until 1982.

In 1958, *Bild*'s absence from "hard" news came to an abrupt end. Springer did not agree with German separation and attempted to intervene in the gridlocked dialogue between East and West (Schirmer 2001). A true patriot, he travelled to Moscow where he endeavoured to discuss his plans for a reunification of Germany with Nikita Khrushchev, the then First Secretary of the Soviet Union's Communist Party. Springer indeed met Khrushchev, but he did not succeed in convincing the Russian of his plans. Upon returning home, the disappointed publisher committed *Bild*'s second editor, Karl Heinz Hagen (who served 1958-1962), to running an austere anti-communist campaign (Brumm 1980).

The sudden change in rhetoric, in combination with *Bild*'s increasing politicization, was met by public reproval; the paper was criticised for its narrative strategies and sensationalised reporting (Minzberg 1999). However, Springer continued using *Bild*'s powerful voice to enforce his political orientation. The paper, at times, resembled a propaganda newspaper, a type of medium that a traumatised Germany no longer tolerated. Circulation soon suffered immense losses. In 1962, Peter Boenisch took over as editor (serving until 1971). Boenisch sought to re-establish the tabloid's mass-pleasing character, without altering its editorial drift (Brumm 1980). Indicating its political orientation, the tabloid still referred to the German Democratic Republic as the 'Soviet Occupation Zone', and continuously put its official name GDR in quotation marks until 1989 (Schirmer 2001: 53-54).

### *Bild* in the Sixties: Ideological Criticism & 'Anti-Springer' Movement

Boenisch significantly re-shaped *Bild*'s style and helped the tabloid to achieve sales of four million by 1962. One of *Bild*'s famous editions during his time as editor includes the front page from 21 July 1969, which ran the headline 'The Moon is a Yankee' (German original: 'Der Mond ist jetzt ein Ami'), displaying an additional title underneath the usual *Bild* logo that read 'Moon Paper'.

By the mid-1960s, public disapproval re-mounted, for *Bild*'s ideological reporting was criticised. Concerns were raised about the paper's distortion of political and social realities (Minzberg 1999: 45-46). Resulting in a new decrease in circulation, *Bild*'s controversial campaigning against the German student movement in the years following 1967, and the students' response in the form of the 'Anti-Springer' campaign, remained the centre of attention. Axel Springer had found his surrogate enemy in the student movement, which to him represented the accumulated front against his publishing empire. At that time, this front included most left-wing and liberal conservative politicians, the unions, the Catholic Church, and a notable number of media outlets, consisting of public service broadcasting providers, current affairs magazines *Spiegel* and *Stern*, as well as *Frankfurter Rundschau*, *Süddeutsche Zeitung* and *Zeit*, two German daily broadsheets and a weekly (Sontheimer 1995).

In the years prior to 1967, *Bild* had already portrayed revolting students as dangerous anarchists (cf. Brumm 1980). On 2 June 1967, however, the student Benno Ohnesorg was killed by police fire whilst participating in a demonstration against the state visit of the Shah of Iran. *Bild* blamed the student movement for violent hooliganism. This confirmed the view held by some of the radical students that Springer was running a chivvy against them. The 'Anti-Springer' campaign was coined, demanding a law against the concentration of ownership. The movement placed Springer (who owned about 80 per cent of the newspapers at the time) at the centre of concerns about the media's manipulative power. Particularly, the tabloid *Bild* was regarded 'the most powerful capitalist instrument for making dull the working classes' minds and deflecting them from its true interests' (Sontheimer 1995: 42). In return, *Bild* started running a witch-hunt in the form of an anti-student campaign. Approaching them as a homogeneous mass, the paper termed students 'left-wing fascists', 'hooligans', 'scatterbrains', 'rowdies', 'half-baked loafers' and so forth (Sontheimer 1995: 42). Highly personalised, the paper's verbal attacks often focused on the activists' prominent spokesperson Rudi Dutschke.

On 11 April 1968, the conflict between Springer's *Bild* and the 'Anti-Springer' movement reached a critical stage, as Dutschke was shot in the head and suffered severe brain damage. The offender was a workman who claimed that the tabloid's reporting had triggered his actions. To the paper's opponents, this was the last straw. *Bild* was blamed for the tragedy and the student movement coined the popular catchphrase '*Bild* joined in the Attack' (German original: '*Bild* hat mitgeschossen'). At its height, the angry protest of a whole generation culminated in major street battles that were later referred to as the 'Easter Riots' (cf. *Spiegel Online* at http://einestages.spiegel.de/static/topicalbumbackground/1780/sturm_auf_springer.html). Berlin, in particular, witnessed violent acts against the tabloid and its publisher, aimed at disrupting the distribution of *Bild*; fire was set to the pickups laden with copies of the paper and windows were smashed at Springer's premises. The following day's edition of *Bild* led with the headline 'Terror in Berlin' (Sontheimer 1995). However, the events had caused a circulation drop of more than one million copies, and Sontheimer, reflecting on the paper's sales peaks and troughs, reiterates that 'too much politics does not do *Bild*'s circulation any good' (ibid 1995: 40).

The question over whether or not it was *Bild*'s reporting that caused the workman to shoot Dutschke remains topical to this day. Only recently, in January 2010, *Axel Springer AG* opened its archives to the general public, re-prompting the debate over *Bild*'s power and responsibility in the case of the Dutschke assassination. Reviewing relevant former editions of the tabloid, a public service radio broadcast entitled 'Springer's Chivvy' (German original: 'Springers Hetze', *NDR Info*, Zeitgeschichte, 23 January 2010) disputed the idea that *Bild* had 'joined in the attack', claiming that radical activists' reactions to the assassination misled public opinion at the time.

## *Bild* in the Seventies & Eighties:
## Charity Campaigns and Journalistic Practices in the Pillory

In the 1970s, *Bild* changed policies again, an action triggered by the takeover of editor Günter Prinz (1971-1981) who soon sought to remodel the tabloid as 'a paper for the people, tailored to the needs of its audience' (Naeher 1991: 265). The tabloid's stances appeared somewhat milder; its editorial content became less biased, and it started carrying more stories focussing on 'emotion and love' (ibid: 265). Prinz is also said to have notably increased the threesome of 'sex, crime, and scandal' (Schirmer 2001: 54). Attempting to restore ties with readers, Prinz significantly introduced a few highly successful campaigns that survive to the present day. In 1978, he coined *Bild*'s fundraising action 'Have a Heart for Children' (German original: 'Ein Herz für Kinder'). Similar to the BBC's 'Children in Need' appeal, an annual 'Have a heart for children' appeal-night is held, which today is joint-hosted by *Bild* and the German public service television channel *ZDF*. The campaign is very popular and enjoys a rather good reputation, consistently raising considerable amounts of money each year (cf. http://www.ein-herz-fuer-kinder.de). In the 1970s, *Bild* started distributing a sticker of the campaign's logo, which soon decorated German cars, bags, doors and so forth, and it is still present today. Moreover, editor Prinz introduced the similarly popular campaign, '*Bild* crusades for you' (German original: '*Bild* kämpft für Sie'). This was designed to revitalise the paper's image as an 'advocate' for its readers – a title introduced by former editor Boenisch (cf. Brumm 1980). Within a few years, *Bild* received two million letters from readers, begging the paper to help in a range of matters. As a result of Prinz' efforts, the paper's circulation rose again, peaking in 1982 with over five million copies sold daily.

The eighties, however, also saw a fierce slump in sales induced by a series of scandalous "disclosures" about the working practices and lack of ethics adhered to at *Bild*. Günter Wallraff caused this crisis through his publications (1977; 1979; 1981; 1985). The author and investigative journalist became widely known for his undercover research at *Bild*. Taking up a job with the paper for a few months in 1977, he collected material for three books, which he filled with allegations about the dismal ethics of reporters, editors and the publisher. His long list of *Bild*'s flaws included the claim that the paper's stories were entirely fictional, or that a false colour was added to them in such a way that distorted facts beyond recognition.

Wallraff also accused the journalists of highly unethical treatment towards the subjects of reports, informants and readers. He blamed the publisher for surreptitiously advertising and running gratis electorate campaigns, depicting the popular '*Bild* crusades for you' campaign as a tool for disguising the paper's true manipulative interests. Moreover, Wallraff lamented the general working conditions at *Bild*, such as the high peer pressure and fierce competition between the journalists (cf. ibid; particularly 1977 and 1979). *Axel Springer AG* reacted by introducing a regular column in *Bild*, entitled 'Wallraff lies', in which it was argued that the author's first book was meant to inspire a conspiracy against the publisher. However, this move only worked to promote the book even more.

Wallraff's accusations hit the paper harder than the student revolts of the 1960s. *Bild*'s sales dropped considerably between 1983 and 1993. Winning many opinion leaders from the German intellectual scene for his cause, Wallraff, indeed, succeeded in setting up a renewed 'Anti-Springer' movement (Sontheimer 1995). Spread across more than 100 German cities, the movement's local branches arranged exhibitions, film viewings, discussions, union conferences and school instruction units on the topic of Wallraff's accusations (Minzberg 1999: 72); bringing the matter of *Bild*'s practices to the attention of a wider public. An aid fund for those impaired by the tabloid's reporting was set up, entitled 'If *Bild* lies, campaign against it!' (German original: 'Wenn *Bild* lügt, kämpft dagegen'). Minzberg (1999: 71) remarks that the paper and its journalistic practices became widely despised, despite the tabloid's best efforts to present itself as a charitable institution. Cultural critics, literary figures and media professionals alike disputed *Bild* (cf., for instance, Böll 1974; 'Plague and Cholera' (German original: 'Pest und Cholera') in *Der Spiegel* from 6 July 1992). Essentially, most voices condemned *Bild* as 'Springer's monster' (Enzensberger 1983: 654).

### *Bild* in the Nineties: Turning Away from 'Turmoil Journalism'

Editor Claus Larass (1992-1997) and his successor Udo Röbel (1998- 2000) represented a new phase in the history of *Bild*. Their predecessor Hans-Hermann Tiedje (1989-1992) was still committed to the "old" ways of tabloid-making, summarised by Michael Haller as being false emotions, shock, and a continued disrespect of all things human (ibid 1995: 9). However, a change in trend can be noted as of 1992, with Larass' takeover, recognisable within the shifting reactions towards the paper that were considerably less indignant in tone. For instance, Wolfgang J. Koschnick (1998: 16) ascertained that *Bild* turned away from its 'turmoil journalism' of the past and evolved into a more 'silent and serious' type of newspaper. Similarly, Evelyn Roll of the *Süddeutsche Zeitung* (1999) described *Bild* as a 'nice, highly professional, liberal tabloid' (cf. also Schirmer 2001: 59 pp.)

*Bild*'s new style was greatly influenced by three guiding principles introduced by Larass. He cautioned to evoke 'real' emotions; to take the readers' concerns seriously; and to provide order to readers' minds, which he believed were overstrained by the televised information-overflow (Schneider and Raue 1998: 129). As a consequence of the changes to *Bild*'s style, Larass was praised for 'humanising tabloid journalism' (Haller 1995: 9). Circulation – although decreasing since its peak in 1982 – saw an upturn, remaining well above the four million mark. The tabloid's public image also improved. Frank Hartmann remarks that the public did not associate 'a certain ideology' (1995: 12) with the paper any more. Aside from the new faces of Larass and Röbel, a further explanation for the perceived change in *Bild* may relate to the post cold-war climate and the relieved tensions in Germany after 1989, which helped in resolving some of the ideological conflicts that the tabloid had previously been involved in (Schirmer 2001). Yet, *Bild* still heads the complaints statistics of the German Press Council in the 1990s (cf. Minzberg 1999; recent statistics are available from http://www.presserat.info/inhalt/beschwerde/statistik.html). Stefan Schirmer, likewise, argues that in terms of journalistic quality, *Bild*'s front page headlines have not improved much (ibid 2001: 133). However, in the 1990s the tabloid seemed to have finally recovered from Wallraff's attacks. Thomas Schuler (1998) remarks in the *Berliner Zeitung*: 'With regards to the notions of objectivity and accuracy, *Bild* does not differ any more from the *Spiegel*.'

## The 21st Century *Bild*

This tabloid has always been shaped significantly by its editors-in-chief. Kai Diekmann, who took over the job in 2001, has also left his mark on the paper's appearance. A most apparent change, Diekmann re-introduced the page three girls (who, in the case of *Bild*, traditionally appear on the paper's front page). Diekmann's predecessor Röbel had attempted to give the paper a somewhat more serious aura by occasionally refraining from printing a half-naked woman on the front page. If the lead, for instance, referred to Steffi Graf, the well-known German tennis player, the pin-up was omitted. Röbel had, moreover, altered the tradition by placing a photo of a lightly-clad man on the front page of 27 October 1999. Yet, since the beginning of the Diekmann period, half-naked girls regularly re-appear on the tabloid's front page, with only very few exceptions. Following the advice of *Bild*'s 'Readers Advisory Board' (p. 40), the paper once more printed a half-naked man on its front page on 16 June 2009. About a year later, on 7 October 2010, the topless photograph was missing, as the lead story featured a new factual television show named *Tatort Internet* (lit: Crime Scene Internet), in which Germany's former Defence Minister's wife, Stephanie zu Guttenberg, sets out to disclose online sex offenders in front of the rolling camera. It would seem that *Bild*'s editors regarded the usual sexy photograph as inappropriate with regard to the subject matter of that particular show.

Having turned 50 in June 2002, *Bild* remains Germany's highest-selling newspaper, although the tabloid's circulation has declined in recent years, alongside that of *The Sun* and many other printed news outlets in many countries around the world. In 2002, *Bild*'s sales dropped to less than four million and they continue to sink. Attempting to counteract this trend, the publisher has launched a few interesting marketing activities. In 2002, a distinct cross-promotion feature was introduced, designed to attract advertising revenues and halt the tabloid's circulation decline. In collaboration with selected business partners, *Bild* established the 'quality brand' of the so-called *Volksprodukte* (lit: the people's products). Allegedly, each *Volksprodukt* is a 'popular, innovative and timely' commodity characterised by an excellent cost/performance ratio (cf. www.axelspringer-mediapilot.de/artikel/ Volks-Aktion-Volks-Produkte_728739.html). Once branded a *Volksprodukt*, individual items, or a line of products, are featured in the editorial text of the tabloid and are aggressively promoted by full-page advertisements in the paper and relevant mono-themed sisters, both online and offline. In addition, a logo identifying the product as a *Volksprodukt* is placed on the relevant item's packaging. Since 2002, the *Volksprodukte* find a ready market and are highly successful (cf. http://www.bildblog.de/schnappchen-furs-volk). The list of *Volksprodukte* includes diverse items such as a *Volks*-mobile, a *Volks*-washing machine, a *Volks*-bible, *Volks*-medicine and a *Volks*-computer. Expanding its cross-promotion efforts, *Bild*, moreover, introduced a low-budget mobile phone and Internet deals in 2007 (cf. www.bildmobil.de), which have since become very popular.

Another interesting activity designed to improve *Bild*'s relationship with its audience concerns the paper's involvement of readers in the production of the tabloid, as of 2006. Meeting current changes in the newspaper landscape, *Bild* regularly invites audience members to share their photos and pass on information about celebrities or other matters that they think may be of interest. Embracing such *Leserreporter* (lit: reader reporter) material, the tabloid frequently publishes content of this kind (cf. Tzortzis 2006, in *The New York Times online*). This move has triggered controversial debates about notions of quality and citizen participation in journalism (cf., for instance, Stumberger 2007 in *TELEPOLIS*; Pohlmann 2007 in the online edition of *Der Tagesspiegel*; Sundermeyer (2006) in the *Frankfurter Allgemeine Zeitung* and Jung (2007) at *sueddeutsche.de*). In a similar way, *The Sun* regularly invites readers to contribute to the production of the paper (Johansson 2007a: 97). However, the focus here is placed on stories readers can suggest for the paper to follow up, rather than on reader-generated material, such as photos and events they have witnessed. *Bild*, meanwhile, has expanded its efforts by launching a 'Readers Advisory Board' (cf. the article 'We are the new Readers Advisory Board' (German original: 'Wir sind der neue Leser-Beirat') in *Bild*'s edition of 29 September 2007). At regular intervals, readers can now apply to become board members for a certain period of time. If selected, they are invited to participate in editorial meetings and offer advice to editors and the publisher with regard to what the paper can do to become even more attractive to its audience.

Yet, public mood toward *Bild* in the first decade of this century can be described as varied. The country's most widely-read and most controversially-discussed newspaper continues to polarise opinions. The only German media outlet without any true rivals, *Bild* enjoys the unique status of a key medium, serving as a prevalent reference to wide parts of the German media landscape (cf. Haller 2001). *The Sun*, in comparison, does not benefit from such singular attention in the UK as it has many tabloid rivals (cf. Chapter 3). However, the British media likewise draws upon popular tabloids frequently, as regular columns in other newspapers indicate. Contemplating the week's red-top stories, examples include the column 'Stop the Week: Shock exchange' in *The Sunday Times*, or 'The Tabloid Week' in *The Guardian*.

*Bild*'s unique role as a key medium can, however, turn sour. This was the case, for instance, in November 2000 when the paper blamed a few young adults for the death of a child in the Saxon village of Sebnitz; a wave of media reporting on the case was triggered. When a few days after *Bild* ran the story it was found that the alleged culprits were innocent, the damage had already been done. Although the case was seen to have shed an unfavourable light on large parts of the entire German media landscape, the responsibility of the tabloid in leading with false accusations was debated extensively, earning it three notices of defect by the German Press Council (cf. Baum 2001). *Bild* has, indeed, frequently been heavily criticised in recent years, resulting in a range of legal actions against the paper. These cases involved, for instance, the infringement of privacy laws, the paper's alleged campaigns for a political cause, as well as stories lacking accuracy and objectivity. Since 2004, *Bild*'s flaws have been painstakingly documented by the public media watchblog www.BILDblog.de. Founded by the broadsheet reporters Stefan Niggemeier and Christoph Schultheis, *BILDblog* set out to correct the tabloid's errors, counteract its exertion of political influence, and disclose its 'mob-rule' witch-hunts and inaccurate, lawless or immoral reporting. Comparable to Wallraff's campaign in the 1980s, *BILDblog* has become something of an anti-*Bild* public sphere. Today, the watchblog ranks amongst Germany's most widely-read weblogs. It is operated by a group of journalists and is supported by a large range of readers who point out fabrications every day (cf. www.bildblog.de). As of 2009, *BILDblog* expanded their objectives to include reporting on errors and untruths in newspapers from Germany and other countries. *Bild* has reacted to the watchblog's popularity by introducing a regular column on page two of the tabloid, in which it now reports and reflects on its own errors (cf. *Spiegel Online* 2006a).

## Distinguishable:
## Editorial Characteristics of the Tabloid Press

Two tabloid newspapers, Britain's *Sun* and Germany's *Bild*, can be identified by a set of editorial characteristics setting them apart from other news media outlets. Having established some of their commercial and historical characteristics, this section am offers a sketch of the genre's classic constituents. Although Sparks cautions that 'there is no very clear definition of what a tabloid might actually be [...]. It is unlikely that I can outline a clear and exhaustive definition that will command universal consent' (2000: 9-10), *The Sun* and *Bild* bear many resemblances regarding, for instance, their content and layout preferences, as well as their use of particular narrative strategies. Essentially, these notable similarities reflect core elements of tabloid journalism that recur, in different shapes, throughout tabloid formats across various media outlets and national contexts (cf. Bruck and Stocker 1996).

### "Outstanding": Conspicuous Visual Layout

A first, rather apparent characteristic of the genre concerns the strong emphasis placed upon matters of visual presentation. As Sofia Johansson (2007a: 87) states, the tabloid 'stands out from the mass of black-and-white print' at the news agent's. This type of newspaper is instantly recognisable by its conspicuous visual layout, its inescapable headlines, the great amount of space devoted to photographs and other pictorial material, as well as the generous use of colour (cf. ibid; Sparks 2000: 13; Bruck and Stocker 1996: 19).

Reflecting its crucial role as the initial draw for readers, the front page of the tabloid is particularly eye-catching. Picture-dominated, with the main story of the day often comprising a large photo and headline which occupy the entire page, (or most of it), the front page thrusts itself upon anyone who looks. Inside the paper, the visual mode of presentation continues with large-sized photos, illustrations and headlines. The stories alongside this graphic material are kept relatively short, and reading them does not require a particularly long attention span. The mix of small, quickly alternating items allows readers to swiftly identify single stories' thrusts and read the paper 'in snippets' (Johansson 2007a: 88). Such a skim-reading mode is furthermore encouraged by highlighted words and phrases within the stories' texts (cf. ibid; Bruck and Stocker 1996).

### Service and Opinion: Components & Journalistic Styles

A moderate amount of the space in popular tabloids is devoted to entertainment and service items such as cartoons, comics, jokes, agony-aunt columns, recipes, horoscopes, crosswords, TV listings and so forth (cf. Bruck and Stocker 1996: 20). A likewise distinctive element concerns the frivolous photographs of bare-breasted women. Indicating their position within the paper, these are commonly referred to as 'page three girls'. However, in the case of *Bild*, photos of lightly-clad ladies usually appear on the paper's front page, while page three displays local news. In terms of the organisation of content, the mixture of news and stories within tabloid papers is punctuated by regular features, which Johansson refers to as '"markers" from which to overview the content' (ibid 2007a: 88; original quotation marks). She mentions, for instance, the two-page 'showbiz' column of *The Sun* as one of these 'markers'. *Bild* has long published a similar column on its pages four and five; however, stories about stars and celebrities are spread across the entire paper. Yet, the sport section placed at the end of both *The Sun* and *Bild* is a fundamental example of such a 'marker' (cf. ibid: 88-89).

Essentially, the specific nature of tabloid reporting is recognisable via the preferred journalistic styles utilized by the papers. Generally, the articles are more feature-based than news-oriented. Leader columns and other opinion pieces dominate the wealth of short items and stories, whilst neutral reports are rather hard to find. However, only very few items can actually be identified as opinion-centred. One of the central features of tabloids, then, concerns their hybrid character of reporting, which is almost entirely marked by a combination of facts and opinion (cf. Bruck and Stocker 1996). Hence, in the majority of the tabloids' articles, judgement and fact can be said, at the very least, to exist in equal shares.

## Tabloid Properties: Content Preferences, News Values & Stances

### 'Human Interest'

Sparks (2000: 15) asserts that tabloids like *The Sun* and *Bild* have 'a strong agenda of scandal, sports, and entertainment' whilst relatively little attention is given to matters of politics, economics, and society. Indeed, when it comes to identifying "classic" tabloid constituents, both *The Sun* and *Bild* score high on "soft" news, maximising matters of sex, sports, celebrities and crime (ibid; cf. also Schirmer 2001; Bruck and Stocker 1996; Rooney 1998). Subsuming the preferred content and news values of the tabloid press under the umbrella term 'human interest' stories, Hartmut Büscher (1996: 12) continues:

'Aside from a fair amount of coverage on readers' idols, i.e. showbiz, film and TV 'stars', Royals, sports heroes and so forth, the stories mostly focus on romantic and exceptional matters, offer juicy and reproachable details from the broad areas of 'love and sexuality', report on something particularly cute and fragile (e.g. infants or animals) or on something particularly horrible and sad (e.g. violence, crime, illness, death etc). Often these issues occur as a mix, for instance, stories about ill showbiz stars or about sex with babies. Almost always, individual fates and (seemingly) sensational details are highlighted, and presented in the form of a narrative.'

As indicated by this telling quote, notions relating to human experience frequently feature in the tabloids' stories; in particular the private experiences of celebrities provide a wealth of material. The tabloids' reports, moreover, often draw on subjective views, highlighting the ordinary and the familiar (Bruck and Stocker 1996: 23; Johansson 2007a: 90; also cf. my discussion of discursive strategies, p. 49). The plots can generally be understood to borrow from common trivial myths, constructing narratives relating to the fulfilment of dreams, last-minute rescue, the punishment of "evil", love overcoming obstacles, the rebellion of ideals, sudden misfortune, ruthless exertion of power and so forth (Saxer 1979: 167-169). Similarly, the subject matter of sports provides popular 'ever-recurring tales of victories and failures' (Bruck and Stocker 1996: 23).

### Politics & Endorsement Traditions

Having established that both *The Sun* and *Bild* prefer non-political content, it should be noted that their reporting is by no means apolitical. Sparks (2000: 15) emphasises that the tabloids also include 'some elements of the news values of the serious press'. However, he notes, referring to *The Sun*, that it contains relatively little 'serious' material relating to politics, economics, and society. *Bild*, in comparison, carries a little more of this content (ibid; cf. also Höke 2004, 2005). The most important cross-national difference between the two newspapers, however, relates to their diverse approaches to stating political opinions. Linking in with British and German journalistic tradition variations (cf. Chapter 3), only the British *Sun* can be recognised to, as Sparks (2000: 15) identifies, 'actively campaign on political issues and in elections'. Indeed, most of the UK press can be recognised as openly partisan. Habitually taking a firm stand on the political views it prefers, *The Sun* has repeatedly portrayed itself as helping particular politicians to power (cf. p. 32). The tabloid's founder, Rupert Murdoch, is accredited with having huge influence on UK politics, and is perceived to intervene through the voice of his red-top titles. Yet, *The Sun* has switched its political patronage on a regular basis in the past, often supporting the party most likely to win an election (cf. Seymour-Ure 1994).

In Germany, *Bild* exists within a different tradition. Since the end of the Second World War, German print outlets have avoided declaring their political views too clearly, as a consequence of past experience with Nazi propaganda media (cf. Chapter 3). *Bild* has, likewise, refrained from overtly stating its political views. The paper also displays the terms 'independent' and 'non-partisan' on its title page (German original: 'unabhängig' and 'überparteilich'); a relic of the past that is still important to its readers today (cf. Chapter 7, p. 185). However, despite its self-portrayal as an independent newspaper, the tabloid is frequently criticised for taking a *concealed* political stance. *Bild* does not tell its readers which party to vote for, but a certain political bias in reporting has, nevertheless, been identified during the past few general elections. In a comparative analysis of 'explicit' and 'implicit' political endorsement in *The Sun* and *Bild*, Frank Brettschneider and Bettina Wagner (2008) reveal that in the German election campaign of 2002, *Bild* supported the Conservative party CDU. However, the tabloid's support appeared rather obscured. Brettschneider and Wagner claim that *Bild* portrayed the CDU's then candidate for Chancellor, Edmund Stoiber, in a more positive light than his rival Gerhard Schröder from the Social Democrats. Albeit not explicitly stating its allegiance, politics associated with the Conservatives featured more often than not in the tabloid's reporting, rather than issues associated with the SPD. Concluding that *Bild* had run a hidden election campaign for the CDU, the authors assume that the tabloid thus attempted to sway readers' voting intentions. However, Germany's Social Democratic Party (SPD) won the majority of votes that year. Still, *Bild* was, again, alleged to have 'implicitly' supported the Christian Democrats and their then candidate for Chancellor, Angela Merkel, in the subsequent election of 2005 (cf. Wagner 2007). Notably, concerns about the tabloid's hidden campaigns for particular political parties coincide with frequent debates about *Bild*'s potential to manipulate readers' views (cf. Chapter 4)[3]. In a way, these issues relate back to the country's past experience with Nazi propaganda media; an alarming scenario which most Germans would not want to let happen ever again. Still, despite concerns that the political impact of both *The Sun* and *Bild* may be huge in either country (cf. Chapter), such perceptions largely remain without empirical foundation. This raises questions

---

3 On a side note, there is some indication that a few printed news publications in Germany – among them *Bild* – have started to express their political opinions more explicitly in recent years. In the forerun of the general election 2002, the regional broadsheet *Berliner Zeitung*, from 21 September 2002, published an editorial clearly in favour of the CDU. Likewise, the national mid-market broadsheet *Die Welt* (also a Springer publication), on the day before the election in 2005, was issued containing an editorial telling its readers to vote for the CDU – an act that would have been deemed impossible just a few years before. On the same day, *Bild* declared on its front page, 'We reveal whom we vote for', portraying a range of celebrities along with their voting intentions. Noticeably, most of the people featured favoured the CDU. Inside the paper, in *Bild*'s traditional politics section on page two, the current Chancellor Gerhard Schröder of the Social Democrats was already bid farewell, despite the fact that the election had not yet taken place. These personal observations lack substantial empirical foundation, but they may indicate a subtle trend in German newspapers towards a more open endorsement of particular political parties.

about the papers' true impact on audiences' views, and about whether or not the tabloids' political stance is of relevance to readers at all.

## National & Local Perspectives

Considering the papers' preferred news values and favoured stances, a further notion is worth noting here. Both *The Sun* and *Bild* can be said to favour a strongly nation-centred perspective, over international or European viewpoints. Textual analyses have shown that the papers invite collective identity positions through providing a range of textual discourses on community and nationhood (Conboy 2002, 2006; Brookes 1999; Law 2001, 2002; cf. Chapter 4). This view is also supported by the typical textual elements and narrative strategies of tabloids, which are often structured around discourses of inclusion and exclusion (cf. p. 49). Yet, the nation-centred focus appears somewhat more pronounced in *The Sun*. Höke (2005: 81) remarks that the British tabloid accentuates feelings of national sentiment somewhat more strongly than *Bild*. Likewise, *The Sun* appears to take a more fervent anti-Europe view (ibid; cf. Chapter 4).

However, local perspectives are highly relevant to both tabloids' reporting. In line with the characteristic discursive strategy of 'familiarisation' (p. 49), the papers frequently forge strong links with their readers through their specific audience address and rhetoric of collective pronouns. Enforcing identification, an aspect specific to *Bild* is worth highlighting here; it concerns the tabloid's focus on regional and local news, which is reflected in the several regional editions of the paper (cf. also the section on 'Production and Distribution', p. 24). This means that each copy of *Bild* contains an identical array of set pages, which are referred to by the technical term *Mantel* (lit: coat). The *Mantel* marks a common editorial frame consisting of several back and front pages. In addition to the *Mantel*, each edition of *Bild* contains an individual local or regional section reporting on the relevant area of Germany in which the paper is distributed. The combination of *Mantel* plus a local section is not unique to *Bild*, for most of the national newspapers in Germany follow this model. However, the tabloid's editorial focus on local news is, indeed, significant, for it demonstrates a certain degree of familiarity with readers' everyday lives.

## Sexuality

A further content preference shared by *The Sun* and *Bild* relates to the strong sexual connotations observed in both papers. As indicated before, the photographs of topless ladies on the front page in the case of *Bild*, and on page three in the case of *The Sun*, are the most apparent examples of sexualised content. Aside from this, Johansson (2007a: 100 pp.) demonstrates through textual analysis that notions of gender and sexuality mark significant textual themes in tabloids, 'preoccupied with how the cultural terrains of femininity and masculinity are to be negotiated' (ibid: 100).

Discussing the papers' representation of female bodies and interests, Johansson argues that the stereotypical 'page three girl' images can be viewed in particular as 'one of the most conservative sites of tabloid discourse on gender' (ibid: 104). Interestingly, the author furthermore points out that the counterpart to this limited representation of femininity can be found in the sports pages, which embody the ideal tabloid masculinity in reporting, photography and sports actors featured (ibid: 104). Johansson concludes:

'The sporting masculinity of these papers, together with the dominant models of femininity [...] must be seen as constituting a dominant, gendered framework from which readers can interpret the rest of the content. The emphasis on sexual difference, with men presented as active and strong, and women as pleasing and controllable, would therefore seem to impact on the overall understanding of the news.' (ibid: 106)

## Humour

While this approach to sexuality and gender is common to *The Sun* and *Bild*, a cross-national difference emerges with regard to the papers' different emphases on notions of humour and joking. Johansson (2007a: 92) identifies a 'constant presence of the joke' in her textual analysis of *The Sun* and the *Daily Mirror*. An essential element to both these papers, 'the joke' recurs in various forms and shapes in headlines, stories and graphics in British tabloids. Pursehouse's description of *The Sun*'s multiple 'voices' also highlights this. He explains:

'One of the loudest voices of *The Sun* would seem to be its effort to raise a laugh and present a 'fun' persona. The paper advertises itself with the self-identity of your 'loadsa-fun *Sun*' and in its mocking headline puns seems keen to laugh at its own sense of humour. The paper takes an ironic stance in relation to traditional expectations of the serious nature of headlines. [...] *The Sun* seeks a friendship with its readers on the grounds of a shared joke.' (ibid. (1991: 96; original quotation marks)

Such a strong emphasis on word play, puns and humour is considerably less observable in *Bild*. Only occasionally, a mocking headline pun appears in the German tabloid. A rather famous example, *Bild*'s front page of 20 April 2005, was, in this sense, singled out for praise. The day after the German cardinal Joseph Ratzinger had been pronounced Pope Benedikt XVI, *Bild* produced the lead 'We are Pope!' (German original: 'Wir sind Papst!') Editor Diekmann was confident that this line had 'captured the mood of the nation' (Hanfeld 2005). A playful pun indeed, 'We are Pope' has triggered a range of reactions in Germany. Clearly addressing a sense of national community, it inspired a rather controversial debate about the patriotic tone implied in the text (with regard to German readers' responses to this context of the headline, cf. Chapter 9, p. 216). Aside from that particular reaction, the headline was thought brilliant by many, for it was toying with several analogies. On first sight alluding to the joyful exclamation commonly associated with winning the football World Cup (We are World Champions), the line drew on the traditional Latin phrase used by the senior Cardinal Deacon to proclaim the new Pope, 'Habemus Papam' (lit: we have a Pope). A further context for the headline's fame, its grammatical structure clearly had an entertaining edge to it. In both the English translation I am using here and the German original, the plural form 'we' of the personal pronoun contradicts the individual subject of the sentence, the (one) Pope. The logic of the verb is also ambiguous, as 'to be' in the way it was used does not normally refer to a person other than the self. Hence, 'We are Pope' was critically acclaimed by the German media, quoted in many media outlets and recurred in various public discourses, ultimately passing into language as a catchphrase[4]. Moreover, the headline earned *Bild* a few media industry awards and was pronounced 'word of the year 2005' by the *Gesellschaft für deutsche Sprache* (Association for the German Language).

Aside from this example, the German tabloid appears somewhat more serious in tone than *The Sun*. *Bild*'s headlines often sum up the gist of a report, rather than feature mocking puns, accentuate jokes and strive for raising a laugh, like *The Sun*. Höke's comparative content analysis of *The Sun* and *Bild* (2004; 2005) reveals that *The Sun*'s stories carry more irony and sarcasm than *Bild*'s articles. This observation receives further support through textual analyses focusing on either one of these tabloids. So far, works on *Bild* have pointed out many things, but have hardly drawn much attention to paper's approach to joking and humour (cf., for instance, Schirmer 2001; Büscher 1996). Unlike *Bild*, notions relating to *The Sun*'s humorous stances have repeatedly been stressed as important textual elements of the tabloid (cf. Johansson 2007a; Pursehouse 1991).

---

4   Illustrating the range of reactions, Ernst Corinth mockingly gloated on 20 April 2005 in the online magazine *Telepolis*, 'Excellent! *Bild* renders all of us Pope!' (German original: 'Das ist der Wahnsinn! *Bild* macht uns alle zum Papst!') An example of a more serious response, the *Frankfurter Allgemeine Zeitung*'s online edition *FAZ.NET* on the same day asked, 'We are Pope. Where do we go from here?' (German original: 'Wellenreiter: Wir sind Papst. Was nun?') Aside from references to the headline made in diverse media outlets, numerous variations of 'We are Pope' pervaded German weblogs, songs and comedy shows throughout the year of its publication.

## Staging Content: Stylistic Devices & Discursive Strategies

Essentially, tabloid reporting can be distinguished from other media formats through the presentation of news and events as stories aimed 'at readers' hearts rather than their heads' (Schneider and Raue 1998: 125). Passions, then, crucially characterise tabloid news values and narratives. Packed with emotive, affective and dramatic words, phrases and expressions (cf. Schirmer 2001), popular papers are often regarded as polar opposites to the more 'rational' reporting of 'quality' newspapers (cf. Sparks 2000: 12). The implications of this view of debates about tabloid media's significance in the public sphere are examined in Chapter 4.

Typically, the reporting of the tabloid press is characterised by the use of particular discursive strategies and stylistic devices aimed at stirring readers' emotions. Peter A. Bruck and Günther Stocker (1996) usefully identify a set of five interdependent discursive strategies of tabloid reporting. Distinguishing these techniques by their effect on the text, the authors refer to them as 'visualisation', 'simplification', 'familiarisation', 'personalisation' and 'melodramatisation' (ibid: 23 pp.) Each of the typical linguistic and stylistic devices used by the tabloid media support the aims of these narrative strategies.

The first narrative strategy identified by Bruck and Stocker, 'visualisation', clearly refers to the visual dimension of presentation in tabloid newspapers, which has already been addressed. This includes both the amount and size of pictures and other graphic material, as well as the use of pictorial expressions and descriptions in the text (cf. ibid: 26).

According to Bruck and Stocker, the second narrative technique of 'simplification' supports the promotion of well-arranged worldviews. Facts and circumstances are generalised, and complex relations are reduced to one aspect or person only; the actions are then ethically and morally judged. Stefan Schirmer (2001: 13) remarks that *Bild* 'interprets circumstances in a way that avoids raising value conflicts between readers and the paper; it is rather keen to maintain clear-cut judgement and encourage black-and-white thinking'. The technique of 'simplification' can, therefore, be regarded as a tool to establish 'emotional equivalence' between the medium and the audience (Büscher 1996: 98). Indeed, tabloid reporting often aims at reflecting readers' worldviews rather than suggesting new perspectives, while the predominant stance ostensibly represents the views of the 'ordinary' men and women (Schirmer 2001: 14; Bruck and Stocker 1996: 25).

The third discursive strategy of 'familiarisation' serves to create feelings of togetherness, belonging and community amongst readers, and between the papers and their audiences, as Bruck and Stocker argue (ibid: 24). Indeed, it would seem that the tabloids frequently present themselves as "one of us", thus appearing to establish strong ties with their readers. The typical audience address revolves around rhetoric of collective pronouns such as 'we', 'us' and 'them', strongly implying notions of inclusion and exclusion. Scholars have demonstrated this, for instance, with regard to the nation (cf. Conboy 2006; Brooks 1999), or the readership community (cf. Johansson 2007a: 95 pp.; Bruck and Stocker 1996: 168). Similarly, clear-cut narrative patterns of "good" and "evil" characterise tabloid reporting, highlighting the familiar and rejecting everything foreign or different (Bruck and Stocker 24-25). Moreover, the text is usually written in a simple, easily comprehensible type of style, using colloquial, day-to-day words and phrases, thereby transporting a sense of closeness to readers' everyday lives. An example of this technique in use is the fact that celebrities are often referred to by "nick-names". By portraying them as "ordinary" men and women, the perceived distance between the average reader and people from affluent socio-economic groups appears to fade away, creating a sense of equality and commonality (cf. Schirmer 2001: 15).

The narrative technique of 'personalisation' (Bruck and Stocker 1996: 25 pp.) is also particularly characteristic to popular papers. As Sparks (1998: 9) points out: 'The individual human personality is the central reference point of the tabloid press.' Indeed, tabloid stories commonly foreground subjective views and focus on individuals rather than institutions. The arena of politics, for instance, appears as a field of cooperation and rivalry between only a few individuals (Nusser 1991: 14). This also applies to notions of economics and society, which are likewise personalised. Even the newspaper itself can be subject to this all-embracing strategy; when it portrays itself as an advocate of "ordinary" men and women, for instance. Bruck and Stocker emphasize that this narrative technique is a tool to make the world appear more straightforward and 'manageable' (ibid: 25), allowing readers to maintain a sense of security whilst navigating the daily flood of catastrophes and scandals.

Finally, the discursive strategy of 'melodramatisation' (Bruck and Stocker 1996: 26) should be noted. Closely linked to the technique of 'personalisation', this approach is reflected in the element of sensation accentuated in tabloid reporting; in stories about personal tragedies, for instance. Likewise, drawing attention to individual actors, the 'melodramatisation' of news and events works to evoke notions of sympathy, and invites identification (cf. also Johansson 2007a: 89 pp.)

In an attempt to complete this list, a further characteristic of the tabloid press deserves some attention. Albeit not directly related to the presentation of content, the issue at stake refers to the typical tabloid ways of framing material. As discussed in some detail in Chapters 4 and 5, a strong social devaluation of the genre can be noted within academic and social discourses regarding popular journalism. To cite John Fiske (1989b: 106), 'the combination of widespread consumption with widespread critical disapproval is a fairly certain sign that a cultural commodity or practice is popular'. Clearly of relevance, this aspect represents a distinctive characteristic of the genre, which will be returned to in due course.

## Conclusions

This chapter has focused on discussing the research objects of this study, the British *Sun* and the German *Bild*. Two classics in the newspaper genre, the tabloids share a number of key characteristics relating to their commercial, historic, and editorial features. This chapter has shown that although they are distributed in different countries, these papers can be approached as similar phenomena. Notably, the two tabloids are Europe's top-selling national dailies, are highly profitable despite falling circulations throughout the entire newspaper sector, and are read across all sections of the population (with a focus on occupational groups in the C2DE categories). Their founders, Rupert Murdoch and the late Axel Springer, are two rather controversial figures whose media enterprises frequently attract considerable unease over notions of concentration in ownership and agenda setting powers.

Looking back on a turbulent history during which they have been intensely debated, *The Sun* and *Bild* have both been recognised as particularly provocative and opinionated media outlets amongst the range of national titles in their respective countries. They have both earned a reputation for publishing less- than-trustworthy facts. Their potential to influence readers has been a strong magnet for concern, and their impact on issue and government politics has been debated excessively. Yet, closely observed by the British and German media landscape and other public realms, the papers frequently attract both admiration and controversy over their scoops and blunders.

In terms of editorial characteristics, *The Sun* and *Bild* would seem truly tabloid in style. A range of typical genre characteristics can be identified in both papers' reporting, including a visual, eye-catching lay-out, a focus on 'human interest' themes, a use of concise and easy-to-relate-to words and language, and – most notably – a set of particular narrative strategies utilised to emotionalise the text. Notably, reviewing *The Sun* and *Bild*'s preferred content and style characteristics, an important specificity of the genre emerges, relating to the observation that tabloid newspapers are hybrids. This means that their reporting seemingly focuses on news, but their discursive strategies and news style create a fictional character for the text. In accordance with other popular media formats, such as Reality TV (cf. Hill 2005; 2007), this hybrid nature of tabloid reporting is a highly significant issue worthy of further examination.

Having established a range of commonalities, it is noteworthy that *The Sun* and *Bild* also differ in some respects. Dissimilarities include, for instance, the handling of local and regional content. Whilst *Bild* is published in several regional versions sharing a common editorial frame, *The Sun* is identical country-wide, with some variation only in the *Scottish* and *Irish Sun*. Moreover, worth re-emphasising are the papers' different approaches to humour and joking. These notions appear much more elaborate in and significant to *The Sun*'s stories than to *Bild*'s articles. A further important difference concerns the papers' diverse displays of their political opinions. While UK newspapers, national tabloids in particular, traditionally state their political stance quite clearly, advising readers which party to vote for in a general election, the German press has avoided such obviously partial content since the end of the Second World War. Yet, *Bild* is recognised as a transporter of its political views via implicit means, inviting regular controversy over this issue. It is also interesting to note that *Bild*'s readers, apparently, do not tolerate an overtly political bias, as circulation decreased at relevant points in the history of the tabloid. A few smaller differences between the papers concern their diverse physical sizes, (*Bild*'s large shape, as opposed to *The Sun*'s small form), as well as the somewhat more pronounced nation-centred perspective of the British tabloid.

Each of these aspects are important to bear in mind when examining readers' responses to the papers. It is worth asking how these issues filter through to audience reactions. Does, for instance, the controversy surrounding the papers reflect on and in readers' attitudes? How do readers approach the tabloids and their texts, and what sense do they make of their hybrid nature? Moreover, what role do similarities and differences play in readers' responses? The evidence suggests that the commonalities between *The Sun* and *Bild* create similar reading experiences of the tabloids. However, it is also likely that the diverse social and cultural contexts of the UK and Germany impact on the papers' reception, causing national variations in readers' responses. Such contextual differences need to be acknowledged as relevant dimensions of variance, which is attended to in the following chapter.

# Chapter 3: Differing Contexts
## Media Systems & Journalistic Traditions in Britain & Germany

Having established a range of similarities between the two tabloids *The Sun* and *Bild*, let us turn to consider their diverse social and cultural contexts. Clearly, a number of similar conditions can be expected in contemporary Britain and Germany, for both countries share a common Western democratic background, and German journalism was modelled after British traditions at the end of the Second World War. Still, it can be argued that *The Sun* and *Bild* exist in different historical, legal and economic conditions, which ultimately impact on the way in which they are read today.

Scholars have identified a range of elements that influence the specific nature of Britain and Germany's journalistic cultures, including the relationship between journalism, the state and the political culture, and the role of journalism in society (cf. Humphreys 1996; Hallin and Mancini 2004); the legal and economic conditions in which journalism operates (cf. Esser 1998); the self-understanding of journalists (cf. Köcher 1985, 1986), their professional ethics, norms and values (cf. Thomaß 1998) and the their working routines (cf. Esser 1998). Examining selected aspects of this 'complex network' (Machill 1997a: 14), this chapter represents a venture into the field of comparative journalism research. Examining key dimensions of variance, the following discussion aims to highlight important differences between British and German media systems and journalistic cultures, indicating their potential significance to the tabloid reading experience in each country.

## PRESS HISTORY

Although Britain and Germany today share a similar journalistic ideal, the press in the two countries operates in quite diverse ways. Relating back to different sociohistoric developments, this section identifies relevant events in the historical processes that have shaped contemporary British and German news journalism[5].

## Press Freedom & the Notion of the Fourth Estate

Essentially, two issues are of fundamental importance to the journalistic ideal in the UK and Germany today: the establishment of press freedom and the idea of the press as fourth estate. However, the events leading up to the implementation of these conditions in each country differ significantly, which has resulted in somewhat diverse performances of the British and German press.

### Britain

Historically, the UK was among the first European countries to establish parliamentarianism, democracy, civil rights and freedom of the press. In Britain, the idea of the press as a fourth estate originated as early as the seventeenth century, a time that was characterized by the rise of the bourgeoisie as the new economically and politically powerful class. In the preceding years, a small minority of aristocrats and a monarch with absolute powers dominated British society. Partly influenced by Enlightenment ideas, however, the bourgeoisie started demanding freedom from this feudal authority. Brian McNair (2003: 32) notes that 'from this basic drive for power developed the political theory of liberalism and the bourgeois concept of freedom: economic freedom, political freedom and intellectual freedom'. Moreover, the dissemination of information was essential to the workings of the bourgeois capitalist class, which resulted in the emergence of news media in Britain. In highlighting the significance of these developments, McNair (ibid: 32) points out:

'Tolerance and diversity continue to be regarded as essential for serving a democratic political system, since such a system depends on rational choice; for enlightening and informing the public, who make the choices; and for allowing the media to stand as a fourth estate over government, thus preventing dictatorship.'

---

5   Many details have to be sacrificed for the sake of conciseness in discussion in this chapter, but it is worth noting that others have provided excellent comprehensive accounts of the origins of journalism in Britain and Germany. For a full discussion of the German development cf., for instance, the works of Fischer (1978); Hurwitz (1972); Lindemann (1969) and Koszyk (1966, 1972, 1986). The history of journalism in the UK is covered extensively by Griffiths (1992); Herd (1952); Seymour-Ure (2001), and a general perspective is offered by Smith (1979) and Wilke (2000).

It is important to note that press freedom in the UK was achieved approximately 150 years earlier than in Germany. However, the struggle for a free and independent press in the UK is usually recognised as a long historical process. It took roughly 300 years, covering a time in which 'the state moved from trying to control all of the outpourings of the press through the use of various forms of direct and indirect controls, to a position where, formally at least, it claimed no power to interfere significantly in the content of the press.' (O'Malley 2000: 1) In mid-Victorian Britain, the stamp duty was abandoned with the repeal of the Stamp Act in 1855 and the paper duty in 1861. At the same time, advertising became increasingly significant with regard to the financing of newspapers. As a consequence of these developments, the press in Britain became independent from the state, and was able to take on its role as a 'public watchdog' (Esser 1997: 115), rising to become a true fourth estate. Free from influence/interference from political parties, the state and other institutions, the press henceforth sought to inform the public, control the government and prevent society from absolutism[6].

Due to this long 'heroic' struggle for press freedom (Curran 2003: 3), as well as its similarly long establishment in Britain, the idea of the press as a fourth estate is a concept deeply implanted in the self-understanding of British journalists, shared also by academics and the general public. As a result, Frank Esser (1997: 131) remarks that the UK press today displays a rather 'pronounced self-confidence', from a German point of view, at times, exercising its rights as a fourth estate in rather 'unscrupulous' ways.

## Germany

Renate Köcher (1986: 45) remarks that contemporary Britain and Germany are 'two countries with extensive freedom of the press'. However, while Britain can be regarded as a precursor in terms of the establishment of press freedom, Germany is the European latecomer in this respect. Historians even speak of a 'peculiar path' to the German development (cf., for instance, Blackbourn and Eley 1984).

---

6  This, at least, is the standard interpretation of press history. There is, however, some disagreement over the issue of the press' true independence. Curran (2003: 6) notes that 'newspapers long remained an extension of the party system' due to the fact that many leading proprietors were Members of Parliament, and some national newspapers received financial support from party funds well into the twentieth century. Other scholars also doubt that the British press today is as free and independent as it is conceived to be (cf., for instance, relevant discussions in Esser 1997; Hallin and Mancini 1997; Requate 1995; Humphreys 1997; Sparks 1999). Although clearly an important issue, this debate exceeds the scope of this book, and therefore does not form part of its focus.

The UK's long tradition of press freedom is contrasted by a very different, yet equally long tradition of authoritarianism in Germany. Political parties and institutions such as the Church were able to exercise massive control over the content of the press, long before the Nazi dictatorship abused newspapers as powerful propaganda instruments. However, there had been attempts to establish freedom of the press in Germany as well – albeit more than a century after those in Britain. Yet, these took place 'under very much less favourable conditions', as Köcher (1986: 45) identifies. She argues that this was due to the fact that eighteenth century Germany was split into a great number of small autonomous states, which represented not one, but many powerful opponents to press freedom. Despite this, Anthony Smith (1979: 79) acknowledges 'various press freedom', arguing that the severity of the restrictions varied from state to state at the time. Overall however, German journalism before 1945 was characterized by authoritarian paternalism, and a severe lack of independence from the state, political parties and the government.

After the capitulation of the Nazi government on 8 May 1945, British and American Allies in West Germany introduced a new democratic ideal to their occupation zones, based upon the standards they had been following for about a hundred years or so. In the course of this process, the German press changed radically. This was the point at which British and German journalistic cultures 'clashed' (Esser 1997: 47 pp.). If there had been few similarities regarding the role of journalism in each society before, a complete rebirth of the German press took place in 1944/45, generally referred to as the 'zero hour' of the German society (Hurwitz 1972). The process that was started then resulted in the adaptation of the German system to the British and US-American model, at least in West-Germany. East-Germany, meanwhile, fell under the Soviet occupation zone, and became the German Democratic Republic (GDR). 43 years later, in 1989, German reunification took place and East-Germany, likewise, adapted to the journalistic model introduced by the British after the Second World War[7].

The re-education of West-German journalists after the Second World War was carried out thoroughly (cf. the detailed account of Fischer 1978), and the significant changes introduced to the German press and media system still apply today. However, as Esser noted in 1997, Germany was still lacking a sustaining blueprint for the idea of the press as a fourth estate (ibid: 122). This was reflected, he argued, in controversial debates on the concept, its use and its true significance, debates that regularly re-occurred within the realms of press laws, politics, and communication research. Moreover, while the British press has acted out their watchdog role ever

---

7   It should be noted that the British liaised with the other allied powers when carrying out these various processes of re-education in Germany. However, as the British model is of major importance to this study, the focus here is on comparing British and German traditions.

since the second half of the nineteenth century, Germany was 'awarded' democracy and press freedom, being more or less devoid of any active participation (Esser 1998: 315). Hence, the heritage of Nazi dictatorship seems more persistent than the British press officers had expected. This became evident, for instance, when German journalists refused to claim 'any political or editorial power' (Esser 1998: 315), as a result of their experiences with Nazi propaganda media during the Third Reich. Esser even regards the persisting traumas of Nazi-Germany as the main reason for the fact that the German press today still appears less aggressive and partisan than the British press (ibid 1998: 126; 315; cf. also Chapter 2 with regard to the diverse endorsement traditions of *The Sun* and *Bild*).

## Development of Tabloid Journalism

These diverse socio-historical processes also impacted on different developments of tabloid journalism in Britain and Germany, the selective milestones of which are outlined in this section.

## Britain

The UK can be recognised as playing a leading role in Europe with regard to its early and elaborate development of tabloid formats. Lucy Brown (1992: 30) notes in *The Encyclopaedia of the British Press 1422-1992* that the history of British popular journalism runs 'from the last dying speeches of condemned criminals of the eighteenth century, through the unstamped papers of the immediate post-war years and the 1830s, and continuing into the later nineteenth century with the emergence of the popular half-penny dailies, led by the *Daily Mail*'.

The nineteenth century can be regarded a crucial time in the history of British popular journalism. A first significant development is marked by the advent of the radical press, which emerged in the early nineteenth century alongside existing newspapers such as *The Times* (launched 1785). Autonomous from political groupings and the state as well as independent from advertising through their low production costs and large sales revenues, these unstamped voices of popular radical expression became a significant political force. James Curran (2003: 6-17) explains that between 1815 and 1855, many of the radical papers were highly profitable, easily outselling the commercial newspapers. The leading titles even managed to reach a nationwide audience. Although the commercial press was regarded as more 're-spectable' (ibid: 9), the radical press had a larger readership. Many of the radical papers were read by a number of people per copy, due to the common practice of sharing a newspaper and reading it aloud at that time (Curran 2003: 10). This could be seen as a parallel to modern tabloid usage, which, likewise, often involves sharing and passing on; for instance, this study confirmed an example of such use amongst a group of colleagues (cf. p. 220). Moreover, the titles of the radical press were particularly popular amongst the working classes, and this aspect also seems familiar in view of today's tabloid press. However, a truly distinctive element of the radical press relates to the fact that a substantial number of the papers were *produced* by members of the working classes, as well as read by them. Many of the proprietors and journalists, indeed, were of 'humble origins' (ibid: 11; cf. also Sparks 1998).

Essentially, the radical papers were able to make a significant political and social impact through their autonomous support of the working class movement. Curran details that the radical journalists understood themselves as class representatives and activists at the same time. Striving to 'establish a relationship of real reciprocity with their readers', the radical press wanted to become a true 'people's organ' (Curran 2003: 11-12). They aimed at representing the views of the less privileged and speaking out for them. Thus playing a vital role in the class struggles of the time, the papers helped the working class movement to a wide-spread recognition, by establishing a growing consciousness amongst their audience members. Read nationwide, they also worked to unify the readership, establishing a common ground among 'disparate elements of the working community' (cf. ibid 2003: 13-16). Again, these issues bear a degree of resemblance to the typical contemporary tabloid self-presentation as "advocates" of the little people, as well as their elaborate audience address and rhetoric of inclusion and exclusion (cf. also Chapter 2). Yet, unlike modern tabloids, the radical papers brought about actual social change through fostering political mobilization[8].

As Brown (1992: 29) asserts, the other important development in Britain between 1800 and 1860 relates to the emergence of popular newspapers 'aimed at the poor and the disenfranchised'. Due to the stamp duty, many of these titles were published once a week only. This led to the establishment of the popular Sunday papers as 'the most significant newspaper publishing development of the 1840s' (ibid). Relatively cheap to produce, the Sundays were sold at a rather low price. Brown explains part of their appeal lay in their inexpensiveness, with the content of the papers acting as a further important draw: 'They used a formula which was already old and tried, compounded of police-court reporting, amazing revelations, and a political point of view that was generally populist, hostile to the rich, the aristocracy, and the monarchy.' (ibid) One of the first Sunday papers was the *News of the World*. Launched in 1843, it passed into the hands of Rupert Murdoch more than 100 years later (in 1969), and is recognised today as the Sunday sister of *The Sun*. Already in the 1840s, the *News of the World* became one of the most widely

---

8   Curran (2003) also regards the development of the radical press in the UK as highly significant to the subsequent establishment of press freedom.

read Sunday papers, soon establishing a style of reporting which, in a similar form, still constitutes part of its success today (cf. Engel 1996: 28 pp.)

Taking a somewhat "lighter" approach to news reporting than the radical press, the popular Sundays heralded a trend that continuously intensified throughout the second half of the nineteenth century, particularly after the 'taxes on knowledge' had been repealed (cf. Griffiths 2006: 92 pp.) Several interlinked developments are important to note with regard to this period. The first concerns the emergence of commercial half-penny dailies in Britain. Originating as 'penny papers' in the United States in the 1830s, these news outlets, for the first time in British newspaper history, combined modern printing technologies with an "on the street" selling technique at a very low cover price (cf. Dulinski 2003: 74). Resulting in a true revolution in news journalism, the half-pennies made news available to large sections of the public, rather than to the society's elites alone. A second, related, issue concerns the advancing processes of the Industrial Revolution, which led to a sustained growth of the urban population, and gave rise to an ever-increasing demand for the cities' mass circulation newspapers, particularly those concentrated in the London area (cf. Sparks 1999: 45). Thirdly, the 'frank sensationalism' (Engel 1996: 44) offered by the US American 'penny papers' rubbed off on their British relatives and caused a shift in the news concept: 'The cheap commercial papers in their turn brazenly asserted their independence from party politics, their advocacy of laissez-faire, their reliance on advertisements, their low price and high circulation, and their emphasis on news from all social spheres.' (Schiller 1981: 8, quoted in Dulinski 2003: 74)

Though not an entirely new phenomenon, this type of news reporting became known as the 'New Journalism' of the period between 1880 and 1914 (a phrase originally coined by the poet and critic Matthew Arnold in 1887; cf. Griffiths 2006: 114). This marked the true birth hour of investigative journalism and the tabloid press in the UK. The *Pall Mall Gazette* (launched 1885) and the *Star* (launched 1888) emerged as the first 'screaming' tabloid titles in Britain (Dulinski 2003: 121). The success of the popular Sundays and dailies encouraged Alfred Harmsworth – more commonly known as Lord Northcliffe – to launch the *Daily Mail* in 1896. Still published today, the *Daily Mail* can be seen as something of a prototype for British tabloid newspapers (cf. ibid). The era of the *Daily Mail* was characterised by the flourishing of popular newspapers and increasing competition in the field. It was also the era of the press barons, and economic controls in the industry were modified during that time (Curran 2003: 36 pp.) In the twentieth century, tabloid news values increased further, particularly from the 1960s to the 1990s (cf. Tunstall 1996: 31 pp.) Murdoch's purchase of *The Sun* in the 1960s, then, is generally recognised as greatly intensifying popular journalism in Britain (Sparks 1998: 8). The recent history of tabloids, therefore, is closely linked to the history of *The Sun*, as outlined in Chapter 2.

Matthew Engel (1996: 46) remarks that with the advent of the half-penny papers, a distinction began to be discerned 'between morning newspapers, which were respectable, and evening newspapers, which were not, rather like the difference between broadsheets and tabloids that exists today'. Echoing the distinction made in the early nineteenth century between the "respectable" commercial press and the "disreputable" radical papers, such binary opposites indicate a significant theme running through the entire history of the popular press.

## Germany

In contrast to the UK, German tabloid journalism made a late arrival amongst the Industrial Western nations. This is despite the fact that the origins of modern newspapers can, indeed, be traced back to medieval Germany, where the invention of the printing press enabled the distribution of daily 'manuscript news-sheets' in the latter half of the fifteenth century (cf. World Association of Newspapers 2005; Höke 2004). However, Ulrike Dulinski (2003: 15) speaks of a 'very long historical latency' of Germany with regard to the development of the popular press. The first popular daily, called *BZ am Mittag*, appeared as late as 1904. It was a local publication distributed in the capital of Berlin only, and it remained the sole popular newspaper sold "on the street" until 1914 (ibid: 121). Although favoured for its emotional reporting and human-interest stories (Höke 2004: 107), and appearing more tabloid in style than other titles published at the time, Dulinski suggests that the *BZ am Mittag* was still 'remarkably serious'. From a contemporary perspective, it appears to resemble the broadsheet *Frankfurter Allgemeine Zeitung*, rather than the tabloid *Bild* (ibid 2003: 121).

Newspapers particularly flourished in Germany in the 'golden' 1920s. However, the years between the First and Second World Wars can generally be regarded a bloom period for the tabloid press; up to 20 popular titles were competing for readers in Berlin at one point during the interwar years (Schirmer 2001: 17). Dulinski (2003: 15) remarks that a similarly high number of rival tabloids have never again occurred in German press history, until the present day. Yet, these publications did not yet reach a mass audience, for their circulation remained relatively low compared to similar titles in Britain, France and the United States (ibid: 123). Still, the Weimar Republic (1919 to 1933) is recognised as hugely important in the development of German tabloid journalism. Sensation gained a stronghold in German press reporting then, due to the emergence of a type of tabloids denounced *Revolverblätter* (lit: revolver sheets). These publications carried news from the red-light milieu, and reported on crime and court cases (Dulinski 2003: 153 pp.) As in the UK, harsh criticism of the papers' 'sensationalist' style of reporting soon emerged (cf. Dovifat 1930). The term *Revolverblatt*, indeed, has survived to the present day, and is still frequently used by readers as a mockingly devaluing expression characterising the type of journalism of *Bild* (cf. p. 197).

Aside from the *Revolverblätter*, a rather famous publication that emerged in the Weimar Republic was the *Arbeiter-Illustrierte Zeitung*, or *AIZ* (lit: the workers' pictorial newspaper). The *AIZ* was a popular, weekly (later bi-weekly), picture-led magazine with a strongly left-wing, anti-fascism and pro-communism stance. Founded and edited by the communist Willi Münzenberg, it was published in Berlin and Prague between 1921 and 1938. The *AIZ* focused strongly on a working class readership, and was designed as a revolutionist proletariat organ with a mission quite similar to that of the radical press in Britain. As such, it was important to the development of the popular press in Germany. The paper was exiled to Prague in 1933 when Hitler came to power, where it died down five years later (cf. Willmann 1974).

During the Third Reich from 1933 to 1945, a German tabloid press was almost non-existent. The Nazis, however, misused some of the titles, and there certainly was a great deal of propaganda disguised as popular news. Generally, the totalitarian NSDAP-regime dictated journalism (and life) in Germany, and only a few newspapers were able to remain independent (cf. Dulinski 2003: 160 pp.) A significant development in the popular press could only be observed again after the Second World War, when the German media system was remodelled on British and US-American traditions. In 1952, *Bild* was founded, and it remains the country's most important tabloid publication (cf. Chapter 2). Dulinski (ibid) also specifies some regional tabloids that were launched or re-established in post-war Germany are still published today, including the *abendzeitung* (1948) and the *tz* (1968) in Munich, the *BZ am Abend* (1949) in East-Berlin, the *BZ* (1953) in West-Berlin, the *Morgenpost* (1949) in Hamburg and the *Express* in Cologne (1964).

# PRESS LAWS

Aside from historical and cultural imprints, some of the reasons for the perception of a less aggressive and partisan approach in the German press (cf. Esser 1998) can be traced back to significant differences in Britain and Germany's legal conditions for journalism.

## Britain

When comparing British and German press laws, it becomes evident that in the UK press rights are far from extensive. Humphreys (1997) points out that freedom of the press has always been regarded as an important, yet self-evident part of the (non-written) British constitution (cf. also Dewall 1997; McNair 1995). Yet, press freedom derives from the individual's civil right to freedom of speech, rather than representing the public's right to gain information (as is the case in Germany; cf. Esser 1997). Although the UK government introduced a 'Freedom of Information Act' in 2000, journalists do not enjoy many occupational privileges.

Esser (1998: 197 pp.) shows that UK courts are also more critical towards the press than the German ones, a fact that adds to the occupational challenges of journalists in Britain. Simultaneously, citizens' rights to take unlawful or unethical reporting to court seem somewhat restricted in the UK, for libel actions in the country are rather expensive (Esser 1998: 215), and British law does not recognize the right to privacy as such. Raymond Snoddy (1992: 94) illustrates this by quoting an English judge, who speaks about the UK's legal conditions: 'It is well-known that in English law there is no right of privacy, and accordingly there is no right of action for breach of a person's privacy'. Similarly, Peter Humphreys (1997: 35) argues that the British tradition of a 'weak state' lacks protection of the private sphere. Only sometimes, the private sphere appears to be 'indirectly protected by actions of trespass, copyright and data protection', as Esser points out (1999: 313; referring to Robertson and Nicol 1992). The British Court of Appeal, however, recently incorporated the 'obligation to protect an individual from an unjustified invasion of private life' (Liz Chong in *The Times* from 21 May 2005) into English law. Yet, privacy in the UK is protected in a much less specified sense than in German press law.

### Germany

Conditions, it would appear, are far more favourable in Germany, both in terms of journalists' professional rights and those of private individuals. Sandra Coliver (1993: 260) notes that 'Germany belongs to the countries with the strongest protection of press freedom of Western democracies'. The three foundations of this are represented by (1) the guarantee for press freedom, which is stated in the country's written constitution; (2) the detailed press rights described in the laws of the German states; and (3) the verdicts of the Federal Constitutional Court, which delivers a judgement in case of conflict. Gerd G. Kopper and Paolo Mancini (2003) regard this extensive system as typical for Germany, arguing that it marks a consequence of the country's Nazi past.

As a result, German journalists enjoy a lot of privileges, most of which are indeed unfamiliar to their British colleagues. Among the range of occupational rights, journalists in Germany are entitled to obtain information from public authorities, if this serves their professional duty of informing the public (Esser 1997: 125). Hence, it is a lot easier for German journalists to access information of any kind. They are likewise free to publish even confidential intelligence material, if it is seen to serve what is perceived to be a 'legitimate public interest'[9]. Another privilege concerns the right to refuse evidence, allowing German journalists to refrain from disclosing facts and sources, even in court. Falling under their right to protect professional secrets and sources, this is a specificity that applies only to a few professions in Germany. People working in the media are especially privileged in this respect, as are medical and clerical professions. However, journalists cannot be released of their right to protect their sources, as it is the case with medical doctors and priests.

At the same time, it is easier for German citizens to take legal proceedings against unlawful or unethical reporting to court than it is for Britons. Germany's differentiated press law system does not only provide journalistic privileges, it also imposes important restrictions on press reporting. Hence, Coliver 1993: 271) states that Germany is one of the few Western democratic countries that explicitly protects the right to privacy and personal reputation in their constitution. Esser (1999: 313) exemplifies:

'In German civil law, a clear distinction is made for three protected spheres (in the rank of growing protection): the individual sphere, the private sphere and the intimate sphere. Sexual behaviour clearly concerns the last mentioned. In general, coverage of this sphere is illegal.'

Hence, the German press appears 'very discreet' in comparison to the British (ibid: 313), particularly with regard to the infringement of personal privacy. The general approach of most German journalists originates in the 'persisting consensus among newspeople, politicians and the public that private matters ought not to be dwelt on in the media' (ibid: 319). Details from the private lives of politicians (relating to their marriage problems, for instance) are rarely mentioned in the German press – very unlike the habit of most British newspapers. Yet, these ethical codes appear to apply to the quality press only, for *Bild*'s reporters would seem to take less notice of such professional principles, as they regularly bridge privacy laws (cf. Chapter 2).

An interesting case exemplifying the different legal protections regarding German and British press reporting, and diverse perceptions of "right" and "wrong", occurred in the year 2003. The British tabloid *Mail on Sunday* published a story on 5 January claiming that former German Chancellor Gerhard Schröder had cheated on his wife. Schröder was said to be enraged by these allegations on the subject of his private life, a reaction that British politicians might, likewise, have shown. However, Schröder took the (from a UK perspective) somewhat "unusual" step of instructing his lawyers to seek an injunction from a German court, ordering the *Mail on Sunday* to refrain from publishing any more accusations, and claiming compensation from the paper. His reaction resulted in a 'tussle' between Schröder

---

9   British journalists can, indeed, claim similar justification for publishing a story. However, they do not enjoy equally extensive professional privileges in general (cf. Esser 1998).

and the paper, and was soon seen to represent a 'clash' of different legal and journalistic cultures (Hooper, in *The Guardian* from 20 January 2003). Further illustrating these national variations, *The Sun*'s publication of photographs of Saddam Hussein in prison on 20 May 2005 marks another example. Seemingly unaware of the fact that photos were taken, the former dictator was portrayed standing in his underpants, washing his socks and sleeping in his cell. Hussein's lawyers reacted by threatening to sue *The Sun*. However, it is interesting that they claimed the photographs breached the Geneva Conventions protecting the privacy and dignity of prisoners of war, rather than basing their arguments on a law protecting an individual's privacy (as lawyers in Germany would have, presumably, reasoned). As a result, legal opinion was quite divided over whether Saddam Hussein would be able to successfully sue *The Sun* at all (cf. Beeston and Theodoulou; Chong in *The Times*, 21 May 2004).

## PRESS MARKETS

Britain and Germany also vary significantly with regard to the economic and structural conditions of the press. While the British newspaper landscape is characterised by competition, concentration, and a dominance of national tabloids, the German press market is marked by intense localisation, a strong tradition for home delivery, and a dominance of broadsheets.

### Britain

With regard to the British press market, the highly competitive nature of the press and the dominance of national titles and tabloid newspapers immediately spring to mind. The newsprint industry in the UK is, indeed, characterized by extensive concentration of, and competition between, national dailies produced in the London area. Tunstall (1996: 2) remarks that the UK's national newspaper market is 'an extreme case within Europe in the extent to which it is dominated by national newspapers published in one city'. He explains that London has a long political and economic tradition of dominance in Britain. The capital emerged as 'the home of the biggest national newspaper press in Europe' from a very early point in press history (ibid: 7-8), which he regards as one of the origins for the contemporary structure of the UK press. Tunstall also points out that competition has intensified even more since 1986, the year Rupert Murdoch moved the production of his newspapers to Wapping (cf. Chapter 2). In the 20 years following Murdoch's move, all of the large newspaper and publishing companies have likewise left their former home in Fleet Street and moved to London's docklands. This transformation is generally recognised as one of the most dramatic events in British press history, leading to a yet larger amount of titles, and an increase in content, selection and aggressive marketing (cf. ibid: 18-30).

While national titles clearly govern the UK press market, regional newspapers in Britain have 'melted down towards the parish pump and local classified advertising' (ibid: 75). However, although national dailies sell well, especially in the south east, they aim at the whole of Britain. Hence, Tunstall recognises a combination of 'supernational' and 'super-local' amongst the national titles produced in London. Most of the London titles are sold at newsstands or on the street. It is, therefore, truly important for them to appeal to readers at first sight, i.e. through their front page. Hence, the UK papers would seem rather unrestrained in comparison to news outlets in most other countries. A further distinctive characteristic of the British press market concerns the traditional importance of Sunday papers (cf. p. 58), which have only recently increased in Germany. What is more, the British newspaper landscape is dominated by tabloids, and there are, by far, more daily and Sunday tabloids than in Germany.

As a consequence, a subdivision within the 'tabloid' category can be observed in the UK. Frequently, the range of popular papers is divided into 'down-market' and 'mid-market' tabloids (cf. Tunstall 1996: 9). Other categorisations include the terms 'popular' versus 'serious popular' papers (Curran et al. 1980: 316). Sparks (2000: 14-15) even distinguishes between three kinds of tabloids, which he refers to as the 'serious-popular press', the 'newsstand tabloid press' and the 'supermarket tabloid press'. Referring to yet another pair of descriptions, McNair (2003: 145-6) categorises 'down-market' tabloids as 'bonk' journalism, distinguishing them from the somewhat 'milder' forms of tabloids, which he refers to as 'yellow' journalism. Although an all-embracing categorisation of the tabloid category is hard to find, it is clear that such distinctions indicate divergent conceptions of journalism. The terms 'tabloid', 'popular' and so forth are frequently contrasted with 'broadsheet' or 'quality' newspapers (cf. Engels 1996: 11). Implying certain evaluations of newspapers, such denominations indicate what is considered reputable or disreputable journalism. Having occurred ever since the birth of tabloid journalism (cf. p. 60), such distinctions would seem to impact on readers' judgements, as well – an issue this book will consider in its third section.

## Germany

In contrast to the UK, concentration and competition is less severe in the German newspaper market. A distinctive characteristic of the country's press landscape, indeed, relates to its extensive localisation. Until 1870/71, Germany was divided into 38 self-governing states, each publishing their own news-sheets (cf. Dulinski 2003). Building on this long-established tradition, local and regional dailies are still highly successful in Germany. A large number of readers take out subscriptions to a regional or national broadsheet, which is delivered to their homes every day. The average German newspaper, therefore, still resembles its original model, carrying much regional and local content, being distributed in mainly one region, and reaching readers via home delivery (Esser 1998). This also impacts on perceptions of what is considered "high" and "low" standard reporting. The most common distinction made between different types of daily newspapers in Germany relates to 'subscription newspapers' (representing "quality" and "serious" journalism) versus papers 'sold on the street' (a selling technique mostly characterising tabloids).

As home delivery is of minor importance to the UK press (cf. Sparks 1999), some variations occur with regard to the newspaper reading habits in Britain and Germany. Tunstall (1996: 215) remarks that readers in Britain frequently do 'newspaper hopping', reading 'one daily on Monday, a different daily on Tuesday, and no daily newspaper on Wednesday'. In Germany, with subscriptions and home delivery being of great importance, the local newspapers are often monopolists in their distribution districts. In addition, the five to seven national daily broadsheets (depending on which newspapers are included in this category) do not overlap much with regard to their key geographical areas of distribution and selling. These conditions create a situation in which German reader loyalty seems more intense, as audience members are rather 'used to reading their regional paper' (Esser 1999: 297).

While tabloids dominate the newspaper landscape in the UK, there are, by far, more national broadsheets than national tabloids in Germany, due to the high number of regional and local dailies. Most of these, to use Spark's categorisation of different newspaper types (2000: 14), can be regarded as 'serious' and 'semiserious' press outlets. Generally, appealing to their readers through the front page is of minor importance to most German newspapers, as the common practice of home delivery guarantees a significant part of the sales, and results in a less 'agitated' and 'obtrusive' type of reporting (Esser 1997: 130 pp.).

With regard to the tabloid marketplace, the German *Bild* does not have any true rivals. Existing alongside a small number of local popular dailies, *Bild* maintains its unique market position as the country's only national tabloid. The paper can, moreover, easily compete with most of the local and national newspapers in Germany. One of the reasons for this can be seen in *Bild*'s editorial focus on regional content, meeting the demands of the German newspaper audience. Likewise, through an extended distribution scheme, the tabloid seems to be one of the most easily available newspapers in the country. Yet, another reason for the fact that *Bild* is able to maintain its singular position in the German newspaper market may relate to its idiosyncratic content preferences, style and narrative features, all of which clearly differ from most other German newspapers (cf. Chapter 2).

## PROFESSIONAL TRADITIONS

The ideal conception of journalism underlying the journalistic cultures in the UK and Germany serves as a model for journalistic behaviour and judgement. This section, therefore, considers important values, ethics and principles constituting the journalistic ideal in the two countries. Some of the principles are understood and accomplished in similar ways; and some differ between German and British press journalists, due to variations in the nations' historical developments. Causing somewhat diverse reporting styles, this would seem to impact upon the way tabloid newspapers are read in each country.

### Objectivity & the Separation of Facts and Opinion

Scholars have argued that the journalistic cultures of the UK and Germany particularly differ with regard to the way the professional principle of "objectivity" is understood (cf. Donsbach and Klett 1993; Patterson and Donsbach 1996; Esser 1997). Before 1945, the German press had operated in an authoritarian surrounding and was lacking autonomy and independence. As a consequence, early professional principles of German journalists included a pronounced display of opinions that conformed to ideas of the state or particular political parties (Esser 1997: 114; cf. Requate 1995). In the nineteenth century, however, conflicts between independent publishers and the state brought about an early form of "resistant" opinion journalism, whereby independent publishers used their newspapers to circulate (alternative) views. An important function of German newspapers back then was to *comment on* what had happened, rather than *report* events in a neutral way (Hurwitz 1972: 41). It can be argued, then, that a strong tradition of opinion journalism existed in Germany long before Nazi propaganda media 'perfected the idea of censorship' (Esser 1997: 114).

This combination of news and commentary within German press outlets was deemed 'dangerous' by British press officers (Esser 1998: 49). Aiming to re-educate German journalists, the British ideal was introduced, placing strong emphasis on the separation of facts and opinion. The press officers were attempting to establish a system by which news would be selected according to their news value, rather than to their political value (Esser 1998: 49). In some ways, however, this request seemed challenging to post-war journalists in Germany; after the Second World War, these reporters felt they were entitled their (political) opinion more than ever. Such initial reluctance could be interpreted as evidence for the view that a free German press, to the journalists in the immediate post-war period, implied a free (and strong) expression of opinions. In their view, having experienced the suppressive Nazi media, neutrality in news reporting seemed a principle that impeded a truly "free" press. However, newspapers in Germany gradually incorporated the British principles, and today, the separation of facts and opinion is regarded as an important standard, indicating journalistic quality in both countries (Esser 1997: 121).

Clearly, the notion of freedom of expression has traditionally been understood differently by German and British journalists, as a result of the diverse historical backgrounds in each country, which has caused variation in the conception of "objective" reporting. Connecting with these initially differing approaches, diverse professional journalistic role conceptions can be observed. Renate Köcher (1985, 1986) remarks in her comparative accounts on the self-understanding of German and British journalists that, 'while British journalists see themselves as bloodhounds – as hunters of news – their German colleagues see themselves as missionaries' (ibid 1986: 63). This is in line with what Emil Dovifat (1927: 214) wrote about the self-conception of German journalists before the Second World War. He argued that they saw themselves as publicists with a mission, determined to have an impact on public opinion by representing and publishing particular political views.

Some implications need to be highlighted with regard to the role of journalism in society and the view of the audience. The main function of British journalism, in theory at least, is to report facts objectively (Esser 1998: 50), whilst balancing different viewpoints; for instance, the positions of all major political parties (Humphreys 1997: 34). British journalists aim to provide readers with the opportunity to attain their own opinion, based on the knowledge of all relevant facts. German journalism, in contrast, 'tends to place a lot of value on opinion and less on news' (Köcher 1986: 43). In particular, during the post-war years, journalistic endeavours focused on the education of readers by means of commentary (Hurwitz 1972). Evidently, these differences cause diverse conceptions of the audience, for it would seem that the British view ascribes more "active" skills to readers – an issue that shall be resumed in the subsequent chapter.

Köcher (1985, 1986) and Wolfgang Donsbach and Bettina Klett (1993) argue that British and German journalists still define their roles and understand their professional values and principles differently. However, opposing positions emerge from the work of Siegfried Weischenberg, Martin Löffelholz and Armin Scholl (1994), as well as that of Klaus Schönbach, Dieter Stürzebecher and Beate Schneider (1994), all of who do not see much difference, claiming that German journalism has more or less aligned to British standards with regard to professional role conceptions. Yet, some differences remain, particularly with regard to contemporary journalists' working routines. The separation of facts and opinion is reflected in the traditional division of labour within British newsrooms. Working on a so-called 'copy flow' principle (Esser 1998: 408), the production of texts follows a fixed succession of stages for controlling and processing a journalistic piece. According to British standards, a reporter is responsible for researching and writing up facts, while articles stating an opinion are written by leader writers, commentators or columnists (ibid: 447). Thus, the separation of fact and opinion is maintained by different responsibilities. The working routines of German journalists, in comparison, do not enhance this principle in a similar way. There is no 'copy-flow', not as much elaborated division of labour, and fewer hierarchical structures in German newsrooms. Instead, any journalist can potentially write commentaries, and it is quite common to have a news report and a commentary on the same issue written by one author. Hence, although separating facts from opinion represents an important professional value to both British and German journalists, Esser (1998: 447) remarks that the realisation of this notion would seem a little 'artificial' in Germany, compared to the British practice.

## Impartiality & Neutrality

A further important cross-national difference relates to the approach to notions of impartiality and neutrality. Academics and journalists in many countries often hold Anglo-American journalism as a model approach to impartial news reporting (cf. Hallin and Mancini 2004). However, separating facts from opinion does not necessarily entail impartiality, at least with regard to the British press (this does not apply to public service broadcasting as much; cf. Curran and Seaton 2003). Although both UK and German newspapers can be situated on a continuum from conservative to liberal titles, British newspapers can be said to be much more overtly partisan than most continental European papers (Hallin and Mancini 2004; cf. Humphreys 1997). This relates to the fact that the UK press looks back on a very distinct, yet independent endorsement tradition (cf. Chapter 2). As Sparks (1999: 45) describes: 'Although newspapers in Britain are obviously and stridently partisan, they are not party newspapers in the formal sense' (cf. Curran and Seaton 2003: 67 pp.) Yet, the British tabloids, in particular, clearly state their political views, frequently campaigning for the political party they prefer. Tunstall (1996) and Esser (1997) even recognise an increase in biased reporting since the Thatcher years, as a result of increased competition.

To the British press, then, the notion of partiality appears to be of vital importance. In comparison, the German press lacks a similar endorsement tradition; at least one not directly influenced by the state or political parties, as was the case during Nazi rule. An equally aggressive partisan press, therefore, did not develop in post-war Germany, despite the fact that newspapers had been recognised for their opinion-centred reporting prior to 1945. An explanation offered by Esser (1997: 130) relates to the structural conditions of the press market. Due to the popularity of local and regional titles, newspapers traditionally target the largest possible audience group of one particular region, rather than aiming at an (inevitably) smaller group of politically like-minded readers.

## Journalistic Ethics

There is some indication that cross-national differences also occur in terms of journalists' ethical behaviour. Connecting with variations between British and German press laws, Esser (1997: 121 pp.) points out that the two countries differ in terms of what journalists regard as "legitimate" methods of research. Drawing on data from surveys focussing on journalists' professional attitudes (cf. Weischenberg et al. 1994; Delano and Henningham 1995), Esser sees particular differences between the British and German journalists' approaches to pressurising sources, paying incentives in exchange for information, as well as in disguising their own identities for investigation purposes(ibid). He remarks that while these techniques seem largely accepted by British journalists, their German counterparts would seem to deem this 'ruthless and illegitimate' behaviour (ibid). Such diverse approaches are reflected in the press complaints statistics, too. German statistics have never reached British "standards", particularly with regard to tabloid newspapers and issues relating to the breeching of privacy rights (Esser 1999: 301).

As mentioned several times in this chapter, the German press appears more cautious than the British press, as a result of diverse issues, for instance, the diverse legal conditions of journalism (cf. ibid). UK journalists do not enjoy as many professional privileges as their German colleagues; hence, they would seem to be forced to employ "unethical" methods of research (Esser 1997: 126). This also relates back to the diverse historical significance of investigative journalism in the UK and Germany. As we have seen, investigative journalism marks an important origin of tabloid journalism in the UK, which looks back on a long-established tradition of the genre. In comparison, German journalism has long operated in authoritarian surroundings, a tradition that can be seen as overshadowing German press reporting until the present day.

Still, there is some disagreement over the issue of whether or not either approach results in quality reporting. Highlighting a contradiction in media policy in the UK, the balance between press freedom and press regulation has been discussed frequently since the beginning of the 1990s (cf. Brants et al. 1998). The UK's current system of self-regulation, which grants the press independence from 'any kind of external accountability beyond the market' (Seymour-Ure 2001: 242), is questioned by some scholars. The notion of the press' "true" independence from 'any kind of external accountability beyond the market' has been contested (Seymour-Ure 2001: 242). Tom O'Malley and Clive Soley (2000: 2) demand that laws should replace self-regulation, claiming that the British Press Council and Press Complaints Commission have failed to stop abuses: 'In the UK at the beginning of the twenty-first century it was still possible for the press to print inaccurate and misleading information about people and be subject, with the exception of a limited number of expensive libel actions, to very little rebuke or penalty'. Tunstall (1996: 380) likewise criticises the Three Royal Commissions on the press (1949, 1962, 1977), which had 'not much to say in terms of policy' (cf. also Curran and Seaton 2003: 346 pp.). Conversely, the fact that German journalists seem to conform to ethical standards rather than attempt further investigation is regretted by some scholars (Esser 1997; Weischenberg et al. 1994).

## Matters of Style and Presentation

Lastly, a few remarks should be added about variations between traditional reporting styles and presentation preferences of German and British printed news outlets. Highlighting the importance of a particular style in writing, British journalists used to mock German journalism after the Second World War. Sefton Delmer most notably, a former journalist of the *Daily Mail* and commissioned to set up the broadsheet *Die Welt* in 1946, wrote about German newspapers as unreadable, putting matters into incredibly pompous words and using such indigestible presentation styles that the German audience was hardly willing, nor able, to take in what they read (Delmer 1963: 642, quoted in Esser 1998: 48). Likewise, Cordelia Becker (1996: 46), reflecting on variations in the training of journalists, quotes Steve Crawnshaw, former foreign correspondent to *The Independent*. Crawnshaw apparently claimed reporters need to possess the skill for presenting serious themes in a human and understandable way. With regard to German newspapers, Crawnshaw observed that they resembled the style of official notes, severely lacking in human touch. Becker also remarks that the training of British journalists traditionally places more emphasis on a sense of humour, while any kind of missionary endeavour (typical for German journalists) is rejected (ibid 1996: 45).

The diverse significance of easy-to-relate-to writing styles and lively presentation of facts have been linked to different audience tastes in the UK and Germany. Schönbach (2000) and Esser (1999: 296), for instance, argue that 'German readers do not go so much for tabloid news value' (ibid), claiming that audiences in the UK are less interested in politics and more interested in human interest stories (cf. also Esser 1997: 129). This has been regarded as one of the reasons for the larger number of tabloids in the UK. However, such arguments have not yet been supported by empirical evidence, indicating that the greater success of popular papers and a certain tabloid style in the UK relates to a particular British audience taste. The situation in the UK could, moreover, also be explained by the rather stable historical and political continuity in Britain. Tunstall (1996: 199) points out that 'editors and journalists [in the UK] have always been looking for celebrities, drama, conflict, 'human interest', and 'good stories'' as a consequence of the fact that the UK has been a country with 'a rather low level of conflict and drama', particularly after 1945. Thus, the British press might have had no other choice than to turn "tabloid" in order to sell; while domestic conflicts in Germany, in contrast, might have provided enough material for newspaper editors to draw on.

## CONCLUSIONS

The aim of this chapter has been to illustrate the conceptual framework underlying my cross-national comparison of tabloid reading experiences further. The basic argument was that *The Sun* and *Bild*, albeit representing similar phenomena, exist in diverse contexts. Idiosyncratic aspects relating to divergent press histories, press laws and press markets in the UK and Germany have been reflected upon, highlighting a range of cross-national variations in the understanding of professional journalistic principles and values.

Summing up the insights gained, it is worth re-emphasising that the British press developed independent from the influence of political parties and the state by the end of the nineteenth century. Around the same time, German journalism moved in quite the opposite direction, a development that culminated in Nazi propaganda media. After the Second World War, German journalism was remodelled on British traditions. These diverse histories, as well as the highly competitive newspaper market in the UK, resulted in a much earlier development of popular formats in Britain. The Sunday tabloid *News of the World* has been published in the UK since 1843 (in London at first, later nationwide), while a comparable title with a national reach did not emerge in Germany until 100 years later, when *Bild* was founded in 1952.

Further important dimensions of variance can be identified with regard to the different legal conditions of British and German journalism. It is noteworthy that journalists in the UK generally enjoy more freedom with regard to what to publish about whom, when, and where. Germany, in contrast, has a considerably stricter legal protection of privacy rights. At the same time, British journalists are at a disadvantage in terms of professional privileges; for instance, when it comes to accessing information from public authorities.

Obvious diversities between Germany and the UK also occur with regard to the characteristics of the press markets. In particular, the tabloid marketplaces differ significantly. The British newspaper landscape is characterised by fierce competition, especially amongst the London dailies, and is dominated by national tabloids. In contrast to this, *Bild* represents the only national tabloid in Germany, existing alongside a few regional and local titles. Generally, the strong tradition of subscription and home delivery in Germany needs to be stressed as a further contrasting feature. Due to these differing conditions, appealing to readers through the front page would seem far more important to British newspapers. In particular, London papers are, therefore, regarded as 'less restrained' than newspapers of most other countries (Tunstall 1996: 3).

Likewise, some variation between German and British press reporting can be observed. For instance, the professional principle of "objectivity" and the role of opinion in news reporting have been understood differently by journalists in both countries, at least during the latter half of the twentieth century. Linking in with divergent conceptions of the audience, British journalists aim at providing all relevant information, in order to allow readers to form their own opinion about various matters. In contrast, German journalists, traditionally, conceive of their professional role in a more authoritarian way, aiming to educate their readers by suggesting viewpoints. The converse applies to the notion of "impartiality". British newspapers, the tabloids in particular, are recognised as clearly partisan, leaving no doubt about which political views they prefer. As opposed to this, German news outlets have avoided stating their political opinion too clearly, as a result of the enduring traumas of Nazi propaganda media. In line with the divergent press laws, the journalists' approach to professional ethics appears to differ as well. British journalists seem somewhat more 'ruthless' in the methods of research they employ than their German colleagues (cf. Esser 1997). Furthermore, British and German journalistic cultures 'clashed' with regard to the significance of an easily digestible writing style and a presentation pleasing to the eye. While these features mark a long-established practice in British journalism, the traditional German approach to news reporting has been described as 'unreadable' (cf. Delmer 1963).

As these principles clearly refer to the theoretical, ideal conception of journalism in Britain and Germany, it is likely that compromises occur when examining the reality in each country. However, the aspects discussed are truly significant as they contribute to shaping the journalistic ideal. Providing the basis for the specific value system by which journalistic endeavours are judged, this ideal serves as a model for conceptions of how journalism ought to be. It is worth keeping this in mind when examining readers' responses to tabloids. Do audiences in the two countries apply different standards when judging tabloid news outlets? And, what happens if popular papers are viewed against the backdrop of the journalistic ideal? How do readers assess, for instance, notions of objectivity, balance or impartiality with regard to tabloid content?

Moreover, a central prerequisite of this study relates to the idea that the varying media systems and journalistic cultures of Germany and the UK create diverse norms and values about tabloid formats that influence the reception. It was interesting, therefore, to examine if and how the differences discussed impact on cross-national variations between British and German audiences' views and understandings of popular papers, through asking questions such as, do tabloids enjoy a greater social acceptance in the UK, due to their longer tradition and current dominance of the market? Can stronger ethical judgements be observed among German readers, as a result of the country's more detailed press laws and the journalists' less aggressive approach to researching and reporting? And, how do readers respond to the idiosyncratic elements of the tabloids; for instance, what are the implications of the fact that *Sun* and *Bild*'s political views are stated differently (explicitly in the case of the British tabloid and implicitly in the case of *Bild*)? Building on a detailed discussion of theoretical and empirical approaches to tabloids in the subsequent section (Chapters 4 and 5), these questions are answered in the third section of the book (particularly in Chapter 7).

# Part II

# Tabloids in the Academic Debate

# Chapter 4: Theorising Tabloids
Approaches to Popular Newspapers

This chapter maps existing theoretical approaches to tabloid newspapers and related formats in the UK and Germany. Reviewing traditional and alternative perspectives, it draws attention to their uses and limitations for the analysis of tabloid audience responses in the subsequent section. The chapter thereby establishes the epistemological and theoretical beliefs that underlie the investigation. An additional thread of analysis running through this chapter concerns the cross-national comparison of approaches to tabloids. Highlighting diverse trends in dominant British and German intellectual traditions and foci within the debate, it reflects on their potential implications for readers' views of tabloids in each country.

## IMPLYING DETRIMENTAL EFFECTS: TRADITIONAL APPROACHES

### Tabloid Journalism & Political Democracy

A dominant drift of thinking can be traced back to liberal theories of the media, conceptualising journalism as crucial to the development and maintenance of democracy (cf. Curran 1991). A representative of this view, Jostein Gripsrud (2000: 294) maintains that 'the core purpose of journalism is and should be about producing and distributing serious information and debate on central social, political, and cultural matters'. In accordance with this position, a range of scholarly works have focused on the relationships between the mass media and political and social life, holding the proposition that 'in contemporary large scale societies, it is only in and through the mass media that democratic political debate, and thus democratic political life, can be articulated' (Sparks 1998: 5).

A substantial number of Anglo-American contributions in this field find their theoretical grounding in the normative concept of the public sphere, developed by the Frankfurt School member and German sociologist Jürgen Habermas (1989). Habermas' bourgeois public sphere and its modern equivalents have been widely discussed and applied to concepts of democracy by academics during the past 30 years or so, and they still represent a common theoretical framework for considerations of the media's role in society. Without launching into a detailed explanation of Habermas' ideas, it is worth pointing out the focus on reason through "serious" political information[10]. This Enlightenment idea is, indeed, very pronounced in the notion of the public sphere, with its ideal model of public discourse as a rational, informed dialogue of equals.

Conversely, entertainment, when considered from this point of view, is commonly disregarded as a 'regrettable diversion from the media's central democratic purpose and function' (Curran 1991: 33). Hence, the significance of popular journalism for democratic communication is questioned. Sparks (1998: 5), for instance, points out that the journalistic conception implied in the concept of the public sphere implies that the media 'make available to the citizen the range of information and opinion essential to reach informed conclusions on matters of public interest', thereby providing the ground for informed rational debate. Popular newspapers and the tabloid media are dismissed by this view as a contamination of "proper" journalism. The argument is that they 'fail to meet (perhaps idealised) criteria as agencies in the public sphere' (Bromley and Tumber 1997: 365; original parentheses) due to their distinctive style features, content preferences, and discursive strategies (cf. also Sparks 2000).

## The 'Tabloidization' Debate in the UK

Such democratic theory positions set the scene for the 'tabloidization' or 'dumbing-down' thesis, an extensive academic and professional journalistic debate in the UK (cf., for instance, Blumler 1999; Brants 1998; Esser 1999; Connell 1998; Marlow 2002; Sparks 1999; Bromley 1998). Referring to a process named after the style and content features of popular papers, the debate concerns an evaluation of perceived changes in the media. It can be located primarily in considerations of the press within British journalism research (cf. Dahlgren 1992), but has also found expression in practitioners' discourses (cf., for instance, Davis 1993; Victor 1994; Sampson 1996; Stevens 1998; Preston 2004). Graeme Turner (1999: 59) describes 'tabloidization' as follows:

---

10 The concept of the public sphere has been outlined and discussed extensively elsewhere (cf. Habermas' detailed explanation in his *Strukturwandel der Öffentlichkeit* 1962). Many scholars have since explained, applied, discussed and critically evaluated the notion of the public sphere, including Garnham (1990), Dahlgren (1991), Thompson (1993), Sparks (1998), Fraser (1992), and Negt and Kluge (1993).

'[...] a shift away from politics and towards crime, away from the daily news agenda and towards editorially generated items promoted days in advance, away from information-based treatments of social issues and towards entertaining stories on lifestyles or celebrities, and an overwhelming investment in the power of the visual, in the news as an entertaining spectacle.'

Linked to changing societal, technological and organizational imperatives, these perceived changes in news values in the British media, towards a 'sharp increase in the extent of tabloid-type material in the newspaper press and on television' (Sparks 1998: 8), have triggered debates about whether or not such changes pose a threat to democracy. Most scholars would conclude that, indeed, these perceived changes are evidence for declining standards. Hence, strong concerns are aired over the question of where journalism is heading. Bob Franklin (1997: 4), for instance, laments the decline of 'hard news' and claims that 'entertainment has superseded the provision of information; human interest has supplanted the public interest; measured judgement has succumbed to sensationalism; the trivial has triumphed over the weighty'. Similarly, Steven Barnett describes 'tabloidization' as 'a pervasive sense of declining cultural, educational and political standards' (1998: 75).

However, studies endeavouring to empirically test the claim that journalism has grown away from its original ideals show an inconsistent picture. While Sparks still noted in 1998 that there was evidence that the perceived 'tabloidization' shifts were not true (ibid: 8), a few empirical studies have since found changes in media content and style. Still, there is no unity as to which characteristics are regarded significant indicators for a process of 'tabloidization'. Various scholars have investigated whether features such as personalisation, human-interest topics, entertainment, or simply 'sensationalism' have increased in a range of media outlets. For example, Mine Bek (2004: 371) found that the news on Turkish public service channels 'personalizes and tabloidizes politics'. Similarly, Howard Kurtz (1993) sees an overall decrease in 'hard news' in US newspapers, and Shelley McLachlan and Peter Golding (2000) show mild changes in content preferences and the discursive style of British broadsheets over the last 40 years. Still, Rodrigo Uribe and Barrie Gunter (2004) note that while the range of subjects covered in British newspapers has not changed much in terms of the content preferences of tabloids and broadsheets, form and style in both print markets have begun to resemble each other more over time.

Hence, several scholars note a lack of exact definitions concerning the conceptual lens of 'tabloidization', and definitions of what elements it comprises (cf., for instance, Sparks 1998; Uribe and Gunter 2004). In fact, it seems that the term is largely used as a 'multi-purpose metaphor' (Rowe 2000: 78) to voice diffuse concerns and disapproval of certain developments in the media and in society, whilst often not comparing 'like with like', as Ian Connell (1998: 11) cautions. McLachlan and Golding (2000: 75-89) have, moreover, shown that 'tabloidization' is not a new phenomenon, as the focus on sports, entertainment, pictures and sensation can be traced in some publications dating from 100 years ago. Similarly, complaints about the journalistic standards of certain media outlets, interpreted as threatening all serious and responsible public discourse, have deep historical roots and are not restricted to contemporary academic and public debates (cf. Sparks 2000; Gripsrud 2000; Örnebring and Jönsson 2004). The conclusion we can draw from this is that 'tabloidization' is neither a static concept, nor a global or unified phenomenon. Instead, it needs to be regarded as a complex and diverse process, taking place with regard to different style and content features, in different media outlets, in different countries, at different times to dissimilar extents (cf. Uribe and Gunter 2004; Sparks 1998).

## The 'Tabloidization' Debate in Germany

Examining the academic debate in Germany, it would seem that the topic of 'tabloidization' has not found its way onto the agenda of German media and communication research as much. Moreover, while the debate focuses on the press in Britain and the US, German discussions are largely restricted to television (cf., for instance, Krüger 1996; Schütte 1996; Custer 1997; Klein 1997; Muckenhaupt 1997). Notions of 'infotainment' or 'convergence' of news and entertainment in television news have dominated the academic agenda in Germany, bearing some resemblance to the UK's 'tabloidization' debate. Soon after the establishment of commercial broadcasting in Germany in the mid-1980s, authors noted a collapsing of boundaries between information and entertainment in German television programmes. Growing concerns focused on the 'converging' of style and content features in public service and commercial news report broadcasting. This perceived trend has – quite similarly to the 'tabloidization' argument in the UK – generally given rise to worries about anti-democratic implications (cf., for instance, Kamps 1998; Krüger 1998; Hohlfeld 1999; Rössler 2002). In terms of a 'tabloidization' of the German media, Wolfgang Donsbach and Katrin Büttner (2005) conducted an empirical study to analyse whether such a process is taking place in German TV news. They concluded that these programmes have, indeed, become more 'tabloidised' in terms of content preferences and presentation characteristics. In contrast to this, a contrary development can be noted in British broadcasting, as there seems to be little evidence for a 'tabloidization' of broadcasting news (cf. Sparks 2000: 22 pp.)

Yet, the press provides a different picture. In the UK, Sparks notes that the circulation of British tabloids has declined over the past 40 years, while the quality market has increased, suggesting that this has been achieved at the expense of 'tabloidization' (ibid 1998; cf. also Bromley 1998). Although an overall decline in newspaper circulation can likewise be noted in Germany, Esser (1999: 306-307) discusses Hans Matthias Kepplinger's (1998) empirical research findings about German newspaper coverage, concluding that there is no evidence for an increase in tabloidised political coverage within the German prestige press. Likewise, Klaus Schönbach, on the basis of his extensive research agenda focusing on newspaper content (cf., in particular, 1997, 2000, 2004), claims that local German subscription newspapers, which increased in tabloidised coverage, suffered circulation losses. Such divergent developments would seem to link in with the diverse media systems in Britain and Germany (cf. Chapter 3).

## Long-Standing Concerns: Traditional Ideological Criticism of *Bild*

Despite the fact that a detailed investigation into a general 'tabloidization' process of the German media has not yet been placed on top of the academic agenda, a related debate occupying academic interests can be observed. Characterised by quite similar concerns, the discussion focuses on the tabloid *Bild*. An impressive body of work on the tabloid exists, which is largely located in the area of literary studies and the field of political communication research. Only a few studies have placed the audience of *Bild* at the centre of attention (for instance, Brichta 2002; cf. also Chapter 5). Still, similar to the UK's 'tabloidization' debate, German scholars investigating *Bild* frequently voice austere concerns about the potentially negative effects of the paper's style, language, content, editorial bias, and discursive strategies, thus placing the tabloid in the centre of a well-rehearsed canon of criticism.

Foregrounding matters of representation and style, a range of textual studies on *Bild* criticise aspects relating to the paper's simplified reporting and personalisation of news and events (cf. Nusser 1991; Virchow 2008); its extensive use of stereotypes (cf. Droege 1968; Link 1986; Jäger 1993); its emphasis on traditional gender roles and sexist (re)presentation of women (cf. Weber 1978; Klein and Pfister 1985; Riedmiller 1988; Geisel 1995), as well as its 'emotionalisation' of content (cf. Vogtel 1986; Büscher 1996; Voss 1999). Other scholars, more generally, lament the 'sensational character' of *Bild*'s reporting, claiming that it lacks journalistic quality (cf. Schirmer 2001; Jogschies 2001). Such arguments would seem helpful in establishing a set of *Bild*'s style characteristics, but they appear of little use to a theoretical conceptualisation of this study's research topic. Moreover, all of these textual considerations of *Bild* offer uniformly pessimistic conclusions about the 'deceiving' effects of the paper's style and world-view. Most authors also maintain a strongly disabling view of the tabloid audience, articulating concerns about the tabloid's negative impact on readers, society and democracy.

This connects with intense disapproval of *Bild*'s ideology and supposedly manipulative political potential. This line of thinking within the impressive bulk of research on the German red-top closely corresponds to the historic events around the paper (cf. Chapter 2). Since it was launched in 1952, *Bild* has been the most controversially discussed German media outlet, and, over the years, historic events around the paper have frequently caused public outrage and resulted in intense criticism of its style and presumed influence. The themes of public criticism have also set the agenda for academic enquiries, which can be grouped into three key areas of concern. The first strand of argumentation views *Bild* as an instrument of manipulation for the masses; the second thread is concerned with the tabloid's political bias, and the third strand questions the journalists' practices, foregrounding, for instance, 'unethical' methods of research. Within each of these argumentative groups, discomfort with the interlinked notions of ideology, manipulation, the assumed (political) power of the paper, as well as the general effects of *Bild*'s reporting on its audience play a major role.

The student revolts of the 1960s and the tabloid's controversial campaigning (cf. Chapter 2) initiated the first academic wave of considerations. These early works are almost entirely based on presumptions about the paper's deliberate manipulative effect on readers. Karlpeter Arens (1971), for instance, gives a detailed account of the paper's potential to manipulate its readers. Other works stress *Bild*'s 'ideologically charged content', arguing that it puts a 'democratic haze' on society (Alberts 1972), or that it deceives its readers with regard to the contrasting differences of the capitalist system (Bechmann et al. 1979; Schäfer 1968). Similarly, Richard Albrecht (1982: 351) describes *Bild* as a 'social institution impacting on the masses'. While these early works derive from conceptual ideas emanating from a tradition of cultural criticism associated with the Frankfurt School, it is worth pointing out that the theme of *Bild*'s assumed manipulative influence still prevails in more contemporary studies.

A second drift of thinking places the tabloid in the context of journalistic ethics, principles and practices. Triggered by Günther Wallraff's long-term investigative project pitched against the paper (1977, 1979, 1981; cf. also Chapter 2), editors and reporters were publicly accused of inventing stories and employing immoral practices and methods in order to acquire the information they required. Consequently, academic considerations focused on the producers of the paper, resulting in an emotionally charged wave of research aimed at 'enlightening' the readers (Albrecht 1982: 353), in order to diminish the paper's powers. Academic analyses from that time point out *Bild*'s 'distorted version of political and social reality' (Minzberg 1999: 45-46; cf. also Sandig 1972; Schwacke 1983; Ionescu 1996; Wende 1990; Küchenhoff 1972), or set out to expose the paper's 'lies' and their effects (cf., for instance, Berger and Nied 1984). The tabloid journalists' ethics and practices have remained a matter for concern in more recent research as well. Martina Minzberg (1999), for instance, in analysing the German Press Complaints Commission's criticism of *Bild*, maintains that most complaints are concerned with a violation of the individual private sphere.

The third strand of argumentation concerns conceptions of *Bild*'s political bias and presumed influence on voters. Studies analysing the tabloid's news coverage in most cases recognise 'deliberate political propaganda' (the German term often used is 'Meinungsmache') in the paper's reporting, implying that readers form their opinion from *Bild*. Many authors assume that the tabloid subliminally supports the German centre-right party CDU (cf. Rust 1984) and condemn the paper for its 'right-wing populism' (Bechmann et al. 1979; cf. also Böll 1984; Albrecht 1986). The historical context of such perspectives can be traced back to paper's early years, during which its founder Axel C. Springer, indeed, used it as a political instrument (cf. Chapter 2). However, notions surrounding the tabloid's alleged political impact also frequently recur in contemporary debates (cf., for instance, Gehrs 2006).

Yet, assumptions about the political bias and influence of popular papers are not restricted to the German debate. Concerns relating to the presumed influence of the outcome of an election can equally be observed with regard to *The Sun* (cf. Chapter 2). Such considerations commonly revolve around the idea of popular papers' impact on their consumers' political opinion formation and citizen behaviour (for instance, Arendt 2009 and Reinemann 2008). Yet, there are opposing views to the argument that tabloids impact on their readers' voting intentions. Shanto Iyengar and Richard Morin (2003) found that US-American news audiences are more attentive to news sources they perceive accordant to their political views and preferences. The authors make the case that 'consumers stick with their preferred (politically compatible) news sources while screening out those sites offering unfamiliar or disagreeable information and perspectives'. However, while the actual influence of tabloids on people's voting behaviour remains an issue scholars disagree about, Iyengar and Morin's findings draw attention to the idea that tabloid newspaper readers may not take advice on which party to vote for, suggesting that the political bias of popular papers is perhaps less important than commonly assumed.

## A Critical Evaluation of the Critical Paradigm

As indicated, a dominant consensus can be noted within British and German academic literature concerning the view that tabloid newspapers are somewhat harmful to society and democracy. The range of democratic reservations held against tabloid news values, popular journalism and a transformation of the media as addressed in the 'tabloidization' argument may be exemplified through a statement by Sparks (2000: 28), who maintains that the kind of knowledge and understanding offered by tabloid journalism marks an attack on the public sphere:

'It is not simply that tabloids and tabloidization constitute a threat to an existing democracy; rather they make its practical functioning an impossibility because they are unable to provide the audience with the kinds of knowledge that are essential to the exercise of their rights as citizens.'

Challenging such arguments without appearing oblivious to political democracy involves facing something of a dilemma. Clearly, there is a case for critical awareness of the state of democracy, the political involvement of its people, and the mass media's role in this. Concerns about perceived changes in the media, such as those raised in the 'tabloidization' debate, also highlight crucial issues relating to the structure of media industries along capitalist lines of production and consumption, and a critical attitude towards popular papers' primary motive to win a large number of readers rather than educate and explain its audience is required (cf. Sparks 1998: 9). Debates such as those outlined, moreover, address valid questions about the power of contemporary popular red-tops published by huge media enterprises such as *News International Ltd.* or the *Axel Springer AG*, raising issues about the significance of ownership concentration. Likewise, it is fair to assume that popular papers are able to set the agenda of a country, and are powerful in repeating a message, as well as in writing for or against someone.

However, such perspectives are limited with regard to their use for a study of tabloid newspaper audiences. Theoretical conceptions implying that popular papers fail to provide sufficient information and threaten political democracy are in line with negative views about popular culture and its audiencecommonly associated with certain members of the Frankfurt School. Such approaches do not account for the popularity of tabloid newspapers, nor do they explain the papers' functions for readers. It is, however, worth tracing the heritage of the critical paradigm, for the conceptual categories by which popular journalism is grasped (particularly in the field of political communication and public sphere theory) clearly emanate from the Frankfurt School's tradition of 'Critical Theory'.

### The Frankfurt School's Continuing Influence

The name 'Frankfurt School' refers to members of the Institute for Social Research at the University of Frankfurt in Germany. The institute was set up in 1923, exiled to New York in 1933, and re-established in Germany in 1950. The term 'Critical Theory' was coined to denote 'the Institute's critical mix of Marxism and psychoanalysis' (Storey 1993: 100). Scholars of the first generation of Frankfurt School members, engaging with popular culture and its role to society, included Theodor Adorno, Max Horkheimer, Walter Benjamin, Leo Löwenthal, and Herbert Macuse[11]. The Frankfurt School was highly influenced by Marxist ideas, for its mem-

---

11 For more detailed accounts of the School's origins and its critical theory tradition cf., for instance, Storey (1993); Strinati (2004); Dörner (2000). More information on the School, as well as the Institute for Social Research's history and prior theories, can also be found in Wiggershaus (1994), as well as the Institute's website at http://www.ifs.uni-frankfurt.de/index.html.

bers drew on Marxism and criticised it simultaneously. Hence, political economy perspectives as well as ideological criticism characterise many of the School's approaches; it emphasised the role of culture and ideology in capitalist societies. Enlightenment thoughts and a critical response to these likewise mark an important context for many critical theory thinkers.

Although some might argue that the ideas of the Frankfurt School are no longer relevant to the study of popular culture, Dominic Strinati (2004) asserts that the School shares much common ground with contemporary mass culture theory. In fact, he sees the School's significance precisely in this continuing influence: 'Along with mass culture theory, the work of the Frankfurt School has set the terms of debate and analysis for the subsequent study of popular culture' (ibid: 46). Likewise, Andreas Dörner (2000) maintains that members of the Frankfurt School have produced some of the most significant and influential works in the field of analyses of modern media culture. The School's influence on contemporary democratic theory approaches to popular journalism continues to be vast, as the cultural criticism positions discussed earlier indicate. Likewise, traditional ideas about the audience of mass mediated products still underpin contemporary approaches.

By far the most cited and influential Frankfurt School work relating to the study of popular culture is the chapter *The Culture Industry* in Adorno and Horkheimer's *Dialectic of Enlightenment* (1972; originally published in German 1942). In their publication, the authors put forward an intriguing argument against modern entertainment culture, or rather, mass media in mass society. Highly influenced by their experiences with Nazi propaganda media, this specific historical context clearly impacted on their views of mass-produced cultural products and their audiences. Adorno and Horkheimer's basic argument was that the 'culture industry' is a form of 'mass deception', as it produces a standardised culture to entertain a mass audience, keeping it dumb and causing it to remain relatively satisfied within the capitalist system. Adorno and Horkheimer saw popular culture products as homogeneously standardised and predictable in their hegemonic messages, and were concerned that consumers might not be able to see through this (cf. Storey 1993; Dörner 2000). They condemned the 'culture industry' as highly manipulative, serving to control or subvert oppositional consciousness and removing any threat to the dominant capitalist class. Furthermore they regarded the audience as an anonymous, and rather media-illiterate, mass easy to manipulate (cf. Gauntlett 2008: 22 pp.)

## Limitations of the Critical Paradigm

In contemporary scholarly works, the academic consensus has moved away from conceptualising audiences as masses, as we tend to regard them as an assembly of individuals or diverse groups of people. Moreover, the idea of an active audience has evolved. If we consider the underlying beliefs of the 'critical lament' (Langer

1998: 289) within the debate of tabloid journalism and popular culture, parallels to classic Frankfurt School positions become apparent. In Adorno and Horkheimer's view, mass entertainment 'corrupts its audiences both morally and culturally' (Curran and Sparks 1991: 216), and the culture industry is therefore responsible for a 'depoliticising [of] the working class' (Storey 1993: 101). Many contemporary scholars still draw on this early perspective of popular culture by condemning popular media outlets as socially, politically or culturally worthless. This implies an intensely negative view of the popular media and tabloid newspapers. "High culture" and "serious journalism" occupy the opposite ends of the scale in this view, fulfilling the valuable democratic functions of enlightening and educating their audiences. As a consequence of this binary opposition, popular newspapers are condemned. The idea that neither popular journalism nor its audience are worthy of in-depth academic attention follows from this. Likewise, traditional critical perspectives often directly or indirectly reproduce and maintain negative discourses and stereotypical beliefs about the readers of tabloid newspapers. Democratic and ideological concerns in contemporary academic works on the subject often imply assumptions about the way audiences read and understand them, about the attractions the papers have for readers, and about their reasons for reading them. Frequently, stigmatizations of tabloid newspaper audiences can be observed; readers are often portrayed as media illiterates (cf. Schirmer 2001), as having an 'apparently voracious appetite for voyeurism' (Barnett 1998: 78) or as entertainment-seeking 'idiots of consumption' (Enzensberger 1983: 659).

Clearly, any perspective on popular journalism is grounded in beliefs and concepts that have their uses and limitations. The influence of Frankfurt School positions is recognisable in the perspectives on popular culture and tabloid journalism outlined above, and some of Adorno and Horkheimer's strong democratic and ideological reservations against mass culture and mass media are prevailing beliefs in contemporary considerations of the popular media. In particular, a strong devaluation of popular journalism in the context of binary oppositions of "high" and "low" culture can be observed. This is based on certain conceptions regarding how and what journalism ought to be like; implied are notions of "good" and "bad" media outlets. In addition, ideas about what can be regarded as "serious" and "quality" information are involved (cf. also Dahlgren 1992). Likewise, a rather passive view of the audience is implied in this, drawing on certain beliefs about how information and learning works, on whom it works, and representing a rather 'disabling perspective' of popular media audiences (Corner and Pels 2003: 4).

Many questions arise from this. Firstly, a discussion of popular media in relation to their "lack" of democratic functions and the assumption that it has detrimental effects on society cannot explain their widespread reception, or illuminate their significance to/for audiences. Moreover, narrow conceptualisations of the functions of journalism leave no room for a consideration of entertaining media content, and the way audiences make sense of this. Likewise, it is not certain whether the ideal model of citizenship through serious, rational debate of public issues represents the only way democracy can persist. Furthermore, the question of what appeals to a mass audience might not be sufficiently understood by applying traditional conceptualisations of "quality" and "information". And lastly, traditional perspectives fail to account for the hybrid character of the tabloid genre, which would seem firmly set in between the poles of information and entertainment (cf. Chapter 2). In order to grasp and understand these issues, theoretical approaches based on the assumption that we are dealing with binary opposites of "good" and "bad" in the study of popular culture and popular journalism require a broadening. Hence, the theme underlying the following sections is concerned with a reflection on alternative approaches to tabloid journalism and popular culture, as well as an evaluation of how these can be of help to a study of tabloid audience responses.

## TURNING TO 'THE OTHER': ALTERNATIVE APPROACHES

### A 'Cultural Studies' Perspective

The intellectual roots of most scholarly endeavours conceptualising popular journalism in different ways to those emerging from traditional approaches can be traced back to an intellectual drift of thinking that has come to be known as 'Cultural Studies'. Evolving as a reaction to Adorno and Horkheimer's cynicism, scholars associated with the Cultural Studies tradition have largely viewed popular culture through a different lens. Yet, defining and clarifying what 'Cultural Studies' comprises and does is not an easy task. Many authors have noted a range of theoretical viewpoints and intellectual disciplines that influenced the emergence of this tradition. Udo Göttlich (1997), as an example, describes it as merging culturalist and structuralist theories; Andreas Hepp (1999: 15) suggests thinking of Cultural Studies as an 'inter or intradisciplinary project'.

The works produced by Richard Hoggart, Raymond Williams, E.P. Thompson and Stuart Hall in the late 1950s and early 1960s are generally regarded as some of the founding texts of the intellectual tradition of British Cultural Studies (cf., among others, Storey 1993; Turner 2003; Göttlich 1997; Jäckel 1997). Subsequently, their institutional home, the Centre for Contemporary Cultural Studies at the University of Birmingham, became a central hub for much significant research produced in the area. Since then, the set of theories and practices labelled 'Cultural Studies' within the humanities and social sciences has profoundly broadened, and branched out to become different academic currents in the UK, Europe, the United States, and other parts of the world. However, explaining Cultural Studies in detail shall not be the focus of this section as others have done so elsewhere, as the impressive amount of books on the subject illustrates (cf. Turner 2003, particularly concerning English language-based academia). Instead, my centre of attention lies on discussing some of the theoretical principles emerging from the British Cultural Studies tradition that seem useful and significant to the study of popular culture audiences, and have influenced alternative academic conceptualisations of popular journalism.

Cultural Studies are concerned with a critical intellectual consideration of culture and the media, as is the Frankfurt School. However, from a Cultural Studies point of view, 'culture' is understood to be a wide range of social practices. Indeed, the originator of this concept, Raymond Williams, argued in his *Long Revolution* (1961) that culture is a whole 'way of life' (ibid: 233), thus refusing to be drawn into an elitist dismissal of the popular. This is contrary to the conception of culture as primarily defined by economic forces, as can be observed in Marxist approaches. While this break with Marxism represents a commonality of the Frankfurt School and Cultural Studies, the differences between the two approaches are even more significant. Research in the tradition of the Frankfurt School maintains ideas of the value of high culture, while at the same time condemning mass culture as stupefying and system-conforming. In contrast to this, Cultural Studies primarily deal not with elite, but with popular culture artefacts, stressing the relationship of culture and the everyday by regarding the popular as a form of lived everyday 'way of life'. Entertainment and "the trivial" are, thus, considered self-evident elements of culture (cf. Jäckel 1997; Turner 2003; Storey 1993).

Aside from a conceptualisation of culture that grants the popular a considerable re-evaluation, a second important principle of Cultural Studies concerns the stress on 'human agency'; i.e. 'the active production of culture, rather than its passive consumption' (Storey 1993: 44). Marking the unifying perspective of Hoggart, Williams, Thompson, Hall and their followers, this view of an active audience is contrary to the audience view of traditional media effects research (which regards the audience as "endangered"), and to classic Marxist and cultural criticism positions of the audience of popular culture. Such an "enabling" perspective of the audience can be traced back to Hoggart's *Uses of Literacy* (1957), which celebrates working class culture and stresses their emancipatory potential. Likewise, Thompson's *Making of the English Working Class* (1963) views 'popular culture as a site of resistance to those in whose interests the Industrial Revolution was made' (Storey 1993: 58). Thompson argues that the experiences, values, actions and desires of the English working class are essential to the understanding of the formation of an industrial capitalist society. Moreover, Stuart Hall's model of encoding and decoding (1973, 1980) as well as David Morley's *Nationwide* audience studies (1980 et seq.) are considered milestones in the establishment of the idea that media audiences actively construct meaning from their consumption of media outlets (cf. Chapter 5).

On a side note, the tension between British and German academic traditions is worth noting here. Essentially, the dominant ways in which popular journalism has been approached vary between German and British academia. Alternative perspectives on popular culture and tabloid journalism, as addressed in this section, have mostly been suggested by scholars working within an Anglo-American academic research arena, while in Germany, a Frankfurt School perspective can be observed as the prevailing approach to popular journalism. This difference is important in itself and in its implications. The variation between the academic domains is reflected in the fact that both Cultural Studies, as well as qualitative audience research, are still relative "newcomers" to German media and communication research[12]. Representing this view, Kerstin Goldbeck (2004) notices a significant gap in the academic research of German-speaking countries with regard to Cultural Studies positions. She claims that only a narrow range of 'certain authors, certain studies and certain methods' can be observed (ibid: 62). Likewise, the number of researchers trying to establish Cultural Studies in German academia by publishing introductory works, readers or textbooks is still rather limited (cf. Winter and Hepp 2006; Bromley et al. 1999; Engelmann 1999). Michael Jäckel and Jochen Peter (1997), Rudi Renger (2000) and Lothar Mikos (2006) have spearheaded this development, arguing that Cultural Studies should be addressed as an alternative approach to dominant, traditional positions within German media and communication research.

In contrast to viewing tabloid journalism through the lens of enlightenment and considering it as hazardous to society, alternative approaches to popular culture and popular journalism, subsumed under the umbrella term of Cultural Studies, seem more useful to a study of tabloid audience responses. Having highlighted the limitations of a rational public sphere point of view, it is worth pointing out the benefits of adopting a 'Cultural Studies' perspective. As Douglas Kellner (1997: 27) phrases it:

'British Cultural Studies overcomes some of these limitations of the Frankfurt School by systematically rejecting high/low culture distinctions and taking seriously the artifacts of media culture. Likewise, they overcome the limitations of the Frankfurt School notion of a passive audience in their conceptions of an active audience that creates meanings and the popular.'

---

12 Göttlich and Winter (1999) regard the fact that German academia is quite narrowly focused on single disciplines as one of the reasons for the reluctant reception of this approach. Another reason might be seen in the expansion of the German 'cultural sciences' – a subject of study at German universities since the 1980s, which Göttlich and Winter think of as a competitor to the British Cultural Studies approach.

Based on Kellner's fundamental insights, the following represents a reflection on key theoretical positions of scholars borrowing from a 'Cultural Studies' drift of thinking.

### Re-conceptualising Binary Opposites

Traditional ideas of "quality" in journalism imply understanding notions of information and entertainment as two binary opposites. Peter Dahlgren and Colin Sparks question this view in their edited collection *Journalism and Popular Culture* (1992). Dahlgren (1992: 4) in particular represents the argument that journalism should be viewed as a form of popular culture, or at least as comprising popular culture elements and themes. Noting a 'concerted juxtaposition of journalism and popular culture', he points out that this can best be studied by adopting a Cultural Studies perspective, as the 'more ambitious and systematic theoretical efforts [of this perspective] often question the separation which journalism draws between itself and other forms of media output' (cf. also Renger 2000; Lünenborg 2005).

Indeed, the contradictions embedded in the popular culture genre are hardly mutually exclusive. John Hartley (1996), for instance, challenges the class- and gender-based binarisms of information and entertainment, hard news and soft news, the public sphere and private lifestyles. He rejects such 'common sense' conceptualisations, claiming they 'reinforce a systematic bias against popular... media'. This, he argues, confirms prejudices such as the idea of 'serious politics' being of concern to men only (ibid: 27). The notion of dissolving boundaries between the traditionally perceived polar opposites within journalism has also been taken up by other scholars. Elisabeth Klaus (1996, and with Margret Lünenborg 2001) claims that the separation of information and entertainment is, indeed, of little relevance to its reception. They argue that audiences gain information from fiction and entertainment, and use information-based texts for entertaining purposes. This view is confirmed by Annette Hill's findings from her empirical research project on factual television audiences in Sweden and the UK (2005, 2007). Hill demonstrates, significantly, that ideas of "learning" are by no means restricted to television programmes that appear more "factual" in content than others (cf. ibid 2007: 145 pp.)

Likewise, the typical tabloid ways of framing issues and actors (cf. Chapter 2) which are often condemned when focussing on popular journalism's "lack" of democratic functions receive re-evaluation in this perspective. Myra MacDonald (2000) challenges the traditional distinction drawn between notions of rationality and personalisation of media texts. Instead, she recognises vital enabling qualities in the personal case studies and testimony of the two current affairs programmes she examined. Arguing that personalised narratives can facilitate political insight and understanding, McDonald draws attention to alternative social uses of narrative techniques, such as those employed by popular papers.

Essentially, this study's intellectual position feeds off these insights. Accepting the view that information and entertainment, rationality and emotionality, "hard" and "soft" news are not necessarily polar opposites with regard to their functions for audiences and society, it is worth asking how readers deal with the contradictions embedded in the genre. What sense do audiences make of the medium's hybrid character? Do readers view tabloid reporting against a backdrop of binary opposites, in line with traditional approaches to tabloid journalism? And, can any significant difference be observed between British and German readers' modes of engagement that might relate back to the diverse academic traditions of the two countries mentioned above? These and related issues are analysed from the point of view of the readers in the third section of this book (cf. in particular Chapter 7).

## Recognising Political and Social Benefits

The ideas outlined so far can be used to shed new light on the concept of the public sphere. McNair (1999) and Hartley (1996) articulate the belief that more than one public sphere exists, suggesting that popular journalism can provide an alternative to the dominant rational and public domain Habermas was thinking of. In this context, Hartley (ibid: 155 pp.) claims that the 'public knowledge project' must be redefined to include:

'... not so much knowledge on public affairs as traditionally defined, but new modes of knowledge which bespeak new ways of forming the public, in communities whose major public functions – the classical functions of teaching, dramatizing and participating in the public sphere – are increasingly functions of popular media...'

Such considerations have led to important re-conceptualisations of popular culture as an alternative public sphere (cf., for instance, Hermes 2005). Scholars have argued that tabloid newspapers can make aspects of the rational public sphere accessible, particularly to those audience members who would otherwise be excluded (cf. Johansson 2007b). Henrik Örnebring and Anna-Maria Jönsson (2004; cf. also Örnebring 2006) claim that popular journalism can even affect social change by granting news access to larger audience sections. They claim that the tabloid media should not be viewed as a threat to democracy, but recognised as fulfilling important social and cultural functions which other kinds of journalism are incapable of. In this view, popular journalism not only provides alternative public spheres, but it offers alternative arenas for public discourse.

Moreover, the belief that democracy requires active and informed citizens has been challenged. John Zaller (2003) argues that 'much criticism of news is based on an ideal of citizenship and a standard of quality that are neither realistic nor necessary for the functioning of democracy' (ibid 2003: 109; cf. also Graber 2003).

Drawing attention to the important ties of popular journalism to the everyday lives of its audience, Jostein Gripsrud (2000: 297) claims: 'The notion of citizenship must clearly include more than the narrowly political, just as there is more to a democratic society than the immediately political institutions and processes.' An alternative to traditional approaches, it has been suggested we should think of 'cultural citizenship' instead. Initially representing the ambiguities of collective belonging to multicultural societies, the concept has been removed from its original context and transferred to the fields of popular culture and political communication. Joke Hermes (1998: 158), most notably, explains that 'the cultural' is the entry to citizenship, and that 'the political value of popular culture is to be found in its contribution to citizenship'. This means that the 'citizens of media' (Hartley 1996: 155) create their social and cultural identities through consuming popular culture. Thus, popular culture provides the grounding for a citizen-identity (Hermes 1998; cf. also Klaus and Lünenborg 2004a, 2004b, 2005). The concept of 'cultural citizenship', then, is useful to the debate about the constitutive role of popular culture in the practice of democratic and political citizenship. Liesbet van Zoonen's book *Entertaining the Citizen* (2005) provides an excellent framework for the consideration of popular culture's social, cultural and political relevance. Highlighting the various connections between popular culture and politics, van Zoonen examines the relevance of entertainment as a resource for citizenship. She explains:

'In the context of citizenship, the first issue is not what entertaining politics does to citizens, but what citizens do with entertaining politics, for citizenship is not something that pertains if it is not expressed in everyday talk and actions, both in the public and the private domain. Citizenship, in other words, is something that one has to do, something that requires performance.' (ibid: 123)

Thus, examining the cultural experience of citizens, van Zoonen reflects on viewers' responses to seemingly apolitical popular movies and television series comprising fictional stories about politicians and politics. She demonstrates that those aspects of popular culture which are frequently condemned by traditional approaches are, indeed, highly relevant to the way people construct citizenship on an everyday level, for notions of personalisation and popularization particularly provide resources for 'discussing, criticizing, and imagining politics for the performance of citizenship' (ibid: 124). Van Zoonen concludes:

'...popular culture does indeed function as a source of gaining insight in politics and as a means to perform citizenship by presenting one's ideas in a public setting. It does not seem to matter much whether the popular text in question is based on true or fictional politics ...., because both fiction and nonfiction of politics draw from the same popular codes about character and narrative..., and because people seem to apply the same frames to make sense of fictional and true politics.' (ibid: 137)

Peter Dahlgren pulls together these and other important strands of thinking in his book *Media and Political Engagement: Citizens, Communication and Democracy* (2009). He discusses popular culture as a space for what he terms 'civic cultures', showing that very significant ties between entertainment and politics exist. Such ideas about the potential social and political value of the popular media serve as the central basis from which to approach audience responses to tabloids. It will be interesting to examine if, and how, forms of citizenship – civic, cultural or other – are endorsed by tabloids. Moreover, how do readers make sense of popular papers in relation to politics and notions of social engagement and participation? These and other questions will be explored in the third section of this book (cf. Chapter 8).

### Providing Resources for Collective Identity Formations

A sense of belonging to a wider collective is of vital importance when people 'perform' citizenship. Hence, it is worth considering the social construction of identities in relation to popular journalism further. Amongst the numerous theoretical and empirical considerations of nationalism, a large body of work deals with national identity as one form of collective identity. Most notably, scholars have embraced sociological perspectives; in examining national identity in relation to civil and cultural citizenship and democracy (cf. Habermas 1996; Buckingham 2000; Schlesinger 1991); in considering the role of nationalism and national identity in increasingly diverse societies (cf. Bond 2006); or in exploring the 'banal' everyday recurrences of symbols of national identity (cf. Billig 1995). An oft-cited work, Benedict Anderson's *Imagined Communities* (1991) stresses the constructed nature of a sense of national identity by arguing that nations are always 'imagined' rather than actual communities, as one member can hardly know all other members. Instead, members of a national community conceive of this community and 'imagine' their belonging. In Anderson's view, printed mass media outlets have played a central role in establishing a common national discourse through providing 'national print-languages' (ibid: 67).

Interestingly, the popular media have been identified as particularly important in providing stories that audiences can use as resources for the 'imagination' of a sense collective belonging. Drawing attention to popular culture's social significance, John Langer (1998) requests that we take television's 'soft' news more seriously, contending that this 'other' material carries important cultural discourses connected to social memory and national identity. In line with this, tabloid newspapers have made a popular target for scholars suggesting that a sense of national identity may be endorsed and nurtured by tabloid narratives. If we consider popular papers' news values and textual characteristics, this connection seems easy to make. The typical audience address, for instance, is characterised by a textual style revolving around constructions of a community of readers. Textual devices around which notions of national and other social togetherness are structured include, for instance, the frequently used pronouns 'we', 'us' and 'them', as well as the pronounced readership address suggesting a conjunction between the newspaper and its audience (Brooks 1999; Johansson 2007a; cf. Chapter 2).

Strongly influencing the conception of what is part of this "self" is also the idea of the "other". This "other" is, likewise, a common textual discourse that tabloid newspapers draw on. As shown in Chapter 2, popular papers quite often include readers in a national community by excluding others. Philip Schlesinger (1991: 299-300) suggested that national identities are constantly changing in response to perceived threats from without and within. Drawing on Schlesinger's ideas, Johansson (2007a: 98) has shown that British tabloids effectively construct communities as 'under threat', by implying notions of togetherness against an external enemy or danger of some kind. Bruck and Stocker (1996: 168), similarly, identified a narrative strategy in Austria's tabloid *Neue Kronen Zeitung*, which they referred to as 'shared outrage' constructed by the text.

Such discourses of inclusion and exclusion, belonging and distinction can also be observed with regard to nationhood and national identity. Indeed, a nation-centred perspective seems particularly favoured by both *Bild* and *The Sun* (cf. Chapter 2). Martin Conboy (2002, 2006), in particular, has provided detailed accounts of the various textual and rhetorical devices British tabloid newspapers employ to construct a national community. Conboy's *Tabloid Britain* (2006) in particular points out the manifold textual resources British tabloids offer for the construction of a sense of national belonging. He argues that by employing various rhetorical devices, tabloid newspapers 'provide a relatively consistent view of the national community' (2006: 46), thus strengthening national belonging in an increasingly fragmented society. Similarly, Rod Brookes (1999: 261) shows that the popular press encourages the nation as 'the dominant form of identity' (albeit, with some national variation in Scotland), through explicit images of nationalism. And, lastly, Alex Law (2002) confirms that tabloids' news values place strong emphasis on the national and local (cf. also Johansson 2007a). These scholars cohere over the view that the popular press have a significant role in nurturing and reinforcing readers' senses of national identity. Such arguments are brought forward in relation to the postmodern view that cultural identities today are increasingly fragmented (cf. Giddens 1991). Indeed, the nation has become less and less significant as a contextual framework of identification in globalised societies today. Hence, while narratives in the media in general mark important resources to national and other social identity constructions, it would seem that tabloids have a special role here. The interesting question is how the papers fit in with the self-conception of readers regarding notions of belonging and identity. This book thus explores audience responses to the papers' invitations to 'imagining' national, cultural, or other social belonging in the readership research (cf., in particular, Chapter 9).

## CONCLUSIONS

Reviewing traditional and alternative academic approaches to popular journalism in Germany and the UK, this chapter has attempted to establish a theoretical framework from which to approach the study of tabloid audience responses. A major conclusion drawn from the review of literature concerns the insight that the genre truly polarises opinions. Essentially, the discussion has shown that two major interpretative trends can be observed among scholarly considerations. Popular newspapers, tabloid news values, popular entertainment, and other forms and denotations of popular journalism and popular culture are either devalued and deemed "hazardous" to the workings of political democracy, or recognised as socially and culturally significant in the way they feed on and add to cultural discourses. The key to unlocking such opposing views lies in their relation to two distinct perspectives of cultural criticism. Notably, intellectual positions emerging from early Frankfurt School ideas mark the one drift of thinking, while approaches drawing on principles emerging from the British Cultural Studies tradition represent the other. Both intellectual traditions are profoundly critical; however, they differ considerably in their presumptions about the role of popular media to society, and in their view of the mass media audience.

Clearly, any approach to tabloid journalism will find its advocates, and each has something to offer to the others. However, I have explained that the intellectual position I chose to adopt largely borrows from a 'Cultural Studies' point of view. In particular, the notion of the active audience provides an essential basis for this research. Likewise, informing the approach here is the idea that popular and entertaining media content have significant social and cultural value, adding to traditional functions of the media, (such as informing citizens and providing for participation within the rational public sphere), rather than replacing these purposes. The discussion in this chapter has particularly highlighted potential functions of popular journalism that revolve around notions of belonging and community, as expressed in the construction of social participation and collective identity, which shall be explored from an audience point of view in the empirical parts of this book.

This chapter, moreover, put forward the claim that the dominant intellectual traditions in Britain and Germany potentially impact on tabloid readers' views and sense-making of the papers. As discussed, a widely shared perspective can be observed in both countries, one that implies a devaluation of popular newspapers in the context of binary opposites constructed around traditional conceptualisations of "quality" and "information". Indeed, such notions of devaluation have even been regarded as essential characteristics of the popular (cf. also Chapters 2 and 3). I am suggesting that this is important in itself and in its implications for the reading experience in both countries, and this will be explored this from the readers' point of view.

However, in contrast to the range of theoretical approaches to popular journalism, the perspective of the audience has so far often been neglected. While this chapter has dealt with predominantly theoretical ideas, the following one, therefore, focuses on findings from empirical research in the field, discussing previous audience studies on tabloid newspapers and related media formats.

# Chapter 5: Milestones Revisited
Building on Previous Audience Studies

Despite the fact that quantitative readership surveys tell us who the readers of *The Sun* and *Bild* are (cf. Chapter 2), such surveys do not offer any insights into how audiences read, interpret and evaluate these papers. Moreover, as pointed out in the previous chapter, democratic and ideological concerns frequently lead scholars to imply a strongly negative image of the "illiterate" readers. Findings from qualitative audience studies, however, suggest that the meaning of the popular media is more complex than assumed. This chapter provides a résumé of previous studies in the field of qualitative audience research and, particularly, tabloid newspaper reception, pointing out what has been done and what needs to be done.

## PROVIDING THE GROUND

As a qualitative audience study, this work stands in the tradition of uncovering what the media mean to audiences. Within this academic realm, scholars have paid particular attention to the way audiences interpret media texts, the way meaning is produced and shared, and the relationship between media reception and the social and everyday contexts of media use. This form of audience research can be traced back to a trend within Anglo-Saxon audience research generally referred to as the 'qualitative turn' of the 1980s (Jensen 1991: 135). Essentially, a consensus has arisen in qualitative audience studies regarding the view that media audiences are active rather than passive, in terms of their construction of meaning from media texts (cf. also Chapter 4). Likewise, media messages are seen as carrying not one fixed meaning only, but offering a *variety* of different interpretations and positions relating to the text, including oppositional readings. Stuart Hall's early conceptual ideas (1973) regarding the 'encoding' (i.e. the producers' intended meaning) and the 'decoding' (i.e. the audience's interpretation) of media texts can be considered a fundamental work in this respect. Aside from that, David Morley's empirical study of the *Na-*

*tionwide* audience (1980) has set the scene for many works that followed. Hall and Morley, indeed, have spearheaded a new consensus in the field, opening up the agenda for a wave of research that is nowadays often subsumed under the term of 'new' audience studies. This section will discuss key findings from this realm that would seem relevant to this study, refraining, however, from giving a detailed overview of the developments, traditions and principles of audience and reception research, for others have provided excellent critical reviews elsewhere (cf., for instance, Morley 1992; Moores 1993; Ang 1990, 1996; Jensen and Rosengren 1990, Jensen 1991, 2002a,b).

## 'Decodings' in Perspective: Contexts of Sense-Making

### The Role of Sociological Variables

Possibly the most fundamental result emerging from the early qualitative audience studies relates to the observation that different audience members show a variety of different readings – or 'decodings' – of media texts. As these various interpretations often seem ambiguous, the primary aim of scholarly research has been to find patterns that offer explanations for different interpretations, as well as to draw relations to sociological variables such as gender, class, or sub-cultural belongings. , David Morley (1980, 1981, 1983 et seq.) provided a major qualitative empirical study considering the significance of social class in the decoding of media texts. Building on Hall's theoretical framework (1973) regarding possible mismatches in media producers' 'encoding' and audiences' 'decoding', Morley explored different social groups' interpretations of the news and current affairs television programme *Nationwide*. He suggested a connection between television viewers' sociological variables and their readings of the programme, using social class as the initial frame for his research. His results, however, revealed that while various audience members showed a range of 'dominant', 'negotiated' and 'oppositional' decodings, he observed that the participants' sub-cultural belongings appeared more significant to their meaning construction than their social class. As a consequence, he concluded that individual viewer's readings could not directly be linked to their social class. Although Morley modified his approach in his later ethnographic studies, he maintained this idea. Drawing on Bourdieu's ideas on cultural capital (1984), he contended in 1983 (ibid: 113):

'It is always a question of how social position, as it is articulated through particular discourses, produces specific kinds of readings or decodings. These readings can then be seen to be patterned by the way in which the structure of access to different discourses is determined by social position.'

Among the various contributions of Morley's research, the idea that meaning production is always context-specific is particularly worth emphasising here. Interpretations of tabloid newspapers, then, need to be viewed in relation to readers' sociodemographic variables as well as their social contexts of reception. In particular, readers' (self-selected) social positions appear to be an important aspect to consider.

Aside from social status, the role of gender has been a concern to many scholars. Exemplifying this, two major studies have set out to examine the reception of women's and men's magazines respectively, exploring readers' gender identities and gender relations. Employing focus group research with (predominantly) male readers of men's lifestyle magazines, Peter Jackson, Nick Stevenson and Kate Brooks (2001) sought to make sense of the appeal of men's magazines and shed light on readers' gender constructions. They observed that while both women's and men's magazines can be regarded as quite straightforward in terms of their stereotypical gender roles, readers' gender constructions in reaction to the magazines seem rather ambiguous. Jackson et al. concluded that men's magazines are used by readers as spaces for the negotiation of one's own position within the 'contradictoriness of modern masculinities' (ibid: 146). Similarly, female gender constructions in relation to women's magazines are not one-dimensional, as Kathrin Friederike Müller (2010) demonstrates in her study. Müller shows that female audience members do not necessarily adopt ideologically dominant positions offered by the text, but make sense of them in relation to other contexts of life. Clear-cut gender stereotypes offered by media texts can even be used as a site of 'resistive' readings. This has been argued by Janice Radway in her study *Reading the Romance* (1984). Exploring the practice of reading Romance novels, Radway investigates the interpretative patterns of female readers. She – like Morley – found that a range of different textual interpretations can be observed. Drawing attention to the fact that Romance readers use the novels' text for advice on how to cope with married life in a patriarchal system, she also highlighted "oppositional" positions as a vital part of this process. Reading Romances, then, seemed to be an activity aiding the negotiation of women's positions, rather than solely maintaining traditional gender roles.

## Everyday and Social Contexts of Media Use

Radway's research (1984) also usefully sheds some light on the role of audience's everyday life contexts in relation to media consumption. As a principle result of her study, she places the activity of reading Romances at the heart of women's day-to-day social practices. Radway highlighted the reading time as a time in which the women did something for themselves; a break from their everyday tasks in the household and family. Quite similarly, Joke Hermes' (1995) research has pointed towards important recreational qualities women's magazines appear to possess. She argued that these media outlets are particularly useful for filling spare time between readers' daily obligations, for they are easily put down and picked up again (for a similar finding cf. Müller 2010). Yet, Hermes has also drawn attention to the way women frame their reading of women's magazines as a largely 'meaningless' and insignificant activity. She concludes that 'general, everyday media use is identified with attentive and meaningful reading of specific texts, and that is precisely what it is not' (ibid 14-15). Thinking about this with regard to the study of tabloid newspaper audiences, we can ask how readers approach popular newspapers. Do they regard the tabloids as a somewhat "light" read, or do they apply an entirely different lens, approaching the papers as "serious" news outlets? Furthermore, it is worth examining the relationship between potentially recreational qualities of tabloids, and the way readers frame their reception.

While the connection between individual audience members' everyday contexts and their interpretations of media texts has been highlighted by the studies mentioned above, other scholars have explored media consumption in relation to its social contexts of use, as well as audience members' interaction with the media and with one another. James Lull's research (part. 1980, cf. also 1988a, 1988b, 1990) offered significant insight into the physical and social relationships audiences can have with the media. Drawing on ethnographic research within US-American families, he established a typology of the 'social uses of television' in a private family setting (ibid 1980). Among his 'structural' uses of television, Lull recognised the television set as providing a background noise and a presence filling the emptiness, for instance, when no other person was in the room. Moreover, he observed that the television schedule structured the day- regulating, for example, mealtimes or bedtime. Lull also noted 'relational' uses, describing how people make use of television in terms of their relation to each other. He claimed that television viewing facilitated communication and sociability among the members of a household on the one hand, and provided a space for individuals to avoid communicative interaction on the other – for instance, when a person chose to concentrate on a television programme rather than talk to others. Other scholars have likewise drawn attention to the structural uses of television in domestic environments; including David Gauntlett and Annette Hill in *TV Living* (1999), Shaun Moores in *Media and Everyday Life in Modern Society* (2000), and John Langer in *Tabloid Television* (1998). Each of these works suggests an interrelation between daily routines, social settings, and media consumption (cf. also Hobson 1982; Moores 1993; Neverla 1992). When carrying out an analysis of tabloid newspaper reception it is particularly useful to keep in mind the general insight that media consumption needs to be understood in relation to its social contexts of use.

## Cultural and National Influences

There is some evidence that cultural and national backgrounds play a significant role in audiences' sense-making practices. In particular, one cross-national comparative project which has gained large recognition offers valuable points to draw on. Tamar Liebes and Elihu Katz have conducted cross-cultural comparative viewing studies of American television drama; most notably of the soap opera *Dallas* (part. 1990; cf. also 1985, 1986, as well as Liebes 1984, 1988). Comparing different ethnic groups' discussions of the programme, they noted that the talks were similar in terms of the themes the show apparently raised (including – among others – issues of success, money and happiness, family relations and sex roles). However, Liebes and Katz pointed out that the individual themes' significance seemed to vary between the different ethnic groups. For instance, a group of Israeli Arabs particularly discussed kinship roles and norms, a group of Israeli kibbutz members were concerned with debating moral dilemmas, and a group of American viewers referred to business relations more often than other groups (ibid 1986: 154). This suggests that while the programme itself can be recognised as setting the agenda in terms of providing a general set of issues to talk about, different social and cultural influences significantly impact on the way these issues are understood, evaluated and debated. These results are highly instructive, suggesting that, in some ways at least, culturally and socially variant tabloid reading experiences can likewise be expected of tabloid newspapers.

## Pleasure, Power and Resistance

Aside from the empirical results discussed so far, some of John Fiske's ideas (1987a,b; 1989a,b; 2003) deserve attention here, although Fiske is not primarily recognised as an audience researcher. His position, based on Michel de Certeau's views (1984), could be regarded as the opposite of Adorno and Horkheimer's in many ways. In contrast to these scholars, Fiske is one of the great advocates for the view that power lies with the audience, not with the media (cf. Gauntlett's discussion 2008: 22 pp.) Fiske argues that cultural commodities and texts carry 'the interests of the economically and ideologically dominant; they have lines of force within them that are hegemonic and that work in favour of the status quo.' (ibid 1989a: 2) However, popular culture texts are, in Fiske's view, open, heterogeneous, and carry a multitude of different possible meanings. This potential plurality of the popular media's meanings, in combination with the presumption of diverse sense-making practices of audiences marks the central contributions of Fiske's work. Although his approach has been widely debated and criticised[13], his ideas have proven significant

---

13 Some critics regard Fiske's views as naïve in their celebration of popular culture's enabling qualities. This position has been advanced, for instance, by Sparks (2000) and

to many audience researchers (for a full discussion of Fiske's contribution to the Cultural Studies tradition cf. Mikos 2009).

With regard to the "resistive" potential of popular texts, Fiske famously argued that popular culture texts carry embedded oppositional meanings, these representing forms of resistance to society's hegemonic discourses (ibid 1989b: 24 pp.; 45). What is more, Fiske regards the mere consumption of popular culture texts as a site of opposition to the irrelevance of abstract politics and high culture (represented, for instance, by "quality" newspapers) consumed by the cultural and financial elites in society. Popular papers, in Fiske's view, are therefore not a threat, but 'evidence of dissatisfaction in society' (1989: 117). Regarding the reading of tabloids as a site through which ordinary people seek to enter the public domain, the consumption of the popular media therefore represents a political act in Fiske's view. Moreover, he suggests that popular news, as opposed to 'official' news, encourages critical awareness in audiences (cf. ibid: 1992b) rather than stupefying the masses, as was Adorno's belief (cf. Chapter 4). These arguments are closely linked to Fiske's conceptualisation of 'pleasure', for popular pleasures exist 'in some relationship of opposition to power' in his view (1989b: 49). He claims that there is a pleasure of resistance, entailing an audience's enjoyment of rejecting the dominant ideological meaning of a text and feeling the power of producing oppositional readings. Explaining this idea, he reviews the findings of Ien Ang (1985) as well as Liebes and Katz (1985 et seq.), maintaining that: 'Buying the programme does not mean buying into the ideology.' (ibid: 1987b)

However, there is more to the idea of pleasure than Fiske's idea of resistant reading modes. Reviewing the considerable range of studies focusing on audiences of television soap operas, Elisabeth Klaus (1998) usefully provides a typology of five different kinds of pleasure viewers can potentially derive from watching these programmes. For instance, she distinguishes between enjoying the content of a programme, and enjoying the formal genre characteristics, such as the narrative strategies. Klaus also emphasises that there is a 'communicative pleasure' that surrounds the consumption of soap operas, for these formats provide a range of subjects for conversation with others. Moreover, she draws attention to the difference between 'imaginative pleasure' and 'realistic pleasure'. Her idea of 'imaginative' pleasure resembles the concept of escapism – grounded in the idea that some media texts offer an escape from everyday life contexts into an imagined world of fantasy. How-

---

McGuigan (1992, 1997), who claim that Cultural Studies has veered off into populism. Other scholars have lamented the missing links between political economy and Cultural Studies (e.g. Garnham 1997; Kellner 1997). Todd Gitlin (1997) even regards Cultural Studies as 'anti-political', thus re-addressing concerns about the value of popular culture to democracy. Detailed criticism of Fiske's concept of pleasure and resistance can also be found in Röser (2000: 59 pp.) and Moores (1993: 130 pp.)

ever, forms of 'realistic' pleasures can also be derived from watching soap operas, for instance, when audience members perceive connections between their personal lives and those of the fictional characters. Fictional experiences, then, can be linked to one's own social reality in many ways; thus allowing for a re-evaluation of real-life experiences and settings (ibid: 337-346; cf. also Klaus and O'Connor's critique of the concept of pleasure, 2000). With regard to an exploration of tabloid reading modes in Germany and the UK, it will be useful to bear in mind these different kinds of pleasure when considering the appeal of these papers. Moreover, if we are to follow Fiske's ideas regarding the resistive potential of popular culture texts, it can be argued that tabloids, likewise, potentially carry the opportunity for opposition. It is worth asking then, if this is reflected in audiences' responses.

## News Reception

While the popular media have been on the research agenda since the advent of the 'qualitative turn' in audience research, news appears to be an under-researched area. Much attention has been devoted to broadcast and printed news as "texts" (cf., for instance, Hartley 1982; Bird and Dardenne 1997a). From the consumers' point of view, it is only television news that has been seriously examined. The audience of the press, however, still represents a rather blank field in media research.

Morley's *Nationwide* studies (1980 et seq.) constitute a prominent project dealing with the audience of television news. Other important works include Peter Dahlgren's meta-analysis of 'viewers' plural sense-making of TV news' (1988), Klaus Bruhn Jensen's account of 'audience uses of television news in world cultures' (1999), and Morley's contextualisation of television news (1999). While both Morley and Jensen remind us of the fact that audiences' conceptions of the world are (at least partly) mediated through news, Dahlgren's publication is particularly helpful in that he pulls together some research trends. In line with the arguments brought forward in Chapter 4, Dahlgren maintains that television news should be recognised as a form of cultural discourse, rather than being regarded as a source of pure information. As such, he emphasises the structural qualities of news to viewers' everyday lives and stresses the fact that the news serves as a reference point for 'making sense of the world around us' (ibid: 287). What is more, Dahlgren identifies various forms of discourse in viewers' talk about news. Suggesting a principal distinction between 'public' and 'private' modes, he establishes several versions of discursive categories – including an 'incorporated discourse' of a factual discussion nature by which the news items' 'dominant political discourse or some version of it' is talked about. However, Dahlgren also observes a 'trivial/random personal association' discourse, whereby viewers link news stories to their everyday life experiences, and a discourse he terms 'media awareness', which is characterised by considerable knowledge about televisual production elements. Both these discourses can be considered to be of a more 'private' nature (ibid: 294 pp.)

## Hybridity, 'Genre Work' and Learning

This leads to the issue of hybridisation, which represents the final aspect I would like to draw attention to in this general overview of important insights from the realm of audience studies. In particular the works of Annette Hill on the reception of factual television in the UK and Sweden (2005, 2007) have proven significant to this study, for they point out the hybrid character of factual television, and the impact this has on viewers' reception processes. Referring to part of the discourse about popular culture and the contradictions embedded in the genre, Hill demonstrates in her studies that the blurred boundaries of factual television formats create difficulties for viewers' categorisation of these programmes. Introducing her notion of 'genre work' (2007: 84 pp.), Hill describes the multiple modes of engagement with factual television she discovered, and shows that viewers are creative and resourceful in classifying and 'working through' (ibid: 91) notions of factuality. She explains:

'Most viewers have a genre map in their head. For some, this map is relatively clear and easy to read; it contains familiar areas, no-go areas, as well as territory in between. For others, this map is moving, and shifts positions depending on changes in the generic environment. One response is to locate genres according to pre-existing knowledge and experience, and also respond to changes along the way. Common genre maps created by viewers are often based on generic techniques, such as the way different factual genres report, document and construct real events. Another way of mapping factual genres is to rely on an information/entertainment axis, with adjustments for new developments and alternative modes of address. Yet another is to create new categories that respond to perceived changes in factual programmes.'

The notions of 'genre work' and 'genre maps' also refer to an issue touched on earlier in this Chapter; namely the finding that audience responses are far from clear-cut, and that meaning-creation is a complex and at times rather contradictory matter. As John Fiske notes, 'a text is the site of struggles for meaning' (1987a: 14).

A further significant insight from Hill's research concerns the various kinds of 'learning' and 'knowledge' which viewers derive from watching factual television programmes (ibid 2007: 145 pp.) Similar to the way viewers employ distinct classificatory practices when 'working through' the genre of factual television, they can be recognised as equally resourceful in learning from the programmes. Broadening notions of learning implied in the 'public knowledge project' which focus on the media's potential to educate and inform citizens with regard to their democratic practices (cf. Corner 1998), Hill identifies several different types of learning from factual television. In relation to cultural, social and personal contexts, she makes distinctions between receiving facts and information about the world (most commonly associated with news and current affairs), getting personally relevant information from a programme (for instance, from a documentary) and learning about the media itself, thereby developing critical media literacy skills. Similar ideas have also been brought forward, as stated in the previous chapter, by Elisabeth Klaus and Margret Lünenborg (2001: 157), who argue that audiences gain information from entertainment and fiction, and use information-based texts for entertaining purposes. From such a perspective, ideas of knowledge and learning are broadened considerably. The basic points made by Hill in particular are significant to my understanding of what tabloid readers may be able to derive from the newspapers. Moreover, I assume that the papers require equally much 'genre work' and classificatory practices, due to their hybrid nature. These issues and their implications for readers' interpretations of tabloids will be examined in the subsequent chapters.

## NEWSPAPER AUDIENCES IN THE SPOTLIGHT

Looking at printed news journalism, it is evident that while television has attracted many scholars, there is only limited knowledge about newspaper audiences. This is in stark contrast to the fact that the press is recognised as the traditional news media, having been granted an important position in media theory. However, what do we know about newspapers and their readers?

### Quantitative Readership Research

Newspapers constitute the second most-used type of media in European countries. After television, which is watched by almost all citizens of European nations, about half of the European public apparently read a daily paper (Badalori 2003: 4 pp.) Both Germany and the UK rank among the countries with the highest scores of newspaper readers. In Britain, 56.6% of the population are newspaper readers; in Germany, 65.5% of all citizens regularly read a newspaper. Both countries also share some of the lowest rates of people declaring they never read a newspaper at all (8.3% in the UK; 10% in Germany). Typically, men outnumber women, and the newspaper readership can be considered as mature, for most of the readers in both countries are between 40 and 54 years old. It is also noteworthy that education significantly impacts on newspaper reading habits. The proportion of readers increases by the level of educational qualification. The common quantitative audience measurements supplied by the *National Readership Survey* in the UK and the *Media An-*

*alyse* in Germany, moreover, provide details about readers' social and economic demographics per title[14]. However, this kind of data does not tell us anything about readers' relationships with the papers; nor can it help us to derive knowledge about the particular attractions of reading popular newspapers or gain insights about the role of the papers in audiences' daily lives.

## Practical Qualities of the Press

Many of the more general uses and functions of the press can be related to formal and structural characteristics of newspapers. In line with what has been detailed above, Shaun Moores (2005) argues that media reception structures daily routines and daily routines structure media reception (ibid: 9). He emphasises the significance of recurring routines and traditions to media reception – in particular stressing the 'cyclicity' of dailies. Their frequency of publication, he asserts, aids the 'ritual function and emotional significance in their [readers'] day-to-day cultures' (ibid: 17). Similarly, Klaus Schönbach and Wolfram Peiser (1997: 16 pp.) argue that the press are unique in the way they provide information. Readers can turn to newspapers at any time that fits their daily schedule. The papers can be carried around, split up in pieces and passed on. Moreover, readers are able to control the speed at which they consume the information provided – a benefit of reading newspapers that does not apply to watching television (at least, this has been the case for a long time, until the recent arrival of new technologies). Schönbach and Peiser also point out that the newspaper is an easily accessible medium which provides a pre-sorted array of information on different themes, and aids a selective search for particular news items (cf. also Rager and Werner 2002). The authors also emphasise the all-in-one quality of newspapers, and regard the medium's combination of 'guidance' and 'freedom' as their biggest asset, which allows for a range of different reading modes and reception styles (ibid: 20). While these characteristics would seem to be becoming less exclusive to the press today, due to the emergence of new technological advancements such as Internet news sources and digital television, the haptic and touchable nature of newspapers remains a unique feature.

## Reading Patterns & Reader Typologies

With a backdrop of falling circulation in the entire daily sector, and concerns that the press may be on the decline as a result of an increasing supply of online news sources, German scholars in particular have devoted a great deal of attention to the

---

14  For a typology of *Bild* and *Sun* readers based on the most recent survey data available cf. Chapter 2, p. 26.

potential hindrances that may prevent people from reading a newspaper. A range of contributions have focused on the most problematic target group of teenagers and young adults, attempting to draw up typologies of readers. The results from these studies show that the particular media socialisation in the family marks an important prerequisite for making printed news appeal to young people at all. Not surprisingly, teenagers from families that consider newspapers as integral constituents of common everyday life are more likely to become regular readers than their fellows. There is also some evidence that notions of media literacy, gender, age and formal education impact on young people's newspaper reading habits. Hence, the typical young reader is male, has obtained high formal educational qualifications, and is slightly older than the average member of his category (cf. Blöbaum 1992; Rager, Rinsforf and Werner 2002; Rager 2003, Rager et al. 2004; Kubitza 2006; Graf-Szczuka 2006, 2007, 2008).

The question of *how* people read newspapers has also attracted some interest. Some intriguing findings in this field derive from Beatrice Dernbach and Judith Roth's behavioural newspaper reading patterns which again focus focusingon teenagers and young adults (2007). Drawing on a variety of methods including in-depth interviews and participant observation, the authors identify two principal reader groups, the 'scanners' and the 'non-scanners' (ibid: 35). While the 'scanner' type inspects the whole of a page, the 'non-scanner' type directly jumps to an item of interest. The authors also observed several sub-categories within these two major groups. The 'scanners', for instance, can be divided into readers focusing on headlines, pictures, or both. The 'non-scanners' appeared to either show a direct approach to reading the paper, jumping to certain content items without attempting to get a general idea of what a page contains overall; else they follow a ritualised reading pattern. Dernbach and Roth conclude that the type of consumer consistently reading every page and news item in a newspaper is ceasing to exist (ibid: 39) – that is, if this type had ever existed before. Mostly, the readers taking part in their study appeared to either start reading a random news item, then jump to the next , or make deliberate choices and turn to reading selected content. Still, it is interesting that a prominently scanning, fast and elusive reading behaviour was under-represented in their results. What follows from this is the insight that newspaper reading is far from being a homogeneous process applying to the mass of audience members. It is, rather, characterised by complex and individual choices readers make; depending on the reading mode they apply and/or particular interests they have.

In terms of readers' relationship with the newspapers, there is some evidence that this is of a rather ambiguous nature; in particular with regard to the notion of trust. In a study conducted by the F&S Medienservice GmbH (2005) on media acceptance in Germany, wide-ranging public scepticism towards media content could be noted. While the public service broadcasting channels ARD and ZDF rank among the sources regarded most credible, the national broadsheets are only trusted by 15% of the German population. What is more, , the information provided by tabloid newspapers was deemed untrustworthy by 99% of all respondents. The UK provides a similar picture. MORI poll data suggests that public trust is lower in newspapers than in radio and television broadcasts, while the BBC is still considered the most trustworthy source of information (cf. Mortimore et al. 2000; Worcester 1998). Still, the role of the press is significant, for newspapers, in particular the popular press, have a large readership in both Germany and the UK. Yet, the material reviewed so far does not allow us to draw conclusion about the papers' roles in audiences' lives, or about the sense-making processes involved in reading them.

## TABLOID NEWSPAPER RECEPTION

As indicated, qualitative audience studies focusing on newspaper reception are scarce; however, some important inferences can be drawn from a small number of previous tabloid reception analyses. After many years of 'academic neglect' (Bruck and Stocker 1996: 10), an emerging interest in the audience of the popular press can be discerned within international scholarly endeavours of the last 15 years. Meanwhile, a few significant works are publicly available. Of particular interest here are the detailed accounts of Peter A. Bruck and Günther Stocker, who have provided a reception study of the Austrian tabloid *Neue Kronen Zeitung* (1996). Similarly significant are Hans Dieter and Ute Klingemann's quantitative analysis of *Bild* readers' likes and dislikes (1983); S. Elisabeth Bird's study of readers of US-American supermarket tabloids (1992); and, last but not least, Sofia Johansson's Ph.D. research, a qualitative reception analysis of the two popular UK dailies *The Sun* and the *Daily Mirror* (2007a; cf. also 2006 and 2007b). A few smaller, more exploratory studies with the scope of Master's theses complete the field. Among these, Marc Pursehouse's reception analysis of *The Sun* (from which he published some findings in 1991), Dorothea Habicht's MA thesis, an analysis of the 'motives' for reading *Bild* (2004; cf. also 2006) and; finally, my own previous research, a small-scale qualitative reception study of *Bild* (Brichta 2002; cf. also 2010).

### Austria's Tabloid *Neue Kronen Zeitung*

In terms of German language-based texts, Bruck and Stocker (1996) provide one of the most comprehensive accounts in the field of tabloid newspaper reception in their book *Die ganz normale Vielfältigkeit des Lesens* (lit: the banal variety of reading). Conducting a qualitative audience study of Austria's best-selling tabloid *Neue Kronen Zeitung (NKZ)*, they compiled five group discussions with readers from different socio-economic backgrounds. For their first discussion, they assembled eight first-year undergraduate students of Journalism, of mixed gender and aged between 19 and 29 years (ibid: 66 pp.) The second assembly was a friendship group of eleven teenage boys and one girl from 'lower social class' backgrounds (ibid: 90 pp.), whom they recruited in a youth centre. The third group was made up of male amateur football players, aged between 16 and 25 (ibid: 118 pp.) For the fourth group, Bruck and Stocker assembled seven men and women between 27 and 60 years from lower socio-economic backgrounds, who 'each pictured themselves as underdogs, as 'little men and women' in one way or another' (ibid: 140; original quotation marks). Finally, their fifth group (ibid: 179 pp.) comprised nine adults from highly diverse socio-economic backgrounds, who had obtained different educational qualifications and were aged between 26 to 82 years.

As a central result of their study, Bruck and Stocker stress a 'qualified resonance' among their respondents, emphasising that the reception of the tabloid varied considerably among their respondents. They elaborate:

'Reading tabloid newspapers like the *NKZ* is not the solid-state process it is assumed to be in nearly all of the textual analyses of the genre. ... There is no such thing as one reading, one meaning and one effect. Instead, reading tabloids emerges as a diverse and fragmentary process, just as the textual elements of the papers are diverse and fragmentary. Above all, reading tabloids needs to be recognised as an active process of sense-making shaped by many different aspects, rather than a passive process in which readers either adopt or dismiss a meaning offered by the text. Indeed, drawing a direct link between the content of tabloids and readers' consciousness would mean to ignore the fact that many different reading modes can be observed.' (ibid: 227)

Substantiating their argument, Bruck and Stocker distinguish between eleven different reading patterns which they observed among the participants of their research (ibid: 236 pp.):

- an *entertainment-centred* reading pattern characterised by the wish for distraction;
- an *action-centred* reading pattern whereby readers prefer editorial content relating to accidents, catastrophes and crime;
- an *information-seeking* pattern that aims to seek out information useful to readers' everyday lives;
- a *skim-reading pattern* focusing on the texts' visual elements or aiming at a casual read;
- a reading pattern the authors term *involvement*, characterised by emotional empathy for those reported on;
- an *oppositional* reading pattern which involves a universal refusal of the text's apparent meaning, leading to oppositional meaning-creation;

- an *arrogant* reading pattern either seeking to fill time (similar to the practice of skim-reading), or characterised by distanced stances to the texts which are seen to target others;
- a pattern the authors name *the NKZ as a show*, focusing on melodrama and sensation;
- a way of reading they regard as working as a *valve*, characterised by shared feelings of outrage in particular;
- a *bourgeois* reading pattern that is engaged with moral judgements which confirm one's own moral norms and values;
- a *strategic* reading, by which readers have a somewhat professionalised interest; for instance through seeking to find out what Austria's highest-selling newspaper says about a particular issue;
- a *voyeuristic* reading pattern whereby readers show little emotional involvement and the reason for reading the NKZ is to know what 'the majority of Austrians read';
- and, finally, a reading pattern the authors describe as *searching for the truth in a world full of lies*; which implies the view that the world is full of conspiracy and the NKZ is the one remaining authentic and honest medium.

Bruck and Stocker acknowledge that most of their respondents showed a combination of different reading modes and alternated between diverse stances to the text. However, attempting to classify readers into categories, the authors sought out relationships between participants' socio-economic variables and their reading patterns. Stressing the significance of social and educational backgrounds, the authors note that readers of a more privileged social status and with higher educational qualifications tended to show reading patterns implying a somewhat 'greater distance' to the text, while readers from poorer groups were more likely to demonstrate patterns characterised by involvement and 'little distance' to the text. Bruck and Stocker assigned, for instance, patterns relating to *entertainment-centred, oppositional* and *arrogant* readings to affluent and well-educated audience members, and associated patterns such as *voyeuristic reading* and *searching for the truth in a world full of lies* to participants who had obtained lower educational qualifications.

These findings significantly underpin the general insight that different audience members approach the media in different ways. It will be interesting to examine if the results emerging from my readership analysis can refine the authors' arguments about socially diverse reading modes, for I will argue against the idea that readers of different social backgrounds generally use tabloids differently or show socially variant likes and dislikes. Instead, my hypothesis is that it is not socially variant readings, but socially variant *valuations* of the papers that are reflected here, and which impact on the way readers understand the tabloid. This issue shall be examined in the course of this study.

There are, however, a few methodological drawbacks of Bruck and Stocker's study which are worth considering. It appears that despite employing the method of focus group discussions, the authors did not make full use of the benefits of this method. This is due to the fact that they approached their material as group interviews, placing emphasis on the quantity of answers rather than, for instance, the processes of meaning-creation in relation to group processes and group opinions. The method of group interviewing, however, produces quite different results than that of group discussions. According to Morgan (1997: 12), in group interviewing the emphasis is on questions and responses between interviewer and participants, with the aim of interviewing a number of people at the same time. One characteristic of group discussions, by contrast, lays in the interaction between the group's members (cf. Chapter 6, p. 132). Moreover, the five questions Bruck and Stocker posed to their participants appear somewhat leading at times, and normatively charged in some instances. For instance, asking 'whose interests does the *NKZ* represent' or 'which emotions does the *NKZ* convey' (ibid: 59) pre-emptively implies that readers' emotions are addressed and their interests are vented. It is, from my point of view, therefore difficult to distinguish between answers reflecting the respondents' views and value judgements and answers that reproduced the anticipated views of the authors. Moreover, Bruck and Stocker, regrettably, do not reflect on their findings in relation to these issues; nor do they address group dynamics which might have impacted on socially desirable responses from the participants. Furthermore, the authors mention that it was not possible to recruit readers of higher socio-economic and educational backgrounds as participants for their research, their assumption being that 'the *NKZ* is apparently not compatible with the social image of these reader groups' (ibid: 56). Yet they observe criticism and devaluing remarks about the paper in each of their group discussions (ibid: 113). However, despite concluding that preconceptions and criticism, emotions and demographic characteristics equally play a role in the reception (ibid: 295), they do not reflect on this in any more detail. For instance, how does the fact that Bruck and Stocker found reading modes with 'greater distance' to the text in readers of more comfortable social positions relate to the paper's image? And does this image impact on other respondents' answers as well; and so, how? I shall aim to give some answers to these questions in the primary analysis chapters.

### Germany's Red-Top *Bild*

Indications of some of the attractions which the German tabloid *Bild* hold for its readers can be drawn from a quantitative survey of 1,052 German readers and non-readers of the paper (Klingemann & Klingemann 1983), as well as from two small-scale studies focusing on the reception of *Bild*: Dorothea Habicht's MA dissertation examining readers' 'motives' for reading the paper (2004), and own my previous research in the area, a qualitative reception study of *Bild* (Brichta 2002). For the latter, I interviewed ten readers from different socio-demographic backgrounds. The respondents were four women and six men between 17 and 78 years. Three of the participants were blue-collar workers (one of whom was a pensioner), a further three worked in skilled or lower managerial jobs (again including one pensioner), and one girl was still receiving compulsory secondary education at a state school. The remaining three interviewees were all in upper managerial positions. The study examined five interdependent research enquiries. It sought to examine the role of *Bild* in readers' everyday life – readers' expectations of the paper as well as the uses and functions of reading it. Moreover, the research attempted to gauge if and how *Bild* addressed issues relevant to readers' social reality; it sought to investigate the participants' reading modes; and finally, it aimed to examine readers' images of the paper and those of the "other" readers. I employed in-depth individual interviews, analysing the material via these five categories and presenting the findings in the form of ten individual portraits of the interviewed readers, following this with a summarising discussion. Dorothea Habicht's MA thesis (2004), emerging two years later, found many of the same themes. Her approach was in line with a considerable corpora of German audience works concerned with examining audiences' 'motives' for media consumption (cf., for instance, Meyen 2004; Donsbach 1991). The conceptual basis for these studies was a 'uses and gratifications'-based approach to media consumption. Habicht's work, therefore, is less concerned with the processes of meaning-creation, and does not offer any detailed explanations of why readers might like one aspect and dislike another. Yet, drawing on four group discussions, her study is instructive as it yields basic points and provides an array of aspects relating to the tabloid's audience appeal, thus helping to confirm and bring together the findings of Klingemann et al. (1983) and my previous research (Brichta 2002).

In terms of general reception practices, it is noteworthy that none of the ten respondents taking part in my study regarded *Bild* as their single source of news – although the scope of participants' "media menus" increased proportional to their level of formal education. However, the results of the study show that both readers' understanding and evaluations of *Bild* depend on ritualised individual reading patterns and reading situations, as well as family traditions. Hence, the research strongly emphasised the interplay between everyday life routines and the reception of *Bild*. The significance of everyday life routines to media consumption has, as discussed, also been stressed in studies like Radway's *Reading the Romance* (1984), Gauntlett and Hill's *TV Living* (1999) and Shaun Moores' *Media and Everyday Life in Modern Society* (2000). These works emphasize the effect of routines and social everyday circumstances on media reception practices. Likewise, reading *Bild* can be seen to structure the day; a fact that both Lull (1980) and Langer (1998), for instance, have noted about television viewing and news consumption. Suggesting that daily routines and media consumption are, indeed, strongly interlinked social phenomena, the findings from my 2002 research also confirm Moore's later arguments about the significance of the mass media's circular nature to everyday routines (ibid 2005: 9; for a full discussion of this issue with regard to *Bild* cf. Brichta 2010: 209-11).

We can, moreover, derive some conclusions about what readers enjoy about *Bild* from my 2002 research project. All participants of that study directly or indirectly commented on the paper's easily understandable language and style, as well as its lucid visual presentation (cf. Brichta 2002: 131). Habicht (2006: 156-57) similarly notes that the tabloid's formal characteristics account for some of the 'motives' for reading it. It is interesting that the social status of respondents significantly impacted on the way they phrased this. While the retired manual worker identified with the easy-to-relate-to language of *Bild* and regarded this as a service quality of the paper, both a university professor and a tax accountant demonstrated more detached stances, describing *Bild* as a light and entertaining read. In line with this, some participants of Habicht's research praised the general resourcefulness of *Bild*'s journalists, particularly with regard to their abilities in headline-making. She refers to a quotation from a man working in PR (ibid: 158), suggesting that this might be an element particularly liked by readers with occupations in the media industry. Supporting this point, a journalist I interviewed demonstrated admiring stances in relation to the professional skills of *Bild*'s reporters and editors (Brichta 2002: 116).

In terms of content preferences, most participants said they enjoy reading the gossip items in *Bild* (Brichta 2002: 131; cf. also Chapter 8, p. 197). However, some gender-related differences evolved concerning the subject matter of the gossip. Women, it emerged, preferred reading about celebrities and showbiz stars, while men liked reading about sports personalities (ibid: 132-34; cf. also Chapter 7, p. 172). With regard to the representation of gender roles, the tabloid's strong sexual connotations also deserve some acknowledgement. My study suggested that notions of gender and sex play a vital role in the reception of *Bild*. Demonstrating that the paper's distinct references to these matters marked a significant element in both men and women's processes of making sense of their own gender roles (Brichta 2002: 135-36), the findings showed that the page three girl invited openly chauvinistic remarks from male readers, in particular from the men with higher educational levels (ibid: 135-136; cf. also the findings relating to *The Sun* and the *Daily Mirror*, p. 117). In contrast to this, the female readers I interviewed were strongly alienated by the way women are commonly depicted by *Bild*, in particular referring to the half-naked ladies on the front page as a negative example that invited detachment.

A further aspect revealed by my previous research and worth mentioning is that notions of sociability and community played a significant role in the reception of *Bild*. Most participants stated that they talked about items in the paper with others; drawing on *Bild*'s reports in conversations and using it as a tool for establishing and maintaining social relations. Moreover, the respondents demonstrated feelings of togetherness in relation to a wider community of tabloid readers (ibid: 137-38). Similarly, some readers made use of the paper via para-social interaction, approaching the tabloid's texts as a substitute for their own experiences (ibid: 79). Identification with others also played a vital role in the receptive process, this being strongly supported by the tabloid's narrative strategy of personalisation. Habicht likewise acknowledges this as serving social comparisons, aimed at confirming one's own view of the world (ibid: 161). The editorial stance of *Bild* – presenting itself as an advocate of the little people – is a further reason for its consumption, as Habicht points out. Many of her readers, she claims, referred to aspects relating to the power of the paper; for instance, the paper's ability to 'disclose' matters and subsequently spark off scandals by publishing the material (ibid: 159). This aspect was also addressed by my study, which has shown that in particular, female working and middle class readers closely identify with the paper, demonstrating highly involved reading modes and maintaining the view that the paper represents the voice of its readers and stands up for them (Brichta 2002: 141 pp.)

Still, the relationship between *Bild* and its readers appears to be marked by conflict, as the early quantitative survey by Hans Dieter and Ute Klingemann's (1983) has indicated. Drawing on a representative sample of the German population, their study provides knowledge about the specific appeal the tabloid has for its audience. However, it also significantly highlights some of the readers' dislikes of *Bild*. Klingemann & Klingemann used a combination of questionnaire and interview methods in order to examine 'the public mood towards *Bild*' (ibid: 240), and discovered a remarkably negative trend in attitudes towards the paper. In particular, their study reveals that readers' attitudes to *Bild* highly resembled the views of non-readers. This means that remarkably negative value judgements could be observed among both non-readers and readers. Looking at what the readers said, it is interesting that – in line with what has been detailed above – their positive comments mainly related to the visual structure and conciseness of the text, the tabloid's topical 'up-to-dateness', the perception that *Bild* provides help and support to its readers, and the paper's sports reporting. Yet, they also criticised a range of aspects of the paper. For instance, readers claimed to dislike *Bild*'s 'sensationalised' style and presentation, its low credibility, and content relating to sex, crime, and celebrity gossip (ibid: 249-50).

This is a highly interesting result underscoring my argument that the negative image of *Bild* and its public devaluation play a significant role in its reception. The results of my own previous research similarly suggest that particularly negative aspects mark a vital part of readers' understanding of the paper, for participants' images of *Bild* appeared largely shaped by diverse, complex and in parts conflicting conceptions and beliefs. While all readers I interviewed showed cautious scepticism and at times strong detachment from *Bild*, I found much stronger notions of alienation amongst the more affluent and well-educated readers. Generally, two different groups of respondents could be distinguished with regard to their images of the paper. The first group consisted of three women (one of middle class background, two of working class background) who saw *Bild* in a rather positive light, largely free of conflict and contradiction. The other group consisted of the six men taking part in the study as well as one woman working as a tax accountant. These participants showed a strikingly negative and conflicted attitude towards the paper. Although they also mentioned positive aspects of *Bild* (most of which have been referred to above), these participants attached a range of negative conceptions and meanings to the tabloid. In particular, traditional perceptions of *Bild* play an important role here. Largely in line with the historical events surrounding the paper (cf. Chapter 2, p. 29), participants' criticism focused on *Bild*'s style and content preferences, its power and impact on society and other readers (Brichta 2002: 144-51). The study has also shed light on socially diverse ways of avoiding the stigma surrounding the tabloid. Participants who had obtained higher educational qualifications demonstrated particular trouble with the paper's negative reputation, showing much detachment from the tabloid and their negative image of the "other" readers. This is an interesting phenomenon which deserves to be looked into in detail and from a cross-national perspective.

### Weekly US-American 'Supermarket Tabloids'

Looking across the Atlantic, S. Elisabeth Bird's study *For Enquiring Minds: A Cultural Study of Supermarket Tabloids* (1992) is an interesting early piece of research investigating the weekly United States version of tabloids. This version differs from its European relatives in more than just its publication frequency. In the US the genre of daily tabloids is commonly referred to as 'yellow journalism', an example being the *Daily News* of New York City, for instance. Presenting itself as a source of news within daily journalism, it resembles papers like *Bild* and *The Sun*. The weekly 'supermarket tabloids', however, occupy a somewhat different position within the continuum of popular print outlets. Focusing almost entirely on scandal, entertainment and sports, they traditionally have a strong element of the mythical and fantastic built into their stories (cf. Sparks 2000: 13-16; Bird 1992: 39-78). Bird's findings must, therefore, be viewed in the context of these genre differences.

Reviewing supermarket tabloids' historical development, their contexts of production and their typical contents, Bird starts her consideration by pointing out that the image of these media outlets as well as that of the readers is 'invariably negative' (ibid: 107). Identifying a strong 'need for qualitative audience research' (ibid: 109), she takes an ethnographic approach to investigating readers' views. Largely in line with Ang's method (1985), Bird solicited and analysed letters from readers. She was able to place a staff-written announcement in the *National Examiner* of 25

August 1987, asking readers to write to her, and received letters from 77 women and 42 men. Bird complemented this material by phone interviews with 15 of these readers (ten women and five men), and added to this one face-to-face interview with a reader, which she had previously conducted (cf. Bird 1992: 109-13).

Bird notes that most of her respondents were sceptical about the tabloid's truthfulness and 'quite selective about the particular phenomena they chose to believe in' (ibid: 120). Yet, she states, readers allowed the paper to 'reinforce their already existing beliefs' (ibid: 121). However, in stark contrast to all other reception studies in the genre, Bird describes her US-American participants' attitude towards the *National Examiner* as genuinely positive. In opposition to the derogatory references she had identified within academic and industry publications, most of the readers described the tabloid as 'fun', 'exciting', 'newsy' or 'interesting', rather than 'sleazy' or 'sensational'. It is also noteworthy that Bird's respondents largely avoided the term 'tabloid', which appeared to carry negative connotations. Instead, participants mostly referred to the paper by using the word 'weekly' (ibid: 114). This interesting result about Bird's participants who 'happily ignore[d] any disapproval' (ibid: 115) needs to be evaluated in the context of the chosen method. The sample she drew on was of a self-selected nature, and, to use the author's own words, 'it is safe to assume that the respondents were more enthusiastic' than many other readers would have been. Although she refers to the activity of writing in this quote, I would suggest that a similar dynamic applies to the general attitude towards the *National Examiner*. Bird's findings could, however, also signal cultural variance within the genre of tabloids referred to above. It may be quite possible that such variations are, likewise, reflected in diverse audience responses.

Bird also observed some ironic and detached responses in what she called the 'self-conscious' reading experience (ibid: 116-19). The author explains: 'The "self-conscious" reading accepts the view that tabloids are "sleazy" and "vulgar", but reading them is an enjoyable kind of "slumming".' (ibid: 118; original quotation marks) Pointing out that this represents a somewhat marginal and 'elite' perception of tabloids (ibid: 114), Bird claims that the different responses to the papers which she found closely intertwine with notions of literacy and class. Among her respondents, she identified only three men who showed 'self-conscious' reading modes; each of whom took care to distance themselves from the people perceived as 'typical' readers. This very much links in with the findings discussed above concerning the somewhat socially diverse images of *Bild* and readers' ways of dealing with this issue. We can also discover similarities to Bruck and Stocker's relationships drawn between detached reading modes and more affluent socio-economic categories. Suggesting that this aspect is similar across different national contexts, studies in the wider field of popular culture have shown that other popular media products likewise attract ironic, detached or 'self-conscious' readings (cf., for instance, Ang

1985). The kind of enjoyment derived from this, then, obviously refers to part of the attraction of popular culture.

Paying particular attention to 'gendered readings', Bird specifically examined female and male readings of tabloids, relating them to traditional gender-related socialisation paths (ibid: 138-61). Bringing together the various threads her of analysis, Bird places the tabloid in a tradition of oral folk culture (ibid: 162-72). Drawing on Fiske (1987a) and others; she argues that the tabloids' narratives resemble traditional storytelling:

'Tabloids certainly draw on and transmit established oral legends, but they themselves also work like urban legends in restructuring diffuse beliefs, uncertainties, and stereotypes in narrative form. ... Furthermore, the media in general, and tabloids in particular, develop their themes and tell their stories in ways that are not unlike the process of oral transmission. As we have seen, readers receive and use the narratives in oral communication.' (ibid: 165-66)

The author claims that tabloids, their producers and their readers are best understood as more or less equal participants in a 'continuing circular process' (ibid: 163). Indeed, she suggests approaching supermarket tabloids as one strand of culture 'existing alongside and because of other cultural phenomena'. Stressing the connections between cultural components, she embraces the (postmodern) notion that 'everything reflects off everything else in ever-repeating images' (ibid: 1-2). Indeed, her arguments fit in well with contemplations of popular journalism by Fiske (1987a, 1989a, 1989b, 2003) as well as Hartley (1996), Renger (1997, 2000, 2002, 2006) and Lünenborg (2005). The common ground of these scholars' ideas rests in the recognition of popular journalism as a cultural process. In acknowledging its cultural significance, this approach emphasises the idea that meaning production is a 'cultural circuit' (Müller 1993: 56).

### Britain's Popular Papers *The Sun* and the *Daily Mirror*

Two works concerned with the British experience complete the picture of preexisting knowledge about tabloid newspaper reception. The first is Marc Pursehouse's qualitative study on the relationship between Britain's red-top *The Sun* and its regular readers (1991). In 1988, with *The Sun*'s circulation at its peak, Pursehouse conducted 13 individual interviews with readers of the tabloid. He sought out young readers' 'uses and opinions' of *The Sun* and offered conclusions about the 'complex relationship between the tabloids, their readers and the wider social processes of which we are a part' (ibid: 90). The second significant work to consider here is Sofia Johansson's Ph.D. dissertation which she published in 2007 (cf. ibid 2007a), a qualitative reception analysis of the two London-based papers *The Sun* and the *Daily Mirror*. Johansson used a combination of focus group research and individual interviews, compiling 11 small-sized real groups with three to six participants each, and conducting 14 additional individual interviews with two female and ten male readers of the papers. In total, 55 readers participated in her research, of whom 35 were male and 20 were female. Her respondents' social backgrounds were in line with those of the majority of the papers' readerships, as was their age range (18-35). Johansson's research emerged at the Communication and Media Research Institute at the University of Westminster at around the same time as this study. Similar in approach and empirical design, her research can be considered one of the key supporting texts for this book. Although the two studies emerged independently, it is interesting that comparable themes were identified. The same can be said of Pursehouse's work, which very much resembles my previous research on the readers of *Bild* in its theoretical approach, scope, methodology, and findings (cf. Brichta 2002). Both Johansson's and Pursehouse's research are, therefore, invaluable to the cross-national comparative aspect of this book. Their results help to identify potential similarities between tabloid reading in Britain and Germany and highlight possible areas of national variation, which can then be examined further in the empirical parts of this book.

Many of the themes and patterns found by Pursehouse and Johansson echo findings from other studies of tabloid reception in other parts of the world. For instance, both scholars confirm the significance of popular papers to daily routines and social relationships. Pursehouse acknowledges *The Sun*'s importance to 'the culture of the masculine working world' (1991: 103), explaining how buying and reading the paper fits in well with traditionally male daily working schedules. Johansson also stresses the significance of recurring day-to-day reception practices, while highlighting familiarity with the chosen paper as a further significant aspect of the reading habit (2007a: 120-22). Likewise, both studies draw attention to the way popular newspapers are resources for sociability and social interaction with others, and can foster a sense of belonging to a wider community (Pursehouse 1991: 104; Johansson 2007a: 148).

Indicating further similarities between the reception of German and English tabloids, both Pursehouse and Johansson found that the papers' scandal and gossip items offer a form of pleasure to (in particular) female and (less overtly) male audience members. Both authors link these kinds of news stories to the tabloids' sociability, demonstrating that the themes, problems and issues offered can easily be related to readers' own lives. On this note, Pursehouse considers scandal as an antidote to the sphere of politics which, in his view, is distant from readers' social reality and provokes feelings of exclusion (ibid: 107). Similar arguments are brought forward by Johansson, who discusses the function of celebrity gossip in relation to social inequality (ibid: 142 pp.; for a detailed argument cf. also Johansson 2006).

With regard to readers' responses to notions of sexuality and gender, the arguments derived from Johansson's and Pursehouse's textual analyses of the tabloids can be confirmed (cf. Johansson 2007a: 100 pp.; Pursehouse 1991: 97; cf. also Chapter 2, p. 46, with regard to typical content features of the tabloid press). Pursehouse, in commenting on the 'problem-free sexual 'fun' of *The Sun*' (ibid: 97), calls the page three girl 'a masculine adult comic' (ibid: 107). Similar to what has been detailed about the respondents of my previous study, Pursehouse notes that some of the male readers he interviewed were 'prepared to be completely honest in their chauvinism' (ibid: 113). The women he interviewed, however, appeared to cautiously refer to the photographs of half-naked ladies as 'normal', rather than drawing on them as a site of resistance to sexist representation of women. Pursehouse concludes that his participants' responses demonstrate the 'solidity of the 'macho' image and the dominance of the male perspective of gender relations, as well as the perceptions of powerlessness still held by many women' (ibid: 114). Similarly, the tabloids' sports pages were generally appreciated, particularly by male readers (cf. Johansson 2007a: 135). Yet, there is also some evidence for the view that the tabloids' representation of sexuality and gender is far from straightforward. Johansson acknowledges ambiguity and counter-discourses within relevant texts in the *The Sun* and the *Daily Mirror* (ibid: 106), pointing out that 'strategies of resistance' can likewise be observed in readers' responses to the papers' displays of gender and sexuality (cf. ibid: 137 pp.)

However, while this book has so far drawn attention to similar aspects emerging from studies of tabloid reception in Britain and Germany, some differences can likewise be observed. Connecting with what both Johansson and Pursehouse identified as typical textual elements of British popular papers, the authors point out that their respondents stressed tabloid reading as 'fun' and 'humorous' (Pursehouse 1991: 106; Johansson 2007a: 133 pp.) In particular *The Sun* was perceived to specialise in amusing narratives and style, for it was singled out by readers for its 'witty nerve' and 'cheeky headlines' (Pursehouse: 111). The *Daily Mirror*, in comparison, was considered less entertaining (ibid: 103), but a paper with 'more brains', as one of Johansson's participants put it (ibid: 128). Also, it was perceived as being less sexist, and aimed at more educated readers. Interesting aspects regarding potential cross-national differences are implied here. Similar to the reception of German tabloids, frequent perceptions of red-tops as 'rubbish papers' (Johansson: 122) occurred in both studies, and much critical detachment was found to the extent that 'even the most avid readers had conflicts and doubts in their relationship with *The Sun*' (Pursehouse: 122). Likewise, both Johansson (2007a: 118) and Pursehouse (1991: 102) assert that their participants turned to other sources of news, mostly televised, for 'truer' reports. Yet, it is interesting that humour, fun and jokes appear somewhat accentuated among British tabloid readers (cf. also Chapter 2, p.43, with regard to differing content preferences of *The Sun* and *Bild*). Additionally it was noted that '*The Sun* was not read in isolation from knowledge of other national papers' (Pursehouse 1991: 103). This is confirmed by Johansson, whose findings indicate that there is a hierarchy of popular papers in readers' heads, resulting in diverse understandings and perceptions of individual tabloid papers (ibid: 127 pp). As with women's magazines (cf. Müller 2010), making comparisons between similar media outlets and claiming to read the "better" alternative helps to enhance, if not sanitise, one's own reading. Preferring one paper over another, then, results in what Johansson describes as 'brand loyalty' (ibid: 127), with '*Sun*-readers contrasting the *Mirror* as for example demanding, 'boring' or 'more technical to read', and the *Mirror*-readers describing *The Sun* as 'tacky', 'embarrassing' or 'extreme' (ibid: 128). In the UK, such comparisons are easy to make, as tabloid papers dominate the market. However, in Germany, *Bild* marks the country's only national tabloid and is unique in this status. It will therefore be interesting to examine if this is mirrored in nationally diverse views of tabloids.

In terms of the relationship between tabloids, their readers, and party politics, more potential cross-national differences come into view that link in with the differences described in Chapter 2. Essentially, Pursehouse asserts that, contrary to his expectations, the respondents of his study made very few articulations about *The Sun* being a Conservative paper. He even claims: '*The Sun* is recognised by its readers without political opinions or messages' (ibid: 113). Somewhat in line with this view, Johansson's participants likewise seemed unfamiliar with any editorial political stance of either paper she investigated. Yet, offering speculations, some of her readers claimed that both *The Sun* and the *Daily Mirror* primarily showed affinity with a majority view rather than any political party's agenda (Johansson 2007a: 129; she also usefully discusses tabloid newspapers as alternative public spheres, cf. 2007a: 155 pp. and 2007b). This appears to contrast German studies' findings which have drawn attention to readers' distinct ideas about tabloids' political stances (cf., for instance, Brichta 2002: 145 pp.)

In general, both Pursehouse and Johansson followed a broad research approach, focusing on investigating individuals' uses and functions of reading. Even in Johansson's study, the methods of data collection, i.e. individual interviews and group interviews with a small number of participants, left much room for examining individual readers' likes and dislikes. Building on these results, then, my study is concerned with more collective processes of meaning creation. I am paying attention to the ways meaning is negotiated in (larger) group settings which can embed and reproduce readers' social reality. Moreover, the research will investigate the impact of different social and cultural contexts to readers' interpretation of tabloids.

## CONCLUSIONS

Set within the domain of media consumption and media audiences, this study is informed by important theoretical ideas underpinning this academic field. Most notably, the paradigms of the form of audience research that can be traced back to a trend within Anglo-Saxon audience research generally referred to as the 'qualitative turn' of the 1980s (Jensen 1991: 135) enlighten my approach – particularly the idea that audiences are active with regard to their meaning-construction from media texts, and the position that media messages generally carry a variety of different meanings. On the basis of these premises, this chapter has discussed previous empirical research findings from the field of qualitative audience studies of popular media formats, newspaper consumption and tabloid reception. The most important findings include the fact that meaning-constructions and positions to popular media outlets are as diverse as the texts. Meaning-production can, indeed, be recognised as invariably context-specific, for individual socio-demographic variables and life-contexts as well as the social context of media use significantly impact on people's interpretation of media texts. Moreover, the relationship between everyday contexts and media consumption has been highlighted, both with regard to the structural and recreational qualities of media use, as well as audience members' interaction with each other through the media. Aside from that, different kinds of pleasure have been described that can be derived from the consumption of particularly popular media formats. This material has also been considered in relation to claims about its "resistive" potential and enabling qualities. In addition, popular media formats have been singled out for their hybrid nature and the classificatory practices and 'genre work' their reception requires.

Having established these premises, this chapter has looked into previous tabloid reception studies from various countries, pointing out important findings and showing that many similarities between the tabloid reading experiences in Germany and UK can be observed. I have drawn attention to possible culturally specific interpretations and evaluations which link back to the diverse characteristics of *Bild* and *The Sun*. There is also some indication that other elements of variance may relate to, for instance, the diverse cultural significance of jokes, fun and humour to the tabloids' discourses. Previous reception studies indicate that while *The Sun* is regarded highly amusing, *Bild* seems to be taken more seriously by its readers. A further indication for cross-national variation concerns readers' perceptions of the tabloids' political endorsement (cf. Chapter 2, p. 44). Moreover, the extended tabloid marketplace in the UK (cf. Chapter 3) is reflected in readers' responses, who perceive a hierarchy of popular papers and apply distinct categorisations when judging diverse tabloids.

A truly significant issue worth re-emphasising here concerns the fact that theoretical and empirical works on popular media formats and their consumption almost unanimously identify a noticeable devaluation of the genre, in both academic approaches as well as from an audience point of view. Nearly all previous reception studies have shown that consumers often frame their reception as an insignificant activity, habitually down-playing the medium and their own consumption habits. Likewise, critical, ironic and detached positions have been highlighted. It is fair to assume that this is truly significant to the reading experience and readers' interpretation of popular papers. Yet, none of the studies so far has approached this as an independent reception category. It is, therefore, worth tracing further the social (d)evaluation of tabloids. However, prior to a discussion of audience responses in the following section of the book, the next step represents a detailed reflection on the research methodology.

# Part III

# Tabloids from an Audience Point of View

# Chapter 6: Methodology
Planning, Devising and Carrying out the Research

This chapter is concerned with elucidating the study's methodology. Having established the theoretical foundations of the research in the previous parts, it is now worth recalling the research aims and questions. I was guided by the desire to investigate and compare reading experiences of the British *The Sun* and the German *Bild*; identifying similarities and differences and (if possible) relating these back to the different national contexts. The research enquiry, therefore, is comprised of two sets of questions relating to two principal aims:

### I. Exploring the tabloid reading experience
- How do tabloid readers make sense of reading *The Sun* and *Bild*?
- How do audience members evaluate the papers?

### II. Comparing tabloid reading cross-nationally
- How do tabloid readers in the UK and Germany differ in the way they make sense of tabloids and evaluate them? How can such differences be explained in relation to the specific social and cultural contexts in either country?
- What aspects of the British and German tabloid reading experience are similar, and how can such similarities be explained?

The following section will explain the methodological choices made to meet the twin criteria of validity and reliability; justifying the value and logic of my approach, discussing the premises and describing the steps leading to the realisation of the project.

## COMPARING NATIONS: CONCEPTUAL FRAMEWORK

As a cross-national comparison, my study poses a range of specific methodological challenges and contradictions that need to be considered. Sonia Livingstone claims that cross-national research needs 'informed choices' (2003: 492). In other words, careful consideration is required for each step, including the choice of the objects of study, the methods and processes of data collection, the analysis of the data, and the interpretation of the findings. Although explication is clearly central to all empirical academic research, the adoption of a cross-national comparative perspective adds further categories to the discussion. Despite this, cross-national (or cross-cultural) research has suffered from a lack of reflection with regard to its methodological principles and challenges, particularly within the field of media and communications studies (as opposed to, for example, sociology or anthropology) and regarding qualitative methods (as opposed to quantitative; cf. Livingstone (2003) who offers a full discussion of this issue). My own theoretical and methodological considerations were particularly inspired by contributions from Melvin L. Kohn (1989), Alex S. Edelstein (1982), Else Øyen (1990a,b), as well as the work of Jay G. Blumler, Jack M. McLeod and Karl Erik Rosengren (1992). Moreover, the cross-national and cross-Cultural Studies of Liebes and Katz (1985, 1986, 1990), as well as the comparative work of Sonia Livingstone and Moira Bovill (2001) proved helpful when thinking through the research design, for these scholars have applied and explicated cross-national methodologies by transferring considerations from other disciplines to the field of qualitative audience studies in media and communication.

One of the more general challenges posed by cross-national research is that of terminological ambiguity. Øyen (1990b: 7) recognises confusion with regard to the terms used to distinguish between different kinds of comparative research. She points out that these vary between such divergent denotations as 'cross-country', 'cross-national', 'cross-societal', 'cross-cultural', 'cross-systemic', and 'cross-institutional'; depending on the researchers' preferences and academic traditions. Claiming that the use of such imprecise terms should be abandoned, she maintains that the essential differences between cultural and national boundaries should be reflected in the vocabulary. Contemplating similar issues, Kohn (1989: 93) prefers the term 'cross-national', for 'nation' has a relatively unambiguous meaning as opposed to 'culture', which could mean a range of diverse groupings , from subculture (e.g. club cultures) to large groupings of nations that share similar cultures (e.g. Western or Eastern culture). In view of these considerations, I have chosen to label my study "cross-national" rather than "cross-cultural". However, this does not mean that all problems can be avoided. Preferring one term over another could also create ambiguities with regard to the interpretational contexts. For instance, when would similarities or differences emerging from my research point to "national", and when to "cultural" contexts? Highlighting that each step within the research requires 'informed choices', I settled on a reflexive contextualisation of the results.

## Why compare *The Sun* and *Bild*, why Britain and Germany?

The obvious methodological choice requiring some attention here is of a conceptual nature and concerns the objects of study I selected for the comparison. Generally, the objects of a cross-national project should reflect the study's primary research aims in terms of their weighting of diversity and commonality, the two dimensions determining the characteristics of each comparative project and its methodological preferences.

According to Kohn (1989), the primary focus of a study determines the degree of similarity or divergence of the objects under investigation. Livingstone (2003: 486 pp.), in drawing on Kohn's fourfold typology of comparative studies, explains the decisions scholars face with regard to selecting nations for comparison. According to her, a study seeking to determine what is distinctive about a nation (Kohn's first model) would treat each country included in the comparison as an autonomous object of study. In this case, fairly similar countries should be selected. If, however, the primary aim of the study is to explore the universality of a phenomenon (Kohn's second model), it would be most useful to choose diverse nations. The third model seeks to test an abstract cross-national theory, in an attempt to understand the diversity of different national contexts. Such an approach would involve identifying multiple dimensions along which nations vary, then looking for systematic relations between them. Lastly, research regarding one nation as a component of a larger international or trans-national system (Kohn's fourth model) would search for a maximum of diversity when selecting countries.

Since the research focus of this study is rather broad, my position with regard to the research and its outcomes was characterised by a high degree of flexibility and openness. Although interested in exploring the diversity of readers' evaluations and sense-making of tabloids across different nations, I was also involved in finding out whether – and if so which – aspects of the tabloid reading experience might be shared across diverse contexts. Thus, categorising my research by aligning it to only one of Kohn's types was far from straightforward. Livingstone and Bovill encountered similar discordances in their *Children and their Changing Media Environment* (2001). They described three parallel phases of their research strategy, which involved following different models of Kohn at different stages of the research. Yet, as Livingstone notes, 'no mapping is perfect...but I would still contend that the organizational effort behind this table [Kohn's typology] is helpful' (2003: 492). Adopting this attitude, my considerations, likewise, share some common ground with several of Kohn's models, due to my desire to seek out differences *and* similarities. Moreover, Edelstein (1982: 15) argues that a cross-national project is 'a study that compares two or more nations with respect to some common activity'. Therefore, he claims, establishing 'conceptual equivalence' is crucial to comparative research. Consequently, the objects of my comparison could not be too much alike, yet needed to be similar enough to be comparable. Thus, choosing to study similar phenomena in different contexts, I settled on comparing reading experiences of the British *Sun* and the German *Bild*. The papers' similarities, representing my 'conceptual equivalence', have been described in Chapter 2. The key dimensions of cultural variance, conversely, mark the discrepancies between British and German media systems and journalistic traditions which have been established in Chapter 3.

Lastly, aside from such theoretically grounded decisions, the choice to compare audience responses to *The Sun* and *Bild* rather than those of any other tabloid in any other country was, among other issues, due to practical issues. Given the specific constraints of a single-authored study, it was necessary to focus on no more than two nations, although a larger scope would surely have produced intriguing results. However, carrying out research in different countries involves working with and in different languages, and dealing with the tensions of different academic traditions. Therefore, I considered it vital to the validity of my comparison to be capable of fully understanding both languages and (not only academic) cultures of the selected nations, in order to be able to adopt both insider and outsider perspectives in the process of the research, in particular when contextualising the data (cf. the section on data analysis, p. 154).

## Dealing with 'a World of Interdependencies'

The value of cross-national comparisons is pointed out by Esser (1999: 294) who notes:

'Although rarely made, cross-national comparisons are essential in communication studies. Without international comparisons one never knows how to evaluate a certain appearance. Is it normal (in the meaning of: shared by others) or an unusual, distinctive feature (in the meaning of: characteristic for a certain country or system)? Internationally comparative studies always bring a fresh perspective to things and very often, new understandings.'

Esser's quote, clearly in favour of cross-national research, represents the view adopted by this study. However, there is some scholarly disagreement over the value of comparative work. Lynne Chrisholm, for instance, acknowledges that 'societies and cultures are fundamentally non-comparable and certainly cannot be evaluated against each other' (1995: 22). Yet Livingstone, in defence of comparative research, points out that 'in a time of globalization, one might even argue that the choice *not* to conduct a piece of research cross-nationally requires as much justification' (ibid 2003: 478; original Italics).

However, as the research progressed, I faced what Else Øyen termed 'problems of doing cross-national research in a world of interdependencies' (1990b: 5), for the world is an ever-increasing array of contexts that can possibly impact on culturally variant readings of tabloids. For instance, what is the significance of Britain and Germany's educational systems to the reading experience of tabloid newspapers? What roles do political structure and social relations play? And what about abstract concepts like mentality? All of these aspects, and many more, probably impact on readers' understanding and evaluation of tabloid newspapers in any given nation. Moreover, these dimensions are also likely to impact on the way readers *talk* about their reading experiences to me, the researcher, which suggests yet more obscurity in terms of the interpretation of the findings. Facing impracticalities with regard to attempting to account for all of these and more possible dimensions, I realised that, indeed, one of the eternal challenges of comparative work arises from this. As Stefan Nowak puts it:

'How do we know we are studying 'the same phenomena' in different contexts; how do we know that our observations and conclusions do not actually refer to 'quite different things'...? Or if they seem to be different, are they really different with respect to the same... variable, or is our conclusion about the difference between them scientifically meaningless?' (ibid. 1976: 105; original quotation marks)

Nowak's questions highlight crucial challenges for any comparative project, for he addresses dilemmas researchers face when attempting to interpret emerging similarities and differences in relation to different national (or other) contexts. I was, therefore, prepared to question my decisions and re-assess the relevance of my established key dimensions of diversity and commonality at every stage of the research.

# DEVISING THE TOOLS: THE RESEARCH DESIGN

## A Qualitative Approach using Focus Groups

This study is concerned with understanding a social phenomenon, i.e. the reading of *Sun* and *Bild*. Considering the nature of this inquiry, I chose to adopt a qualitative research approach which would allow for a general openness to the respondents' views and opinions and the study's outcome (Lamnek 1995: 21). Moreover, Anders Hansen, Simon Cottle, Ralph Negrine and Chris Newbold (1998) suggest that qualitative methods are required when attempting to explore how audiences make sense of and relate to media (ibid: 257). Hence, after weighing up the benefits and drawbacks of different qualitative methods in relation to the aims of this study, I settled on focus group discussions as the method of data collection.

Focus group discussions were traditionally used as a technique in commercial market research in the Anglo-American world, and became an established method of academic media audience research in the 1980s and 1990s as a response to the 'discontent with the 'passive' audience view and the stilted view of media influence' (Hansen et al. 1998: 259; cf. also Chapter 5, p. 97). There is, however, some cross-national variance with regard to the development of the method's methodological basics and terminological conceptualisation in the UK and Germany that is worth tracing. In reviewing the method's development in British, American, and German language-based academia, Peter Loos and Burkhard Schäffer (2001: 15 pp.) point out that distinct trends can be identified. German textbooks and reference works often make clear distinctions between different sub-categories of the method, emphasising methodological differences between 'focus groups', 'group discussions', and 'group interviews'. According to them, the methods of 'group interviewing' and 'group discussion' are particularly likely to generate divergent results. David L. Morgan (1997: 12) explains that group interviewing is a method used for interviewing several people at the same time; aiming at an assembly of individual opinions. By contrast, group discussions can be employed for exploring group members' interaction with one another; allowing for group processes and group opinions to emerge. However, despite the fact that the method has been developed in considerable theoretical detail in Germany (cf. Loos and Schäffer 2001; Bohnsack 2000), it is not very commonly used in German media audience research.

Such thoroughly specific terminological distinctions cannot be observed within British media audience research (cf., for example, Hansen et al. 1998 and May 2001). Yet the method has become a popular tool used frequently in audience studies (recent works include, for instance, Hill's research (2005, 2007). Commonly referred to as both 'group discussions' and 'focus groups', the different conceptualisations discernible in German handbooks have largely merged in the British view. Group discussions today are used by UK researchers to examine collective meaning production as well as individual views, depending on the individual study's aims and objectives. These issues are significant as the methodological grounding of this study largely draws on the British context, but also borrows from German considerations. This research, for instance, subscribes to the view that a distinction needs to be made between group discussions and group interviews. Approaching the fieldwork with this in mind, care was taken to compile groups that consist of more than four participants, for this number has proven the minimum sufficient for the emergence of a discussion between the members, rather than with the moderator. Groups with less than four participants, conversely, are likely to resemble group interviews, which were not intended as the method of this study (cf. p. 137). Hence, the focus group discussions were approached as a tool for examining collective meaning creation rather than individual views and opinions.

## Qualitative Depth, Openness and Flexibility

One of the reasons for selecting the method relates to the fact that using focus group discussions allowed this researcher to adopt an active meaning-constructing view of audiences. The primary aim of focus groups is to explore and understand a specific topic. This permits the researcher to explore audience members' creation of meaning from media texts in some depth, investigating their interpretations and uses of media consumption, as well as the participants' interaction with each other. Moreover, one of the major strengths of the method as opposed to, for instance, a survey questionnaire, can be seen in its openness and the 'flexibility it offers for participants to respond, at length, in their own 'language' and their own terms' (Hansen et al. 1998: 273). Focus groups are, moreover, particularly useful for the aims of this research, for they are likely to generate a wealth of qualitative data concerning the reception of tabloids which can be used to map the field and generate themes for subsequent studies.

Clearly, both qualitative depth and exploratory potential apply to other qualitative methods as well, notably participant observation and in-depth individual interviews. Why, then, use focus groups? Focus group research involves an organised, focused discussion of a set of questions about a certain topic with a selected group of individuals (cf. Gibbs 1997; Kitzinger and Barbour 1999). Hence, they are well suited for gaining information about several different experiences, attitudes, opinions, values and conflicts around the same topic (Lamnek 1989: 74; Kitzinger and Barbour 1999: 5). In comparison to individual interviews, a broader range of opinions and reactions can be obtained through focus group discussions, as the group participants may inspire each other to respond frankly and candidly, and direct each other's attention to aspects that are yet missing from the debate (Lamnek 1989: 74). Such potential is crucial to this research and beneficial to the exploration of the research questions.

On a more pragmatic level, it should be acknowledged that conducting focus groups allowed me to gain insight into the views and experiences of a larger number of people than would have been possible with individual interviews or observational methods. Anita Gibbs (1997) argues that participant observation in particular 'tend[s] to depend on waiting for things to happen', which raises the practical question of available resources for conducting research. Moreover, the focused nature of a group discussion was crucial to the choice of method for this study. This is due to the fixed set of questions that would be discussed and would therefore allow me to raise and explore specific issues identified as important in the literature on tabloid journalism. Yet, the fact that focus groups are organised events and thus not entirely spontaneous instances of communication and behaviour can be seen as one of the drawbacks of the method that needs to be considered when analysing the data and interpreting participants' responses.

## Meaning-Creation as a Collective Activity

In foregrounding the benefits of focus group discussions in comparison to individual interviews, Hansen et al. state:

'The generation of meanings and interpretations of media content is 'naturally' a social activity, that is, audiences form their interpretation of media content and their opinions about such content through conversation and social interaction.' (ibid 1998: 261; original quotation marks)

Focus groups then, through providing a close-to-natural setting for communication amongst the participants, can provide insight into this process. This argument links in with the idea that group discussions allow for an investigation of the 'details of complex experiences and the reasoning behind... actions, beliefs, perceptions, and attitudes' (Carey 1994: 226). Such potential is valuable to the exploration of British and German readers' understandings and evaluations of tabloid newspapers, as well as in examining how these two categories influence one other.

Group discussions allow for an investigation of social processes by observing the collective activity of sense-making through communicative negotiation. Krüger (1983: 93) asserts that the range of opinions within a group is revised, adjusted and re-articulated through group interaction. Thus, focus groups provide the chance to examine how a shared attitude is formed and how contextual meaning is created. Hence, the method is suited to this study as it allows for an exploration of the way evaluations and understandings of tabloids are articulated, judged, contrasted and negotiated (cf. Lamnek 1989: 130). Focus groups, moreover, can provide insight into the specific idiosyncratic and conflicting processes involved in meaning-creation from tabloid newspapers, for the method leaves enough room for contradictions to emerge in the views expressed by respondents.

At the same time, focus groups provide the opportunity to study how individual group participants' views emerge within a discursive context that resembles everyday life communication, as well as allowing shared social values to be identified. Through observing this, an understanding of how common frames of interpretation emerge can be gained. Focus group discussions, therefore, can generate knowledge about the wider social and cultural group to which the participants belong; thus, capturing attitudes, decision-forming and opinion-forming processes of specific social groupings (cf. Bohnsack 2000; Bruck and Stocker 1996; Lamnek 1998). The method also provides the chance to observe the significance of 'peer communication and group norms' within the process of negotiating meaning (Kitzinger and Barbour 1999: 5). Hence, focus groups are well suited to exploring readers' evaluations of tabloid papers in Britain and Germany and the significance of specific social and cultural characteristics to this. The method is ideal for exploring the production of discourses around tabloid newspapers, for these are likely to emerge when participants talk about their reading of *The Sun* and *Bild*. Likewise, insights about direct and indirect discourses concerning the valuation or devaluation of tabloids can emerge from conducting group discussions, allowing for a deeper understanding of how meaning and evaluation influence each other and merge in the reading experience.

However, as with all research projects, there are limitations to what this study can accomplish. It needs to be acknowledged that only limited conclusions can be drawn from my research about individual participants' views and opinions. While in-depth interviews may provide insights in respondents' individual perspectives, problems, and desires (cf. Lamnek 1989: 79), Gibbs (1997) points out:

'It should not be assumed that the individuals in a focus group are expressing their own definitive individual view. They are speaking in a specific context, within a specific culture, and so sometimes it may be difficult for the researcher to clearly identify an individual message.'

Hence, this study might have benefited from a combination of several different forms of scholarship rather than using one method of data collection only. Supplementing the group discussions with individual interviews, for instance, would have made a valuable expansion, allowing me to gain in-depth understanding of respondents' individual contexts and biographies, and to fully explore the personal uses, interpretations, functions and meanings of tabloids in the everyday lives of their readers. However, private and individual points of view and the impact of individual biographies on media use are not the primary concerns of this study, for these issues have been explored in detail in previous studies (cf. Chapter 5, p. 117).

## The Research Instruments

### The Standard Demography Questionnaire

A standard demography questionnaire was prepared and handed out prior to the start of each focus group discussion. Both English and German copies included the same set of questions focusing on age, sex, education, occupation, and living situation. One additional question concerning the nationality of participants was included in the English questionnaire, so as to be able to later distinguish between British readers of *The Sun* and those from other national backgrounds living in London. It did not seem necessary to include this item in the German questionnaire, for the variety of foreign immigrants living in Northern Germany does not compare to London's diversity. Both German and English questionnaires also included items regarding participants' "media menus" (i.e. their general media consumption habits) as well as details of their specific reading habits with regard to *The Sun* and *Bild* (i.e. their frequency of reading, their preferred days of the week, etc.). A further question was included asking whether respondents usually bought the paper themselves; and if not, where they were likely to pick up a copy.

A last question asked the participants to briefly list their likes and dislikes of *The Sun* and *Bild*. Designed as a preparation for the first part of the discussion, the information provided in this section was also drawn on occasionally during the data analysis. Moreover, the question was designed to help individuals clarify their position before discussing their views with others. In this, I was influenced by the method of Bruck and Stocker (1996: 58 pp.), whose group discussions were characterised by a short interval following each question, in which the moderator asked the participants to note down their thoughts before discussing the issue with the group. Although it was decided not to introduce such intervals, for they were likely to disrupt the flow of a discussion, the idea behind this measure seemed apposite. Bruck and Stocker argue that asking participants to note down their thoughts helped to counterbalance responses in the manner of *'I was going to say that, too'*. They had anticipated these as a result of participants' possible intimidation with regard to the tabloid's social stigma. I had also identified considerable evidence for the existence of a social stigma around *Bild* and *Sun* (cf. my discussion of the recruitment, p. 143), and therefore decided to include a similar question in this study's questionnaire.

### The Focus Group Guide

The focus group guide represented the primary tool for the discussions, for it was used as a template for the moderator to work from. The guide included a series of open questions regarding readers' understanding and evaluation of *Sun* and *Bild*, both general and in relation to specific themes. The guide's sequence of questions resembled a 'funnel-approach' (Hansen et al. 1998: 274); that is, the discussions were planned to move from general matters to more specific themes. Structured by five key themes, the guide included a general open question about readers' general likes and dislikes of the paper as the opening question. To better understand specific aspects of the tabloid reading experience as well as to identify differences and similarities, a series of media stimuli was then introduced (front pages of *Bild* and *The Sun*) to the groups. This was intended to direct the discussion towards readers' responses to specific aspects of tabloids, thereby moving away from an undirected, general conversation about likes and dislikes. For example, participants were encouraged to discuss themes such as the tabloids' approaches to notions of nationhood, politics, and scandal. These had been identified as important aspects of popular papers in the review of literature; however, I was open to participants' views and additional themes raised by them. In the last part of the discussion, the agenda was opened up again towards a more general conversation about the tabloid's reputation, readers' ideas and responses to this. While these topics and questions were specified for all groups, the sequence in which the media stimuli were introduced to direct the discussion could vary. Likewise, frequency and intensity of probing questions altered, depending on the status of participants' interaction with one another, and on which issues they had brought up.

I tested the guide in more than one pilot group in each country, revising potential problems with the chosen media stimuli, the sequencing, as well as the framing and wording of questions. Once tested and adjusted, the guide was followed consistently throughout all of the group discussions to ensure comparability (cf. Hansen et al. 1998: 274). I also worked towards making the focus groups from both countries comparable by, for instance, describing media stimuli introduced in the German groups to the UK participants and *vice versa*, in order to capture possibly divergent reactions towards the tabloids' front pages. With regard to timing, May (2001: 125) suggests allowing 1.5 to 2.5 hours for the duration of a group discussion. However, I settled on about 15 minutes for each key topic and planned on a total of 75 minutes per focus group. This margin could generally be maintained, albeit with some natural deviation as some groups were not as talkative as others. A copy of the focus group guide used for the British part of the study can be viewed in the appendix.

## The Focus Group Reports and Fieldwork Journal

Directly after each discussion, a brief report was prepared, in which was noted particularities of the group, the overall content of the discussion, the group's consensus and the main issues raised by participants during different stages. In addition, I reflected on the general atmosphere and included remarks on the group's individual members, the location and the setting, as well as problems with the media stimuli and details of any questions asked (which sometimes occurred). These reports were useful in capturing important observations and thoughts during the process of carrying out the research, highlighting, for instance, discussion themes that recurred in several of the groups. Furthermore, the reports reflected on my role as a moderator, and included remarks noted down by the assistant who acted as an observer to the group discussion[15].

---

15 In the UK, a few students from the University of Westminster kindly assisted me in the focus groups; in Germany, my friends and family helped out.

In addition, I kept a detailed "Fieldwork Journal" which proved a highly valuable tool during the fieldwork stage, and represented an important resource for the writing up. A similar journal was also kept by Ute Bechdolf (1999: 59), who drew extensively on her reflections in her study. My journal is a record of the changing decisions and reflections involved in carrying out the research. It contains accounts and reflections on experiences and observations, and captures ideas that would otherwise have disappeared from memory. The journal helped to engage with questions, articulate problems and develop solutions to these, particularly aiding the recruitment, as this phase of the research was characterised by a hugely self-reflexive approach, and any progress depended on the reflection of my individual experiences. The focus group reports and the fieldwork journal, therefore, represent significant tools for this research.

## LINKING PRINCIPLES AND PRACTICE: THE RESEARCH EXPERIENCE

### Identifying Equal Samples

A certain degree of methodological equality across countries is crucial to the validity and reliability of cross-national comparisons (cf. Livingstone 2003: 487 pp.) However, while attempting to achieve this can be seen as a guiding principle of my work, practical challenges need to be acknowledged. Eric Michaels (1985: 57-58), in identifying 'categories of error' in cross-cultural communications research, notes that 'demographic errors' in the sampling should be acknowledged as one of the most important methodological problems. This also applied to the sampling of this study.

On searching for categories by which to identify equal samples in Germany and the UK, I noticed that the readership statistics provided by the British *National Readership Survey* and the German *Media Analyse* use different classification systems. According to the British *Market Research Society (MRS)*, the practice of allocating people to social classes represents the 'common currency' in social classification (MRS 2005). Hence, the UK's *National Readership Survey* uses the social grades A, B, C1, C2, D, and E for organising readers into different categories. Indeed, social class is one of the most important categories along which audiences are commonly classified in the UK (cf., for instance, Bocock 1993; Seymour-Ure 2001). Still, the dividing lines of class segregation are unique to the British system. Moreover, readers' social grades are based on the occupation of the chief income earner of the household in the *National Readership Survey*. This suggests a superior importance of one person's income and occupation over that of any other household members. Likewise, income and occupation are seen as more important social markers than other demographic variables, such as education. Tunstall (1996: 8) highlights the 'fuzziness' implied in this. He claims that while one partner in a marriage might have a 'white collar' job, the other could might be classified as 'working class'. Yet, they both may read *The Sun*. A dissimilar sorting system can be observed in Germany. The most common form of readership analysis is provided by the *Media Analyse*, which focuses on individuals rather than the chief income earner of the household. Moreover, social class – albeit not commonly termed as such – would always include a consideration of individuals' educational qualifications. As an example, a Ph.D. researcher would be designated a member of the 'skilled working class' (C2) in the *NRS* categories, due to their typically low income. In Germany, a Ph.D. student would, by contrast, be considered of higher social status due to their educational qualification – although admittedly, this varies across different surveys, depending on the statistical focus.

Due to such national variation, neither social grade nor educational qualification seemed a suitable category for identifying equal samples in Germany and the UK. There is, however, a useful similarity between the national readership analyses which considers the category of professional occupation. Indeed, the largest proportion of *Sun* readers is spread across the social grades C1, C2, D, and E, a spectrum which bears similarities to the occupations of the largest group of *Bild* readers. The German category of 'skilled workers' resembles C2 occupations; the 'non-managerial employees and clerks' is comparable to the C1 category; and the group of 'unskilled workers' resembles D occupations (for an overall composition of the two national readership groups cf. Chapter 2, p. 26).

## Ideal and Real Sample

As a result of these considerations, my ideal sample consisted of eight to twelve focus groups in total, with an equal number of groups in each country, and similar characteristics of the participants. Although my research did not aim at statistical representativeness, it did strive for findings that would permit a degree of generalisation. Hence, I aimed at a total of at least 60 participants. It was, moreover, my intention to capture 'most shared or common attributes' (Fern 2001: 163); therefore, I planned to set up 'full groups' (i.e. groups consisting of eight to ten participants; Greenbaum 1998: 3), attempting to conduct a minimum of two groups per characteristic (cf. Knodel 1993). As the fieldwork was designed to examine participants' collective meaning creation, a homogenous assembly was sought, in order to approach the consensus that has been noted in focus group research (Hansen et al. 1998: 270). In terms of the sampling criteria, I settled on focusing on the largest occupational group within both national readerships. In terms of age, I intended to recruit readers between 30 to 49 years. Yet, participants in individual groups were to be no more than 15 years apart, in order to prevent generation gaps from emerging. As gender is one of the most frequently used variables for controlling homogeneity in focus groups (cf. Fern 2001: 35), I aimed at clustering the participants by their gender characteristics, composing both single-sex as well as mixed-sex groups.

A further important criterion consisted of participants' regularity of reading. I intended to focus on regular readers, who routinely bought and read the papers. Jeremy Tunstall's claim that most people read their daily paper only three to four days per week rather than seven (1996: 1) was adopted as a specification for the "regularity" of reading I aimed at. The participants should, moreover, be reading the printed weekday edition of *The Sun* and *Bild*, rather than the online version or their Sunday sister-editions. I also intended to compose "artificial" rather than "real" groups; i.e. groups consisting of participants not acquainted with each other prior to the discussion (with the exception of friendship pairs). This initial plan was due to my wish to avoid the exclusion of some common experiences from the research, as it has been noted in real groups (cf. Kitzinger and Barbour 1999). Moreover, I had hoped that groups of strangers would help to 'reduce fear and enhance making revelations' among the participants (ibid: 9). Finally, I planned not to pay incentives due to the hazards of a self-selective sample this might imply.

However, a number of changes had to be made to the sampling criteria whilst recruiting for the groups (cf. p. 143). Consequently, the ideal and real samples differed somewhat. Ultimately, 104 readers in total took part in the research, participating in 18 focus groups spread across the two countries. Each of these groups marked a valuable contribution to the research experience. However, only six German and six British focus groups were similar enough with regard to their composition to be subjected to a detailed analysis. I also omitted pilot groups and largely concentrated on analysing discussions with more than four participants. Although the degree of group interaction generally varied, I noticed that the number of people participating often impacted on the respondents' willingness to engage in a discussion. In groups of less than four participants, the members tended to be less active – expecting the moderator to ask questions, then answering them in turn, and waiting for the next question (except for fg11-UK, which was marked by a very lively interaction between the four female participants; cf. tables overleaf).

Hence, the sample which the primary readership research is based on consists of twelve focus groups: six in each country, with a total of 74 participants. I included four groups composed of female participants, four groups with male participants, and four mixed-gender groups – two of each in Germany and the UK. Overall, 41 German and 33 British respondents participated, aged between 20 and 69 years. 33 participants were women, 41 participants were men. Most of them worked in semi-skilled and skilled occupational categories. The German groups were conducted between 16 August and 18 September 2005; the British groups subsequently, in the period from 28 February to 11 May 2006. Five discussions took place in a formal university environment (three in Germany, two in the UK); four groups were conducted in domestic settings (two in Germany, two in the UK); two groups in the UK were set up in a workplace environment, and one group discussion in Germany took place in a pub. The average duration of the discussions was 75 minutes; the shortest took 45 minutes, the longest 100 minutes. Due to modifications made to the sampling criteria during the recruitment, my sample included assemblies of people who were part of a pre-existing group ("real" groups), as well as groups in which participants were not acquainted to one another prior to the discussion ("artificial" groups). However, I carefully balanced real and artificial group settings. The overleaf tables represent an overview of the participants and group composition. Table 1 illustrates the core set of German focus groups; Table 2 refers to groups that took place in the UK. Table 3, then, gives an overall summary of the sample, indicating the proportional allotment of participants' gender, age groups, regularity of reading, and country of residence. The overleaf tables only include the twelve core groups which I based my analysis on. In the interest of anonymity, each participant has been given a pseudonym.

*Table 3: The German Sample*

| FG1-G[16]: female *Bild* readers | FG2-G: female *Bild* readers |
|---|---|
| Artificial group | Real group (neighbours) |
| *Location*: University of Hamburg | *Location*: domestic setting, Reihen |
| *Duration*: 100 minutes | *Duration*: 75 minutes |
| 1. Maria (f), shopkeeper, 49<br>2. Lena (f), taxi driver, 50<br>3. Hannah (f), assistant clerk, 50<br>4. Sofie (f), retail saleswoman, 54 | 1. Ilona (f), legal assistant, 28<br>2. Sarah (f), clerical assistant, 29<br>3. Vera (f), electronic technician, 29<br>4. Amelie (f), labourer, 35<br>5. Natascha (f), shop assistant, 37<br>6. Kathrin (f), unemployed, 39<br>7. Maike (f), shop assistant, 42 |

| FG3-G: male *Bild* readers | FG4-G: male *Bild* readers |
|---|---|
| Artificial group | Real group (colleagues) |
| *Location*: University of Hamburg | *Location*: a pub, Lippstadt |
| *Duration*: 90 minutes | *Duration*: 75 minutes |
| 1. Alexander (m), shop assistant, 45<br>2. Max (m), painter, 46<br>3. Felix (m), unemployed, 48<br>4. David (m), retail salesman, 50<br>5. Paul (m), technician, 56 | 1. Dirk (m), service technician, 27<br>2. Mario (m), carrier, 33<br>3. Olaf (m), techn. supervisor, 36<br>4. Harald (m), locksmith, 41<br>5. Phillip (m), welder, 42<br>6. Reiner (m), turner, 43<br>7. Lutz (m), engineer, 43<br>8. Matthias (m), locksmith, 44<br>9. Thorsten (m), turner, 45<br>10. Chris (m), turner, 52<br>11. Hannes (m), operator, 57 |

---

16 The 'G' included in the focus group's name signifies that this discussion took place in Germany. The British groups, obviously, are indicated by the letters 'UK'. These denominations are used in order to distinguish between German and British groups in the discussion of findings. Providing such orientation, the names are included when referring to any of the focus groups in the subsequent chapters. On examining quotations from group number three, for instance, the relevant reference is [FG3-G], indicating both the group and the country it took place in.

*Table 3: The German Sample (continued)*

| FG5-G: mixed-sex *Bild* readers | FG6-G: mixed-sex *Bild* readers |
|---|---|
| Artificial group<br>*Location*: University of Hamburg<br>*Duration*: 75 minutes | Real group (neighbours)<br>*Location*: domestic setting, Hamburg<br>*Duration*: 75 minutes |
| 1. Nadia (f), clerk, 36<br>2. Franziska (f), clerical assistant, 41<br>3. Bertram (m), lorry driver, 44<br>4. Tanja (f), unemployed, 44<br>5. Jens (m), unemployed, 44<br>6. Simone (f), postal clerk, 45 | 1. Tracy (f), child nurse, 26<br>2. Michael (m), technician, 26<br>3. Ingo (m), clerk, 35<br>4. Eva (f), medical secretary, 40<br>5. Sandra (f), factory worker, 40<br>6. Ludwig (m), plumber, 47<br>7. Babs (f), assistant med. techn., 49<br>8. Kristian (m), executive producer, 69 |

*Table 4: The British Sample*

| FG7-UK: female *Sun* readers | FG8-UK: female *Sun* readers |
|---|---|
| Artificial group<br>*Location*: University of Westminster<br>*Duration*: 75 minutes | Real group (neighbours)<br>*Location*: domestic setting, London<br>*Duration*: 90 minutes |
| 1. Denise (f), beauty consultant, 37<br>2. Alice (f), science communicator, 38<br>3. Kaiya (f), pers. dev.trainer, 41<br>4. Emma (f), shop assistant, 42<br>5. Cynthia (f), tutor, 66 | 1. Cheryl (f), adm. manager, 31<br>2. Paula (f), housewife, 36<br>3. Claire (f), housewife, 40<br>4. Anna (f), bank clerk, 47<br>5. Sally (f), housewife, 47 |

| FG9-UK: male *Sun* readers | FG10-UK: male *Sun* readers |
|---|---|
| Artificial group<br>*Location*: University of Westminster<br>*Duration*: 60 minutes | Real group (colleagues)<br>*Location*: a construction site, Harrow<br>*Duration*: 45 minutes |
| 1. Ed (m), decorator, 24<br>2. Andrew (m), adm. officer, 35<br>3. Ethan (m), care taker, 40<br>4. Ricky (m), training officer, 44<br>5. Roger (m), postal clerk, 44<br>6. Edgardo (m), service technician, 48<br>7. Juan (m), information assistant, 53 | 1. Josh (m), roofer, 34<br>2. William (m), worker, 34<br>3. Matthew (m), drywall fixer, 43<br>4. Daniel (m), worker, 43<br>5. Garett (m), roofer, 44 |

*Table 4: The British Sample (continued)*

| FG11-UK: mixed-sex *Sun* readers | FG12-UK: mixed-sex *Sun* readers |
|---|---|
| Artificial group | Real group (colleagues) |
| *Location*: domestic setting, London | *Location*: an office, London |
| *Duration*: 75 minutes | *Duration*: 60 minutes |
| 1. Carla (f), bartender, 20 | 1. Lewis (m), local gov. officer, 28 |
| 2. James (m), sales assistant, 26 | 2. Jessica (f), local gov. officer, 35 |
| 3. Quentin (m), event manager, 35 | 3. Dustin (m), local gov. officer, 35 |
| 4. Samuel (m), actor, 35 | 4. Jerry (m), local gov. officer, 39 |
| | 5. Amanda (f), local gov. officer, 40 |
| | 6. Adam (m), local gov. officer, 43 |
| | 7. Susan (f), local gov. officer, 52 |

*Table 5: Overview of the Focus Groups Participants (FG1-G – FG12-UK)*

| | German participants | | British participants | |
|---|---|---|---|---|
| Total | 41 | 100 % | 33 | 100 % |
| Women | 19 | 46 % | 14 | 42 % |
| Men | 22 | 54 % | 19 | 58 % |
| 20-29 years | 6 | 15 % | 4 | 12 % |
| 30-39 years | 7 | 17 % | 12 | 36 % |
| 40-49 years | 20 | 49 % | 14 | 43 % |
| 50-59 years | 7 | 17 % | 2 | 6 % |
| 60-69 years | 1 | 2 % | 1 | 3 % |
| "Regular" Readers | 28 | 68 % | 17 | 52 % |
| "Occasional" Readers | 13 | 32 % | 16 | 48 % |

## Organising the Groups

The practical organisation of the groups in both Germany and the UK emerged as a challenging and at times frustrating task, mainly due to the severe difficulties faced in the recruitment of readers for my research. These challenges led to adjustments being made to the recruitment strategies and sampling criteria, in an attempt to access potential participants for the groups. It is interesting to note that despite the considerable wealth of practical and methodological guides, textbooks and reference works on focus group research (cf. for example, Barbour and Kitzinger 1999; Fern 2001; Morgan 1997), very few publications actually include a reflection on strategies for the recruitment of participants. Reflections on the methodological implications characteristic to the recruitment phase in the research are, likewise, very hard to find. Moreover, while practically oriented guides for market research offer advice on best practice, they do not discuss methods for the recruitment of participants at all (cf. *The Association for Qualitative Research*'s website at http://www.aqr.org.uk/refsection/recruitment-bestpract.shtml). I am, therefore, including a rather detailed account of my experiences here; explaining the strategies I adopted, discussing and reflecting on my experiences and observations in both countries, and examining the analytical implications. It appears particularly vital to share these insights in view of the lack of discussions focusing on the recruitment stage. Operating on the basis of personal face-to-face, telephone and email conversation, I am drawing on my extensive Fieldwork Journal (cf. p. 135) as an important resource for the accounts given here.

### Recruiting in Germany: Observations, Experiences, Implications

Aiming for my ideal sample, I started the recruitment of *Bild* readers in Germany by using a personal networking approach; i.e. I employed the techniques of 'snowball sampling' (May 2001: 132). This initial attempt involved contacting about 100 friends, relatives and acquaintances, asking them if they knew any readers of *Bild*, and if so, whether they would be willing to nominate potential participants for my research. While a few helpful contacts resulted from this form of "non-probability" sampling, it is worth noting that my query generally caused considerable consternation amongst those I contacted. I received a large number of replies stating in an almost offended manner that they *'definitely did not read Bild, had never done so and did not intend to ever do so, and certainly did not know anyone who did'*. I had expected to encounter such difficulties when trying to involve members of affluent and well-educated social groups in my research, due to previous experiences (cf. Brichta 2002). A 'general unwillingness of some target groups' (Greenbaum 1998: 3) has, moreover, been noted in the study of Bruck and Stocker (1996: 56), who failed to recruit well-educated and affluent readers of the Austrian tabloid *Neue Kronen Zeitung*.

Still, it was puzzling to encounter such widespread hostility. Clearly, this posed questions to the recruitment approach. If most of my personal contacts appeared to interpret my query as offensive, this pointed to a strong social stigma of the paper. Perhaps, then, the force of their reactions was due to the limitations of my own personal network, tending to comprise too many "non-readers" of *Bild*. Attempting to expand the reach of my target group, I therefore supplemented the personal network approach by initiating word-of-mouth recommendation. Announcing after each focus group that I was still looking for people to take part in the research, readers who had already participated, indeed, proved highly valuable to finding further respondents. Furthermore, I employed a form of "street pick-up" – approaching people at random in shops or newsagents, in the tube or on the train, on building sites, or in popular public places such as the plaza in front of the town hall. I asked them whether they sometimes read *Bild* and if so, would they like to take part in a group discussion about the paper. However, while the personal network approach tended to include several regions in Germany, both street pick-up and word-of-mouth-recommendation were confined to my hometown Hamburg, a city of two million inhabitants in Northern Germany, due to reasons of practicability and access.

I soon noticed a recurring ambiguity surrounding the reception of *Bild*. Contrary to my anticipation, this did not seem to explicitly correlate with particular socio-economic characteristics. Many people I approached simply stated *'I don't read such crap'*. Similar to this, even the builders I saw reading a copy on a building site told me that they normally did not read the paper, and therefore could not be 'proper' participants in the research. Many others said they only read the paper because of its sports section, or because they had picked it up somewhere, and therefore did not have anything to say about it. Such detachment was often accompanied by considerable scepticism about my research and my persona, which contributed to the overall difficulties in recruiting readers. While most participants seemed to sense some reassurance once I had mentioned that the research was associated to the University of Westminster, a general scepticism seemed to persist with regard to the topic of the study.

Endeavouring to improve the recruitment progress, I identified several potentially problematic issues. Firstly, motivating a number of people – mostly strangers – to come to a particular place at a particular time to take part in a group discussion lasting about one hour generally seemed a challenging task. I also noticed that there did not seem to be something like a natural desire to talk about the reading of Germany's most widely-read tabloid. On the contrary, many people were reluctant to speak about their consumption of *Bild* at all. All these factors raised the prospect of time, effort, and financial constraints becoming potential obstacles for research participation. Those who did agree to take part, however, might have belonged to a particular group of readers sharing a keen interest to voice their views and opinions, rather than representing "common" readers' views. Attempting to balance this, I started recruiting in the areas where the discussion was to take place (targeting, for instance, shops and cafés around the University of Hamburg where I had booked a room), for it appeared useful to have a date and place ready when talking to potential participants.

As a further response to the emerging difficulties, I started paying incentives, which greatly increased readers' general willingness to participate in the research. I offered €15 (and, subsequently, £15 in the UK) to each respondent in return for their time and effort. This proved highly beneficial to the recruitment, even though the amount was less than what is commonly paid in commercial market research. Paying incentives also improved readers' overall commitment to the arrangement. It was generally necessary to recruit several more participants than actually needed for a discussion, for at least 1/3 of those recruited did not show up; however, this changed somewhat when I started paying incentives. Yet, it needs to be acknowledged that paying incentives also posed potential problems to the quality of the sample. By asking respondents a few screening questions about their reading habits before notifying them that incentives were paid, however, I endeavoured to rule out those who did not read the tabloid but took part because of the money involved.

A further challenge concerned respondents' assessment of their personal safety. This was particularly the case with female readers who seemed less confident than male respondents. Women were generally more likely to participate if they were asked to bring along a friend. Still, female participants were considerably more difficult to recruit. Gender particularly seemed to interrelate with the issue of "reading along" v "buying" *Bild* (cf. p. 146). While one reason for male readers being more forthcoming towards me may be due to my own gender, another possible explanation relates to traditional gender roles and stereotypes. Men often explained to me that they read *Bild* only because of the 'very good' sports section, or because of the photos of half-naked ladies. Traditionally masculine-dominated domains, the issues of sports and sex were, indeed, frequently raised during the recruitment of men. In contrast, a particular interest in (seemingly "stigma-free") sports coverage or pictures of lightly-clad women did not apply to the female readers I approached. This could be an explanation for the considerably stronger detachment they showed. However, the somewhat unequal number of female and male participants reflects the tabloids' readership composition in which men, likewise, outnumber women (cf. Chapter 2, p. 26).

Linked to this, the method of group discussions itself posed challenges. It was evident that even if I had won a person's interest, many appeared to sense an intimidating tension once I mentioned that this would involve taking part in a group discussion, and some of the respondents became uncertain about the research. This clearly interrelates with gender differences. I noticed that inviting women to participate in a group discussion correlated with conceptions of traditional gender roles. Indeed, many of the female respondents I asked referred me to their husband or male colleagues when being confronted with the idea of being required to "publicly" debate an issue. On the basis of these observations, gender seemed to play a significant role in many respects, including content preferences, readership composition, and discussion habits. The issue of gender roles in focus groups is discussed in detail by Fern in relation to both 'cultural value orientation' of individual group participants as well as 'normative behaviour'. He explains that anticipating gender roles in a discussion is based on the notion of gender-specific socialisation: 'males are taught to behave in active, dominating, and provocative ways. As a result, men... are more likely to engage in instrumental behaviours (e.g., giving opinions or information). Conversely, females are raised to behave in passive, submissive, and reactive ways [...]' (Fern 2001: 35 pp.) As a result, I composed single-sex focus groups, in addition to mixed-sex groups. By separating men and women in about half of the discussions, possibly unequal contributions from male and female participants could be balanced. This move also aided the establishment of an atmosphere in which women were encouraged to articulate their views.

However, the idea of voicing and perhaps defending an opinion in a group of strangers appeared to create timidity amongst both women and men during the recruitment. This appeared to be due to a form of "exam nerves", as some respondents seemed to be afraid to not be able to answer my questions. Such apprehensiveness was obviously due to respondents' fear of censure. Participants seemed insecure about their role in my research and about the fact that their reading of *Bild* was placed at the centre of attention. This was clearly a response to the research objects of my study, for any socially "unproblematic" issue such as their experiences with baby food, for instance, would not have provoked such insecurity. As a response to the mixture of caution and scepticism I met, I adjusted my manner and the questions I asked when approaching potential participants. Attempting to address the issue of *Bild*'s problematic image within the recruitment stage, I attempted to act as non-judgemental and reassuring as possible. I mentioned, for instance, that I did not think *Bild*'s readers were different from any other newspaper readers (neither less literate nor less sophisticated), acknowledged that I read *Bild* myself and made jokes about the social stigma of the paper. This improved the recruitment and proved a helpful approach; even though I had initially planned not to raise the notion of *Bild*'s negative reputation during the recruitment, in order to avoid distorting readers' original contribution to the research. However, my remarks about *Bild*'s social image, indeed helped to put my respondents at ease, encouraging them to chat to me about their reading habits, likes and dislikes, and gain interest in the research.

These observations also led me to rephrase my introductory lines when approaching potential participants. I noticed essential differences in the way most people reacted when I asked '*do you occasionally read Bild?*' as opposed to '*do you sometimes pick up a copy of Bild and flick through it?*' While this seemed particularly to be the case when speaking to women, both men and women appeared more willing to talk to me if I phrased my question about their reading of *Bild* in this more casual and light way. Interestingly, the significance of *reading* as opposed to *flicking through* both *Bild* and *Sun*, likewise, recurred in the analysis of the data (cf. Chapter 7, p. 160). Most people I talked to clearly distinguished between 'buying' the paper and 'picking up other people's copies', indicating that in their eyes, reading other people's copy was not a "proper" kind of reading of *Bild*. Such distinctions were often followed by the argument that respondents were not suitable for my research, for they were no 'real' readers. As mentioned above, the idea of sometimes reading the tabloid without actually buying it seemed even more significant to women than to men. Such "reading along", indeed, emerged as a significant activity. Hence, I decided to expand my recruitment criterion ("regular" readers) by including those respondents who did not buy the paper themselves.

I also relaxed other sampling criteria, broadening the margins towards a slightly more generic sample while still aiming at a mix of occupations associated to C1, C2, D, and E categories. Despite now striving for a broader age range, I took care to maintain homogeneity within single discussions by composing focus groups of participants who were, ideally, no more than 15 years apart in their age. Moreover, I altered my intention to compose only non-pre-existing groups; expanding my efforts towards including real groups as well as semi-real groups from 'naturally existing constituencies' (Hansen et al. 1998: 284). Clearly, both group structure and group cohesion needed to be considered when analysing and interpreting the data. Interestingly however, participants from real group environments often voiced their delight about having discussed issues and discovered opinions not known to them prior to the discussion. This is interesting as it indicates that tabloids have not been the objects of frequent discussion within the respective real and semi-real groups. It also suggests that the conditions under which opinions and views about the paper are negotiated and articulated, through the interaction in the focus groups, resemble those of the non-pre-existing group discussions in my research.

### Recruiting in the UK: Observations, Experiences, Implications

Striving for equivalence constituted the overall principle of my fieldwork; hence, I was guided by the desire to replicate the German sample in the UK. Ideally, I aimed at a sample of six focus groups composed of a generic mix of *Sun* readers with C1, C2, D, and E occupations, particularly manual low-level and skilled workers. The groups were to be clustered according to the variable of gender in order to match the German sample. I also endeavoured to compose groups with British citizens in the main, thereby not considering the views of London immigrants.

Despite employing similar recruitment strategies and tools in the UK, some compromises need to be acknowledged. I altered my recruitment strategy slightly by enlisting the help of two students at the University of Westminster in London[17]. This proved invaluable to the recruitment of *Sun* readers, for my personal contacts in the UK were not as extensive as in Germany, and I was able to additionally draw on the students' social networks. Moreover, a considerable amount of sensitivity

---

17 I selected two students who did not attend any of my seminars. The students were thoroughly informed about the study, and trained by me in recruitment aims, strategies, and best practice. In total, both spent between 10 and 15 hours each on my research in the period between January and February 2006. Additionally, one of them, and a third student, took turns to assist during half of the group discussions in the UK, taking notes and observing the discussion.

and insider knowledge concerning nationally specific cultural norms and values were required when dealing with the recruitment drawbacks I had met in Germany. Working with Britons allowed me to draw on their social and cultural insider knowledge and to better understand and respond to specific challenges of recruiting in the UK. Yet this teamwork approach also posed challenges for the equivalence of data collection, as my experiences from the German part of the fieldwork were not shared by the two students. They could, therefore, only act upon my account of these (for example, concerning the opening lines that had worked well in Germany) but were not able to gauge whether there were differences in the responses of readers in the UK. In order to balance this, we kept in close contact during the recruitment, and had regular meetings at the University to discuss and reflect on our experiences.

Significantly, notions of embarrassment, shame and reluctance recurred during the recruitment of *Sun* readers, and proved to be similarly important. One distinctive impression relates to the sense of fear of being judged for one's reading habits, which has also been pointed out as characteristic to the German study. This indicates that a similar social stigma is attached to *The Sun* in the UK as there is to *Bild* in Germany. A comparable reluctance to talk about reading habits was, likewise, noticeable among *Sun* readers. This was combined with an almost instinctive putting down of the paper. Such observations clearly relate to readers' comments about 'picking up' and 'browsing through' rather than 'buying' and 'reading' the tabloids. Experiences from the recruitment in both Germany and the UK suggest that issues of identity, status and taste are addressed when talking to *Sun* and *Bild* readers about their reading habits. As an example, I chatted to Saturday League Football Teams in London's parks about my research, trying to recruit members for the focus groups. Assuming that it must be easy finding *Sun* readers amongst football fans and players, I was surprised to find that most of the teams' members instantly said they did not read *The Sun*. One of them, however, who had bought a copy of the paper that morning, became increasingly intimidated through the team mates' jokes about his reading of the paper. As a consequence, although the man seemed initially interested to take part in the research, he soon withdrew. Another interesting reaction included that of a few builders who I saw reading a copy of *The Sun* on a construction site. They told me that they could not be suitable participants, as they read the tabloid only because they had not enough time to read other papers in their lunch break. Illustrating the range of detached positions, reactions of this nature shall be restated and reflected on in the discussion of findings.

A few distinctive experiences from recruiting in the UK are worth noting, for they point to national particularities that presumably influenced the flow of the group discussions. To begin with, the introductory lines used when approaching potential participants needed to be adjusted. This was due to the fact that the rather direct and straightforward way of putting forward my query which had worked well in Germany was met with reservation by respondents in the UK. As a result, the whole of the recruitment in Britain was marked by considerably more "chattiness", and characterised by a higher degree of polite caution. As an example, rather than simply asking people whether they occasionally read *The Sun*, the most common opening line used in the UK was of a more apologetic and cautious nature, for instance *'Excuse me, could I ask you a silly question'*; or *'Sorry, I see you're on your lunch break, but can I just ask you a few quick questions?*

Similar caution was applied to the general manner in which the whole of the conversation with readers moved along. While this may be a sign of different norms relating to social behaviour in everyday life conversations, it is of significance to the comparison of the group discussions, for it indicates differences in the 'cultural values' of the two countries – an issue of non-demographic nature referring to possibly diverse discussion habits of British and German focus group participants. 'Cultural value' is discussed by Fern (2001: 24) as possibly impacting on the process of a single focus group. He states that 'countries differ in terms of the degree to which they are individualistic or collectivistic' (ibid: 24). He refers to Triandis (1995: 6), who speaks of 'individualism' and 'collectivism' as elements that define 'shared beliefs, attitudes, norms, roles and values' of any given group of a particular language, historical period and geographic region. Esser (1998: 82), similarly, argues that Britain and Germany differ in their consensus about social norms and values. Considering the British attitude to originate in a positivistic and empirical way of thinking, Esser sees this reflected in the tendency to strive for compromises and reject ideologies. By contrast, he argues that the German mentality is based on idealism, social discontinuity and a weak resistance towards ideology. Such differences reflect my experiences in the recruitment of readers, and need to be considered when attempting to compare participants' norms and values about tabloid journalism.

A further nationally specific characteristic concerns the fact that many people approached during recruiting in the UK were reluctant to give away their contact details for the subsequent arrangement of the group. An issue much less problematic in Germany, where participants seemed to be confident to give me their phone numbers, this may relate to the presumably more cautious attitude of inhabitants of large cities like London. Unfortunately, none of the respondents unwilling to disclose their contact details got back in touch with me, nor did they show up for the group discussion. As a result, it was more difficult to set up groups in neutral locations such as university rooms in the UK. Another difference relating to the groups' composition concerns the variable of age. It was much easier to recruit younger participants for the British focus groups, whereas the reverse applied to Germany. Hence, German group participants tended to be slightly older than in the UK; however, this reflects variances in the readership's composition (cf. Chapter 2, p. 24).

While it was generally difficult to involve female readers, my recruitment endeavours in the UK produced an interesting side-effect that pointed to gender particularities. I had spread the word about my search for *Sun* readers among my personal contacts in the UK. However, I had not expected that some of my personal contacts would try to help me by putting up information sheets about my research in a few public places in London, such as the town hall, for instance. As a consequence, I was surprised to receive phone calls from five different ladies who had seen this notice and wished to vent their views about *The Sun* with me. It would seem that these ladies need to be handled in a different way than the rest of the fieldwork, as they represent a self-selected sample. Yet a focus group was set up which resembled that of all other discussions in terms of the questions I asked. However, it was interesting that the animated debate between the ladies was characterised by almost exclusively negative views about *The Sun*, for they were all "non-readers" and seemed highly infuriated by the paper.

The experience highlighted cross-national differences regarding gender-related differences in dealing with the tabloid's negative reputation. I had initially planned not to advertise for focus group participants due to concerns about the confinements a self-selective sample would imply. Moreover, as Kitzinger and Barbour (1999: 9-10) put it, 'focus groups are ideal for individuals whose views you wish to elicit, but who protest they do not have much to say on the topic in question'. Yet, as a response to the recruitment difficulties in Germany, I had decided to put up notices on blackboards in cafés, pubs, and public places, giving details of my research and my contact number, thus allowing interested readers to call back. However, this attempt to recruit participants failed completely, for not a single person contacted me. A similarly ineffective recruitment strategy involved attaching information sheets with details about the research and my contact numbers to copies of *Bild*. No-one called back in Germany: thus, it is striking that in London, five ladies responded to the poster about my research, volunteering their "*Sun*-haters" views.

Lastly, a further cross-nationally variant experience concerns an interesting side-effect of my research. In both countries, I had started the recruitment by letting my personal contacts know that I was trying to find participants for the research. While this was met with reluctance in Germany, I was surprised and pleased to receive considerably more interest and willingness to help me in the UK. In particular, this applied to responses from academics who frequently replied to e-mails I posted to different mailing lists. I was intrigued to receive several helpful tips and ideas on how to approach the recruitment from researchers all over the country, who demonstrated a keen interest in my study. Their reactions were, in fact, the inverse of the scarce responses and somewhat offended tones implied by German colleagues. Such disparity is worth noting, for it suggests that tabloid newspapers are approached differently in Germany and the UK, a fact which might, in turn, be reflected in readers' responses, as well.

## Informed Consent

Once initial contact to interested readers was established, I followed a standardised procedure by handing each respondent an information sheet which – as suggested by Hansen et al. (1998: 279) – included a summary of my research project, details of the nature, object and duration of the discussion, and my contact details. This sheet also included information about me – stating that the project was an independent academic study rather than commercial market research, and that the study was associated to the University of Westminster. Likewise, it reassured participants of their confidentiality and the anonymous use of the material, informed them that the discussion would be recorded, and that incentives would be paid. All of this is in accordance with the regulations of the University of Westminster's *Code of Best Practice Governing the Ethical Conduct of Investigations, Demonstrations, Research and Experiments* (2005) as well as the *Qualitative Research Guidelines* provided by the *Market Research Society* (2006).

Each potential participant was, moreover, asked a few screening questions concerning their demographics (age, profession, highest educational qualification obtained), and concerning their reading habits, in order to be able to assemble homogeneous groups. I also enquired if they could think of any other readers amongst their friends, relatives or colleagues who they might like to bring along to the discussion. Each participant was asked their phone number for later confirmation, and whether they were free on one of days the groups were set up. If they agreed to take part in the discussion, they were handed a written invitation to the relevant focus group specifying location, time, and date of the discussion. This invitation sheet also made reference to respondents' rights to withdraw and withhold information. Following up, I contacted each respondent a few days prior to the discussion to confirm. The procedure was slightly altered when dealing with real and semi-real groups, which were mostly set up with the help of gatekeepers. However, every participant was thoroughly informed about the purpose of the discussion, as well as the principles by which it was conducted prior to the date the discussion took place, and in addition I repeated everything in my introduction to the group discussion.

## Conducting the Groups

### Moderating and Asking Questions

Overall, the focus groups were characterised by a medium level of moderator involvement. The aim was 'to 'facilitate', 'moderate', and 'stimulate' discussion among participants, not to 'dominate', 'govern', or unduly 'lead' such discussion' (Hansen et al. 1998: 272). Thus, I supported participants' interaction by occasional probings and promptings specifically aimed at initiating and maintaining the discussion among the group's members. Frequent questions included '*what do the others think about that?'*, whereby I carefully tried to address the group at large rather than individual participants, in order to encourage them to concentrate on one another. This was particularly important in the first few phases of the discussion, during which participants were still warming up and a self-aiding discourse needed to be initialised[18]. At the same time, the moderator's role also included tending to a balanced involvement of all participants by displaying 'compensatory behaviour' (Bruck and Stocker 1996: 46). This involved, for instance, breaking off eye contact with very talkative speakers and looking to others; or supporting silent participants by, for instance, asking them probing questions such as *'could you explain that a little more?'* However, in-depth probing of individual opinions and views was not possible, as the interest of all participants needed to be maintained.

The focus group guide included key questions and presented a template for the moderator to work from; while the nature and extent of probing questions depended on each discussion. The media stimuli were used to ignite a discussion on specific themes. At times, however, debates about topics less relevant to the research emerged as a result of these. Thus, part of the moderator's role was to keep the discussion gently on course, and occasionally direct it back to the central theme of the study.

In terms of the equivalence of conducting focus groups in Germany and the UK, it needs to be acknowledged that I occasionally faced linguistic challenges when moderating in Britain, which posed difficulties to understanding the context of a country other than my own. As a result, I probed for clarification much more in the British groups than in the German study. Yet this could also be recognised as a quality of the research. Asking questions which native speakers might not have asked encouraged participants to explain themselves and their views some more, thereby supporting my aim of gaining in-depth information about readers' views and opinions.

The groups also differed in the degree of interaction that took place between the participants, for the atmosphere seemed more relaxed in some than in others. With hindsight, it needs to be acknowledged that a somewhat stiffer atmosphere was more likely to emerge in groups conducted in formal settings, as well as in groups of strangers. Conversely, groups including participants known to each other prior to the discussion were characterised by specific discussion habits. Participants in real group discussions would, for instance, frequently draw on insider knowledge not

---

18 Lamnek (1989: 145) identifies five phases in a group discussion. In the first phase, 'strangeness' is the most important characteristic, and group members' responses are noncommittal and careful. In the second phase, the 'orientation' stage, views and opinions are voiced, explained and justified. The third phase is marked by 'adjustment' due to emerging commonalities. In the fourth phase, 'familiarisation' can be observed through general collective accordance of group members' views. And finally, in the fifth phase, 'conformity' is most dominant, for participants express the group's opinions.

familiar to me as an outsider, which at times resulted in a less detailed explanation of their views, and led me to ask more probing questions such as *'Can you give me an example for this?'* or *'What do you mean by this?'* A third influence on the general atmosphere of a group was harder to control: the presence – or absence – of personalities who, for instance, made jokes throughout the discussion, helping others to relax. Clearly, both the composition and ambience of the individual groups influenced the process and content of a discussion, and was therefore considered when comparing the findings.

A further issue worth noting concerns the fact that I acted as the moderator in all of my focus groups. Hansen et al. (1998: 273) sees an advantage in the researcher and moderator being the same person, for they are 'fully aware of the nature of the research and its objectives'. However, this could also be recognised as a disadvantage. When moderating, I deliberately tried to keep my own pre-conceived expectations of the research and readers' responses in mind, in an attempt to avoid steering participants' responses towards my expectations.

**Location and Atmosphere**

Hansen et al. (1998: 272) note that 'it needs to be borne in mind that the setting – any setting – inevitably exerts a 'framing' influence on the nature of the participants' responses and on the group discussion as a whole'. For this reason, it was my initial intention to conduct all focus groups in very similar settings. Despite the frequent advice of many researchers to use domestic settings as these create a more "normal" atmosphere, and participants are more likely to feel at ease if they are familiar with the venue (cf. Kitzinger and Barbour 1999; Liebes and Katz 1990; Hansen et al. 1998: 271), I aimed at a neutral environment and setting – for instance, a university room – in order to enhance the comparability of the groups. However, as explained above, this had to be counterbalanced with the fact that I faced severe recruitment difficulties. As a result, I chose the venue for single focus groups largely according to convenience and practical feasibility.

As much as I was able to, I tried to keep each venue 'quiet, comfortable, free from interruptions, [and] protected from observation' as Kitzinger and Barbour (1999: 11) describe the ideal setting. Though acknowledging that researchers 'often have little choice' concerning their use of locations, Kitzinger and Barbour (ibid) claim that 'researchers should consider [...] the different messages that are being given to participants when we select different venues'. This clearly applies to my research, as the mix of formal and informal settings is likely to impact on the comparability of the discussions. However, in order to create a casual atmosphere in each of the discussions, drinks and snacks were provided, and I made sure to arrange the available seats and tables in a round shape so that the participants would be able to see and interact with one other. In terms of the University venues, I prepared the room prior to the arrival of the participants. This was not always possible when discussions took place in domestic or workplace settings. According to my experience, however, involving participants in the setup preparations proved beneficial to the discussion and served as a 'natural warm-up', as Loos et al. (2001: 49) have also noted.

## REACHING CONCLUSIONS: THE DATA ANALYSIS

### From Recordings to Texts

I used an analogue audio recording device in combination with an external stereo microphone to tape each discussion on a 120 minutes compact audio cassette. Tape recorder and microphone were placed in the middle of the table or in the centre of the seating arrangement, in order to capture all participants' contributions equally well. The audio recordings were later transformed into mp3 files for further handling and storage on my personal computer. As I had decided to analyse the focus groups as texts, the audio recordings were subsequently transformed into text. An advantage of doing so relates to the fact that the pace of reading a text is generally slower than listening to recorded speech. The analysis of a transcribed discussion can, therefore, generate considerably more depth and detail. Moreover, several meaningful layers can be identified in a text, and it is easier to engage with, for instance, marginal opinions.

Hence, the groups' recordings were transcribed in full. Half of the transcriptions were done with the help of a transcription machine; the other half by using a foot switch with my computer. During transcribing, I used the German software *f4*. In order to transform the recordings into text that resembled the characteristics of speech, I fully transcribed each focus group discussion, writing down what I heard exactly in the way I heard it, and attempting to translate every sound on the tape into text. I transcribed half of the focus groups myself and was able to pay third parties to do the remaining half. This was particularly helpful with regard to the British focus groups' transcriptions, for I faced difficulties when attempting to identify slang and colloquial expressions, as well as certain accents of British participants. Endeavouring to ensure the comparability of transcripts produced by different parties, I compiled a list of transcription conventions, following the examples given by Judith Green and Laura Hart (1999). My conventions included details on how to put certain characteristics of speech into writing, such as stuttered parts, filler words (e.g. *'er, erm'*), grammatically incorrect sentence structures, or compound expressions (e.g. *d'y'know'*). Likewise, I included suggestions on how to handle interruptions, pauses in speech, occasions when participants were talking over each other, sudden turns of speech, strong emphasis of certain words or phrases, and speech-accompanying noises such as laughter or groaning.

Although the dominant language of the research is English, I decided against translating the German transcripts, with the exception of one German focus group used as a basis for supervisory discussions about the fieldwork. The other transcripts remained in German, in order to allow linguistic idiosyncrasies to remain in the text, which convey meaning and are non-transferrable. However, all German quotations referred to in the discussion of findings have been translated into English.

Once all focus groups had been transcribed, the material to be analysed amounted to a total of about 150,000 words. The transcripts were anonymised, each participant being given a pseudonym, which I also refer to in the discussion of the findings. The other names also proved valuable to my approach to the data analysis, for they allowed me to adopt a fresh perspective on individual contributions.

## Coding and Classifying the Data

The analytic steps undertaken in organising the material into meaningful themes combined both inductive and deductive approaches. I drew on the groups' transcripts as well as my fieldwork journal and the focus group reports, which were highly revealing in terms of their notes on atmosphere, conflicts and important themes discussed in the individual groups. As a first step, a list of themes and subcategories was compiled, based on my research questions, the queries posed in the focus group guide and my ideas and observations noted down during the fieldwork. This list represented a matrix used for coding the material, thus reducing and conceptualising the data set. Initially, I organised the voluminous material into passages that broadly related to the dichotomy of readers' likes and dislikes of the two papers. This was followed by further steps of coding: breaking down the raw text and giving emerging phenomena names, thereby capturing their essence. For instance, I used major labels such as "community", "politics", or the papers' "social reputation". In adding category-layers to the text, many passages received multiple codes. However, as the material was highly complex, themes and categories often interrelated and overlapped, and I discovered further phenomena as I worked through the text. The pre-set categories were therefore approached as open groupings, for they were examined, compared, re-grouped and modified according to the evidence extracted from the material. My procedure at this point resembled both a deductive qualitative textual analysis (cf. Mayring 2003), and a more inductive grounded theory approach (cf. Glaser and Strauss 1967, 1978). The computer-assisted qualitative data analysis software *NVivo* aided this step.

Having identified a multifaceted network of themes emerging from the corpus, several more inductive analytic steps constituted the subsequent analytic procedure. Aiming at developing my categories, I sought out properties and dimensions for the most important ones. This involved analysing them in some depth and detail, thereby discovering repetitions and relations, and adding observations along the way. As an example, I looked at the way recurring themes were discussed by examining when and on which aspect participants' agreed or disagreed; this would reveal how participants negotiated a group position. In addition, I profiled typical readers, identifying dominant and marginal ideologies underlying their positions, examining if relationships between socio-demographic variables and their viewpoints could be identified and determining how this interrelated with the way the group discussed the theme. The evolving pattern from this detailed analysis served as a model for the organisation of the three chapters discussing findings.

## Towards Comparability and Contextualisation

Each of the categories identified was, moreover, subject to careful investigation with regard to the cross-national comparative aspect of this study. Yet, the question of whether – and to what degree – focus groups can actually produce comparable sets of data needs to be reconsidered in this context. Indeed, there is some scholarly disagreement over whether quantitative or qualitative methods are better suited for comparative research – a controversy which Livingstone notes is 'in accordance with the familiar etic vs emic debate' (ibid). Supporters of the quantitative position claim qualitative data is context-dependent and the transcripts are written in different languages, arguing that facts and figures are more comparable. Opposing this view, Livingstone (2003: 488-489) demands:

'Why does comparing focus groups across different cultural and linguistic communities seem self-evidently more challenging than the often unspoken but surely equally demanding task of translating questionnaires, ensuring consistency of survey procedures or determining how a measurement of 75 percent in country A compares with one of 68 percent in country B?'

What this implies is that the context *always* needs to be considered when it comes to the interpretation of results, regardless of whether the research compares opinions or percentages. However, one of the eternal challenges of comparative research is addressed here. It concerns the question of how to interpret emerging similarities and differences in relation to different national contexts. In terms of my own interpretation and contextualisation of findings, my resolution was inspired, again, by Livingstone. She recommends identifying appropriate dimensions of comparison, while acknowledging the relation of each dimension to other potential categories (ibid 2003: 490). I therefore settled on a compromise: aiming at a reflexive contextualisation of the results. Hence, the similarities and differences between *The Sun* and *Bild*, British and German media systems and journalistic traditions, established in Chapters 2 and 3, represent the theoretical foundations for the contextualisation of the results. However, the discussion of findings rests upon a reflexive approach. While I am highlighting relations between the results and my established key dimensions of diversity and commonality wherever possible, I approach these as flexible variables; prepared to question their relevance and consider other social and cultural factors, as well.

## CONCLUSIONS

Representing a detailed discussion of the methodology, this chapter comprised observations and reflections on all stages of the research. As outlined, my work was inspired by Livingstone's suggestion that each step of comparative work needs 'informed choices' (2003: 492). The conceptual framework for the cross-national comparison, then, has been devised carefully in consideration of the study's research aims, and the two dimensions of commonality and diversity that determine the nature of each comparative project. The objects of this study, the two national tabloids *The Sun* and *Bild*, have been deemed suitable for a cross-national comparison – albeit some challenges of comparative research have been acknowledged, such as the eternal dilemmas scholars face when attempting to interpret emerging similarities and differences.

As discussed, a qualitative approach to the research was chosen to meet the study's aims and objectives which required some qualitative depth, flexibility and openness towards audience responses. Choosing focus groups as the method of data collection allowed me to investigate meaning-creation as a collective activity, while exploring readers' understanding and evaluation of tabloid papers and the significance of specific social and cultural characteristics to this. The instruments devised for carrying out the research have, equally, reflected the cross-national angle of the study, for the research approach and strategy have been carefully refined and adapted to the relevant national context. I have also reflected on my experiences involved in carrying out the research in the UK and Germany, and detailed the analytical underpinnings of the approach to analysing the material.

Notably, the challenges faced during the recruitment of readers impacted on the research approach, and changes were made to the sampling criteria and recruitment strategy. The extended discussion of recruitment experiences in this chapter has, moreover, highlighted essential aspects surrounding the reading of tabloids. Important issues include the distinction readers make between the activities of 'reading' (seemingly "proper") newspapers and 'flicking through' tabloids. The fact that reading popular papers does not necessarily involve buying them, likewise, illustrates the wide-spread conception of these news outlets as "throw away" commodities. The implications of these issues to the reading experience will be examined in the subsequent chapters, which each deal with a key aspect emerging from the research. Chapter 7 is concerned with the tensions and contradictions surrounding the reception. The potential of tabloids to foster communicative, social, and cultural participation is discussed in Chapter 8, and the papers' ability to contribute to notions of community and identity is examined in Chapter 9.

# Chapter 7: Balancing Tensions
The Politics of Reading Tabloids

This chapter will critically assess one of the most important results from the research. The issue at stake relates to the finding that more similarities than differences could be observed between British and German audience responses to *The Sun* and *Bild*. This is significant, for it suggests that there are shared ways of reading tabloids across different cultural and national contexts. This chapter maps generic (and, at times, nationally variant) audience responses to the two tabloids, discussing four principal modes of engagement with popular papers that form two opposing pairs. These modes of engagement, which I refer to as "views" of tabloids, each include a set of idiosyncratic arguments, themes, attitudes and reading styles that create a distinctive cognitive, emotional and intellectual framework through which popular papers are made sense of. I hope to demonstrate that these differing yet co-existent views of tabloids represent a crucial source of friction that shapes the relationship between the readers and their papers.

## TRIVIALISING TABLOIDS:
## THE "LIGHT ENTERTAINMENT" VIEW

Contradicting the idea of daily newspapers as traditional information media, there is a strong case to be made for the argument that most readers do not take *The Sun* and *Bild* too seriously as providers of news. It is clear from the focus group discussions in both countries that, in many ways, readers' expectations of popular newspapers are rather rigid with regard to traditional notions of journalistic quality such as objectivity, neutrality and accuracy. The first pair of opposing views, then, relates to readers' perception of the papers as lacking such qualities. One way in which audiences respond to this is to regard tabloids as "light" and "entertaining" reads – an important approach which can be observed in both Germany and the UK. Adopting a mocking attitude towards typical tabloid news values and style elements, readers state that they enjoy the 'funny headlines', the dramatised and sensationalised coverage, the debatable truthfulness of the stories, the gossip, the sleaziness, and the excesses of tabloids. Elisabeth Bird, in addressing a similar result emerging from her research, sums this up on the back cover of her book (1992) by claiming: 'The tabloids are popular precisely for the reasons they are despised'.

Typical arguments relating to the "light entertainment" view of tabloids are exemplified in the following extract [FG8-UK]:

SALLY: I think *The Sun* is very easy reading, tell y' truth.
CLAIRE: Yeah, I like all the captions in it, and the funny headlines! It's cheeky, it's sort of indiscreet. It's light at heard, innit. It's not... very serious (short pause) can be. But it's not.
SALLY: Yeah, it doesn't bore you.
PAULA: And some of it is a bit unbelievable, as well. Cos they have like, SHOCK... shock sort of stories. ...so it's a bit, like, bold, and unbelievable. But that's funny.
CLAIRE: Yeah, I think sometimes it's like a comic, isn't it? That was what I meant to say. It's a bit fierce, a bit funny: it's a comic!
PAULA: Yeah, it's sensationalist, it's biased, and it's tacky.
SALLY: And that's why we like it!
[laughter and 'yeah' from all sides]

Significantly, similar parallels drawn between *The Sun* and purely narrative media such as comics recur in the majority of British focus groups. This illustrates how participants move the tabloid away from an information-centred frame towards one of entertainment when approaching them as "light reads". Yet, in emphasising the papers' entertaining and enjoyable qualities, readers demonstrate their refusal to take them seriously as news outlets. Similar perceptions relating to the "lightness" of reading have also been found in other reception studies of the genre. Pursehouse (1991: 106), Bruck and Stocker (1996: 238), as well as Johansson (2007a: 125) stress these as key elements of popular papers' audience appeal, linking them to one of the mass media's core functions – that of providing means of entertainment and recreation (cf. also Chapter 5, p. 98). Readers, indeed, often associate recreational qualities with the tabloids' conciseness, simple text, everyday language, short narratives and easy flow. QUENTIN [fg11-UK], for instance, observes: 'When I'm feeling that I don't want to test myself too much, you know, I don't wanna strain my brain too much, I buy *The Sun*'. In many focus groups, frequent descriptions about reading popular papers chime with this, as the short extract below illustrates [fg2-G]:

ILONA: Reading *Bild* is a little bit like a holiday.
KATHRIN: Yeah, it's a very relaxing read.
NATASCHA: You don't have to put too much effort into reading it.
SARAH: Yeah, It's like a time-out.

ILONA: You don't have to think too much.
NATASCHA: You don't have to reflect.

Such remarks, foregrounding conceptions of holiday and leisure-time, relaxation and neutral engagement of the brain, exemplify typical positions involved in the "light entertainment" approach to tabloids. Clearly, highly pleasurable merits are attached to this. In summarising what she enjoys about *Bild*, KATHRIN [FG2-G] stresses an engaging all-in-one quality about the paper:

'Well they are kind of filling a gap, aren't they. I mean, which paper has got the main stories of the day, as well as the gossip, and the horoscopes, and lightly-clad women, and the sports, and bizarre, comical stories? They've got EVERYTHING, haven't they! That's an art in itself, isn't it. If you think they're actually putting everything in one paper!'

This idea of popular papers as "all-rounders", offering something to everyone, was shared by many participants. In relation to this, some readers even address an element of addictiveness in reading tabloids. KATHRIN [FG2-G] again, speaking self-reflexively about her reading of *Bild*, declares: 'I just can't help myself. If I can get hold of a copy of the paper I will read it. It's just too tempting!'

The "light entertainment" approach to tabloids also relates to practical arguments regarding the way reading popular papers fits in with daily routines; particularly during gaps the day. Participants frequently stress the view that reading *Sun* and *Bild* facilitate a picking-up and putting-down routine, for instance when commuting or taking a break from work. As discussed in Chapter 5 (p. 99), similar notions attract audiences of related media products, as Hermes (1995) and Müller (2010) have pointed out in relation to women's magazines. Many readers of this study stress that the tabloids' concise and often blatant phrasing is useful in getting 'the gist' of things; as DUSTIN [FG12-UK] phrases it:

DUSTIN: With *The Sun*, you just get a ROUGH idea of what's going on. For instance, like today: 'Disgrace!' It's, like, if you read this headline – it's about Kenneth Clark, he's freed one thousand foreign criminals – you don't really need any more information than that. You just get the gist of what the story's all about [some participants start talking at the same time]... I mean, if you really want to know then you can just go and get another paper {SU-SAN: yeah} or listen to the news {ADAM: or go on the Internet} yeah, or the Internet. But you get the rough idea of what's going on just by a couple of sentences in *The Sun*."
SUSAN: Yeah, it's bite-sized news, isn't it.
ADAM: Yeah, it's like listening to the radio when we're here at work – it's almost like reading the radio.

The "lightness" of reading in this extract is reflected in expressions like 'bite-sized news', and the comparison to a casual activity such as listening to a radio playing in the background. Hovering between rejecting tabloids as news outlets and taking them seriously as sources of 'rough' information, there is some indication here that although reading popular papers is not entirely considered a "serious" form of engagement with news, it is at least partly seen to provide some means of information. While important notions of sociability and participation are implied in this (cf. Chapter 8), readers link the idea of "proper" information to notions of work, seriousness, rational thinking – and other media outlets, for instance, more mid-market tabloids or broadsheets. SAMUEL [FG11-UK] claims: 'I read *The Sun* in the morning but then I'll read the *Evening Standard* if I want real news (laughter). But I like *The Sun* better because it's quite comical, and they normally have a funny headline'. Although other newspapers are considered more informative sources of news, they are also frequently referred to as 'boring' (DENISE [FG7-UK]); 'pretentious' (CARLA [FG11-UK]); 'too complicated' (SANDRA [FG6-G]); or too time-consuming to read (ADAM [FG12-UK]). Expecting 'in-depth' stories and 'real news' elsewhere underscores the perception of *Sun* and *Bild* as "non-serious" news outlets, thus emphasising the "light entertainment" view of tabloids.

Concurrent with this, a variety of highly significant mechanisms of detachment characterise audience responses. Approaching *Sun* and *Bild* as "light entertainment" facilitates detachment from the paper due to the distanced and sometimes mocking stances implied in this view. The vocabulary readers use to describe the activity of reading is of particular significance here. Crucially, the overwhelming majority of participants in both countries made sharp distinctions between the activity of 'reading' newspapers (referring to broadsheets), and 'flicking through', 'skimming through', or 'looking at' tabloids (referring to *The Sun* or *Bild*). This distinction emerged as a crucial issue of the research (cf. also Chapter 6, p. 146). JERRY [FG12-UK] explains: 'There's a difference between sitting down and reading *The Times* and picking up *The Sun* and flicking through it'. Similarly, many readers of this study emphasised that they did not buy a copy of the papers, but read it when they 'found it lying around somewhere' (ADAM [FG12-UK]). However, the difference between "buying" and "reading along" did not appear to significantly impact on the actual reading habits of the study's participants. Most audience members who had referred to themselves as 'marginal' or 'irregular' readers, in effect, showed rather regular reading habits judged by the frequency and regularity in which they engaged with the papers. Often, such self-defined "irregular" readers read *Sun* or *Bild* in a similarly ritualised way to "regular" readers, i.e. at similar times every other day and in similar or the same settings. For instance, many of them stated that they 'always' flicked through the tabloid on their lunch break, or on their way to work. Hence, any such verbal distancing from a regular reading of *Sun* and *Bild* neither reflects a distinctive activity, nor a diverse reception situation. Still, phrases down-playing one's reception habits proved of great significance to the research in many ways. They served to motivate readers to participate in the research in the first place, as discussed in Chapter 6, indicating that participants found it easier to identify with a "flicking through" reception mode rather than with the idea of properly "reading" tabloids. Moreover, such verbal differentiations highlight readers' perceptions that the papers are not to be taken seriously. The significance of detached positions, then, evidently relates to the social stigma surrounding tabloids (cf. the "ideological imposition" view of tabloids on p. 179; as well as Chapter 9, p. 199).

While these aspects are shared by German and British participants, some interesting cross-national variation is worth highlighting. With regard to the "light entertainment" view of tabloids, intriguing differences emerged in relation to "fun"-centred perspectives of popular papers. Humorous interpretations of tabloid style and content surfaced more clearly in the British study, where a "fun"-centred view of *The Sun* proved very popular amongst the majority of participants. Shared by most readers, remarks relating to this, moreover, occurred very early in the discussions, and were re-emphasised at several points throughout. A mocking detachment from the genre was, for instance, reflected in recurring claims made by UK participants that they take *The Sun* 'with a pinch of salt' (ADAM [FG12-UK]; cf. also Johansson 2007a: 133 pp., for a similar result). In Germany, by contrast, joking exchanges were not as common and occurred less frequently. Participants were, moreover, more likely to raise such notions when prompted to do so by the moderator – for instance, through direct questioning such as: 'Is there an element of fun involved as well in reading such exaggerated stories like the one you were just talking about?' Enjoying typical tabloid features as "fun", indeed, represents a minority position in the German study.

A venture into *Bild* readers' responses to one of the media stimuli introduced to the German groups is highly instructive here, for it illustrates key national variations. *Bild*'s front page of 20 April 2005 displaying the headline 'We are Pope!' (German original: 'Wir sind Papst!') was used in the focus groups to stimulate talk. Leaving aside readers' responses to the patriotic tone of the headline (cf. Chapter 9, p. 216), the fact that it was critically acclaimed and celebrated by the German media as linguistically felicitous in its humorous play-on-words is of importance here. Toying with a variety of analogies and alluding to several different contexts, the bemusing grammatical structure of the headline carried a considerable potential to entertain. Many *feuilleton* writers of German broadsheets made references to 'We are Pope'. The line became a vibrant catchphrase, quoted many times in both media outlets and other public discourses (cf. Chapter 2, p. 47).

Judging by the way 'We are Pope' has been celebrated by the German media it is somewhat surprising that, in the majority of cases, *Bild*'s headline failed to win its readers' approval. Indeed, humorous interpretations were only marginally noticeable, for the majority of German readers' reactions to the front page were largely negative. Some feelings of discomfort surfaced, relating to the perception that *Bild* was patronising their readers, and some participants even suspected that the paper's editors were laughing at them. The grammatical structure of the headline attracted particularly negative comments. Common reactions include a variety of depreciative value judgements ranging from 'stupid' (HANNAH [FG1-G]), 'obnoxious' (LUDWIG [FG6-G]), 'ridiculous' (LENA [FG1-G]), 'absurd' (MAX [FG3-G]), to 'inadequate' (FRANZISKA [FG5-G]), 'inappropriate' (ILONA [FG2-G]) and 'irrational' (MARIO [FG4-G]). Notably, a great proportion of participants dismissed the line as 'incorrect German' (TANJA [FG5-G]). Exemplifying the strong opposition to the literalness of 'We are Pope', DAVID [FG3-G] exclaims: 'That is just bollocks! THAT MAN is Pope, not WE!' It needs to be acknowledged that a large part of readers' irritation was directed towards the nationalistic tone and context of the text as well as the subject matter of Catholicism (cf. Chapter 9, p. 226). Still, their responses illustrate that humorous and joyful interpretations of *Bild* did not play a major role in the majority of German reactions to the paper.

There is some indication that readers' socio-economic variables have an impact on this. In the German study, affluent readers tended to enjoy *Bild*'s word-play a lot more than participants from social categories representing the largest group of readers. This becomes evident if we look at two German discussions with affluent and well-educated upper and middle class readers, which were conducted in addition to the core focus groups this analysis is based on. Although the two extra discussions were excluded from the detailed analysis due to their restricted cross-national comparative potential, referring to them here highlights the point I am making. Significantly, the 'We are Pope' headline was positively celebrated in both of these groups. Participants elaborately appreciated its entertaining qualities, in stark contrast to all the other German discussions in which the line was forcefully dismissed. The example extract below relates to these participants' initial responses to 'We are Pope':

MODERATOR: *Let me show you a few examples (showing 'We are Pope')*
(loud roaring laughter, participants talking all at once, making joking remarks, laughing)
FABIAN: Yeeeeeeeah, great!
ANKE: That was a really, really brilliant line!
NORBERT: Very funny. Very funny indeed, putting the whole country as one man, great idea.
EMIL: This line is absolutely genius language-wise. Someone did really very well there. It's casual, light, and amusing. And a picture of the old guy to go with it. Can a tabloid's front page get any better than this?
GABI: Yeah, it's simply brilliant. I was laughing so hard when I first saw it! I still keep a copy of this edition.
ANKE: Yeah, I also keep a copy; I've put it up on the door to my office (general laughter)

Such celebratory tones echo the German media discourses about the headline mentioned above. However, in all of the other German focus groups, affirmative remarks praising *Bild*'s style and word play occurred only occasionally. Themed around an appreciative engagement with the aesthetics of the genre, such sporadic comments, likewise, tended to be offered by the "atypical" participants of a somewhat more privileged socio-economic status. As an example, OLAF [FG4-G], the only technical supervisor in a group of manual and skilled workers, admires the headline's composition and the tabloid editors' ability to capture the moment:

'*Bild*'s journalists are artists. They juggle with words. Taking three words and composing a well-fitting statement like that – really, that's not bad at all! It's the first time in five hundred years or so that there's been a German Pope, and they've managed to convey this novelty in a single line.'

As discussed, remarks of this nature were uncommon in the German discussions, for most participants rejected both the headline's content and its linguistic construction. A humorous interpretation of typical genre characteristics, therefore, can be recognised as a somewhat privileged perspective in the German part of this study. This idea receives further support in view of Bruck and Stocker's findings, who found that the Austrian University students taking part in their research took very similar reading positions (cf. ibid 1996: 88).

In contrast to this, a "fun"-centred view of *The Sun* proved very popular amongst the majority of British audience members. UK readers' responses were, indeed, infused by remarks of a humorous nature, raised early on in every discussion, and re-emphasised at several points throughout. Such strong mocking detachments, reflected in fun-centred perspectives of the genre as "light entertainment" refer to an issue I touched on earlier when reviewing *The Sun* and *Bild*'s characteristics as well as previous audience studies. Evidently, readers respond to different characteristics of the newspapers and the diverse significance of humour, joking, and a mocking stance to the tabloids' texts (cf. Chapter 2, p. 47). However, *The Sun*'s speciality in composing witty headlines and conveying a humorous style may be a consequence of the fierce competition between the UK national tabloids, which leads to a greater diversity among the national tabloids (cf. Johansson 2007a). It is therefore likely that these variations reflect both a culturally diverse significance of humour, and highlight variations within the national tabloid marketplaces of each country.

## SCRUTINISING TABLOIDS:
## THE "FLAWED JOURNALISM" VIEW

Sparks (2000) suggests in *Tabloid Tales* that the distinction between tabloid and serious news outlets is maintained, for they represent dissimilar forms of journalism. From what has been argued so far, this can be confirmed, for readers primarily define *Sun* and *Bild* against "quality" journalism when approaching them as "light entertainment". However, despite claiming not to expect notions of journalistic quality of tabloids, most audience members taking part in this study disapproved of their absence at the same time – voicing intense criticism about the lack of quality in reporting. By elaborately accentuating the flaws of popular papers, readers view them as synonyms for improper journalism. As a result, unambiguous standpoints towards popular papers can hardly be observed among British and German audience members, for one and the same aspect of tabloids is both criticised and valued by their audiences. This greatly contributes to the tension-filled nature of the reading experience. Moreover, readers' distinctions between tabloids at one end of the scale and "serious" newspapers on the other become blurred, as they rapidly alternate between divergent viewpoints. Intriguingly, while dismissing popular papers as "proper" providers of news when approaching them as "light entertainment", readers take the papers rather seriously as news media when applying notions relating to the journalistic ideal. Hence, it would seem that the two opposing views of tabloids as "light entertainment" and "flawed journalism" emerge as a response to the hybrid character of popular papers.

Without a doubt, it is easy to dismiss tabloid newspapers as deficient when searching for established traditional notions of "quality" in journalism. In accordance with this view, a considerable degree of scepticism can be recognised throughout the majority of the focus groups. As part of the various mechanisms of detachment mentioned earlier, a strikingly critical discursive practice can be noted among the readers of this research. In both the UK and the German study, the tabloids' truth claims, discursive strategies, treatment of people, morals and methods were subject to intense scrutiny, and attracted many unfavourable judgements. For instance, readers criticised the papers for presenting 'incomplete pictures' and 'shortened versions' of reality; for telling 'half-truths' and 'lies'; for exhibiting 'scandalous', 'dramatised' and 'sensationalised' reporting; for 'mixing news and opinion'; and for breeching moral journalistic principles by 'haunting', 'defaming', 'insulting' and 'exploiting' people. The following exchange between German readers illustrates this [FG5-G]. A high degree of suspicion towards *Bild*'s "tales of reality" and its stereotyped character of reporting can be noted in this conversation.

SIMONE: I don't like that there are so many half-truths in *Bild*. The stories are often unreasonably blown up.
NADIA: Yeah, they will always write more than there actually is to a story. I don't like that either. The stories often aren't true. Sometimes, if you happen to know the background context to a particular event, it's clear that they put a sort of fairy tale version in the paper. That really gets to me! Actually, I think that's pretty bad.
SIMONE: Yeah that's bad.
JENS: What really annoys me is their sensationalised coverage as well, like the stuff they said about Pit Bull Terriers recently. I mean, I've never read one single nice thing about these dogs in the paper. I am a dog owner myself, and I know how sweet-natured they can be. But *Bild* really polarises the debate surrounding this silly 'fighting dogs' issue. It's the owners who are to blame, aren't they – not the dogs! It really annoys me how they vilify the dogs.
BERTRAM: Yeah – though that's the sort of thing they'd regularly do, don't they. They make allegations without having a single bit of proof. They don't mind adding a false colour to things when they want to come out with a good story.
JENS & NADIA: Yeah

Readers echo the critical canon about popular papers identifiable in academic and public debates (cf. Chapters 2 and 4). At the same time, their responses mirror diverse characteristics of British and German media systems, and reflect key variations in the concerns brought forward by academics and media critics in both countries. While the "flawed journalism" approach to tabloids needs to be recognised as a generic element within both British and German readers' sense-making processes, a few national variations in readers' discussions can be observed. Part of this relates to the diverse thematic foci of the debate. In the UK study, readers quite often concentrated on the tabloids' breeching of privacy rights when discussing *The Sun*, along with the common perception that the paper's paparazzi were frequently harassing people for their photographs. Playing an important part in UK readers' discussions, *The Sun*'s treatment of people attracted a lot of critical remarks and was frequently dismissed both ethically and morally. For instance, readers deemed the tabloid's 'moral failures' as 'horrible' (KAYA [FG7-UK]), 'hypocritical' (LEWIS [FG12-UK]), or 'dangerous' (SALLY [FG8-UK]). Such elaborated criticism of the issue in the UK clearly relates back to diverse trends in the press laws of Britain and Germany (cf. Chapter 3). If we look at recent statistics of the UK's Press Complaints Commission, for instance, it is clear that privacy complaints represent a key component of their work. One of the recent reports states that 329 rulings were made, up 35 per cent from 2007, most of them relating to newspaper journalism (cf. Press Complaints Commission 2008). This links in with frequently reiterated demands to introduce stricter mechanisms for the regulation of the UK press. Currently, UK newspapers can publish practically any photographs or facts that are in their possession. The Press Complaints Commission, it is argued, have failed to stop abuses resulting from this (cf. O'Malley 2000). Hence, notions relating to privacy laws, the power to deciding what is the public interest, and the balancing of regulation and freedom of the press represent key issues of concern in the UK. Clearly, this discourse filters through to readers and is echoed in their debates about *The Sun*. Indeed, readers in the UK addressed and discussed these issues often and in detail. Germany, by contrast, has some of the world's strictest privacy laws, and although *Bild* (and other German media outlets) likewise disobey these rules at frequent intervals, criticism relating to this did not emerge as a similarly forceful theme in the German study. With the exception of occasional remarks about *Bild*'s 'lawlessness', German readers tended to foreground other matters when viewing the tabloid through the lens of the "flawed journalism" view – in particular, concerns about potentially harmful effects of the paper's reporting on others (cf. the section on the "ideological imposition" view) were emphasised.

Aside from such thematic variation, important differences emerged with regard to the degree and dominance of audiences' criticism. There is some indication that the "flawed journalism" view generally tends to be more prevalent among German readers, while UK audiences are more likely to approach tabloids as "light entertainment". Looking into this, the amount of critical remarks arising from the group discussions seemed telling. On organising the material into themes, it emerged that *Bild* readers' remarks referring to negative value judgements about the paper's content, form, style, and morals greatly outnumbered those made by *Sun* readers. Concurrent with this, a greater amount of positive comments about the British tabloid appeared in the UK study. Although a variation difficult to verify, this observation still marked a tentative indication worth following up[19]. Indeed, looking at the way argumentation patterns developed reveals that a "flawed journalism" stance was a particularly dominant viewpoint among German readers. In most German focus groups, participants appeared highly critical of *Bild*. Despite the fact that criticism was, in the majority of cases, raised by one or two readers, this always affected the entire group, heavily impacting on the way communal viewpoints evolved. Even participants who tended to show more affirmative stances towards the paper echoed these critical remarks, even if this contrasted what they had argued before. In the following exchange between VERA and ILONA [FG2-G], this is illustrated:

---

19  Yet, a number of variables pose challenges here, including the choice of method (being of a qualitative nature, this obviously lacks fully standardised interview questions and categories which could be compared quantitatively), the significance of individual participant's characters and the group atmosphere, the role of the moderator, as well as different cultural norms and values impacting on the degree to which such criticism relates to 'socially accepted behaviour' (Schnell et al. 1993: 363).

VERA: I really like the pictures in *Bild*. I think it's good that you can actually SEE what's going on. Particularly, when really big, horrible things happen, like the floods. I mean, I don't necessarily need to see photos of dead bodies lying around, but I don't think it is a good idea to sugar-coat these things either, 'cos you can feel for the victims when you see this. Sometimes it can be difficult to grasp the scope of such terrible disasters and really get an idea of how terrible it actually is; so I do think that in the end it is actually GOOD that *Bild* shows it, and–

ILONA: [interrupts] –but *Bild* ever so often crosses the line {VERA: mhm}, particularly in cases like disasters, accidents, and so forth you get these pictures of dead bodies and blood ALL OVER *Bild*.

VERA: Yeah, but if you watch the *Tagesschau* [daily public service news broadcast], they show pictures of dead bodies, too. They sometimes show images you wouldn't even want to see in a horror film.

ILONA: Maybe, but *Bild* clearly has a strong inclination for sensationalism.

VERA: Yeah, yeah, it does. That's true.

The discussion process here is characteristic of many of the German groups. At the beginning of the quote, VERA raises important notions of emotional sharing fostered by *Bild*'s coverage (cf. Chapter 8, p. 193). Her points, however, are disputed by ILONA, whose arguments are framed by normative ideas of how journalism ought to be like. VERA attempts to sanitise *Bild*'s reputation by comparing it to the reputable television news programme *Tagesschau*; however, she fails to win ILONA'S approval. As a result, VERA agrees to ILONA'S dismissal of *Bild*'s 'sensationalised' reporting, abandoning her own argument about this positive value. What this illustrates is how difficult it is for *Bild* readers to oppose the dominant "flawed journalism" view of tabloids, as this stance seems to be more 'socially accepted' (Schnell et al. 1993: 363), and supported by the majority.

On a side note, an advantage of the method is revealed here. Focus group discussions allow for an investigation of collective viewpoints emerging from social interaction. Thus, they mirror social processes by representing socially negotiated meaning-creation as it occurs in wider social settings beyond the research, while individual views are more difficult to identify (cf. Krüger 1983: 93; Lamnek 1989: 130; cf. also Chapter 6). Personal face-to-face interviews, in contrast, stress the individual respondent's opinions, allowing them to explain at length, and without any influence from others (aside from the interviewer), what it is that they really think. The differences between these methods of data collection can generate quite diverse results. Illustrating this, it is worth reconsidering some of the results from a previous research project, a qualitative reception study of *Bild* (Brichta 2002; also cf. 2010). The findings of that study revealed that in individual interviews, readers of *Bild* tend to express themselves freely and in detail about what they enjoyed about reading the paper. Notions relating to emotional sympathy, such as VERA raised in the example above for instance, were addressed by several readers who explained and reflected on this in detail (ibid. 2002: 144 pp.) In the focus group discussions of this research, however, even readers indicating that they enjoy the tabloid's style for one reason or another (like VERA) soon became critics of exactly the same aspect when communicating with others. It is interesting that audience members, if asked in isolation, apparently seem happy to raise aspects they think are qualities of *Bild*, but in larger social settings such as a group discussion start criticising the paper or agree with the criticism of others. What this highlights is that social norms and values about tabloid journalism strongly impact on the view participants' take in a group setting. The study can, therefore, shed light on dominant social and cultural norms impacting on the collective construction of understandings and evaluations of *Sun* and *Bild*. Recurring argumentation patterns, as indicated, can therefore signify the position tabloid journalism holds in the British and German society and media systems.

Some further evidence for diverse discussion trends in Britain and Germany can be found in the temporal sequence of arguments brought forward in the focus groups. Much of what German participants criticised about *Bild* was raised very early on (often, even before the moderator had posed the opening question prompting for 'likes and dislikes') and was re-emphasised at several points. Such a high level of self-motivated criticism is significant, for it did not resemble the discussions between *Sun* readers. Similarly, as most German groups started off with a round of criticism, *Bild* readers only gradually voiced aspects they liked or enjoyed about reading the paper. In addition, the discussions' tone often appeared somewhat more outraged than in Britain. Opposite trends emerge from the UK study. Here, notions of "lightness" and "fun" tended to be addressed more often and were established as the dominant position (as shown above). British readers also seemed a lot friendlier towards *The Sun* and tabloid journalism in general, in their tone and attitude. This is reflected in the fact that in the UK, readers more often began chatting about their likes, before moving on to addressing aspects of *The Sun* they disapproved of. As such, these group dynamics can be interpreted as a result of what readers conceive of as 'socially accepted' behaviour or viewpoints.

There is, however, a highly conspicuous exception to the rule. Both German and UK audiences greatly distinguish between sports-related and all other editorial content of *Sun* and *Bild* when making judgements. Interestingly, all criticism is discarded when readers talk about the tabloids' sports coverage. The following conversation between *Bild* readers exemplifies typical stances towards the sports section [FG6-G]:

**KRISTIAN**: I read *Bild* particularly because of the sports pages. That's basically why I buy the paper {**INGO**: Yep, me too}. Cos the sports pages are really very good. You get detailed information about all sorts of different sports. I mean, I would say *Bild*'s other content often is a little bit shallow, but the sports part is really in-depth.

LUDWIG: Yeah, the sports pages are quite good. The rest of the paper I find not critical enough in many ways.
KRISTIAN: What amazes me about the sports is how often they are the first to publish a story! Sometimes three, four days before other newspapers have it. The reporters really do a great job; it's incredible what sort of things surface once they start digging into the depths of a football club or something. They've really signed up some quite professional sports writers.
INGO: Yeah, the sport is informative and authentic. And, most of the information is actually true. You don't get half-truths and stuff like that as much as in the rest of the paper. And what I also like, there's not so much gossip in the sport section, either {agreeing mumbles from several others}. Because I really don't like all that gossip in *Bild*, I think it's absolutely irrelevant {KRISTIAN: Yeah}.
*MODERATOR: But when they, as you said 'dig into the depths of a football club' and then maybe publish a story about a footballer who had an argument with the manager and is asked to leave the team or something like that, is that not gossip as well?*
INGO: That's not gossip. That's football.
KRISTIAN: Yeah, how is that gossip? If you asked me, the sports pages don't contain any gossip. They contain pure information, and well-researched too. And if a footballer changes to another team then that's a fact, not gossip. And it's quite an important piece of information actually.
*MODERATOR: Okay – and how about a story about Michael Schumacher and his brother engaged in some sort of family argument – you know, like the article they published a few days ago?*
KRISTIAN: The only purpose of something like that is to fill the pages. They've got a pile of these articles ready, and when they need to fill a page they just use one of them.
LUDWIG: Yeah.

Note the shift in readers' responses, from disregarding *Bild*'s 'other content' to praising the tabloid's sports coverage. This contrast between affirmative remarks made about the sport, and a delimitation of 'the rest' of the paper marks a common theme recurring in most of the German and British focus groups. Significantly, readers reproduce many of the dual opposites constructed around common conceptions of information and entertainment, "quality" and "tabloid" journalism when talking about sports-related content. This involves alternating between modes of identification and dis-identification. Many readers appear to identify with the tabloids' sports coverage with greater ease than with other sections of the papers. As a result, rather unambiguous stances can be observed in relation to this, marking a strong contrast to the often detached and scepticism-filled viewpoints reading tabloids also entails. In the extract above, this contradiction is exemplified in participants' dismissal of *Bild*'s 'other' content as 'not critical', 'shallow', and containing 'half-truths', in contrast to their approbation of the tabloid's sports section as 'in-depth', 'detailed', 'authentic', 'informative', 'well-researched'; and their praising of the reporters' skills and expertise by referring to them in technical terms such as 'professional sports writers'. Such approval is interrelated with high levels of identification.

This relates to a somewhat gendered pattern constructed around certain tabloid material – in particular the celebrity gossip items in *The Sun* and in *Bild*. As shown in the example above, the male readers of this study frequently criticise the tabloids' "fixation" on gossip, stressing they do not like this material. JOSH [FG10-UK], for instance, claims: 'I skip that bit. I'm really not interested in who's getting married and who's got bigger boobs. I'm just not interested'. Likewise, ALEXANDER [FG3-G] asserts: 'I can't bear these stories about celebrities' affairs. There's way too much of that in *Bild*.' By contrast, women seemed more likely to admit they enjoy reading stories about celebrities. Elisabeth Bird (1992: 138 pp.), in noting a similar phenomenon among her respondents, suggests that such "gendered readings" are largely due to 'different paths of moral development' (ibid: 138) between men and women in Western culture. A woman's role, she argues, is traditionally defined in terms of her ability to care for others and maintain social relationships. Clearly, the desire to know about what other people (in this case, stars and celebrities) are thinking and doing could be related to such traditional sociological gender paths.

Yet, this contrasts with the result that an interest in reading and chatting about gossip in a wider sense could be observed among both male and female readers of this research, but there appears to be a gender divide with regard to the subject matter men and women feel attracted to. While women tend to show an interest in news stories focusing on showbiz celebrities and Royals, men seem more fascinated by reports about sports personalities, as illustrated in the extract above. However, concluding that women are generally more entertainment-oriented than men would seem misleading. If we look at the structure of sports events in popular papers (and elsewhere), as well as the featured plots and discursive strategies of this kind of material, it is clear that their dissimilarity to reports about showbiz celebrities lies primarily in the thematic focus of the stories. Discussing British tabloids' sports reporting, Dick Rooney (1998: 105), for instance, points out: 'Both the Mirror and *The Sun* recognized that many people wanted to see the stories behind the event they had already witnessed on television, so the main ingredient of the sports pages were rather more feature-based than news-oriented'. Similarly, Elisabeth Klaus (1996: 411-412) argues that sports coverage in the media is a kind of male soap opera.

However, the social evaluation and classification of celebrity gossip and sports reporting differ considerably. While demonstrating an interest in sport appears a socially accepted reason for buying and reading popular papers, it would seem that enjoying the celebrity gossip involves a sense of "guilty pleasure". Reading gossip was, indeed, often felt to be something one does not do; something "dirty" that evokes shame and embarrassment. Interestingly, the women taking part in this study often showed intense self-criticism with regard to their reading interests. HANNAH [FG1-G], for instance, reflecting on the fact that she enjoys reading about celebrities' lives, speaks about this in a somewhat apologetic tone:

'I know I really shouldn't care about these kinds of stories. And I'm normally not a person who likes slagging off. But I must admit that despite that, I do indulge in the gossip sometimes.'

Responses of this nature could, by contrast, not be observed amongst the male readers of this study. Klaus and Röser (2005) have termed a similar phenomenon the 'gendering' of information and entertainment. According to them, dualisms of information and entertainment are gendered, with one side being associated with maleness and social desirability, and the other with femaleness and problematic media developments (also cf. Röser 1998).

Much of this links in with the fact that sport is often placed in the context of a more information-based frame. As evidenced in the exchange above concerning the "non-existent" elements of gossip in *Bild*'s sports coverage, readers make an effort to keep their immaculate image of *Bild*'s sports section free of any flaws, by arguing that it comprises purely information-based facts and rejecting the moderator's provocative remarks that imply a connection between gossip and sports reporting. This, of course, is very much in line with the traditional treatment of sports as an often integral part of broadcast news and current affairs programmes in both the UK and Germany. By contrast, stories about celebrities are commonly identified as 'gossip', and classified as 'tabloid news'. Although the validity of such dualisms and the value systems they are based on have been challenged recently (cf. Chapter 4), it is not entirely surprising that audiences sense a connection between sports and news. Reproducing these dualisms, they associate sports reporting with notions of factual information rather than with entertainment. Suggesting that an interest in sports represents a socially constructed "acceptable" reason for reading tabloid newspapers, many (in particular male) participants frequently claim they buy the papers 'only because of the sports pages'. Again, this can be viewed as evidence of the mechanisms of detachment I have touched on a couple of times in this chapter. Readers in both countries employ these mechanisms when engaging with popular newspapers on a day-to-day basis. In fact, the entire "flawed journalism" view of tabloids is vital to taking up a distanced position, for the criticism involved in this approach serves to re-evaluate one's own reading. Illustrating this, ILONA contemplates: 'Okay, maybe I read *Bild*, but I also criticise many things in the paper'. This quote addresses a certain detachment from other readers who, in ILONA'S view, might not take up critical stances. This is where the "flawed journalism" approach is strongly inter-related with the positions involved in the "ideological imposition" view of tabloids, which revolves around readers' versatile ideas about popular papers' negative effects on other audience members (cf. p. 179).

Overall then, this first important pair of contrasting views of tabloids coexisting in readers' responses is largely concerned with notions of genre knowledge and genre expectations. Depending on the lens readers choose to apply, the perspectives on *The Sun* and *Bild* differ considerably, as do the value judgements. Audiences fluctuate between being attracted to the aesthetics, content, style features and discursive strategies of the genre; and dismissing these in search of established principles entailed in the journalistic ideal of the two countries. In balancing two contradicting sets of value judgements, readers oscillate between taking the tabloids seriously as news outlets and trivialising them as entertainment media. 'It's news, but then, it isn't news' is how SUSAN [FG12-UK] describes her difficulties in classifying *The Sun*. Much of this relates to the tabloids' hybrid character as news outlets employing the narrative strategies more commonly associated with entertainment and fiction – challenging readers in classifying and unambiguously viewing popular papers on an imaginary axis of information and entertainment. This relates to a general phenomenon surrounding popular culture and its reception. As we know from other studies (notably, Hill 2005; 2007), the embedded contradictions and blurred boundaries of the genre are mirrored in audiences' responses, and create challenges for the categorisation of popular formats. It is important to note that the tension between the two poles – news and information on the one hand and entertaining content and narrative discursive strategies on the other – must be recognised as a generic feature of tabloid reading across the two countries under investigation, a feature that causes readers to frequently apply conflicting criteria when engaging with popular papers.

## ENDORSING TABLOIDS: THE "SOCIAL VALUE" VIEW

While the "light entertainment" and "flawed journalism" views both reflect the hybrid character of the medium, the second significant pair of conflicting views revolves around readers' ideas of the newspapers' power and the effects this has on individuals and society. Generally, audiences believe that *The Sun* and *Bild* are enormously influential. Exemplifying this, SOFIE [FG1-G] offers: '*Bild* is very powerful, it has a powerful position in society because it reaches a large audience. And that's good sometimes – it can be quite positive. But it can also be very negative.' As highlighted by this quote, the presumed power of the tabloid attracts ambiguous value judgements and differing views. Readers' responses entail both positive and negative interpretations of this, depending on whether or not they perceive a connection between the papers' power and their social reality. Much of what audiences approve of in relation to the tabloids' alleged power can be subsumed under the "social value" view of tabloids. The modes of engagement introduced so far involve rather distanced standpoints (mocking and amused stances with regard to the "light entertainment" approach; sincere scepticism in relation to the "flawed journalism" view). As opposed to this, the "social value" view of popular papers is characterised by strong involvement, for readers draw close relations between the papers and their everyday lives when approaching popular papers in this way.

Significantly, in all of the focus groups in both countries, recurring arguments emerged relating to differing kinds of assistance, aid and support provided by *The Sun* and *Bild*. The idea of a tabloid newspaper as "the people's champion", then, marks a central theme of this study. A large part of readers' arguments are grouped around positive value judgements of the papers' appeals, relating to the perception that *The Sun* and *Bild* are able to positively impact on issue- politics. In the UK study, readers often emphasised *The Sun*'s 'naming and shaming' campaigns. In particular, the paper's long-running crusade against paedophiles was highlighted as being a valuable example of *The Sun*'s attempts to inform the public and promote safety in one's own neighbourhood. GARETT [FG10-UK] exemplifies this perspective: 'It's good that they put his face on the front page. I mean, it could be that he's living next door to you, and you'd never know!' In Germany, readers showed a high regard for *Bild*'s ability to 'disclose and publicise things' (THORSTEN [FG4-G]). Examples raised by the participants include individual abuse cases such as 'when parents mistreat their children' (FELIX [FG3-G]), as well as notions of wider social interest, for instance, 'when the gas companies announced that the prices would go up, *Bild* demanded to 'first prove to us that you really need to increase your prices', asking them to publish a profit and loss statement' (KRISTIAN [FG6-G]). While significant arguments relating to the tabloids' presumed capability to provide substantial support and help could frequently be observed in both national reader groups, some minor variations surfaced with regards to readers' general ideas of the scope of the papers' power. These variations can be traced back the differing social histories of tabloid journalism and some of the specific features of *The Sun* and *Bild*.

In the UK study, readers particularly highlighted *The Sun*'s impact on matters of society as a whole – for instance, as a forum for social safeguarding. As mentioned, the British discussions often focused on *The Sun*'s appeals, campaigns and petitions. Readers recognised these as 'fair' (SALLY [FG8-UK]) and 'tactful' (JESSICA [FG12-UK]) and by and large interpreted them as valuable examples of socially responsible ways in which the tabloid should employ its power. Such appreciative stances indicate that *The Sun* is perceived to foster social safety and maintain social equality. Essentially, readers draw on idiosyncratic features of investigative journalism in these cases. This indicates that *The Sun*'s social inheritance is, indeed, of continuing significance to the way it is read today. The paper's roots in investigative journalism can be traced back to the 'New Journalism' period between 1880 and 1914 (cf. Chapter 3, p. 59). Stemming from this particular kind of journalistic fact-finding and critical scrutiny, *The Sun* is still perceived by its readers as serving important social functions by disclosing, drawing attention to and tackling issues of interest to a wider social public.

In Germany, readers' predominant conception of who should be benefiting from *Bild*'s initiatives differs somewhat. Campaigns of a wider-ranging scope were only to a marginal extent referred to by participants – for instance, *Bild*'s appeal to raise money for the victims of natural disasters such as the 2004 Asian Tsunami. Arguments in the German study revolved much more around conceptions of *Bild* as a personal aid, attending to individual readers' needs rather than those of a larger social group. Interestingly, none of the German participants stated they had had personal experience of the tabloid "helping" them in any way. Yet, most of them shared the belief that, in the event that they got into trouble, *Bild* would be there for them, and they could always "go to the paper" as a means of getting help. In all of the German focus groups, readers reported non-personal experiences of this nature. VERA [FG2-G], for instance, recounts:

'Just recently, *Bild* helped a man who had a cerebral tumour. He wasn't able to pay for surgery, and his health insurance wouldn't pay for it either. So he rang *Bild*, and the paper published an appeal to donate money for him, and they actually raised the entire costs for this treatment! *Bild* can really make a difference.'

Although raising money generally marked an important theme of support which participants in both countries associated with *The Sun* and *Bild*, this was more often seen to benefit individuals in Germany. Examples readers referred to included, for instance, a case in which the paper had backed a family in enforcing a claim for social benefits. *Bild* had, apparently, succeeded by 'exerting considerable pressure on the authorities' (OLAF [FG4-G]). Another case mentioned by readers involved the shortening of sofa legs for a woman who was too small to sit on it. MARIA [FG1-G], recounting the story, remarks that the furniture store had refused to refund the woman, who had subsequently approached *Bild* for help. This move had led to the adaptation of the sofa's legs by the furniture store. Common to these examples is a strong inclination towards the highly personal, banal, everyday life significance readers perceive surrounding the tabloid's support. This perception, in fact, reflects the public self-image of the paper which traditionally presents itself as a tool for individual aid and support in the minor and major challenges of readers' everyday lives. As a particularly famous example, *Bild*'s late owner Axel Springer introduced the campaign 'Have a Heart for Children' in 1978, which marked the beginning of the tabloid's long-standing tradition of raising money for children from poor German families (and, later on, for children in need in all other parts of the world).

Hugely successful both commercially as well as in terms of increasing the paper's public reputation, *Bild* continues running this campaign to the present day (cf. Chapter 2, p. 37). It is interesting that although *The Sun* likewise 'continuously demonstrate[s] its capability to take action on readers' behalf', as Johansson (2007a: 97) reveals in her textual analysis, the idea of a tabloid newspaper as a rather *personal* aid and assistant in everyday life matters is somewhat unique to the German study. A comparable theme emerged in none of the UK focus groups, with one exception: similar issues were raised in a discussion among female *Sun* readers [FG8-UK]. However, this exchange followed direct prompting from the moderator, rather than representing an issue raised by the participants themselves, as was the case in the German focus groups.

A further theme to the "social value" view common to both the British and the German study connects with readers' approval of some of the genre's style characteristics. Recognising *Bild*'s presentation as vital to her understanding of complicated matters, VERA [FG2-G] observes:

'When the government proposed to decrease taxes last month, *Bild* published a large table showing how much everyone's salary would increase.... They've explained everything in detail. I really thought that was good because I wouldn't have understood it otherwise.'

As this quote indicates, the tabloids' idiosyncratic style is, indeed, important in making news accessible to some reader groups (cf. Chapter 8). However, praising the papers' conciseness and comprehensibility also relates to perceptions of popular papers as "service" journalism, which occurred in many of the focus groups. Readers of *The Sun*, for instance, often found the promotional items occasionally included in the paper a welcome addition, which highlights the tabloids' ability in framing matters of readers' everyday lives beyond the actual reception of the paper. In Germany, *Bild*'s local section proved a popular topic singled out for praise when readers commented on the tabloid's "service" quality, thus reflecting a specific feature that is not shared by *The Sun* (cf. Chapter 2, p. 24). *Bild*'s regional pages include local news as well as features such as a regional job market or notes on events taking place in the area. An example discussion extract focusing on the paper's regional section is given below [FG1-G]:

**MARIA**: What I really enjoy is the bit about local events and things going on in the area. Where else would you get this kind of information? If there is a special event, or an exhibition opening, or a restaurant that offers a 10 course menu for 10 Euros, you would find this in *Bild*. No other newspaper would be as good at this as *Bild*.
**LENA**: Yeah, I also enjoy reading the Hamburg section.
*Moderator: What is it you like about that?*

LENA: Well, it is quite detailed. And they report on the little things, as well. Like, if someone has found something.
MARIA: You mean like events, or restaurants....
LENA: No, I mean the little things! Not the big stuff – the little, down-to-earth matters, like the restoration of a playground or something similar.
HANNAH: Yeah, they're quite good at highlighting everyday life matters that really concern us. I also think their job market is much better than that of other newspapers. I mean, *Bild* carries so many more and better job offers than the *Morgenpost* [local Hamburg tabloid] or the *Abendblatt* [local Hamburg mid-market broadsheet].

As evidenced in this quote, *Bild*'s regional pages, similar to the sport section of the tabloid, attract many positive remarks. Moreover, readers in all of the German focus groups uniformly consider the tabloid's local section as 'better quality' than similar material in other newspapers. Catering to local audiences' needs, *Bild* forges strong ties with readers through its regional pages. Moreover, as illustrated, the focus on regional and local content enforces strong identification with the tabloid and encourages feelings of belonging and community (cf. Chapter 9). In the German study, a specific example of this this revolved around the regular column of Heiko Brost, a *Bild* commentator to the tabloid's Hamburg edition, whose articles were well-received by most of the German participants. In his column, Brost comments on small everyday nuisances occurring in and around Hamburg. Typical responses are exemplified in the piece of discussion below [FG3-G]:

DAVID: I like this column of, what's his name, Heiko Brost! I find the stuff he writes about Hamburg excellent (soft laugh). It's remarkable what he discovers in all sorts of places. For instance, there's an overgrown traffic sign that cannot be viewed any more from the road; or someone has dumped off their old refrigerator somewhere; or anything like that. Brost would publish it. And, amazingly, it makes a difference, because the authorities take action. I think that's great!
FELIX: Yeeeeeeeeeeeaaah, I loooooove that column!
(all start talking at once)
MAX: It was just yesterday that he took up the issue on Hamburg's playgrounds. How many of our playgrounds are totally crap these days, so that children really shouldn't be allowed to play there anymore. And, immediately after it was published they blocked one of these playgrounds! It's that sort of thing that makes the column so valuable.
PAUL: Yeah, it really makes a difference.

Such praise is telling, for it illustrates the idea of *Bild* as representing their readers and fighting for their concerns. Brost's column, indeed, marks a tangible service of practical use in readers' day-to-day lives. Moreover, the little changes brought about by his publications are verifiable by one's own experience, which adds a highly reliable touch to the reporter's self-set mission, and creates a sense among readers that the tabloid 'matters' and 'really makes a difference'.

Having said that, it should be emphasised that despite valuing such qualities, readers in both countries demonstrated that they were fully aware of *The Sun* and *Bild*'s roles as commercial enterprises aiming to make profit. Perceiving a certain 'hypocrisy' (CYNTHIA [FG7-UK]) about tabloids, a common argument in the focus group discussions related to the idea that the papers' editors make the most of what they think is a good story, while discarding anything that will not sell. The idea of tabloid newspapers as assistants and advocates of their readers was somewhat impaired by this. In Germany, readers demonstrated great cynicism, in spite of their belief that the paper would be there for them if they approached it for help. A typical remark comes from MARIA [FG1-G], who limits her own ideas of the assistance she might possibly be getting from *Bild* by suggesting: '*Bild* is not a charitable society. They will only stand up for a cause if it sells.' Similar arguments recurred among the British participants. Grouped around the commercial value of stories, a frequent claim was that *The Sun* 'will write whatever sells well' (QUENTIN [FG11-UK]). This ties in with the general contradictions implied in readers' responses in relation to the hybrid nature of the genre.

## DISMISSING TABLOIDS:
## THE "IDEOLOGICAL IMPOSITION" VIEW

As explained above, viewing tabloids through the lens of the "social value" view implies seizing the potential of *Sun* and *Bild* to positively influence matters relevant to individuals' everyday life, as well as benefiting larger social groups. However, the papers' power to make an impact needs to be recognised as an equally strong magnet for criticism and unease, articulated through wide-spread concerns among readers about its potentially *harmful* consequences to individuals and society. This and related themes worrying readers epitomise the "ideological imposition" approach to popular newspapers. Often implying rather abstract standpoints "from above", this view is characterised by three significant principles. Firstly, readers draw sharp distinctions between their own reading and interpretation of the text, and that of other readers. Secondly, readers' image of these "others" is habitually negative, and infused by speculations about the others' low media literacy skills, credulity and naivety, vigorous bad taste, and dangerous susceptibility to manipulation. Thirdly, readers implicitly or explicitly highlight their own media and genre literacy skills as being more elaborate than those of others, thereby raising their profile and exempting themselves from their own negative image of the tabloid audience. Significantly, these mechanisms are notable amongst the overwhelming majority of readers across the two countries irrespective of their socio-economic status and regularity of reading.

Resting upon serious ethical, moral and political concerns voiced by readers in disapproval of *The Sun*'s and *Bild*'s style and content characteristics, this view features very close links to the positions involved in the "flawed journalism" approach. Criticism relating to the tabloids' conciseness, truthfulness and, in particular, their strong opinions and bias fed into pessimistic assumptions about how this might affect 'the masses'. A central theme was concerned with criticism of the papers' lack of distinction between news and comment, which attracted concern relating to the impact this might have on other readers' opinion-formation. It is worth re-emphasising that the tabloids' stances are both praised and despised, depending on the view readers choose to adopt. They may make positive value judgements about the papers' strong opinions, regarding these as helpful in terms of raising issues and stimulating a debate when adopting a "social value" view (cf. Chapter 8, p. 201). Yet, audiences in both countries caution that *The Sun* and *Bild* are able to make a considerable impact on (other) readers' views. Foregrounding concerns that these others might form a (wrong) opinion from reading the paper, ILONA [FG2-G] is convinced that, 'if *Bild* entertains a certain view, the majority of readers will adopt it.'

Other characteristics of tabloids are also perceived as problematic. Again, the same aspects are both appreciated and condemned depending on the lens readers apply. In line with arguments relating to the "light entertainment" approach, *Bild*'s ability to provide the 'gist of things' is highlighted as hugely enjoyable and convenient, for instance, by SOFIE [FG1-G]. At the same time, she argues a little later in the discussion that the papers' concise texts are dangerous because 'the majority of readers gain an incomplete picture of reality from such abbreviated reporting'. A similar dynamic applies to the notion of truthfulness. JERRY [FG12-UK], who says he derives pleasure from what he mockingly refers to as *The Sun*'s 'tale-like quality of reporting', addresses concerns relating to other readers' interpretations of this, suspecting that 'a lot of readers, the majority probably, believe everything that is said in the paper'. Generally, readers apply the "ideological imposition" view of tabloids to various themes and subject areas. Two issues – the treatment of people and the political sway of the papers – shall be highlighted in the following section, for these issues were discussed in each of the focus groups (partially through the help of media stimuli; cf. Chapter 6, p. 179; Appendix).

*Sun* and *Bild* readers equally stressed the papers' impact on public opinion with regard to the portrayal of individuals. The central argument was that the tabloids are ethically and morally disrespectful towards those they report on, and that they 'make and break people', particularly celebrities and politicians. Linking in with scepticism concerning the papers' discursive strategies and style, the 'breaking' of people was particularly relevant to readers' "ideological imposition" approach. Attracting much concern relating to the filtering of *The Sun*'s judgement through to audience members, the exchange below refers to the paper's coverage of the UK's former Deputy Prime Minister John Prescott and his affair with one of his secretaries [FG7-UK]:

KAIYA: *The Sun* stir up certain things with a certain style of reporting, and... maybe not all over the place, but there are people who buy into it {Several: Yeah!}. I don't know I mean look at this week's stuff. John Prescott has had an affair... I mean I'm not supporting what he did, I'm just saying the style in which they report it is one-sided, and offensive if you ask me.
ALICE: 'From Two Jags to Two Shags' you mean?
KAIYA: Yeah! Yeah I mean, it's like – alright, this man, he is cheating, he is disloyal. But for a newspaper to say 'Two Shags', that's ridiculous. And it conveys a certain judgement.
CYNTHIA: This is why I can't take it seriously as a provider of news.
[talking over each other, incomprehensible]
ALICE: Yeah, but as you said, many people buy into it. And that's why this marks the end of his career. *The Sun* can make and break people because it becomes common vocabulary what they say.

What is notable in this quote is that the speakers forcefully detach themselves from other audience members and their assumed understandings. Such conceptions of the tabloids as imposing their ideology on a faceless mass of "others" was frequently accompanied by readers' great efforts to make it clear that the papers have no such effects on them. A German reader sums up this issue by implying that he is critical and able to see through the assumed persuasive mechanisms of *Bild*, pointing out that 'you need to know how to read trash' (DIRK [FG4-G]). Similarly, a crucial argumentation pattern emerging from both German and British readers' responses concerned the truly negative view of the tabloid audience, and readers' detachment from other audience members. Such detachment was often voiced implicitly, for instance, by raising concerns about other people's potentially lower media literacy skills. Yet readers' detachment also took more explicit forms. For instance, TANJA [FG5-G] claims, 'In terms of political information, I rely on other media outlets rather than on *Bild*'; and QUENTIN [FG11-UK] maintains: '*The Sun* certainly doesn't influence me in my principle views'. Resembling positions involved in the "flawed journalism" approach, a ritualised distancing from the mass of other readers, therefore, represents a fundamental aspect of the "ideological imposition" view of tabloids.

Still, the reading experience is, obviously, framed by nationally and culturally specific norms and values. To exemplify this, it is worth looking at readers' responses to one of the media stimuli used in this research. Aiming at encouraging talk about the relationship between tabloids and party politics, relevant front pages of *The Sun* and *Bild* were introduced to the focus groups. I used copies of *Sun* and *Bild* both published in the lead-up to the general elections held in both countries in

2005. The clippings each dealt with possible outcomes of the election. *The Sun*'s front page from 21 April 2005 expressed a clear opinion in support of the then Prime Minister Tony Blair. Referring to the traditional smoke signal announcing the election of a new Pope and juxtaposing it with the colour of the Labour Party, the paper claimed on its front page *'Sun smoke goes RED for Blair. One Last Chance'*. Similarly, in the main story of *Bild*'s chosen edition from 24 May 2005, the then candidate for chancellor and leader of the opposition Angela Merkel was pictured rather flatteringly with a headline asking *'Merkel v Schröder: Will she really do better?'*; whilst the word 'really' was printed in very small letters compared to the rest of the headline.

Generally, when speaking about issues relating to the narrowly political realm, readers in both countries voiced concerns about the tabloids' lack of objectivity. Participants suspected that the papers' political opinions filter through to other readers', thereby strongly impacting on public opinion. However, despite maintaining that *Sun* and *Bild* have considerable political sway, readers portrayed themselves as unaffected by the papers' stances. The discussion extract below [FG10-UK] exemplifies a typical argumentation pattern focusing on this issue.

JOSH: *The Sun* is a big voice, isn't it. But it doesn't speak for everybody. Just because I buy it doesn't mean –
GARETT: – I wanna read it.
JOSH: Yeah, it doesn't mean I wanna read it. I don't think they should be promoting a particular –
GARETT: – party.
JOSH: Yeah. As far as politics is concerned, *The Sun* is trying to influence people on what it's… on what it… THEY think is the right party to run this country. But they should be leaving it to the individual. If I wanna hear it, I'll go and listen to the politicians' talk, and let them comment and tell me what their parties are gonna do. And then decide for myself. Rather than let *The Sun* tell me what's right and what's wrong and trying to sway my opinion. Because that will never happen. So, yeah, I can tell you I voted for Tony [laughing] but not because of *The Sun*! I did it cos I made a mistake [laughter from all]. That's what I'm saying, I did it of my OWN opinion. I didn't need to be influenced by *The Sun*. Or by any other paper. So, if *The Sun* wants someone to vote Labour, all right, but that doesn't influence me.
GARETT: But it's influencing many others, that's pretty sure!
JOSH: Yeah! I mean they're putting their beliefs on the front page which is capturing everybody's attention!
DANIEL: But that doesn't mean it's always good what they're saying.
GARETT: Yeah, that's true.
JOSH: Yeah, and you don't want their opinions shoved in your face like that.
DANIEL: No, that's true.

These responses are somewhat in line with what Martin Linton (1995) suggests about the relationship between British tabloid readers and the papers' political position. Arguing that newspapers are read not *because* but *in spite of* their political stance, he notes even before *The Sun* switched allegiance from Conservative to Labour in 1997, half of its readership were already Labour voters. Clearly, the findings of this study are confined with regard to the issue of whether or not *The Sun* and *Bild* increases readers' political knowledge, awareness or expertise; nor are they considerably telling in relation to the papers' effects on readers' voting intentions. However, the participants' discussions of the tabloids' political bias and impact can still be viewed as a form of discussing politics and matters of the (normative) public sphere. In that sense, the papers can be recognised as playing a role in contributing to notions of civic participation (cf. Chapter 8).

The true significance of these findings is to be found in the observation that readers habitually state that the papers are not influencing them, without having been prompted to comment on this issue. In raising such notions, they make important distinctions between themselves and other (presumably less media literate) audience members. Reflecting the common sense expectation that people do not want to state that the media is influencing them, a similar phenomenon, known as the 'Third Person Effect' (Davison 1983), has been noted. Referring to the notion that media consumers generally conceive of greater effects on audience members other than themselves, this effect has been confirmed by a number of academic studies (for an overview, cf. Jensen 2002a,b). Notions of detachment also recur in other reception studies within the genre of popular news. Hill (2007), for instance, recognises that television viewers are often concerned about the potentially negative effects of popular factual programmes on other viewers. This indicates a generic feature of popular culture and its consumption. Significantly, such patterns could be observed in the overwhelming majority of readers taking part in this research, irrespective of their social and cultural background. An indication for the impressively negative image of tabloids and their readers, a ritual distancing from the genre and its audience can be observed- perhaps as a means of wiping away the stigma of tabloids and justifying one's own reading. Readers' detachment, then, needs to be recognised as a crucial element of the reading experience across the two national contexts, demonstrating how the image of popular papers impacts on the way they are interpreted.

Hence, striking similarities can be observed between British and German readers in terms of their "ideological imposition" approach to tabloids. The image of the tabloid audience is equally negative in both countries, grouped around unflattering ideas of the less critical, less literate, and less capable "others". Having said that, there is some evidence that somewhat differing trends emerge from the two national reader groups with regard to their approach to the papers' potential to impact on other readers' opinions. Again, readers' debates about the tabloids' political impact provide some evidence for these claims. In the extract above [FG10-UK], a note of anger is evident in JOSH'S response concerning the idea that *The Sun* might influence his views. Many readers in the UK, indeed, took offence at this idea, foregrounding their right and will to have their own opinion. Although British readers were by no means unconcerned about *The Sun*'s power and impact, there was a strong sense that opinion-formation, in the end, is a matter of individuals making up their own minds. Suggesting that *The Sun*'s stances, therefore, have only a marginal impact on people's political persuasion, JERRY [FG12-UK] argues:

'I think probably most people have their political views ready. *The Sun* might be able to change one or two things about the way they think, but in general people will just pluck out bits in the paper they want to agree with and just ignore the rest.'

Such views link in with readers' responses to the different traditions to endorsing political parties of the UK and German press (cf. Chapter 2, p. 44). In the UK study, participants frequently pointed out that all of the national tabloids are biased, as the exchange below [FG8-UK] exemplifies:

ANNA: Every paper is biased. That's universal to all of the newspapers; they've all got their allegiance to certain parties. They think there's no need for a sort of unbiased point of view.
PAULA: I've put that down in my 'dislikes' section in the questionnaire actually – they're all politically biased {SALLY: *The Sun* 's very Labour} yeah {ANNA: yeah, they are} yeah.
CLAIRE: Whereas the *News of the World* is more Tory.
CLAIRE: And the *Daily Mirror* is more Tory {PAULA: mhm}, it is, yeah.
ANNA: The *Daily Mail* is more Tory {CLAIRE: yeah, definitely} *The Express* is more {PAULA: definitely Tory} yeah, sort of, but a bit milder.
PAULA: Yeah, it's got a milder Tory persuasion.

Hence, the British press' long-standing endorsement tradition impacts on readers' responses to popular papers. As the contributions above show, UK audiences somewhat naturally expect a political bias from any tabloid newspaper. Although a feature they do not necessarily approve of (as PAULA indicates), this is perceived as an eternal aspect of the popular press, and hardly attracts much criticism or debate. Concurrent with this, the diversity of popular papers, or rather the diversity of political opinions that follows from this, allows British participants to confidently categorise popular papers according to their political allegiance. This contributes to readers' sense that they are the ones choosing between the divergent news outlets – for instance by selecting one that reflects their views rather than putting up with a paper's political persuasion if they do not agree with it. As such, the belief that the choice to voting for a particular party is made by the individual relates to an important idiosyncrasy of the UK's tabloid marketplace, which is characterised by strong competition between the national tabloids.

By contrast, *Bild* is the only popular newspaper with a national scope in Germany. This is reflected in readers' responses, for they inevitably draw fewer comparisons to other tabloids, accentuating the paper's somewhat unique status within the German media landscape. As a consequence, *Bild* is often at the centre of attention and criticism, both in the public realm as well as among its readers. Moreover, as the genre is not as common as in the UK, some uncertainty could be noted among German readers with regard to how to classify the tabloid. TANJA [FG5-G] for instance, says that she is displeased with the paper 'more and more becoming like a tabloid newspaper'. Similarly, many German participants' approached notions of the paper's political power in slightly different ways to the British readers. The idea of a newspaper openly supporting a particular political party was, indeed, alien to the German audience. *Bild* readers recognise a distinct political stance in the tabloid's reporting, but they describe the paper's position as 'indirect' or 'subtle'. This attracts even more criticism, for any such 'indirect' editorial attempt to endorse a political party is considered extremely hazardous. Hence, *Bild* is often seen to subliminally impact on public opinion. A common conviction expressed by German readers concerns the view that the tabloid manipulates the masses to voting for a particular political party. Such vocabulary is telling. Recurring in many German discussions, the term 'manipulation' pervades readers' talk, along with other strong expressions and phrases depicting the paper as an ideological propaganda instrument attempting to sway audiences' political persuasion, as exemplified below [FG5-G]:

JENS: *Bild* can easily win an election campaign for a political party.
SIMONE: Yeah, I agree.
FRANZISKA: It's frightening how much influence they have.
JENS: Yeah, if they continue portraying Angela Merkel as the most wonderful person in the world –
SIMONE: [interrupts] – then the majority of readers will think 'I'll vote for her, cos she's good'!
JENS: Yeah, exactly.
FRANZISKA: They're pitching themselves up as the CDU's propaganda paper.
BERTRAM: In my view they are dumbing down the masses. Because most readers buy into what the paper says – they read the paper and they agree with everything it says. They're thinking 'if *Bild* says so, it must be true', and they form their opinions from the paper.
NADIA: Yeah, but that's what *Bild* wants! They want to manipulate readers' opinions. They want to have political sway. They may not be stating their opinions directly, but they say things like 'oooh, this isn't right' or 'look at how Gerhard Schröder has got it all wrong

again' or 'surely Angela Merkel would do better'. So, they're clearly not as impartial as they claim on their front page. They're instilling a certain persuasion into readers.
BERTRAM: Yeah and there's a certain danger to that. I mean, they're SUBLIMALLY manipulating readers' opinions, and I'm not entirely sure that readers are actually aware of that.
NADIA: Absolutely.

Essentially then, the dominant argument among German participants is that *Bild* can originate a belief or an opinion in its readers, thereby 'manipulating' their views. British readers, by contrast, tended to believe that *The Sun* amplifies an opinion, a theme, or a discourse that already pre-existed in the public domain b. It is also notable from the examples referred to in this section that UK participants' discussions about *The Sun*'s ability to influence public opinion appeared somewhat less agitated in tone and nature, including less forceful assumptions about *The Sun*'s power than it was the case in German readers' discussions. Interestingly, the perspective of British participants, likewise, appears somewhat more in line with conceptions of an 'active' media audience: a notion that has notably been advanced by the British Cultural Studies tradition. This indicates that audiences respond to the divergent intellectual traditions which can be observed in either country (cf. Chapter 4), and reproduce important viewpoints entailed in the divergent academic trends. In terms of perceptions of media consumers and the mass media's power, it could be argued, then, that German readers' arguments are more in line with a classic Frankfurt School perspective, foregrounding notions of manipulation and passive media audiences. A significant context to this relates to the specific political and social histories in either country. In particular the German discussions revealed that the legacy of Nazi Germany needs to be acknowledged as still highly relevant to readers' responses to *Bild*, particularly with regard to the "ideological imposition" view of tabloids (cf. also Chapter 9, p. 216). Emerging from unpleasant past experiences, readers in Germany conceived of a much greater liability for the audience to be manipulated than readers in the UK did. Linking in with this, although the idea of tabloids as delivering political propaganda disguised as news attracts concern among readers in both countries, German participants were considerably more distressed by this thought. In a similar way, the UK's long-standing democratic tradition could also have some influence on the way readers react towards *The Sun*'s political stances. The country's social and political history may, likewise, be reflected in the way *Sun* readers insist that political opinion formation is a matter of individuals.

The second important pair of contrasting approaches to tabloids, then, represents the theoretical antagonisms entailed in the "social value" and the "ideological imposition" view. Both of these revolve around ideas of the newspapers' power and the effects this has on individuals and society. However, the key distinction relates to abstract conceptions of the papers' power on the one hand, and perceived concrete effects on the other. This is in accordance with the degree of closeness or distance readers draw between the papers and their domestic lives. The "social value" view entails conceiving fairly close ties between popular papers' power and one's own social reality. When approaching tabloids in this way, readers sense concrete effects on their everyday lives. This involves highly identified modes of engagement that lead to positive value judgements. By contrast, viewing popular papers through the lens of the "ideological imposition" view implies thinking about the newspapers' power in a more abstract and conceptual way, distant from the realms of one's own day-to-day concerns. Accompanied by strong means of disidentification, audiences' interpretations of the papers' power tend to be highly negative in the "ideological imposition" view. Readers' assumption about the tabloids' substantial political sway gives rise to concerns about the effects this may have on the opinion-formation of a faceless mass of "others".

## CONCLUSIONS

Examining one of the most important results from the research, this chapter has focused on discussing crucial commonalities emerging from British and German audience responses to tabloids. The complexity of the tabloid reading experience has been highlighted, and generic modes of engagement with tabloids have been offered. Overall, the findings reveal that the reception process needs to be recognised as a constant struggle: critical tensions and contradictions characterise the reading of popular papers in both countries, for criticism and enjoyment can frequently be observed with regard to one and the same aspect of tabloids. Reading *The Sun* and *Bild*, then, essentially means having to involve two or more apparently contradicting forces. Audiences' responses therefore combine potentially conflicting expectations, evaluations and perceptions of tabloids, which are reflected in contradicting value judgements. This leads to a highly tension-filled character of the reading experience.

As outlined previously, four principal modes of engagement with popular papers have been established. I approach these as "views" of tabloids, indicating that each is characterised by specific themes, arguments, and argumentation patterns contributing to a distinct cognitive, emotional and intellectual framework within which popular papers are made sense of. Depending on the lens readers choose to apply, the perspective on *The Sun* and *Bild* differs considerably, as do readers' value judgements. However, the somewhat ideal distinction presented here does not entirely reflect the reality of readers' engagement with popular papers. In line with Bruck and Stocker's claims with regard to the reception of Austria's tabloid *Neue Kronen Zeitung* (1996: 227; cf. also Chapter 5, p. 108), the reading of tabloids emerges as a 'diverse and fragmentary process' that involves various modes of engagement, applied individually or in combination, in dissimilar ways and at differing times in this process. Hence, although none of these views exists in isolation, and more forms and blends could be identified, the majority of British and German readers applied a combination of the herein- established views of tabloids to their reading of *Sun* and *Bild*. Yet it is important to note that the modes of engagement with tabloids introduced in this chapter represent not a typology of individual reading styles, but one of discursive practices as they are invented, negotiated and established by a group of people. As such, these patterns shed light on the construction of tabloid reading modes in wider social settings.

The first pair of contrasting yet co-existing views of popular papers is reflected in the "light entertainment" and the "flawed journalism" view. There is a strong case to be made for the argument that most readers do not take *The Sun* and *Bild* entirely seriously as providers of news. This is expressed in the joys of reading articulated in the "light entertainment" view of tabloids. Yet, despite claiming not to expect journalistic quality from tabloids, readers frequently disapprove of its absence. Intensely criticising the tabloids' news style, they judge the papers through the lens of the "flawed journalism" view. This first pair of views clearly relates to the hybrid character of the medium. Tabloids present themselves as news outlets, but employ narrative strategies associated with entertainment and fiction. This challenges readers in classifying them and defies the unambiguous positioning of tabloids on an imaginary axis of information and entertainment. The second significant pair of conflicting views relates to the way in which readers conceptualise the newspapers' power and its effects. Interlinked with either abstract detachment or the concrete ties readers draw between the papers and their everyday lives, two opposing approaches can be observed, which have been termed the "social value" view and the "ideological imposition" view of tabloids. The "social value" view places popular papers at the heart of readers' daily lives. The papers are regarded as powerful advocates of the "little people" when viewed in this light. In contrast to this, the tabloids' power represents a strong magnet for suspicion and concern, particularly with regard to the perceived harmful effects on "others" , as implied by the "ideological imposition" view of popular papers.

With regard to the cross-national comparison, the key differences are in variations in the dominant discussion patterns emerging from the British and German focus groups. In Germany, a dominant critical-concerned movement could be identified, while in the UK, a critical-light movement characterised the discussions. Other cross-country variations concerned, for instance, the diverse significance of fun-centred approaches involved in the "light entertainment" view of tabloids, which appeared more pronounced in UK. On the one hand, diverse textual characteristics of the two papers are reflected here; on the other, these differences relate back to variations in the two countries' national press markets. Further differences between German and British readers' responses include reactions that relate back to the nationally diverse endorsement traditions of newspapers, and to the differences in the histories of tabloid journalism.

While this chapter has dealt with cross-nationally shared tabloid reading modes on a very broad level, the two subsequent chapters will concentrate on distinct aspects of the popular press, foregrounding matters of participation, inclusion, sharing and community fostered by *The Sun* and *Bild*.

# Chapter 8: Fostering Engagement
## The Participatory Potential of Tabloids

Having established the tensions and contradictions surrounding the tabloid reading experience in Germany and the UK, the next two chapters explore the role of popular newspapers in contemporary Western society. Examining the potential of tabloids to facilitate significant notions of inclusion, sharing, belonging and identification, my arguments are divided in two parts. Chapter 9 takes a closer look at tabloids as tools for social belonging. This chapter, meanwhile, builds on basic points made about the "social value" view of tabloids detailed previously, attending to important ways in which popular newspapers foster significant social and cultural engagement and participation, by activating and stimulating their readers.

Before launching into a discussion of audience responses, a preliminary note on the idea of participation I am referring to deserves some attention. Participation in this chapter is understood as affording the opportunity for individuals and social groups to take part and engage in a variety of communicative, social and cultural settings that largely exist outside the narrowly political field. I examine several aspects of this, pointing out rational and emotional types, real and symbolic functions, as well as smaller and wider effects. By consciously approaching the concept in this very wide sense, its original realm of political involvement in the democratic project is broadened, thus providing the grounding for an understanding of some of the important societal benefits of tabloids. Such reasoning also implies abandoning the underlying dualisms of "information" v "entertainment", "quality" v "popular", "reason" v "emotion", "public" v "private" and so forth, which inform the controversy around tabloids and other popular media formats (cf. Chapter 4). My approach concurs with the idea that *hybridity* marks the key to understanding popular papers and their audiences (cf. Chapter 7). This reasoning has been greatly inspired by Liesbet van Zoonen's arguments in *Entertaining the Citizen* (2005). Van Zoonen looks at seemingly "apolitical" popular culture artefacts, stressing their engaging potential to audiences. Addressing the various interrelations between popular and political culture, she highlights the everyday experience of citizens, arguing that more attention should be given to the role of entertainment when examining matters within the political and civil sphere. While van Zoonen's focus is on the political, I will largely be examining other spheres of social and cultural participation here. Building on some ideas of John Langer regarding the symbolic qualities of 'soft' news on television (1998), the significance of typical tabloid content preferences, news values and narrative strategies to various social and cultural discourses is investigated.

## ACCESS TO NEWS

There is no doubt that *The Sun* and *Bild*'s news style play a vital role in providing news access to large audience sections. Indeed, one of the most important qualities setting the papers apart from other media outlets concerns the effortless ease with which readers state they 'can relate to' the tabloids' texts. The way the papers communicate with audiences is central to this. Many readers cherish the impression that popular papers speak clearly and in their terms, rather than using 'complicated words and long sentences' (GARETT [FG10-UK]). The concise and comprehensible news style of tabloids has been described as an 'appropriate level of complexity' for working class readers (Bruck and Stocker 1996: 177), resulting in the idea that this represents the central motivation for reading tabloids (ibid). Although such claims do not reflect the complexity of the reading experience (cf. Chapter 7), important notions of social participation in the democratic project can be derived from this. It is clear that the easily understandable, 'bite-sized' (SUSAN [FG12-UK]) presentation of facts and stories is the key to making news accessible, at least to some audience sections. SALLY [FG8-UK] remarks: '*The Sun* is pretty broken-down English so that everyday people can read and understand it.' Moreover, participants in both countries agree that other newspapers, in comparison, lack the right level and fail to communicate with them. In particular broadsheets were perceived as exclusory in this sense. SARAH [FG2-G] elucidates: '*Bild* can easily be understood by anyone. But, if you look at other papers, you'd have to read their articles twice at least – and then you still wouldn't understand what they're talking about.'

Hence, in accordance with general social purposes of the media, tabloids offer orientation and reference points to audience members who might otherwise be excluded from such important functions. This brings to mind arguments revolving around popular papers' contribution to the rational public sphere (cf. also Chapter 4, p. 77). In many scholarly considerations, the "quality" press is often held as an ideal communicative space for participatory debate and the development of critical political discourse, while popular journalism is seen to harm democracy and civic culture (cf. Habermas 1989; Postman 1985). However, popular journalism appears to offer important social and cultural functions to a mass audience, which other kinds of journalism seem less capable of doing. An important argument deriving from this concerns the idea that tabloids have a role in promoting civic behaviour through providing alternative approaches to news and making aspects of the rational public sphere accessible (Örnebring and Jönsson 2004; Örnebring 2006; Johansson 2007b). Following Fiske's claims (1992), tabloids can, therefore, be regarded as important sites through which readers seek to enter the public domain.

## Melodrama & Emotion

Such arguments are rooted in the idea that popular culture formats, including tabloid newspapers, have a range of stimulating and activating effects on audiences. It is worth examining the emotional appeal of tabloids in this context. Henrik Örnebring and Anna-Maria Jönsson (2004: 15) assert: 'The often criticised appeal to emotion can actually stimulate political participation by speaking to the senses and feelings as well as the rational mind.' Indeed, on examining audience responses to *The Sun* and *Bild*, it is evident that both papers possess the ability to raise readers' emotions. Clearly, readers respond to the discursive strategies of tabloids, in particular to the 'melodramatisation' of news and events (Bruck and Stocker 1996: 26; cf. also Chapter 2, p. 51). Peter Brooks (1984: 11-12) has defined melodrama as 'the indulgence of strong emotionalism; moral polarisation and schematisation; extreme states of being, situations, actions; overt villainy, persecution of the good, and final reward of virtue'. Although this marks a stark contrast to the detached and rational way of experiencing news, which is commonly associated with civic participation, it is clear that popular narratives speak to readers more effectively. Indeed, encouraged by the emotive presentation style, audiences respond to *Sun* and *Bild* in equally emotional terms. A distinct element of sharing derives from this, represented in emotional and empathic reception modes. This is illustrated by VERA [FG2-G], who, commenting on a report about the severe 2005 floods in Germany, remarks:

'I really like the pictures in *Bild*. I think it's good that you can actually SEE what's going on. Particularly, when really big, horrible things happen, like the floods. I mean, I don't necessarily need to see photos of dead bodies lying around, but I don't think it is a good idea to sugar-coat these things either, 'cos you can feel for the victims when you see this. Sometimes it can be difficult to grasp the scope of such terrible disasters and really get an idea of how terrible it actually is. So I do think that in the end it is actually GOOD that *Bild* shows it.'

Reviewing *Bild*'s coverage of the floods, VERA demonstrates a highly emotional engagement with the text and the images displayed. Identifying with the victims, she feels for them, working through the tragic event by applying a great deal of sympathy. Through grasping the disaster on an emotional level, she gets 'an idea of how terrible it actually is', thereby coming to terms with what has happened. Friedrich Krotz (1993: 489) has pointed out that emotional news reception is indeed important to cognitive processes through which audiences draw relations between themselves and the world. VERA effectively combines affective and rational responses. Despite showing shock, horror, and empathy, a more rational and self-reflexive mode of reception can also be observed in her response. This is represented in the matter-of-fact way in which she speaks of the 'dead bodies lying around', relating her emotional reactions to the genre's presentation style. Indeed, the idea of emotional and rational responses merging into a cross-fertilising process underscores other findings from the area of popular culture consumption. Suggesting that social and emotional learning in particular can be derived from watching factual and reality TV programmes, Hill (2005; 2007) demonstrates that the significance of news does not only lie in informing us about what is going on in the world but also serves important psychological functions. She recognises news as an 'information-rich environment but one that is hard to connect with unless there is some personal investment in a news item' (2007: 97). Emotionally framed news consumption can be recognised as a form of 'personal investment'. Hence, the 'melodramatisation' of the text, in combination with the tabloids' simplified and concise style, makes news and current affairs accessible and easy to relate to – and not only to audience members with minor media literacy skills.

Aside from that, it is worth examining some further ideas about the general role of feelings in media consumption. The observations made so far could, for instance, be related to arguments about the potential benefits of violent media content. A remarkable position from this field of research relates to the belief that the reception of violence can have cathartic effects (Feshbach and Singer 1971). Although the theory has been disputed, the advocates of this hypothesis claim that people's aggressive impulses can be reduced through the consumption of violent and graphic material in the media. Following on from this, the tabloids' potential to raise feelings in readers could be seen as attending to basic human needs, for reading about horror, catastrophes and violence provides for a certain emotional balance, thereby serving societal interests such as stability and safety. Similar points have been picked up by Dolf Zillmann in relation to his 'mood management' theory (1988). Taking up a uses and gratifications-based approach to the consumption of media violence, Zillman argues that people turn to certain content in order to balance their emotional state of mind. In simple terms, accidents, catastrophes, and similar dramatic events can be experienced (emotionally) "as if" they were taking place in one's own life. At the same time, people are (rationally) aware that their life is unharmed. In accordance with the entertaining and recreational functions of the media, an engagement with such arousing material, it is argued, can balance monotony.

It is clear that emotional news reception potentially fulfils a range of purposes that exceed the functions of merely providing for feelings in a rationalised world, as has previously been seen (Bruck and Stoker 1996; Rogge 1988). As explained, the style of popular papers facilitates significant social participation by making news easy to relate to. Emotions, in particular, can be regarded as equally significant to vesting societal interests. Dahlgren highlights this by explaining:

'In simple terms: passions have *reasons*: there is some object or vision that is valued, cherished. Passion is based, at some level, on '...*first, a* concept *and interpretation of the object's nature and qualities; second, a* judgment *that the object is valuable in some way; and third, an* intention *to pursue the value of that object in one's life'*. (Hall, 2005: 15–16). Thus, passion is not blind, it involves a vision of the good, something to be attained, something to strive for, and often also involves some notion as to how to achieve this good.' (ibid. 2006: 26; original Italics)

This reasoning is intriguing, for it suggests that 'passions' have important social benefits. If we accept this view, the idiosyncratic news style of popular papers needs to be recognised as evoking readers' 'vision of the good'. Thus, in addressing the 'concepts', 'judgements' and 'intentions' underlying this vision, tabloids can be regarded as aiding the negotiation of individual and collective norms and values.

## A Currency of Communication

Important notions of communication and inclusion are implied in the points raised so far. A truly significant aspect of the tabloid reading experience in the UK and Germany relates to *The Sun* and *Bild*'s extensive sociability. The findings of this study reveal that the papers provide continuous opportunities for conversation and social interaction, both within the reader community and beyond. As SOFIE [FG1-G] points out:

*Bild* informs me about what is going on in the world in its short and concise way. It gives me an array of politics, serious stuff, stupid stories, celebrity gossip and the sport. If the paper didn't exist I would have to go through a lot of trouble trying to assemble the various bits and pieces myself! [...] Reading *Bild* on my way to work, I get the gist of the latest news and events and have something ready to talk about with anyone. I can chat about the latest football scores with my workmate, about the floods with my boss, and about who snogged who last night with the lady in the cafeteria. This does make things a lot easier.

As indicated here, tabloids clearly possess the ability to foster talk and sharing through providing material for various kinds of everyday conversations. The "all-in-one" quality of the papers, moreover, supplies a vital sense of knowing what is going on in the world and being able to 'move along with the currents', as KATHRIN [FG2-G] puts it. Aside from that, the perception that the papers provide 'the gist of things' relates to practical arguments about the way the papers fit in with daily routines, contributing to a casual and relaxed mode of engagement (cf. Chapter 7, p. 161). While these issues link back to general functions of the media, it is interesting that the tabloids' sociability is perceived as significantly bridging social differences. DUSTIN [FG12-UK] explicates:

*The Sun*'s got ALL the main stories that all the other papers have, but it's also got stories that NONE of the other papers would have. Like 'the bloke who slept with next door neighbour's goldfish' or something similar.... So, if you spoke to someone that was high-brow, you could talk to them about maybe the layman's version of what happened in politics. And if you went down to the pub, you could talk to your mates about the bloke that DID sleep with a goldfish, or any other story that you've read in *The Sun*.

The important connective functions of tabloids addressed here are neither confined to one's own social surroundings nor to the reader community. Instead, participants address a vital sense of being able to join in a conversation with *anyone*, regardless of their social background. Thus, by offering a currency of communication for various private and public realms, *The Sun* and *Bild* provide essential means of communicative participation and contribute to notions of community and belonging.

### Sharing a Joke

By stimulating talk and easing social interaction, tabloids offer several opportunities for jointly experiencing elements of the papers. One important aspect of this concerns the sharing of a joke. In the quote above, DUSTIN indicates that *The Sun* carries amusing stories like 'the bloke who slept with next door neighbour's goldfish'. Bound to provoke laughter and joking, remarks of this nature often occurred in the group discussions. Generally, as shown in Chapter 7, humour and fun-centred perspectives played a more important role in British participants' responses to *The Sun*; however, a humorous detachment from the genre could also occasionally be identified among German readers. The sharing of a joke about *Bild*'s debatable truthfulness and sensational presentation style is a particularly important aspect to this. Drawing on these issues, the term *Revolverblatt* [lit: revolver sheet] was often used in reference to the German tabloid. Stemming from the 'golden' era of tabloid journalism in Germany in the 1920s, this colloquial expression originally referred to the then popular type of tabloids (cf. Chapter 3, p. 60). Along with a few other stereotypical sayings about *Bild,* this phrase has endured up to the present day and is still popular among readers. Yet, it nearly always has a humorous edge to it, as illustrated below [FG4-G]:

PHILLIP: Us colleagues really enjoy reading aloud items in the paper {REINER: oh yeah}, in particular some of these sensational stories, you know; stories that are so ridiculous they just cannot be true. {REINER: mhm} Those are the kinds of stories proving that *Bild* really is a *Revolverblatt.* It's a bit like a penny dreadful.
CHRIS: A penny dreadful (laughs) yeah that's a good term! (laughs)
PHILLIP: But we enjoy reading these kinds of stories 'cos we laugh about them.
OLAF: Yeah, especially stories written in the manner of '*Bild* got an exclusive off the dead man'.
REINER: No, stories like '*Bild* got an exclusive off the dead man who shot himself with a rope'!
(all laugh)

This piece of discussion demonstrates shared ironic and sceptical stances which are constructed in relation to the perceived truthfulness of the tabloid's content and presentation style. Entailing significant detachment from the genre, such reading positions relate to recreational qualities of consuming tabloids as well as the observation that readers in both countries habitually down-play the genre and their own reading. This is articulated by frequent devaluing terms in which participants speak of *The Sun* and *Bild*. For instance, when comparing popular papers to other news outlets, readers refer to tabloids as 'trash' (LUDWIG [FG6-G]) or 'rubbish papers' (GARRETT [FG10-UK]), representing 'bad taste' (CHERYL [FG8-UK]). Similar observations have been pointed out in other tabloid audience studies (cf., for instance, Brichta 2002: 145-152; Johansson 2007a: 122-124; Bruck and Stocker 1996: 113); indicating a generic feature of the genre's reception. As can be observed in the example above, the exchange of such devaluing stereotypes significantly works to symbolise belonging to a community – in this case, the group of colleagues (cf. also Chapter 9).

### Gossiping

Other aspects of tabloids also facilitate sharing and inclusion. Celebrity gossip is particularly noteworthy in this respect, for talking about celebrities' lives and affairs crucially facilitates a certain "moving along with the currents". KATHRIN [FG2-G] points out: 'My mates and I really enjoy indulging in the gossip. I always read every bit of it, so that I know who has done what, when, where, why and with whom, and then I can chat about it with my mates.' In addition to providing material for conversations, the connective character of celebrity gossip becomes evident in the focus group setting. Gossiping about celebrities provided a topic all participants could effortlessly contribute to, even if they had been formerly inactive. Some of the responses to *The Sun*'s front page of 16 September 2005 are telling in this respect. Used in order to stimulate talk about scandal and the treatment of people, the paper of that day depicted an unflattering photo of Kate Moss on its front page, along with the headline *'Kate's £200 a Day Coke Habit'*. This report marked one of the first in a series of articles, features and commentaries on the issue that followed in the time after this edition's publication. The fashion model's drug abuse, the impact it had on her career, the police questioning she underwent, and her subsequent residence in a drug-rehab clinic made the headlines for several weeks in 2005[20].

Demonstrating the connective character of such material, it is worth paying attention to AMANDA in the discussion extract below [FG12-UK]. She had taken the role of a silent observer until the talk turned to Kate Moss' drug abuse. Suddenly, she joined in the conversation and fell silent again when the subject ceased. AMANDA'S singular engagement illustrates how chatting about the fashion model's affairs got all participants involved. Her responses displayed here marked the only contribution she made to the entire discussion:

MODERATOR: *[showing Kate Moss' clipping] I was wondering what you thought to this.*
JESSICA: I think that was really horrible, because it ruins her career. And she's got a child to support! That really pisses me off –
AMANDA: [interrupts] But if she's got a child to support then why is she even shoving coke up her nose? {LEWIS: Yeah!} {DUSTIN: Mhm!}
JESSICA: Because people do that, and we know she's done it, cos they've outed her. So, don't grind her down now, so she can't pick herself up again.
AMANDA: But that's what it means for someone to be ground down, so they realize and then they pick themselves back up.
DUSTIN: Yeah – but what it does is, you can highlight the problem that coke is today, highlight it to non-celebrities.
JESSICA: But Kate Moss, I mean the amount of drugs that girl has been doing – and she looks fantastic every bloody time! There's TEENAGE girls that are looking at that! And she always looks fabulous, she's always well dressed – that is just so bad for young girls to see that kind of thing.
AMANDA: But she's got a make-up artist, that's why.
JESSICA: But does a fourteen year old girl know that?

---

20 The British group discussions took place in the spring of 2006. Participants, therefore, drew on the *Sun*'s entire coverage of the issue.

AMANDA: I think actually they know more than you would think; they know most of the stuff about her, like that she's anorexic and so on.
LEWIS: Yeah, that's true, they all know about that. And she does looks very thin too. But then you've got all these young kids wanting to look like her {JESSICA: Exactly} {AMANDA: Yeah} And saying 'all right, she's got a drug habit', but she's looking all nice and sexy.
AMANDA: Yeah, that's definitely the wrong message.
JESSICA, DUSTIN, LEWIS: [all at once] Yeah, yeah.

As this illustrates, the lives and affairs of celebrities provide significant resources for communication and sharing. The integrative function of stories about stars and celebrities in tabloids, which can be observed in many of the focus groups of this research, has also been noted in other studies (cf., for instance, Bird 1992; Johansson 2007a). Hill (2007: 162) suggests that gossiping can even work to unify a nation: 'When viewers gossip and debate about these [factual TV] programmes they become part of a social, sometimes national, event'. Going even further, Uwe Hasebrink (2006: 60) raises the interesting point that entertainment news can work as a form of trans-national social glue:

'There is a high potential of global fascination for all kinds of *glamour* and *top stars*. Royals, Hollywood Stars, sports heroes, etc. attract audiences all over the world and provide an important part of the "communicative substance" of the globalized world: those issues we can talk about with anyone from anywhere.' (original Italics)

Gossiping, then, can foster a sense of togetherness and sharing both on a micro and a macro level, sometimes even passing beyond the boundaries of nations and continents. As a side note, it seems important to re-emphasise that gossiping in a wider sense could be observed among both men and women during this research, but the subject matters men and women felt attracted to differed somewhat: while women tended to show more interest in news and stories about celebrities, stars and Royals, men seemed more fascinated by reports about sports personalities (cf. Chapter 7, p. 172). The implications of this are significant. Conboy (2002: 168 pp.) explains part of *The Sun*'s success by relating it to oral traditions of sensational and hyperbolic gossip. He argues that the paper draws on the 'grotesque and bodily humour of the carnivalesque' (ibid: 169). Both celebrity gossip and the sport can be seen as showing elements of this. Picking up on similar points, Bird views the scandals favoured by tabloids as 'folklore', arguing that they draw on and contribute to existing narrative traditions (1992: 162 pp.; 1997).

Following these thoughts, the act of gossiping can be understood as a form of moral tale-telling constitutive to human society. As can be observed in the example above, readers talk about this material "as if" it affected their own life, thus allowing conversations to start concerning what they perceive as "right" and "wrong".

Bird (1997: 102) points out: 'I believe that this is the key to the enduring appeal of scandal – that it is *one* type of narrative that helps people structure their view of what the world is and how it should be' (original italics). In the example quote from FG12-UK above, participants agree on the morally charged issue of the effects Kate Moss' behaviour has presumably had on her child and on other young girls who might read about the fashion model's drug problem. This works as a conflict-reliever. The atmosphere in the group had been rather tense before as opposing positions were raised; however, readers' ideas of "right" ways of motherhood and the personal traits of a role model provided issues to unite around. Representing their sense of 'what the world is and how it should be', this brings to mind Dahlgren's argument about the 'vision of the good' entailed in 'passions' (2006). Chatting about scandal and gossip, then, could be regarded as stimulating this 'vision of the good', encouraging readers to discuss, negotiate, and cohere around morally and socially important matters, at the same time fostering a sense of orientation, stability, and community. In accordance with Langer's demand (1998) that we regard 'trivial' media content as equally important as 'hard' news, the ritualistic and symbolic functions of such material are brought to life here (cf. also Connell 1991; 1992). The tabloids' "trivial" story-types can, indeed, be recognised as beneficial to the social and cultural engagement of audience members, through providing spaces for meaningful talk about social norms and values.

## SPACES OF NEGOTIATION

### Representing 'un-pc' Opinions

A further aspect to this relates to readers' perception of the tabloids as 'big voices' in society (JOSH [FG10-UK]). The papers were regarded as somewhat autonomous in the way that they state their views. This is, for instance, addressed by VERA in the quote referred to at the beginning of this chapter. Commending the fact that *Bild* does not 'sugar-coat' the shocking details when reporting on the floods, she indicates that this kind of 'shocking' coverage is typical for *Bild*, but unusual if viewed in the context of the German media landscape. Indeed, a distinct element of 'daringness' (MATTHIAS [FG4-UK]) and 'indiscretion' (BERTRAM [FG5-G]) was pointed out by many German participants, involving the view that *Bild* regularly 'breaches social taboos' (INGO [FG6-G]). Similarly, in the UK, *The Sun* was singled out for its 'un-pcness' (SAMUEL [FG11-UK]), and referred to as 'outspoken' (DENISE [FG7-UK]), 'naughty' (ADAM [FG11-UK]) or 'cheeky' (PAULA [FG8-UK]). Participants in both countries considered other printed media outlets (in particular broadsheets) as incapable of such qualities, describing them as 'rather well-behaved' (ALEXANDER [FG3-G]), 'a bit too conforming' (BERTRAM [FG5-G]) or 'too afraid of the consequences' (CLAIRE [FG8-UK]). These arguments are significant to the idea that popular papers can provide communicative spaces for the rehearsal and negotiation of social and cultural norms and values. As elucidated by RICKY [FG6-UK]):

'Sometimes, you know, in this pc world, you want a voice to say something totally un-pc and regard it in this way. And that's something quite good about *The Sun*. I sincerely believe that a little titillation is not bad.'

Using strong language, *The Sun* and *Bild* are seen to violate social norms. However, as indicated, readers praise the papers for this ability, describing them as 'talking straight' (SIMONE [FG5-G]), 'telling it as it is' (JOSH [FG10-UK]) and 'tackling sensitive issues in society' (JESSICA [FG12-UK]). Such notions suggest that the tabloids raise arguments which need airing, but which rarely find expression elsewhere. Indeed, readers view the papers as somewhat refreshing counterparts to hegemonic discourses in this respect. QUENTIN [FG11-UK] maintains:

'Obviously when you read *The Sun* you will get strong opinions. And I wouldn't say that I necessarily agree with it at all times, but what I enjoy about it is that it kind of gets a response out of you, a reaction of some sort. That's good – I mean, it may not sway my opinions, but it does make me think, you know.'

The papers' 'strong opinions' thus activate readers, for they endorse views that are otherwise felt to be suppressed within society, which leads to important talk and reflection.

## Venting Social Discourses

As discussed above, notions of stimulation and challenge also come into play with regard to the emotional appeal of popular newspapers. *The Sun* and *Bild*'s sentiments were met with particular enthusiasm if participants considered them as somewhat 'un-pc'. Some of the reactions to *The Sun*'s front page from 30 July 2004, used as a media stimulus for the UK study, can illustrate this. Displaying the headline 'Got the Bastards', the main story of that day covered the arrest of four alleged London bomb attack suspects earlier that month. It is clear that 'Got the Bastards' was considered a provocative statement, addressing emotional rather than intellectual reasoning. CARLA [FG11-UK] self-reflexively asserts: 'I think the intellectual in me says it's not appropriate, but the emotional part says 'YEAH!'. In a similar way, RICKY [FG9-UK] admits: 'They are saying something where you're ashamed that you're actually thinking that too.' These remarks suggest that readers experienced inner conflicts in response to the headline. While feelings of outrage, anger and revenge in relation to the alleged culprits of the London bomb attacks appeared to be shared by the UK participants of this study, actually expressing these emotions raised problems for readers in terms of their reasoning about why they felt that way, and whether it was tolerable to feel or say such things. Indeed, there is some indication that such feelings were considered too close to notions of racism and xenophobia, which were deemed taboo by many. Hence, feelings of anger and outrage appeared to have been considered 'un-pc' by the participants, evoking shame, embarrassment, and a certain fear of exposure. The great deal of controversial debate stimulated by the 'Got the Bastards' headline in all of the British focus groups echoes these conflicts. On the one hand, many participants referred to *The Sun*'s exclamation as 'jingoistic' (JAMES [FG11-UK]), raising concerns that it might 'incite racial hatred' (ADAM [FG12-UK]) and demonstrating detachment from *The Sun*'s morals. On the other hand, a large number of readers took the view that the paper had effectively 'captured the mood of the nation' (RICKY [FG9-UK]) in its front page headline. Exemplifying the controversy over 'Got the Bastards', it is worth examining a longer passage taken from FG12-UK:

MODERATOR: *I'd like to show you a few examples [showing 'Got the Bastards']. I was wondering: what do you make of this? I don't know if you remember the headline* {SUSAN: yeah}, *it was published after the* {SUSAN & DUSTIN: July the 7$^{th}$} *yeah, after the London bombs.*
DUSTIN: Yeah I remember that, cos it was what the general public were feeling at the time–
SUSAN: [interrupts] –yeah, it got the mood right–
JESSICA: [interrupts] –but I don't think it did a lot to help in other situations. You know, with the big thing going on about immigrants these days–
ADAM: [interrupts] –think it's a dangerous headline because it incites racial hatred. And that is irresponsible, really–
JESSICA: [interrupts] –it is irresponsible NOW, but it wasn't at the time.
DUSTIN: If that was an IRA person and they had come up with a headline like that it wouldn't have been deemed a racial thing either {SUSAN: and you'd still say, 'Got the Bastards'!} Yeah, it is regardless of their ethnic background.
SUSAN: I don't think there was any racial element or anything intended.
ADAM: I'd say everybody KNEW that they were Arabs, or of that persuasion.
So, if there was going to be any anti-Arab movement–
DUSTIN: [interrupts] –but then it would've been 'Got the ARAB Bastards'–
ADAM: [interrupts] –no, what I mean is that an anti-Arab movement would have been there anyway, regardless of the headline {JESSICA: yeah} {SUSAN: ye-ah}. But, the question is, did that inFLAME it or make it worse.
[all start talking at once, Susan prevails]
SUSAN: No I REALLY don't think that was inflammatory.

LEWIS: Well, I'd say MOST people are level-headed enough control their feelings on it. You might get the odd one or two, but most people were probably rational enough to think it through.
DUSTIN: It is exactly what someone down at the pub would have said. You can't tell me that when you were at the pub no one said it.
JERRY: Yeah, they might have, but–
DUSTIN: [interrupts] –see, exactly! So THAT's whole point! *The Sun* was saying exactly what the bloke down at the pub would have said.
JERRY: Yeah. But if that person was someone emotionally unstable–
[several start talking at once]
JESSICA: [drowns the others] –but these people blew up Moslems as well {JERRY: I know, I know} they blew up Asian Moslems as well!
JERRY: Yes, and I think they are AWful people {JESSICA: mhm}, but some innocent people are gonna be BRANded along with those awful people. And that's where the danger comes in.
[several start talking at once]
SUSAN: No, really! It doesn't say 'GOT THE BLACK MUSLIM BASTARDS' it just says 'Got the Bastards'!
JERRY: Yes, but you get SOME people that are–
DUSTIN: [interrupts] –but those people would have held those views before anyway
SUSAN: Ye-ah!
JERRY: They might have, but then if you push it a little bit further.
LEWIS: It's like with the movies, isn't it. They're always gonna blame the movies for the violence. But people are going to be violent anyway. I don't think it made a difference that *The Sun* ran that headline.

This conversation is telling for various reasons. The rather passionate mode in which 'Got the Bastards' was discussed in the UK study is exemplified here, reflected in participants' heated engagement with one another, the headline, and its meanings. Linking in with readers' inner conflicts addressed above, the discussion also refers back to specific cultural discourses in the UK. Any media stimulus introduced to the focus groups naturally drew on themes specific to the nation or region in which it was published. In the case of 'Got the Bastards', *The Sun* ran the headline during a time of fierce discussion about the increasing level of ethnic diversity in Britain and the question of whether there is such a thing as a coherent British 'heart'. Indeed, contemplations of 'Britishness', it appears, have become 'the key issue of the moment among politicians, journalists and ordinary people alike' (Baldwin 2008: 1). Acknowledging the increasing national and ethnic diversity of contemporary Britain, the question of how to balance variety and commonality plays a vital role within the debate (cf. ibid). In history, Britain has always integrated other people, allowing difference and diversity. However, the 'Britishness' debate revived in 2005 in the aftermath of the London bombings. Further prompting the debate, the 'Life in the UK Citizenship Test' was introduced in the same year, meaning that those wishing to obtain British citizenship needed to demonstrate their 'sufficient' knowledge of social norms and values in the UK. Meanwhile, media debates about multi-culturalism in the UK frequently include fierce debates about racism (cf. www.media-diversity.org/articles_publications/Media%20debates%20 multiculturalism.htm). Julian Baggini (2007), for instance, asks in *The Guardian* from 23 January: 'How racist is Britain?'

This suggests that *The Sun*'s 'Got the Bastards' front page, by referring to the latest terrorism attacks in London, also addressed important social discourses surrounding notions of diversity, immigration and racism in Britain. Indeed, readers' discussions of the headline mirror this. As evidenced, *The Sun*'s polemic raised intense debate about the headline's true meaning and its effects, reflected by the participants' argument about whether or not it should be considered racist. Some readers understood that *The Sun* had implied a connection between ethnic origin and terrorism; others believed it had simply seized the public mood about the London bomb attacks. This example illustrates the great deal of differentiated debate on the issue occurring throughout the UK groups. A range of participants criticised the strategies employed by the tabloid, showing scepticism about how accurately the paper portrayed modern British society. Voicing such discontent, JESSICA seemed particularly disappointed that *The Sun*'s coverage did not 'help in other situations'. This indicates that she would expect the tabloid to take on the role of appealing to a more diverse Britain – promoting diversity and strengthening matters of social cohesion rather than inciting racial hatred. The debate also revolved around notions of the potential 'dangers' of the headline, merging into a discussion of media effects in general. In particular, JERRY and ADAM represent the view that unspecified "others" may be influenced by *The Sun*'s front page headline in a negative way, while portraying themselves as able to see through *The Sun*'s text[21]. While these readers displayed opinions in opposition to the headline, it is clear from DUSTIN and SUSAN'S passionate reactions that the tabloid's claim worked as a powerful emotional smokestack for them, allowing them to clearly vent their feelings on the issue. Such different viewpoints demonstrate that *The Sun*'s reporting invited a range of opinions, rather than causing readers to uniformly agree with the paper. Such 'struggles for meaning' (Fiske 1987a: 14) are noteworthy, for they reflect the 'struggles for meaning' in society. Linking back to the perception that the papers frequently violate social norms by presenting 'un-pc' stances (cf. p. 200), *The Sun*'s blatant posture encouraged participants to take up positions in opposition to hegemonic (or,

---

21 This connects with my idea of the "ideological imposition" view of tabloids, and the phenomenon of the 'third person effect' occurring in each of the focus group discussions of this study (cf. chapter 7).

indeed, politically correct) discourses raised by other audience members. A distinct sense of 'the good' can, again, be noted in their responses, for ideas about right and wrong ways of addressing ethnic diversity, immigration, racism and related matters in the UK were implied in the discussion. The Sun's headline thus served as a resource for discussing, reviewing, and reassessing socially sensitive issues surrounding the London bomb attacks. Analogous to what has been established above concerning the balancing of individuals' emotions, popular newspapers can be recognised as capable of providing a "negotiative space" for the articulation of (minority) positions by representing views, opinions and sentiments that would otherwise be suppressed in society. Offering interpretations that seem politically incorrect at times, the tabloids provide significant resources for readers to draw on when making sense of important social and cultural discourses. Thus, they contribute to debates in which both majority and minority positions can be brought forward.

## A Sense of Empowerment

A related aspect concerns *The Sun* and *Bild*'s oft-declared focus on the concerns of the "ordinary" people. Indeed, the "ordinary" represents a key to understanding the papers' ability to speak to their readers. Jostein Gripsrud (2000: 289) maintains that 'various brands, forms, and concerns of popular journalism do after all have important ties to the everyday lives, values, and interests of "ordinary people"'. It is often suggested that speaking to these "ordinary" men and women is a powerful tool for success. Johansson (2007a) explains British tabloids' audience appeal and economic success by referring to this ability, amongst other things. Similarly, Stuart Hall (1983) argues that Thatcherism became successful because it managed to communicate in terms that addressed the concerns of the 'ordinary people', thereby promoting a right-wing political agenda.

Without a doubt, many readers of this research similarly believe that *The Sun* and *Bild* truly know their audiences well and are highly familiar with the social reality of the "ordinary" readers. The tabloids' narrative style is, quite clearly, tailored to give that impression. As GARETT [FG10-UK] states: 'It's our language. That's how we'd speak.' Like this reader, many participants felt that the papers essentially 'get the level right' (REINER [FG4-G]) when communicating with them. Moreover, readers see important aspects of their life-worlds reflected in the text. Grounded in the belief that the papers are familiar with their readers' concerns, participants frequently state that they crucially 'address what we feel' (DUSTIN [FG12-UK]), as discussed above. These perceptions contribute to a sense of belonging and togetherness between the papers and an assumed reader community consisting of "ordinary" men and women (cf. also Chapter 9, p. 232). What is more, encouraged by the tabloids' self-portrayal as "the people's organs", participants assume that *The Sun* and

*Bild* have a mission in fighting on their readers' behalf, and for their concerns. In many of the focus groups of this research, a feeling that 'something has to be done' runs through participants' discussions – and they assume that the papers are able to make a positive impact on individual lives and issues of wider social interest (cf. Chapter 7, p. 174). SALLY [FG8-UK] explains: *'The Sun* matters. It sees the people's point of view {ANNA: yeah, the people's view} {PAULA: yeah} and it puts it across.' Very similarly, INGO [FG6-G] maintains: '*Bild* is the only one to care about the burning questions of twelve million people in this country.' Approaching *Sun* and *Bild* as amplifiers and advocates for "the people's voice", readers expect the tabloids to serve the function of watchdogs, safeguarding social justice and equality.

The implications are significant. Viewing tabloids as powerful voice-amplifiers for those whose positions are not heard often in society gives rise to conceptions of popular papers as adjuvant antipodes to the perceived powerlessness of the individual in an increasingly complex world. Indeed, readers' impression that tabloids express what they think in a way that speaks to them creates a vital sense of having a say in issues that otherwise seem distant from their everyday world and realm of control. Such a perceived extra level of support and access contributes to a distinct sense of empowerment observable among the participants in both countries. Essentially, a challenging of existing social power relations is implied here. Johansson (2007a: 98) points out in her textual analysis that British tabloids can be recognised as taking an 'anti-establishment' stance whilst constructing the average reader as 'someone dissatisfied with, and indignant of, those in positions of authority'. Similarly, Rod Brookes (1999: 256) interprets the purpose of the collective pronouns 'we' and 'us' which can frequently be identified in the tabloids' texts, as follows: ''we' is defined as oppositional to government health officials and cabinet ministers, part of a populist discourse which opposes 'us' with politicians in general and bureaucrats, where 'we' would seem to refer to a more vague notion of 'the people''. Such rhetoric brings to mind Fiske's notion of community defined against the 'power-bloc' (1989a: 8) in society. Indeed, the participants of this research demonstrated positions in accordance with this. A certain feeling of neglect also emerged, expressed in the view that one has to resign to the will of those in power. *Sun* and *Bild*, however, were perceived as combatting this through (symbolically) deconstructing such relations.

This transpired in several ways in the focus groups. It is evident, for instance, that readers perceive a certain "fairness" about the tabloids, reflected in the popular view that all men and women are equal before *The Sun* and *Bild*, regardless of their social status. Celebrities and politicians in particular were seen to receive their "just desserts" from the papers. SALLY [FG8-UK] claims that *The Sun* treated Tony Blair in a "fair" way: 'They might have backed him at first, but then afterwards, when he didn't keep his promises, they gave him a really hard time'; and DAVID [FG3-G] reviews *Bild*'s coverage in similar ways: 'It doesn't matter who is in power, if it's the CDU or the SPD – *Bild* won't mince matters. If one of them politicians up there did wrong, the paper will cause a huge stir about it.' A reassuring sense of justice is implied in such tones, rooted in visions of a world in which virtually no-one gets away with an act of wrongdoing. Bearing links to the normative notion of the press as a fourth estate, the idea of tabloids as watchdogs for social justice emerges here – attending to the "equal" treatment of politicians and "ordinary" men and women alike. Important articulations of existing power relations in society are implied in this, as popular papers can be used for the symbolic derogation of social inequalities (cf. also Johansson 2006, who recognises similar functions with regard to the consumption of celebrity stories). Moreover, talking about politicians' performance and virtues entails communicating one's view of what is "good" politics and politician-behaviour. Thus, readers engage in reflections on personal and social values, undermining my argument that tabloids provide spaces for the negotiation of social and cultural discourses.

Approaching popular newspapers as enabling tools for the empowerment of readers, however, raises questions about the nature, scope, and implications of the type of power involved. If the papers are seen to stand up for those who are not socially privileged, this may be interpreted as a form of opposition to the 'power bloc' in a Fiskian sense. Fiske (1989a, b; cf. also Chapter 5, p. 101) argues that the 'resistance' of popular culture audiences takes place within the realms of meaning-creation rather than on a practical, 'radical' or even system-attacking level. Yet he asserts: 'The interior resistance of fantasy is more than ideologically evasive, it is a necessary base for social action.' (ibid 1989a: 10) However, while such forms of dissociation from hegemonic and elite discourses may provide the ground for social change, there are limits to the actual empowerment of the tabloid readership. Richard Seaman (1992) objects to the idea of a potentially insubordinate audience, arguing that oppositional readings serve to stabilise the system and merely channel feelings of dissatisfaction rather than representing the basis for social action. Other than, for instance, the radical press in nineteenth century Britain, today's tabloid newspapers are commercial enterprises rather than autonomous political and social forces. Sparks (1998: 9) notes that while the radical press had a 'didactic intention… to explain, to enlighten, to teach the readers about the world', the primary motive of today's tabloids and their owners is to win the largest possible readership, sell well, and make profit – aims that are achieved, he regrets, 'through entertainment, not education' (ibid; cf. also Chapter 3, p. 57). The commercial role of *The Sun* and *Bild* is, however, reflected in audience responses. Readers clearly demonstrate that they are fully aware of the papers' commercial aims, and even expect them to publish stories that sell well rather than stories that aim at social change (cf. Chapter 7, p. 179). Yet it is important to emphasise that despite this awareness, many participants obtain a crucial sense of empowerment from *imagining* the country's biggest-selling newspaper on their side, speaking and fighting for them. Although the material of this study does not allow for conclusions to be made about whether or not this actually leads to social action, it is noteworthy that readers derive crucial feelings of involvement and belonging from the idea.

## CONCLUSIONS

This chapter has addressed some of the societal benefits of popular newspapers by examining in what ways the tabloids are able to promote notions of social and cultural participation. As will have become clear from the discussion of audience responses, *The Sun* and *Bild* are highly accomplished in reaching their readers, activating and stimulating them, and encouraging them to engage with important social and cultural issues. I have added evidence for the view that the tabloids' news values and presentation style, such as the conciseness of the text and the emotionalised narratives, facilitate alternative access to news which other (more "quality" or "rational") media outlets are less capable of. With regard to the emotionally framed modes of reception invited by tabloids, some of the societal benefits of such 'passions' in media consumption have been pointed out. The emotional sharing that derives from this, for instance, makes news more accessible and easy to relate to. I have, moreover, picked up on Dahlgren's notion of the 'vision of the good' (2006: 26) in which emotions are rooted, arguing that the tabloids' emotionalised texts create a sense of 'personal investment' for readers (Hill 2007: 97). Showing that – crucially – this inspires them to address and discuss 'their view of what the world is and how it should be' (Bird 1997: 102), the tabloids have been regarded as providing a space for meaningful talk about social norms and values; essentially, inspiring audience members to get involved in important social and cultural processes of meaning creation. In support of this view, I have drawn attention to the social aspects of reading tabloids. Fostering talk, providing collective reading experiences, and encouraging social interaction both inside and outside the reader community, the tabloids' sociability is remarkable. In particular their "trivial" content – for instance, stories about celebrities, sports stars or Royals – fulfils such functions. Moreover, relating back to van Zoonen's arguments about the important crossovers between entertainment and information (2005), an engagement with and communication about entertaining material in the tabloids has been interpreted as one way in which readers develop their conceptions of right and wrong, and communicate their 'vision of the good' to others.

The tabloids' content preferences and narrative strategies represent the key to their activating potential. In particular, the understandable and easy-to-relate-to language is valued by readers, contributing to a strong sense that the papers speak to them in their own terms. This, likewise, applies to the readers' idea that the papers tackle issues of relevance to their everyday life-worlds. Contributing to the overall impression that *The Sun* and *Bild* are familiar with the concerns of the "ordinary" people, the tabloids' ability to address the emotional aspects of audiences' lives marks an essential element. Significantly, it is the readers' impression that popular newspapers are somewhat "courageous" in the way they voice 'un-pc' views and sentiments that are not addressed elsewhere in society and need airing. In doing so, the papers stir and vent readers' feelings, particularly on socially sensitive issues. As a consequence, popular papers are seen to lend a voice to their audiences – expressing what readers feel and think on behalf of them. Partially as a response to the tabloids' typical self-portrayal, many participants of this research conceived of *The Sun* and *Bild* as voice-amplifiers and advocates for their readers. This often implied expecting the papers to take on roles of watchdogs for social justice and equality.

There are important opportunities here for readers to sense notions of representation and empowerment. Popular papers provide spaces for voicing opinions that oppose the dominant hegemony by addressing views and sentiments that appear 'un-pc' at times, encouraging readers to likewise articulate such notions, alongside more socially accepted views. Allowing both minority and majority opinions to be brought forward, tabloids thus contribute to essential conversations about socially and culturally significant issues. Rather than limiting the kinds of reader positions possible (as noted by many textual analyses), the papers' polarised stances and strong opinions in fact invite diverse views on an issue, as has been shown. Hence, the papers have an important contribution to make to the social and cultural participation of audiences, for they crucially engage readers in the processes of producing, negotiating, rehearsing and re-inventing important social and cultural norms and values. Overall, then, *The Sun* and *Bild* can be recognised as providing and maintaining alternative forms of social participation. They are capable of addressing socially relevant issues in ways that speak to a mass audience, crucially stimulating their readers and encouraging them to contribute to the processes of cultural meaning production. The papers thus foster audiences' involvement in the reassessment and re-negotiation of social and cultural norms and values.

I have demonstrated that these issues apply to tabloid audiences in both Britain and Germany. However, the responses to *The Sun*'s front page referred to as a case study in this chapter exemplify that the papers' texts as well as their readers' meaning-creation always draw on and contribute to nationally and culturally specific discourses.

The discussion within this chapter has raised important questions about tabloid newspapers' contribution to various notions of community and identity. I will attend to these issues in the following chapter, which deals with popular papers as tools for social belonging and distinction.

# Chapter 9: Managing Identity

## Tabloids as Tools for Social Belonging

The previous chapter's discussion has raised important questions about the community value of *The Sun* and *Bild*. This chapter, in turn, draws attention to audience responses grouped around feelings of togetherness and community. Textual analyses have shown that popular papers offer a range of resources for the construction of a sense of belonging (cf. Chapters 2 and 4). As discussed earlier, scholars have thought about this in terms of the reader community and the context of the nation. As *The Sun* and *Bild* are two national newspapers, the themes of nationhood, national belonging and unity, as well as patriotism, run particularly through this chapter. It has been argued that tabloids nurture and reinforce readers' sense of national belonging significantly (Conboy 2002, 2006; Brookes 1999; Law 2001, 2002; cf. also Chapter 4, p. 93). Yet, these issues have thus far not been examined from an audience point of view.

The following discussion deals with readers' responses to the tabloids' textual construction of regional, national and other collective social belongings. Drawing on Hall's ideas of national and other cultural identities as diverse, contradicting, and constantly re-forming concepts, constructed through strategies of exclusion and inclusion (e.g. 1996), this chapter examines audiences' processes of identifying (and dis-identifying) with the tabloids' text. Exploring how the papers fit in with readers' self-conception, the ways in which *The Sun* and *Bild* can be recognised as having a role in promoting a sense of territorial loyalty and social cohesion are highlighted. Benedict Anderson's concept of 'imagined communities' (1991), likewise, underlies the analysis in this chapter. Anderson foregrounds the social construction of nationhood in the sense that its members, who construct this community by believing that it exists, ultimately create feelings of belonging to a community (cf. also Chapter 4, p. 93). This chapter explores the tabloids' contribution to the establishment and deconstruction of social differences, underscoring the papers' role as resources for 'imagining' diverse modes of social belonging and distinction.

## Rehearsing Nationhood:
## 'The Trouble with this Country'

Both German and British readers of this study leave no doubt that they expect and frequently observe nationalistic tendencies in the two newspapers. As a typical remark, PHILLIP [FG4-G] asserts: 'Addressing patriotic matters and national pride is definitely one of the things *Bild* often does.' Despite this, however, participants raise the idea that precise forms of nationalism and patriotism, such as flags in the front garden or other displays of generic patriotic sentiment, represent somewhat improper behaviour in their country. Frequently, they compare their homeland to other countries, stressing the impression that nationalistic feelings seem more socially acceptable elsewhere. The following exchange illustrates this view [FG12-UK]:

JERRY: The problem is that it's taboo to be patriotic in this country! Everyone's being told it's wrong to say 'I'm proud to be British'.
SUSAN: Yeah!
MODERATOR: Really?
JERRY: Yeah!
SUSAN: Oh ye-ah! Haven't you noticed?
MODERATOR: Erm...
DUSTIN: Yeah, people think you're racist, or associated to the British National Party, or both, if you say you're proud.
JERRY: Whereas in the States, they've all got their flags up, and they all say that America's great, and they celebrate all things American. It's very different from here, the way society's gone.
JESSICA: Yeah, they do that kind of thing in Greece as well.
DUSTIN: And in Poland.
SUSAN: Yeah.

A very similar approach can be observed in the German groups. Discussing patriotic sentiments in *Bild,* readers frequently debated what they self-perceptively termed a 'typical German attitude' (BERTRAM [FG5-G]). As in the UK, the way in which patriotic attitudes are displayed in other parts of the world was regarded as contrary to "the German way", endorsing readers' impressions that the issue is handled with overly tentative social vigilance in their country, as in this example quote [FG6-G]:

INGO: There's a fundamental touchiness concerning notions of national pride that is very typical this country. If you think of the US, for instance, they don't have issues with that. But here in Germany, it always becomes some sort of a problem. Every time we could potentially

be proud of something, any expression of this will automatically be suppressed and questioned, like, 'is this right?', 'is this ridiculous?', or 'is is it even wrong?' I think that's very typical German.
MICHAEL: That's true. Perhaps it's because of our past. There's still a general feeling that we are not ALLOWED to be patriotic in this country, so it just doesn't feel right to flag German nationhood.

Frequently emerging from readers' discussions of the papers' discourses relating to national collectiveness, it is interesting that (as in the quotation above) traces of irritation can be observed in relation to the idea that any exhibition of national pride is immediately scrutinised in 'this country'. This suggests ambivalent feelings towards notions of nationalism and patriotism in both countries. Themed around issues of social acceptance, the examples given demonstrate considerable reservations on both sides, addressing a certain social stigma audiences perceive with regard to recognising themselves as British or German. Indeed, open displays of national pride, of one's own nationality and national belonging are considered somewhat 'unsexy' (RICKY [FG9-UK]). Susan Condor, who acknowledges that English patriotism is a very delicate matter, confirms this. She reports that the respondents in her research were, likewise, highly reluctant to 'adopt an explicitly national footing or to display a sense of patriotic national pride' (2000: 175). Similarly, patriotic sentiment appears a very "un-German" behaviour. As argued by the news and current affairs magazine *Spiegel Online* (2006b): 'National pride, especially when it comes to publicly displaying a love, or even a mid-affinity, for Germany is still simply taboo.'

### Embracing Nationalistic Sentiment: the British Response

Despite perceiving generic nationalistic sentiment as taboo, many readers in the UK demonstrated affirmative stances towards patriotic tones addressed by *The Sun,* approaching the tabloid as an important instrument working to restore pride in their country, as shown in this short exchange [FG12-UK]:

SUSAN: It may not be ok to be patriotic in this country, but I think there's absolutely nothing wrong whatsoever with showing a bit of national pride like *The Sun* does.
JERRY: Yeah, actually I find the paper quite refreshing in that respect.
DUSTIN: Yeah! If there was a bit more national pride in this country we would probably be in a better state than we are now.

There is a note of irritation here, which indicates that these readers do not necessarily agree with the hesitant attitudes towards patriotism and nationalism they perceive in their social surroundings. A theme discussed in Chapter 8 (p. 201) recurs here, revolving around ideas of the tabloids as frequently violating social norms and challenging established values. Indeed, in line with the point about tabloids as spaces for addressing 'un-pc' opinions and sentiments, UK readers feel that *The Sun*, significantly, counteracts the normative trend by representing a 'refreshing' perspective on patriotic attitudes. Such issues in the paper were, quite frequently, referred to as one of the tabloid's main qualities throughout the UK groups. It appears, then, that there is an essential social need for such sentiments, which is met by the tabloid, providing something like a last bastion for feelings of nationhood, patriotism, national loyalty and unity.

This becomes clearer if we consider some of the readers' responses to *The Sun*'s edition of 30 July 2005, displaying the headline 'Got the Bastards'. As discussed in Chapter 8 (p. 201), most UK participants argued that the line had 'captured the mood of the nation' (RICKY [FG9-UK]) and expressed 'what the general public were feeling at the time' (DUSTIN [FG12-UK]). Aside from venting readers' feelings on the recent terrorist attacks in London, *The Sun*'s exclamation was often linked to a sense of nationality, as in the following excerpt of discussion [FG10-UK]:

MODERATOR: *[showing 'Got the Bastards'] I was wondering, what do you think of this?*
[significant uproar; participants talking over each other; it is impossible to single out individual voices]
DANIEL: ... (incomprehensible in parts)... Every English person would say it! It's the way we are, isn't it. We always want to catch the person who did bad things to us.
JOSH: Yeah, it's expressing what we're thinking, that is. In our language.
GARETT: Yeah, right-on! That's standing up for every Englishman, that is. Doing what a lot of us would like to do!

It is evident from this example that *The Sun* addressed issues important to the readers. Speaking to their sense of nationhood and national identity, the headline was seen to have articulated an opinion on behalf of 'every English person'. Elements of *The Sun*'s text, then, are central to readers' construction of a sense of who they are. This is significant if viewed in the light of Michael Billig's arguments (1995) concerning the implied discourses of community and togetherness in the national press, which, as he argues, are symbols of everyday 'banal' nationalism. Billig claims that such symbols are evident in quality as well as popular newspapers; however, it is particularly the language of the latter that has often been recognised as transporting a sense of nationalism (cf. Taylor 1992; Conboy 2002, 2006; Brookes 1999; Law 2001, 2002). There are several ways of articulating this, for instance through the use of structures relating to somewhat opposing conceptions of "us" and "them", often relating to quite xenophobic representations entailing stereotypical images of "good" and "evil". The tabloids' common editorial stance of representing the voice of the little man adds to this, as shown in Chapter 8 (p. 205). All of these aspects can be subsumed under the heading of strategies of inclusion and exclusion, which represent typical genre characteristics (cf. Chapter 2, p. 49). Common to most reception studies in the field is the result that audiences of popular newspapers welcome such notions of inclusion and exclusion offered by the text (cf. Johansson 2007a; Bruck and Stocker 1996; Habicht 2006). With regard to the issue of nationality, a further significant aspect comes into play: the tabloid press' potential to vent readers' emotions. In the particular case of 'Got the Bastards', *The Sun* conveyed both the anger and frustration caused by the recent acts of terror, as well as the triumph at capturing the alleged culprits, as we have seen in Chapter 8 (p. 201). CARLA and QUENTIN [FG11-UK] explain how this relates to their sense of nationality:

CARLA: I think it was just a very scary time, you know. The phrase 'culture of fear' was mentioned a lot round that time. And after the bombings, *The Sun* had these 'we are not afraid' things in it, you know. They made it very clear that ok you can bomb us but we're not going to capitulate ['yeah' from all]. It's that kind of national resistance thing. When something really bad happens like 9/11 or the London Bombs, you want to feel united as a country. And *The Sun* does fulfil that kind of function; it makes you feel like being part of a bigger group.

QUENTIN: Yeah, it will generally cheer you up. There will always be something in *The Sun* where, you know, you're not gonna think 'Oh God the world's so terrible'. Because even if bad things are happening *The Sun* will have an angle on it that says 'yeah, ok, it's bad but, you know, we're gonna get you!'

Important elements specific to the British part of this study are exemplified here. Strengthening feelings of national resistance and solidarity, *The Sun* is seen as an important resource to counteract "the bad" in the world. This greatly contributed to UK readers' sense of national unity. Indeed, the idea of people pulling together in a crisis strongly marked British participants' responses. As a consequence, they were more than willing to embrace feelings of national togetherness and belonging, in response to the outside threat of terrorism addressed by the tabloid.

Ideas of who we are, then, are essentially constituted by ideas of who we are not. Indeed, the notion of "the other" is highly significant to the construction of a national sense of self (cf. also Bond 2006). *The Sun*'s text triggered readers' collective consciousness by addressing notions of 'shared outrage' (Bruck and Stocker 1996: 168). Displaying such sentiments has been particularly highlighted as an important narrative strategy in the popular press (ibid: 244). Philip Schlesinger (1991: 299-300), for instance, argued that national identities are constantly reformed in response to perceived threats from within and without. Drawing on these ideas, Sofia Johansson (2007a: 98), likewise, points out that both the *Daily Mirror* and *The Sun* portray their reader communities as 'under threat' by frequently addressing notions of danger, terror and angst. Hence, in implying an evil "outside other" set upon harming the UK, the 'Got the Bastards' front page of *The Sun* powered readers' sense of solidarity and resistance. Sharing these sentiments, participants experienced a degree of companionship within the group and a sense of social cohesion that fuelled feelings of belonging to a national community. It is clear then that *The Sun*'s headline was seen to promote a positive spirit of nationalism. However, it is also evident from readers' reactions that this particular front page addressed culturally specific discourses of racial hatred, immigration, diversity, and xenophobia, as the previous chapter's analysis into this showed. Working through these related discourses, readers discuss significant notions of inclusion and exclusion, thereby exploring, developing and rehearsing their sense of nationality.

### Avoiding Nationalistic Sentiment: the German Response

The German part of this study marks an intriguing contrast to what has been established so far. It is worth taking a closer look at readers' responses to 'We are Pope', *Bild*'s front page headline of the 20 April 2005 edition, which was used as a media stimulus in the German focus groups to inspire talk about matters of patriotism and nationalism (cf. Chapter 2, p. 49). Evidently, this particular *Bild* title possessed a high recognition value. Introducing it to the German discussions, participants demonstrated great familiarity with the line. This is reflected in the intensity of their responses, which was unparalleled by any other media stimulus used to aid the fieldwork. Clearly, the paper's headline hit a nerve[22].

Similarly to the UK study, participants in Germany took the view that emphasising the national context and accentuating feelings of national pride needs to be understood as a key characteristic of *Bild*, leaving no doubt that they regarded the 'We are Pope' exclamation as an appeal to expressing feelings of national pride. PHILLIP [FG4-G] offers:

'It is obvious that 'We are Pope' is meant to speak to our sense of nationality. It's supposed to stir our collective pride. *Bild* regularly does that; it often displays patriotic tones and national pride.'

In contrast to the UK, however, a great deal of disconcerted feeling and irritation emerged in the German study. Much unlike the laudatory tones characterising pub-

---

[22] Yet, an important context of this relates to the media event created around the death of Pope John Paul II, the election procedures of the Papal Enclave, and the subsequent appointment of Joseph Ratzinger as Pope Benedict XVI (cf., for instance, Döveling 2005; Thull 2005a,b). Capturing the attention of audiences around the world, the subject prevailed in media discourses for quite some time in 2005.

lic reactions to 'We are Pope', *Bild*'s title failed to win audiences' approval[23]. In fact, readers' largely negative responses mark the inverse of the celebratory acclaim discernible in German media debates. To illustrate this, it is worth looking at how readers phrased their disagreement, and which notions they referred to. Significant discomfort and disagreement emerged with regard to linguistic and grammatical attributes of 'We are Pope'; suggesting that a large proportion of *Bild*'s audience did not appreciate the headline's ironic twist and linguistic playfulness (cf. Chapter 7, p. 163). Readers had particular trouble with the idea of being included in the collective 'we' of the headline, showing some degree of confusion and irritation in response to this category. There was, for instance, much bewilderment concerning the question of whom this 'we' was meant to comprise, and whether or not it was ok to include oneself in this group. The following exchange [FG6-G] exemplifies this:

**TRACY:** ... 'We are Pope' – who is we? {**KRISTIAN**: yeah} All of us? The whole country? Or who is we?
**KRISTIAN:** I suppose it's meant to address all of us {**TRACY**: yeah} but the trouble is we can't relate to it.
**LUDWIG:** Exactly!
**SANDRA:** Yeah, I can't relate to it at all. {**LUDWIG**: no} This we, this we – exactly WHO OR WHAT is meant by we??

The readers' frustration with the collective pronoun shows that they are discontent with *Bild*'s text. As discussed, *The Sun*'s implied discourses of community and togetherness, by contrast, were appreciated by its audience, confirming findings from other reception studies (cf., for instance, Johansson 2007a; Bruck and Stocker 1996; Habicht 2006). However, German readers' frustration with the category of the 'we', and their claim of being unable to relate to the headline's exclamation contrasts with such results. Indeed, participants in Germany did not seem to appreciate notions of national unity and inclusion addressed by *Bild*. Particularly if viewed in light of the general result that readers in both countries expected to find easy-to-relate-to texts in tabloids, German readers' confusion and anger suggest that *Bild* failed to satisfy readers' expectations. Thinking about this gap, it could be argued that audiences' frustration was due to a sense of feeling misunderstood, caused by disappointment about the fact that *Bild* neither represented their views nor spoke on their behalf or even in their language. This, then, suggests a certain alienation of the paper from the majority of its readers' views, representing quite the contrary to editor Diekmann's claim that 'We are Pope' had expressed 'what the nation feels' (Hanfeld 2005). Foregrounding their refusal of being included in the 'we', readers

---

23 For some examples of the celebratory public reactions to the headline see the section on 'humour' in Chapter 2, p.49.

put their opposition to the literal sense of the headline in quite straightforward terms. Clearly touching on matters of dis-identification, LENA [FG1-G] criticises the linguistic 'absurdity' of *Bild*'s statement: 'This is just so silly! WE ARE NOT POPE!!' Similarly, DAVID [FG3-G] explicates: 'This WE, 'We are Pope', we Germans, that's bollocks! THAT MAN is Pope, and that's that. But not WE, not all of US!' Such claims, constructed around the argument "it's him, not us", recur in many readers' responses, highlighting their disagreement with being included in the national 'we'.

A second theme concerns the relative absence of ironic understandings (cf. Chapter 7, p. 163). It is important to remember that the participating readers demonstrated considerable genre knowledge and expectations, and largely agreed with the view that 'We are Pope' was meant to address feelings of national pride. Despite this, some uncertainty about whether or not the tabloid's statement should be taken seriously emerged. A few participants wondered if *Bild* was mocking its readers, as the following extract [FG6-G] shows:

MODERATOR: *So – would you then say this is a sort of tongue-in-cheek headline, or do you think that it is to be taken seriously?*
(short pause)
INGO: No, I think they were pretty serious about it.
(short pause)
KRISTIAN: Well, I would assume that it's supposed to be taken seriously. I guess we can assume that. Otherwise it would perhaps say–
MICHAEL: [interrupts] I don't think so, I–
LUDWIG: [interrupts] Nay, they were quite clearly taking the piss!
MICHAEL: Yeah, that's what I wanted to say.
INGO: Mh, I don't know.
LUDWIG: Yeah, come on. They were taking the mickey out of their readers – at least that's what I think. Cos, I mean, 'We are Pope', please! They just can't be serious about that!

As evident in this quote, there is no unity with regard to readers' ideas about *Bild*'s intentions. This relates to a more general aspect of tabloid reading discussed in Chapter 7: readers' responses to popular newspapers are by no means free from conflict and contradiction. As established, audience members in both countries were quite vocal in criticising *Bild* and *Sun*, and many readers detached themselves from the papers and their texts by stating that the 'exaggerated presentation' and 'far-fetched stories' cannot be taken seriously. Yet, in other respects, *Bild* and *Sun* were taken quite seriously, as in the case of the 'We are Pope' headline. The various feelings of discomfort emerging from readers' responses highlight the level of serious scrutiny. The idea that *Bild* might have been mocking them, and the fact that the paper did not live up to their expectations in terms of the way it spoke to them, resulted in frustration and annoyance.

Much of this relates to the fact that the overwhelming majority of participants in Germany were deeply resentful of patriotic discourses addressed by the tabloid. It is interesting to observe that their detachment from the text can be linked to discomfort regarding Germany's political past. Markedly, the Second World War and the legacy of Nazi-Germany are not as remote to readers in Germany today as it might seem. This is evident from readers' vigorous responses to 'We are Pope', which frequently touched upon notions of Germany's social inheritance. Clearly, then, we need to look beyond readers' relationship with the tabloid to extract what is revealed about German national identity and the role *Bild* plays in the construction of this. Essentially, there is a political element entailed in audiences' disagreement with the headline. In each of the focus groups, parts of the discussions revolved around participants' criticism of the appropriateness of perceived resemblances to Adolf Hitler and Nazism. CHRIS [FG4-G] explains:

'The resemblance to a certain period in our past worries me. By no means do we want something like that again! But there's this ONE PERSON on the front page of *Bild*, and he is a GERMAN, and he appears all over the world. So, he's something like TOP LEADERSHIP, cos he's the most senior authority in the Catholic Church. And then, there's this 'WE', like, 'WE GERMANS.''

CHRIS is not alone in making allusions to the Third Reich, and in dismissing such tendencies. Attaching a certain political edge to the persona of the Pope, his appearance and his views, many participants found it difficult to identify with the idea of collectively celebrating one German with a certain ideology. Readers' forceful disidentification with the tabloid's text can, therefore, be understood as a consequence of their repulsion towards the notion of "one man for Germany". Tainted with ideas about the worst of Germany, this concept is met with considerable reservation.

Emphasising the political dimension of such views, part of readers' dissociation from Nazism analogies rests on ideas about *Bild*'s general political bias. Talking about the tabloid as an agent for matters of nationhood, participants frequently emphasised the view that *Bild* typically accentuates the national context. However, the way in which this was voiced often involves detached stances, as PHILLIP [FG4-G] exemplifies:

'In my point of view, *Bild* is very – very FIXATED on Germany. And I would even call it rather hostile to European matters. You know, it is not exactly a – a cosmopolitan paper, it's rather fixated on German matters.'

Observations like this, foregrounding perceptions relating to an anti-European stance of the tabloid and a hegemonic representation of Germany, are often linked to concerns about *Bild*'s political intentions. As illustrated in the sequence below [FG10-G], the paper's patriotic headline caused readers to discursively negotiate its relation to political extremism:

CHRIS: It may seem inappropriate to say this, but I'm convinced that if any extreme right-wing party came to power in Germany again, *Bild* would put on its front page something like 'Yes! Finally, we are German again!'
(short pause)
MATTHIAS: Well, I don't know.
OLAF: Oh no, no. No no no
DIRK: Nah
LUTZ: No
CHRIS: I don't think so.
REINER: Chris is being a little (?snotty?) again.
OLAF: I think that's putting it too blatantly, I don't really believe they would do that.
MATTHIAS: I would agree that *Bild* tends to incite people. I mean, I used to compare the paper to another one that we used to have here; it was called *Der Stürmer*[24]... {OLAF: but Axel Springer was Jewish} Yeah, but even Jews can trim their sails to whatever wind is blowing {HANNES: no} {REINER: no} Yeah, I sometimes think that *Bild* tends to bend the rules quite a bit, and that it vigorously borders on an incitement of people.

Although *Bild*'s headline about the Pope might appear apolitical at first sight, it gave rise to a debate about the tabloid's political position. Some readers even assumed extremist nationalistic tendencies by drawing lines between *Bild* and the Nazi propaganda paper *Der Stürmer* – albeit this issue was disputed, as the example shows. However, conversations like this frequently occurred throughout the German groups, indicating that the tabloid's expression of patriotic sentiment invoked concerns about the assumed dangers of German national consciousness.

Although 'We are Pope' provided an opportunity to indulge in a somewhat "light" interpretation of national pride due to its ironic twist and celebratory request, it is interesting that most of the participants' reactions, in fact, represented the opposite of this. The implications are significant, for they tell a story about what *Bild*'s headline meant to readers, and what a generic sense of German national pride means. Obviously, German patriotism is still rather negatively charged in the eyes of most participating *Bild* readers. Clearly, there is a significant gap in their repertoire to react to discourses of patriotism, national pride and related matters, for no-

---

24  *Der Stürmer* was the name of a weekly Nazi propaganda newspaper published in Germany between 1923 and 1945.

tions of national collectiveness almost self-evidently evoke a historic-political frame of reference that reminds them of the traumas of Nazi-Germany. Viewed in this light, it is not surprising that they forcefully reject the tabloid's patriotic celebration. Moreover, there is considerable evidence for the claim that there is a link between readers' perception of patriotism's lack of social acceptance, and concerns relating to the way outsiders might judge public displays of German national pride. In fact, the notion of "the image outside" appears crucial to German audience responses to 'We are Pope'. Marking an important cause of their refusal to indulge in *Bild*'s Pope-induced patriotism is this illustration below [FG5-G]:

*MODERATOR: Could you tell me a little bit about what it is that makes you groan when you see this headline?*
TANJA: I don't know, I just find it soooo embarrassing!
*MODERATOR: Yeah? What is it that makes it embarrassing?*
TANJA: I don't know, it's just... well I can't really say why. It's just embarrassing. And... so cheesy {FRANZISKA: yeah} I don't know.
SIMONE: Yeah–
(all start talking at once; incomprehensible in parts)
FRANZISKA: That headline, it just comes across so pretentious! I can certainly do without that.
*MODERATOR: What is it that–*
FRANZISKA: [interrupts] –When I read the line for the first time, I immediately turned away and thought: oh my God! If the English or the French read this {NADIA: embarrassing, isn't it} they will go berserk! {NADIA: yeah} They will think: the Germans, they're mad (someone laughs), they're off their rocker {NADIA: (agreeing) mhm}!
*MODERATOR: What is it a French or a British newspaper would have done differently?*
NADIA: It's the whole headline, it would have been completely different {FRANZISKA: yeah}, except in England, of course. THEY would have written something like that too, the Brits. Cos they have a quirky sense of {FRANZISKA: humour?} err, yeah. Not only humour, but they would have written something like that, I don't know why. Maybe because they are a bit weird with their newspapers anyway {SIMONE: mhm}, with the headlines and so forth. But for Germany, I find it a bit sad. I mean, okay, the British tabloids, they frequently make a gaffe {BERTRAM: yeah}, so over there they're accustomed to that {FRANZISKA: mhm}, you know, they're used to the fact that something like that occurs every now and again. But THIS [forcefully taps onto *Bild*'s 'We are Pope' edition, lying on the table in front of her] is just EXTREMELY embarrassing.
FRANZISKA: Yeah. 'We are Pope'. Honestly, the moment I read that, I wanted to leave the country.

A highly significant theme surrounding notions of shame and embarrassment emerges from the way these women made sense of *Bild*'s text. Foregrounding concerns about Germany's image in the outside world, the tabloid's exclamation is viewed as a definite national *faux pas*, causing them to feel embarrassed. It is interesting that insecurities regarding what outsiders might think have been recognised as essential characteristics of German national consciousness (cf. Thomas 2003). The way in which this is expressed here is noteworthy. A remorseful tone can be observed in the women's talk, indicating a somewhat apologetic tone in consideration of the tabloid's text. This points to a somewhat inferior German sense of self in relation to the outside world, while issues of rivalry between nations are likewise implied. The participants above specifically mention Britain and France in this context, two nations whose historical relationship to Germany is notably marked by their opposition to Hitler in the compound of Allied powers. The theme of disagreement with hegemonic ambitions of Germany can also be recognised here again, as the underlying perspective can be traced back clearly to the historical context of the Second World War. We can, likewise, observe that the women here construct a somewhat "worse" alternative to *Bild* as the relevant "other", represented by British tabloids, which are considered even worse. Again, the understatement implied in this comparison demonstrates the level of caution and reservation typical for the way in which German readers handle issues of nationality in the focus groups of this study.

However, it needs to be acknowledged that whilst refusal marks the most dominant theme among the responses to 'We are Pope', a few more optimistic tones also emerged from German readers' responses. Although only one woman out of 41 German participants took apparent pride in the fact that a German was elected Pope, expressing her joy in unambiguous terms, a few others cautiously stated that *Bild* significantly endorses a form of 'healthy' form patriotism, making a positive impact on the overall German reluctance. DAVID [FG3-G] phrases it like this:

'I'd say *Bild* is great because it gives us a bit of HEALTHY patriotism. Really, I think it would do Germany good to show some more national pride and all that. So, it's great that the paper sometimes advances this a bit. It sort of transports a sense of 'yes, we are entitled to love ourselves and our country'! Plus, *Bild* is the ONLY newspaper in Germany prepared to print the German flag on its front page. They dare to do so, and that's what we need.'

Although rare, contributions like this highlight that German readers also occasionally viewed the tabloid's patriotic sentiments through the lens of the "social value view" (cf. Chapter 7, p. 174). In accordance with what has been detailed about the 'British response' (p. 213), participants articulate the view that *Bild* is 'refreshing' in the way it addresses the delicate matter of patriotism. Still, there appears to be a gap between what readers recognise as a certain social necessity for German patriotism, and the actual public display of such sentiments. While it may be acceptable to sense German national pride, it is certainly not suitable to publicly display this, particularly in front of other nations. Illustrating the intense tension surrounding these issues in the German part of the study, these points tell a story about what readers conceive of as "socially accepted" ways of performing (or, indeed, avoiding) "Germanness".

In studies of nationalism, the significance of a common past to notions of nationality and national identity has been pointed out (cf. Gellner 1983). Often, a glorious past has been particularly stressed. However, the findings of this study reveal that a traumatic past plays an equally important role in the formation of a sense of common national identity, as the trauma of the Second World War marks a central focal point from which German readers draw in their construction of a sense of national consciousness. Indeed, *Bild*'s coverage of the Pope's election significantly facilitated ways of thinking and talking about nationhood, national identity and national pride – albeit not in straightforward terms. It could be argued that the way German readers worked through their nation's past and sense of nationality tells a story about the way they rehearse issues to do with the construction of a collective German consciousness. Emotionally contaminated in Germany, the issue of nationalism is not regarded as a particularly good quality of *Bild*. Indeed, the readers participating in this study worked hard to avoid showing any form of collective pride, as shown, devoting a lot of energy to avoiding patriotic sentiment. This strongly relates to what Nina Eliasoph (1998) observed in *Avoiding Politics*. The participants of Eliasoph's research worked hard to demonstrated indifference towards political matters. However, she spectacularly shows that what they do is, indeed, essentially political. Thinking about this in relation to matters of national identity, I, in turn, would argue that avoiding German patriotism and nationalism is essentially German and thus, has a lot to do with constructing national identity. Displaying national collectiveness and national pride appears a very un-German behaviour. Hence, a significant aspect of "Germanness" to the readers of this study consists of disidentification with *Bild*'s text and a lack of national pride. As we have seen, readers often felt the need to show that contemporary Germany bears no resemblance to Nazi times any more. Hence, there is an apologetic tone involved in what might be considered a collective German sense of self. This gives rise to thinking about patriotism's social acceptance with regard to the context in which it is placed.

# FLAGGING NATIONHOOD: SOCIALLY ACCEPTED CONTEXTS OF PATRIOTISM

## Local and Regional Belonging

Having discussed the differences emerging between British and German readers' responses, it is interesting that important similarities can be observed with regard to socially accepted contexts for patriotic feelings. Significantly, audience members demonstrate that *The Sun* and *Bild* can be used as important resources for the construction of a spirit of regional and local belonging.

## Celebrating 'Englishness'

In the UK study, many participants perceive *The Sun* as an essentially British icon. This is evident from remarks such as: '*The Sun* is quintessentially BRITISH, it's like fish and chips, roast beef and Yorkshire puddings' (SUSAN [FG12-UK]); or '*The Sun* is a British institution, that's what it is' (JAMES [FG11-UK]); and '*The Sun* is an important part of the British culture' (ANDREW [FG9-UK]). The territorial context of such views refers to the British nation, of which the tabloid is regarded as an imperative part. However, while such remarks imply a sense of identification with a wider national community, readers' responses to the paper's patriotic discourses often relate to their sense of 'Englishness', rather than 'Britishness'. It is, indeed, significant that the tabloid represents an important resource for celebrating regional (in this case English) identity in a social environment that is otherwise perceived as less and less nationalistic, as we have seen. SALLY [FG8-UK] explains:

'*The Sun* is clearly one of the best papers for celebrating ENGLISHness. They're the only ones that bring up St. George's flag. They don't give a carrot about the Scottish or the Welsh, or the Irish, for that matter! We love it!'

This is interesting if considered in the context of the UK's extended 'Britishness' discussion, touched upon in the previous chapter. Indeed, the notion of 'Britishness' deserves some further attention with regard to the idea that *The Sun* nurtures a sense of regional identity. Essentially, participants of the UK study interpreted the tabloid's patriotic stance as significant in restoring pride in England. This must be viewed against the backdrop of the history of the British Isles. Historically, national unity in the UK is not a straightforward matter, as pointed out, for instance, by Keith Robbins (1998), Norman Davies (2000), and Tom Nairn (1981). Demanding that the United Kingdom needs to be recognised as four nations rather than one, these scholars claim that England, Wales, Scotland and Northern Ireland should, indeed, be regarded as four quite distinct countries. In view of such arguments, an overarching definition of British identity appears hard to find.

Looking at the respondents of this research, debating patriotism with regard to *The Sun* was primarily infused by the desire to strengthen English national identity, while implying notions of detachment from the other British nations. The idea of 'Britishness', then, poses challenges, for ideas about what it is to be considered 'British' differ considerably depending on whom and where is asked[25]. The British Social Attitudes survey reports that fewer people think of themselves as British (Park et al. 2008), and it is clear that the readers taking part in this study also struggled with the notion of 'Britishness'. A lowering sense of British community is, likewise, mirrored in the findings, for the type of belonging readers responded to clearly referred to the region they resided in, or stemmed from. Challenging assumptions about a link between British national identity and the British press as a whole, Brookes (1999: 250) argues that 'the idea of the 'British press' is itself problematic'. He takes up the argument of Britain consisting of four nations, pointing out that Scotland, in particular, has significant national newspapers of its own. Some national titles, including *The Sun*, are even published in Scottish editions (cf. Chapter 2, p. 24). Hence, this study's results can be tied back to the region in which the fieldwork took place (Greater London), for it can be assumed that if the study had been carried out in Scotland or Ireland, the findings would supposedly have shown readers seek to nurture a sense of "Scottishness" or "Irishness", rather than 'Englishness'[26].

In re-emphasising the importance of a relevant "other" to the construction of a sense of national identity, these arguments highlight that whatever is excluded from the community essentially constitutes the 'imagined' borders of the object one senses belonging to. While earlier in this chapter, the relevant "other" in the UK discussions referred to an outside threat linked to other nations, the "other" here relates to the other regions within the British nation. This demonstrates that the 'imagined' communities vary, depending on the context of inclusion and exclusion constructed by the tabloids and sought by their readers.

---

25 A detailed summary of the 'Britishness' versus 'Englishness' debate would exceed scope and purpose of this chapter; however, the matter has been examined in detail elsewhere. Notable works include Linda Colley (1992); David McCrone (1997); Keith Robbins (1998); Norman Davies (2000); Phoebe Griffith and Mark Leonard (2002); Krishan Kumar 2003; Sonya O. Rose (2003); and Richard Weight (2002).

26 There is a particularly lively body of research on the role of the press in Scottish national identity constructions (cf., for instance, Smith 1994; Higgins 2004).

## "Local Patriotism"

A similar theme can be observed in the German study, although readers in Germany generally displayed more reluctance with regard to indulging in *Bild*'s nationalistic and patriotic sentiments, as already shown. However, there is strong evidence for the view that displaying *local* forms of patriotism and territorial belonging are perceived more socially acceptable than the display of generic pride and belonging to the *national* community. The findings show that the majority of participants in Germany demonstrated such territorial loyalties. In examining the discussions of 'We are Pope' again, constructions like 'us up here in the North', as opposed to 'them down there in the South', transport this significantly, as illustrated in the sequence below [FG6-G]:

KRISTIAN: The Bavarians down there in the South, they will have celebrated when they saw the 'We are Pope' headline {LUDWIG: yeah, the Bavarians} cause they're all Catholic down there, aren't they?
INGO: Yeah, you kind of wonder whom *Bild* wanted to address with this headline.
SANDRA: Yeah.
INGO: You know, sometimes it really annoys me that *Bild* scarcely puts something on the front page that would be important to us up here in the North {KRISTIAN: absolutey}. For instance, if a large cruise ship anchored in the Port of Hamburg, or something similar. Clearly all of us would go 'yay!' if they put that on the front page, and the harbour would be full of people, and you wouldn't talk about anything else for days. But the rest of the country? They wouldn't give a damn.
LUDWIG: Yeah, the Bavarians don't give a damn about our ships. And we don't give a damn about their Pope.
SANDRA: Exactly. Because we cannot relate to it.
KRISTIAN: Yeah, right. Are we all Catholic up here in the North? No, quite clearly we're not!
INGO: Right!

The overarching theme of such reflections is, again, concerned with matters of inclusion and exclusion from a collective. As established, the majority of participants consider the paper's attempt to resume the entire country in one general 'we' as problematic. Aside from the Nazi frame of reference, the lack of identification with the subject matters of Catholicism and the Pope play a significant role here. Indicating that issues of Catholicism are of little importance to their everyday lives, the participants in the stretch above foreground matters of exclusion from those to whom the text might have spoken; i.e. Catholic communities in Germany. Such disidentification connects with regional divisions of religious denominations, for Protestants tend to dominate in the North and Northeast, and Catholics tend to prevail in the South and Southwest of the country (cf. the recent statistics issued by the

German Federal Statistical Office at http://www.destatis.de). As most of the German part of the study took place in and around Hamburg in the North, it is not surprising that Catholicism did not find many followers amongst the participants. What is more, some irritation was notable from readers' responses in relation to their perception that, despite the fact that *Bild* addressed the nation as a whole, its headline did not speak to people in Northern parts of Germany. Relating to the idea that readers expect tabloids to be familiar with their everyday life concerns (cf. Chapter 8, p. 205), some disappointment and confusion emerged. Highlighting that, indeed, identification with the subject matter is a crucial prerequisite for displaying feelings of national belonging and collective pride, the notion of Catholicism clearly marks an important context for readers' refusals to be included in the national 'we' of 'We are Pope'.

This relates back to general findings from the area of media consumption that suggest that audiences prefer local media content over national and international coverage. Indeed, the 'cultural proximity' factor has been emphasised as the key to audiences' engagement with media content, suggesting that cultural and historical familiarity, as well as local tastes, attract the most attention (cf. Straubhaar 1991; Hasebrink 2006). This is echoed in the responses of this study's participants. The subject matter of Catholicism evidently lacks such 'cultural proximity', at least from the point of view of readers in Northern Germany. Conversely, the local section of the tabloid was valued rather highly. Consideration of the answers given to the pre-discussion questionnaire's section relating to readers' likes and dislikes about *Bild* (cf. Appendix I) confirms this. Significantly, two thirds of all German participants wrote down aspects relating to *Bild*'s local section in their 'likes' column (for instance, the tabloid's coverage on local events; local job adverts; reviews on new theatre productions or restaurants; scores of local sports teams, etc). In many of the German discussions, readers' felt rather passionate about *Bild*'s local section (cf. Chapter 7, p. 177). Little reservation emerged with regard to the idea of including oneself in a collective 'we', if this referred to the geographical region readers' lived in or felt attached to, rather than the entire country. Such notions of confined territorial loyalty even evoked strong feelings of affection, as reflected in the participants' collective pride in the Port of Hamburg, which can be observed in the previous focus group extract displayed on p. 226. Indeed, feelings of belonging and loyalty were clearly expressed with considerable more ease if these referred to the regional community rather than to the nation. It is clear, then, that tabloids have an important role in providing resources for the construction and maintenance of feelings of belonging to a local community, for readers actively sought such aspects in the papers' text. Yet, it appears that the criteria for territorial attachment lay beyond the papers' textual construction, for whilst they may be able to amplify such feelings, they cannot fundamentally change or redirect these towards the nation. Moreover, local territorial loyalty appears to be interpreted as a form of socially accepted patriotism in the eyes of the readers', whilst a sense of national collectiveness and pride attracts more ambiguous feelings.

In view of these results, Anderson's concept of 'imagined' communities (1999) can be refined. In particular, in the case of *Bild*'s 'We are Pope' headline, this chapter has shown that despite the fact that *Bild* substantially offered textual resources for the construction of nationhood, patriotism and national identity, it is not the nation which attracts readers' feelings of belonging, sharing and inclusion. Indeed, in a society in which various identity constructions are possible, this broad territorial category needs to be divided up into smaller and more precise parts, to which the concept of 'imagined' communities might be applied. Such detachments from the original link of belonging and pride to the nation-state have also been suggested by other scholars, who recognise multiple, 'intersecting local, national, and global loyalties and identities in different contexts' (Gavrilos 2003: 333). Moreover, it seems necessary to expand the definition of patriotic feelings. While 'love' and 'devotion' for one's *country* have often been recognised as the main characteristics of patriotism (cf., for instance, Bar-Tal and Staub 1997; Viroli 1997), Tamir (1997: 31) suggests that the term 'loyalty' is more suitable 'to describe in accurate terms the wider and more general type of feelings, on which abstract patriotism must rely'. The findings of this study, indeed, demonstrate that feelings of *regional* territorial belonging were welcomed much more by British and German readers than feelings of *national* loyalty and pride – with some national flavours, as discussed. In parts, these findings relate back to some of the tabloids' distinctive characteristics, in particular *Bild*'s regionally various content, as well as the different English, Scottish and Irish editions of *The Sun*. Tabloids today, then, can be recognised as important tools in establishing and maintaining a sense of regional and local community and belonging.

## National Sporting Events as Arenas for Unconstrained Patriotic Sentiment

In thinking about context-specific displays of national pride, belonging and unity in relation to tabloid reporting, it is impossible not to touch upon the subject matter of sports. The national context in which stories are told is most explicit in sports reporting (cf., for instance, Blain et al 1993; O'Donnell 1994). Interestingly, sports indeed take on a special role in readers' eyes, quite similar to the distinction many of them make between the "high quality" of the sports reporting and the "low quality" of all other tabloid content (cf. Chapter 7, p. 170). Audiences in both countries confidently demonstrated stark patriotic sentiments in response to the papers' sports coverage, while a generic sense of national pride addressed by *The Sun* and *Bild* was something many felt uncomfortable with. In particular, stories focusing on national football events appeared significant in inviting feelings of national collectiveness and pride. National football support, in particular, was understood as firmly intertwined with patriotic celebration, of which feelings of collective solidarity were regarded an integral component. Singling out the Football World Cup as a strongly patriotic event both for the tabloids and their audiences, the extract below exemplifies this [fg8-UK]:

CLAIRE: I think we're quite patriotic when we've got the World Cup {ANNA: yeah}, the football World Cup.
ANNA: Yeah, and *The Sun*, they say 'have everyone round, and put your flag up' {CLAIRE: definitely}, and–
SALLY: [interrupts] –and they even print the flag on their front page, *The Sun*.
CLAIRE: Yeah, they do that sort of thing.
ANNA: Yeah, and then we go out and put up our flag in our front gardens!
SALLY: Yeah!

Such responses stress the relationship between football and forms of patriotism focusing on the nation-state. Re-considering reactions to *Bild*'s 'We are Pope' headline in this context, it is interesting to note that German readers worked hard to explain the difference between feelings evoked by this line, and feelings evoked by an imaginary football-related exclamation such as 'We are World Champions'. This is further illustrated in the extract below [FG5-G]:

*Moderator: OK now, could you perhaps explain to me why it is you say that 'We are Pope' is not comparable to something like 'We are World Champions'?*
Simone: It is not comparable, it's not comparable at all! It's different with football–
Nadia: [interrupts] –if it was 'We are World Champions' then that is something that we had actually ACHIEVED. OUR team would have worked hard for that {**Franziska**: yeah}, whoever was on the team would have worked hard {**Simone**: yeah}. And football is a lot of FUN, too! But 'We are Pope' really has little relation to that {**Simone**: exactly} {**Franziska**: yeah} because there is only ONE Pope, it's only one person, it's not US.
*Moderator: But in football, is it really WE, I mean, all of US here in this room? I mean, none of us plays football, do we? And so it would not be US, either, would it?*
Franziska: No, but WE hang on the edge of our seats, WE are excited, US Germans! We share–
Nadia: [interrupts] –it's true though that it's not US playing there.
Franziska: Yeah but WE SHARE THE EXCITEMENT in football, we cross our fingers, we join in the frenzy, we are engrossed in watching them play. But we don't do that with a Pope or something (someone laughs).
Nadia: Mhm, yeah… true.
Bertram: Actually, with respect, the comparison to 'We are World Champions' seems quite far off! I mean, in football it's all about the game. And if we become World Champions it's

possible to completely live out the joy without any reservations {**Franziska**: yeah}. Like, you can act it all out {**Franziska**: yeah} in great big arenas or in front of the TV or wherever. I mean, take me for instance: I always meet up with the lads in a pub, and we cheer and shout and drink beer and all of that, and it's just a lot of fun to be part of it, you know.
**Nadia**: Exactly. Whereas it doesn't feel right to celebrate Catholicism and the Pope. As you said, it's completely different with football, 'We are World Champions' just feels completely different.
**Bertram**: It does. With football, you get a kind of patriotism that is totally ok. But with 'We are Pope', you get nationalistic tendencies. That's not ok.

The exchange exemplifies readers' sense that patriotic sentiments are socially acceptable in the context of national football events. As observable from the statements made, indulging in football was seen to significantly transport feelings of community, inclusion and participation. The readers' decided willingness to be included in a national 'we', and their apparently celebratory desire to be patriotic in relation to sports is significant. Throughout the German and British focus groups, there was very little concern about the appropriateness of displays of national pride and collectiveness with regard to national football. This confirms arguments from previous works, which have recognised sports as significant for imagining and constructing national communities. Scholars researching the wider field of nationalism studies have argued that sports, indeed, bear close links to matters of national identity, nationhood, nationalism, and patriotism. Billig (1995), for instance, regards sports as a symbolic modern war between nations, claiming that the signalling of national solidarity in sporting events is an important expression of nationalism. Albeit the existence of a relationship between sports and a sense of nationhood is not universally applicable, (for it can take on several different forms and shapes in different national and regional contexts (cf. Smith and Porter 2004)), the media has frequently been recognised as playing a crucial role in fostering such relationships (cf. Hobsbawm 1990). Press coverage about national sporting events, in particular, with newspapers' vernacular of war and conflict, constituting an arena for symbolically acting out rivalry and competition between nations, are understood as providing important resources for the construction of nationhood and national identity ( cf. Abell et al. 2007; Bishop and Jaworski 2003; Alabarces et al. 2001; Maguire et al. 1999).

These arguments are noteworthy if considered in relation to typical tabloid news values and properties. Popular papers in particular often toy with symbolic rivalries between nations (cf. Chapter 4, p. 93). This could, for instance, be recently observed when England played Germany in the World Cup 2010 quarter-finals. A classic for football fans, *The Sun*'s front page prior to the game alluded to the Second World War, calling its readers to 'Get Ready for the German War Machine – the Old Enemy has Posted the First Knockout Round against England'. Backing

England's team, the online edition of the tabloid on the same day launched a video entitled: 'Your Boys will get one Hell of a Beating!' On the day after the match (which the German team won), *The Sun* titled: 'You let your Country down', whilst *Bild* gloated: 'England got Muellered-out!' (German original: 'England weggemüllert') Clearly, a political function of sports coverage is mirrored in these headlines, for they highlight that modern rivalry between nations can be played out symbolically in sports (cf. Smith and Porter 2004).

Given that sports are a traditionally important subject matter in tabloid reporting, it is perhaps not surprising that the findings of this study confirm such well-rehearsed arguments that foreground a link between media content, sports, and the expression of nationalism and national pride. It is, however, important to stress that a large part of the significance of popular papers' sports reporting lies in the typical narrative strategies of the genre. As can be observed in the quotes offered in this section, indulging in national football support is nearly always intertwined with the sharing of strong emotions. The joint excitement, joy, or disappointment involved when witnessing one's favourite team's performance is, indeed, vital to transporting a sense of participation in a national event, and being part of a national community. Tabloid reporting, as demonstrated in the previous chapter, is generally able to address and raise readers' emotions significantly. Coverage about national sporting events in particular is charged with emotions surrounding rivalry, winning and losing, and feelings of collectiveness, suggesting that popular papers are able to nourish feelings of national unity, pride and identity through their sports coverage. It is, indeed, quite evident that a national sporting consciousness exists among the readers of this study, reflected in the lightness involved in displaying affirmative and celebratory feelings of collectiveness, nationhood and pride in relation to sports. However, it is also clear that such feelings defy a transfer to other arenas of life, for generic patriotic and nationalistic attitudes still seem to raise rather ambiguous feelings in many participants, as shown (cf. also Abell et al. 2007; Condor 2000). This underscores the proposed argument that patriotic reactions to *The Sun* and *Bild*'s texts are essentially context-specific, rather than a straightforward matter.

On a side note, in line with what has been detailed about the 'British response' and the 'German response' to nationalistic and patriotic tones in *The Sun* and *Bild* (p. 213), there is some evidence for cross-national variation regarding the display of national belonging and loyalty in sports, too. While it seems quite natural for England's football fans to flag their support whenever the national team plays, similar displays of patriotic loyalty have long been frowned upon by many Germans, since the end of the Second World War (cf. my discussion regarding 'the trouble with this country', p. 212). However, triggered by the Football World Cup in 2006, which was hosted by Germany, the country experienced a sudden boost in patriotic spirit and flag-waving, which increased during the event as the national team went undefeated until the semi-finals. The enthusiasm with which German people flagged their support was, indeed, interpreted as evidence of the rise of a 'new German patriotism', causing a large number of media reactions. Some exemplary headlines included 'It's Okay to be German Again' in *Spiegel Online* (2006c), as well as 'The Magic of Joy' (German original: 'Magie der Heiterkeit') in *Zeit Online* (2006). Not surprisingly, a constant stream of patriotic exclamations and symbols likewise permeated *Bild*'s coverage during the event. To name a few examples: the front page of the German tabloid on 12 June 2006 read, 'Black-Red-Glorious' (German original: 'Schwarz-Rot-Geil'); on 4 July the paper demanded, 'Now more than ever: Unity and Justice and... FINALE! (German original: 'Jetzt erst recht: Einigkeit und Recht und... FINALE'). Such high-spirited flagging of "Germanness" highlights the ability of national football to lift the mood of a nation. However, it also exemplifies the huge significance of sports in matters of patriotism and national consciousness. Although the euphoria in Germany died down somewhat after the World Cup in 2006, patriotic celebrations were easily resumed in 2010, when the subsequent World Cup took place in South Africa. This indicates an increasing trend towards establishing national football events as socially acceptable arenas for experiencing and celebrating German nationhood and pride.

## Belonging and Distinction: Notions of Status and Class

In addition to the promotion of regional and national identifications, readers' responses in both countries highlight that popular newspapers offer considerable resources for the symbolising of other forms of social belonging and distinction. There is, undoubtedly, an element of class implied in the consumption of tabloids, which is intertwined with notions of status and taste.

### Symbolising Social Status

Recurring in many focus groups of this study, issues of class and taste were closely tied to the reception of different media outlets (also cf. Pursehouse 1991: 118). This might not come as a surprise, as the UK's newspaper market in particular is commonly recognised as 'sharply segmented on social class lines' (Tunstall 1996: 7). However, interesting in the context of this chapter's theme are readers' ideas about the audience of *Sun* and *Bild*. Significantly, most focus group participants drew sharp lines between tabloid readers and people reading other newspapers. The following extract [FG8-UK] exemplifies this:

CLAIRE: I think the main core of *The Sun*'s readers are working class.
SALLY: Yeah, working to middle class.
PAULA: Yeah. To me, the typical *Sun* readers is, like, a builder, or a painters, or decorator.
SALLY: Yeah, the normal working everyday class person. People like us. 'Your Average Jo Public'.
CLAIRE: Yeah!
PAULA: Yeah.
ANNA: That's right, you'd never see a businessman sitting on a train {all shouting at once} –
CLAIRE: Nah, they wouldn't read *The Sun*! They'd read *The Times*, the *Independent* and the *Guardian*, but they wouldn't read *The Sun*! They think it is... {SALLY: below their level} yeah, they think it's below their level. Because it is such an EASY read {SALLY: mhm} and they like to think that they're above us and that they can read more (mocking voice) l-o-n-g, c- o-m-p-l-i-c-a-t-e-d words.
ALL: Yeah!

As seen in this quotation, *The Sun* was quite often identified as a true 'working class paper', closely resembling German readers' perception of *Bild*. It would seem that such perceptions are grounded in the belief that the papers express and promote the views of "ordinary people" (cf. Chapter 8, p. 205), leading readers to think of them as 'the people's paper[s]' (e.g. SALLY [FG8-UK]; MAX [FG3-G]), or 'paper[s] for ordinary men and women' (e.g. JESSICA [FG12-UK]; SIMONE [FG5-G]). This indicates that a sense of being part of a wider community of readers is essentially grouped around occupational categories, which are often linked to notions of class, taste, and social status. Certainly, participants from working and lower middle class professions found it easy to identify with an 'imagined' community of working class readers, as the example above illustrates. These readers can, indeed, derive significant feelings of belonging from this. However, ideas about those who do not read popular papers are of equal importance. As in the example above, the image of the "others" is, without exception, characterised by occupational groups and newspaper reading habits less familiar to the participants, and clearly less important to their everyday social practices. This results in bipolar ideas of "who we are" and "who we are not", indicating that rather clear-cut conceptions of "us" and "them" are tied to the reception of particular media outlets. This can be partially understood as a response to the frequent stereotypical narrations offered by tabloids (cf. Chapters 2 and 8). Yet, the key to unlocking the way in which tabloids can be used as resources for social identity constructions lies in readers' identifications with an 'imagined' community of "others" who are conceived of as leading a similar lifestyle and having a similar taste in newspapers. Tabloid newspapers, by reflecting important aspects of such conceptions, can therefore symbolise parts of readers' identities.

Conversely, readers derive a sense of belonging from the idea that the activity of reading popular papers is spread across all socio-economic groups, thus representing a break through well-established social boundaries. A highly recurrent argument among both countries' participants, indeed, related to the belief that virtually "everyone" consumes popular newspapers. This view was reflected, for instance, in habitual comments such as 'posh heads read *The Sun* as well' (JAMES [FG11-UK]); 'the German Chancellor also reads *Bild*, just like any ordinary workman does' (BERTRAM [FG5-G]); and 'University professors, and people with a first class honours degree read tabloid newspapers, too' (HANNAH [FG1-G]). Thus, audience members express their sense of inclusion and belonging to a fairly comprehensive community of readers, illustrating that *Bild* and *Sun* can be used significantly in bridging social differences. These points also relate to readers' ideas about all men and women being somewhat "equal" before *The Sun* and *Bild*, receiving their "just deserts" from the papers, regardless of their social position (cf. Chapter 8, p. 206).

## Spoiled Identities & Stigma

Despite sensing such important qualities about tabloids, the evidence also suggests that a strikingly large proportion of this study's participants perceive a strong social stigma surrounding the reception of *Sun* and *Bild*. The following piece of discussion [FG11-UK] exemplifies this.

SAMUEL: Some people, if they see me reading *The Sun* they give me dismissive looks. It's like as if they were saying: 'You philistine! You're just such a complete uneducated moron'! (spread laughter and agreeing murmurs)
QUENTIN: Absolutely! If you're carrying *The Sun*, there's certain perceptions being made of you {SAMUEL: yeah, automatically} (all talking at once, agreeing noises) It's like, as if you're not a THINKING person. People assume that you're less intelligent if you read *The Sun*.
JAMES: Yeah, people go mad about it, don't they. Like, they're going, 'oooh *The Sun*, what a load of rubbish' and 'it's all scandal, tits and arse'. And they think that you don't care about really important issues, about how the world works and stuff. It's a badge.
QUENTIN: Yeah.

These arguments, together with a multitude of other discomforting experiences recounted by readers of all socio-economic backgrounds, clearly point to a strong element of judgement and categorisation, which audiences perceive in their social surroundings. Evidently, reading *Sun* or *Bild* transports certain social information that is not always welcomed by readers. Addressing a sense of exposure when engaging with popular papers in public, a note of frustration can be observed in the example above; relating to unflattering stereotypes about tabloid readers as less intelligent, uneducated, immoral, voyeuristic, and page three-fixated. Such devaluing ideas clearly correspond to the negative comments made about popular papers' lack of journalistic and social value in many academic and public discourses about the genre (cf. Chapter 4). Filtering through to readers, the papers' negative images thus impact on their understanding and judgement of tabloids. Indeed, there is a strong case for the existence of a certain "internalised" devaluation of popular papers (cf. also Chapter 7, p. 166)[27]. This is reflected, for instance, in the fact readers regard *The Sun* and *Bild* with cautious scepticism. KATHRIN [FG2-G] explains:

'Some people's reactions make me feel quite uneasy. For instance, my husband always complains about me reading *Bild*. Like, he says to me 'why are you spending money on such crap?' So, of course I think twice about buying *Bild* if everyone around me insists that I shouldn't read it.'

Traces of an "internalised" social devaluation of popular papers can also be found in some observations made in earlier chapters. Notably, both German and British participants habitually referred to *The Sun* and *Bild* in devaluing terms, describing them as 'trash', bad taste', 'crap', and 'rubbish papers', thereby demonstrating disconnected attitudes towards the tabloids' news style. Aside from this, this work has shown that readers' employ various strategies of detachment, using expressions like 'flicking through' rather than 'reading', exerting extended criticism, and claiming the tabloids may have harmful effects on "others" (cf. Chapter 7, p. 162). It would seem that these positions represent reactions to the social stigma audiences perceive regarding tabloids. Interestingly, similar critical and detached views recur in many other audience studies of the genre (cf. Ang 1985; Hermes 1995; Jackson et al 2001; Hill 2005, 2007). This indicates that a certain taste in media outlets is commonly associated with a certain lifestyle, a certain social status and, indeed, a certain social identity, in the eyes of both audiences and those who do not engage with the relevant media formats.

Pierre Bourdieu's study of *Distinction* (1984) and Ervin Goffman's notes on *Stigma* (1963) are useful in placing these thoughts into context. Concerned with the relationship between taste, individual lifestyle and social position, Bourdieu explains how our social identities are shaped by the choices we make. He argues that taste and value judgements are socially constructed, famously asserting: 'Taste classifies, and it classifies the classifier' (1984: 7). Goffman, likewise, maintains that the representation of self often involves using objects (such as media outlets) to

---

27 I am leaning on Röser (2005: 28) with regard to this term. She has observed a similar phenomenon among the readers of women's magazines, and referred to this as 'internalised deprecation'.

give a particular impression to an external audience, explaining that 'society establishes the means of categorizing persons and the complement of attributes felt to be ordinary and natural for members of each of these categories' (1963: 2; for similar arguments cf. Mackay 1997; Baudrillard 1996; Corrigan 1997). Applying these insights to tabloid readers' "internalised" social devaluation of *Sun* and *Bild*, we can assume that this serves to repulse the off-putting image of the "typical" tabloid reader, counteracting unwanted social information in order to re-assess one's own social position.

## Seeking Distinction

Notions of distinction are also highly important, not only to middle class audience sections, but also to participants who would be happy to include themselves in a community of 'working class' readers. Despite viewing popular papers as media outlets that are consumed universally, participants in both countries sharply distinguish between those who admit to reading them, and those who do not. Particularly significant, a recurring theme concerns readers' ideas about people of a somewhat "higher" social status who read the tabloids in secrecy. This is illustrated in the following extract [FG11-UK]:

CARLA: I think it's the class association. You'd associate *The Sun* with working class, so you're not gonna get city bankers on their way to work reading it.
JAMES: But they do read it! That's where you're wrong. It shouldn't really just be classed as a working class paper cos it isn't!
CARLA: Yeah, that's true, but all I'm saying is that they would NEVER read it on the tube or on their tea break, because it's not like the paper has got an associated image with the bankers.
JAMES: But they'd pick it up on their way back home, and then they'd read it behind closed doors! [general sounds of agreement, some spread laughter] That's the difference. I mean, I don't need to hide the paper. I stand up for what I read {MANY: yeah!} 'cos it doesn't show what character you are, it doesn't show the person that you are.
CARLA: Yeah, it doesn't bother me in any way if some people think it's rubbish.

The idea of city bankers reading *The Sun* stresses my argument that tabloids serve to symbolically bridge social differences. It is interesting, however, that audience members' notions of distinction regarding social positions other than "one-self" are equally important. Again, ideas of "us" and "them" come into play, as JAMES and CARLA forcefully dis-identify with those who are not honest about their reading of *The Sun*, claiming that they themselves are not embarrassed about their reading habits. A sense of belonging to a community of readers is, again, reinforced here.

However, in this case the community is believed to consist of people who confidently admit to reading the tabloid.

Yet, the idea of people hiding their reading of popular papers deserves further attention. Notably, the more affluent and well-educated the participants of this study were, the less they wanted to be perceived as readers of *Sun* and *Bild*. JUAN [FG9-UK], for instance, acknowledges: 'I only read *The Sun* when nobody is looking, because I am ashamed (spread laughter). I would never carry *The Sun*. For my life, I wouldn't carry it!' Similarly, a short exchange between SAMUEL and QUENTIN [FG11-UK] highlights that reading *The Sun* can be socially problematic:

SAMUEL: To be honest, I would never turn up to meet my lawyer with a copy of *The Sun* under my arm, or when I go to see my accountant.
QUENTIN: Definitely, there are certain people that I wouldn't advertise the fact that I read *The Sun* to.
SAMUEL: Yeah, there's just too much of a statement behind it.

It would seem that tabloids' stigma poses intense challenges to affluent and well-educated readers, who apparently fear disapproval from their "high-brow" environments. This calls for some of Bourdieu's arguments (ibid) about social power relations and symbolic media power. In his view, the cultural elites (in the quotes above represented by occupational groups, such as lawyers and accountants) retain the ability to dictate over questions of taste by legitimizing their taste and delegitimising the tastes of the working class. It is understandable that delegitimisation is something readers would like to avoid; hence, some audience members portray themselves as having a non-tabloid taste in newspapers. In doing so, they rehearse social norms and values to do with what is commonly associated with good or bad taste, reproducing a hierarchy of taste, and maintaining social differences. This particularly applies to the educated women of this study. ALICE [FG7-UK] confirms: 'It's a class barrier. There are lots of middle-class and perhaps upper-class people, especially women, who read *The Sun* and who can't come out and declare it.' Similarly, ILONA [FG2-G] elaborates on the issue using the significant term 'image-trap':

'To be honest, it is a bit embarrassing to be seen with *Bild*. I mean, if you asked around in the lawyer's office where I work, no-one would admit to reading the paper. I personally would never dream of sitting down for my coffee break and taking out a copy of *Bild* to read it. You fall into an image-trap if you do, because people automatically judge you, no matter who you are. And most people I know just don't want to put up with this image. So, the way it works at the office is, you carry the *Spiegel* [up-marked current affairs magazine], and you read *Bild* – but only secretly, when you're at home.'

This quote tells a story about how belonging and identity can be symbolised through tabloids. Essentially, avoiding being seen reading popular papers can be recognised as a form of social distinction. If Bourdieu is right and we constantly position ourselves in our social surroundings (1984), then any form of dis-identification with tabloid newspapers and their audiences represents the construction of a particular socio-economic identity. Popular papers, clearly, provide a range of resources for readers to draw upon and identify with a social grouping of their choice. Yet, social identities are mental categories rather than factual objects, and community constructions are essentially created by those who believe they exist (cf. Anderson 1991). The examples given in this section, therefore, illustrate how shaping one's own social identity in relation to tabloids involves distinct acts of self-positioning and self-presentation: audiences construct and perform their social identity by including themselves in an 'imagined' community of readers, or an 'imagined' community of non-readers. This links back to Hall's (1996) arguments about identities as not fixed entities but varied constructions, differing according to the setting and the relevant norms and values collectively agreed on in a specific setting. I argue that popular newspapers qualify even more for the construction of social identities over other media outlets, for tabloids represent particularly powerful symbols that transport additional social information to both readers and non-readers.

## Conclusions

The findings presented in this chapter provide ample evidence of how *The Sun* and *Bild* can nurture a sense of community and belonging by offering significant resources for the construction and performance of various social identity formations. It has devoted much attention to analysing ways in which the tabloids nurture constructions of nationhood, national identity, unity and pride in contemporary Britain and Germany, for a range of relevant textual resources endorsing these issues have previously been identified in popular newspapers (cf. Chapter 4, p. 93). However, the results of this study also shed light on the significance of popular papers in the construction of other modes of social belonging, in particular with regard to an 'imagined' belonging to (or, indeed, detachment from) particular social groupings.

As discussed, readers in both countries share the belief that open displays of generic patriotic sentiment are considered socially undesirable in their society. However, whilst this emerged as a common pattern, significant cross-national differences could be identified with regard to audiences' judgement of discourses of national collectiveness addressed by *The Sun* and *Bild*. The specific historical context of each nation plays a central role here, impacting on the ways in which readers construct nationhood and collective belonging in response to the text. In the UK study, most participants were pleased with the nationalistic tones in *The Sun*, interpreting this as a welcome change to common social discourses. The tabloid was seen to bring in a breath of fresh air, much in line with the "social value" view of popular papers (cf. Chapter 7, p. 174), and the idea that the papers "daringly" address sensitive subject matters and vent social discourses (cf. Chapter 8, p. 200). Similar appreciative stances emerged to only a very limited extent in the German part of the study, which was, by contrast, characterised by readers' strong rejection of patriotic sentiments. German participants were highly suspicious and resentful of the appropriateness of nationalistic and patriotic meanings in *Bild*, and an engagement with these matters was often channelled towards discussing the social inheritance of Nazi-Germany.

The issues around which a sense of shared nationhood truly evolved in relation to tabloids proved essentially nation and context-specific. In the UK study, readers' national consciousness and feelings of unity and pride were triggered by notions of resistance in response to an outside threat, as well as the idea of solidarity amongst the British people, who would pull together in times of crisis. If this is viewed as an expression of what readers consider part of their national awareness and sense of self, the tabloid, indeed, provides significant resources for the construction of a sense of national belonging in an increasingly complex and diverse British society. In Germany, a unifying perspective can be seen in the way readers mutually agreed on the view that any articulation of national belonging and pride is fundamentally un-German, suggesting the country's Nazi history has left a deep scar on German national consciousness, which reverberates in their sense of nationhood. In discussing norms and values relating to the tabloids' handling of these issues, readers identify significant aspects of their collective national sense of self, thus working through, negotiating and rehearsing what they conceive of as German or British nationhood.

Aside from referring to nationally diverse discourses addressed by the media stimuli, such variant constructions of nationality and nationhood stress the significance of specific cultural and historical backgrounds in meaning construction taken from the media. This chapter has highlighted that it is not necessarily the nation that readers draw on in their sense-making of belonging. On the contrary, forms of territorial loyalty appear to be of particular importance to readers if they refer to local and regional communities, rather than being linked to the nation-state. Participants in the UK study, for instance, responded a great deal more positively to patriotic discourses articulated in *The Sun* if these fuelled their sense of 'Englishness', rather than 'Britishness'. Similarly, it emerged that *Bild*'s nurturing of what may be termed readers' sense of "local patriotism" was of central importance. Moreover, in both countries, national sporting events emerged as significant arenas for patriotic sentiment and the celebration of nationhood, with some cross-country variations, as discussed. Adding evidence to the point about the construction of territorial belonging as a fundamentally context-specific affair, it can be argued that *The Sun* and *Bild*, indeed, facilitate ways to think and talk about nationhood and national identity. However, it is notable from the responses discussed in this chapter that the most significant criteria for the display of territorial attachment lay beyond the media's textual offers. Hence, tabloids may be able to amplify such feelings, but they cannot fundamentally change or redirect them towards contexts and subject matters other than those chosen by the readers, as the example of *Bild*'s 'We are Pope' headline has shown.

Finally, with regard to other collective social identity formations in relation to tabloids, significant notions of inclusion and exclusion from an 'imagined' community of readers have been pointed out. Evidently, there is a strong social hierarchy implied in consuming tabloid newspapers, reflected in common ideas of a largely 'working class' readership. Notions of inclusion have, indeed, proven equally as important as notions of exclusion, for this chapter has demonstrated that tabloids provide a range of resources for symbolising class, lifestyle, taste, and social status in readers' daily lives. A further key aspect of this relates to the tabloids' social stigma that audiences perceive, as well as the common stereotypical beliefs about the tabloid readership circulating the public domain and filtering through to readers. Senses of self and community can, therefore, be constructed by means of either identification or detachment from popular papers and the 'imagined' audience. Hence, the act of including or distinguishing one-self from the community of tabloid readers represents a highly significant strategy for communicating particular social information and, indeed, identity to others.

# Chapter 10: Tabloid Modes of Engagement

Popular newspapers like the British *The Sun* and the German *Bild* are some of the most contentious media outlets in the UK and Germany. They regularly invite controversy over their morals and methods, their power and responsibility, their political influence and social impact. At best, their reporting is rejected as trivial, vulgar and tasteless; at worst, it is deemed hazardous to the workings of democratic society. The tabloids are, nevertheless, able to attract large audiences, and contribute significantly to the daily lives of millions of readers in Britain and Germany. Yet, they are often accused of 'dumbing down' the masses and manipulating readers' views. On the backdrop of this controversy, this book has considered popular newspapers from the readers' point of view, asking how they view and make sense of tabloids, and investigating the role of the popular media in two democratic Western societies. Examining the crucial relationship between news and entertainment from an audience perspective, this study has provided essential empirical evidence for the social and cultural significance of popular newspapers, calling for an opening up of the agenda and for fresh perspectives on the popular media.

By exploring the reception of two national tabloids from the UK and Germany, the study was characterized by a cross-national comparative perspective and a qualitative design in particular. It has highlighted important similarities between British and German readership responses, and emphasised cross-culturally shared modes of engagement with popular papers. Yet, it also stressed the impact of specific national and cultural contexts on the reading experience, offering significant insight into shared elements, and elements specific to a particular society or system. The cross-national comparative angle has been maintained throughout all stages of the research, for the study has consistently highlighted similarities and differences between Britain and Germany. Building on an extensive discussion of *The Sun* and *Bild* and their individual national contexts, culturally specific trends in dominant academic approaches to the genre have been pointed out, and, finally, readers' responses to the two national tabloids have been compared.

The book was guided by the desire to investigate audiences' reading experiences and explore how readers make sense of the tabloids. It was also guided by a wish to examine cross-national differences and similarities between the two national readership groups. Extensive qualitative material was derived from the responses of 104 diverse adults who participated in 18 focus group discussions spread across the two countries (cf. Chapter 6). Seeking to compare readers' responses to national tabloids in different countries, *The Sun* from the UK and *Bild* from Germany were chosen as the case studies for this research, for these two newspapers can be regarded as similar phenomena in differing contexts. They share a number of key characteristics relating to their commercial, historical, and editorial frames (cf. Chapter 2); yet they exist within differing media systems and journalistic traditions, with particular regard to the divergent tabloid marketplaces and the histories of popular journalism in each of the two countries (cf. Chapter 3). The research sought to explore if these similarities create common reading experiences, and in what ways the different national contexts influence readers' understandings of tabloids.

The theoretical approach this study has taken has largely drawn upon intellectual thinking emerging from the British Cultural Studies tradition (cf. Chapters 4 and 5). In both countries, popular media outlets have been condemned as either trivial or dangerous to the workings of democratic society. Yet, the advocates of the genre (Anglo-American scholars in the main) have demanded the tabloid media and the interests of the audience be taken more seriously, approaching popular papers as important cultural artefacts, and claiming that the papers cannot sufficiently be understood from a rational public sphere perspective. Borrowing from this view, the social and cultural experience of audiences has been brought to the fore in this book.

The findings have highlighted the role of the tabloid media into increasingly diverse societies with rapidly changing media landscapes. The tensions and contradictions surrounding the reading of *The Sun* and *Bild* have been considered, and attention has particularly been drawn to the similarities between audience's responses from the two countries, by showing that four generic modes of engagement with tabloids could be observed (cf. Chapter 7). The book has also sought to shed a more nuanced light on some of the social meanings of the popular press in modern day Britain and Germany. It has considered the papers' potential to fostering social participation (cf. Chapter 8), and explored how *The Sun* and *Bild* fit in with readers' self-conceptions with regard to notions of territorial and other kinds of social and cultural belonging (cf. Chapter 9).

# Reading Popular News

One of the key results of this study concerns the fact that generic modes of engagement with popular newspapers can be identified across the two diverse cultural contexts. Participants in both countries were, overall, involved in discussions with much the same agendas, and the networks of meanings derived from the readership analysis could be grouped around very similar key themes. These patterns suggest that the politics of reading tabloids are, indeed, very similar. If we look at the largely comparable characteristics of *The Sun* and *Bild* described in Chapter 2, it is perhaps not overly surprising that the nature of tabloid storytelling and reporting, essentially, produces such strongly generic modes of engagement. Indeed, common features such as the conspicuousness, the service and opinion journalism, the 'human interest'-centred stories, the polarised stances, the emotion, the personalisation, and the melodrama all contribute to generating a variety of sometimes rather contradictory responses from readers, which are shared across the two countries.

## Genre Knowledge & Classificatory Processes

This book has devoted much attention to exploring the complex classificatory practices employed by readers of *Sun* and *Bild*, demonstrating that participants in both countries confidently alternate between "public" and "private", "serious" and "trivial", "rational" and "emotional" modes of engagement. Some of Peter Dahlgren's early arguments (1988: 294 pp.), from his meta-analysis of various forms of discourse in viewers' talk about news, add a useful context to these findings. As discussed in chapter 5 (p. 103), Dahlgren suggests a principal distinction between 'public' and 'private' viewing modes, by establishing several versions of discursive categories. Among these, he specifies an 'incorporated discourse' of a factual discussion nature. The news items' 'dominant political discourse or some version of it' is the primary subject of this form of talk about news. Dahlgren refers to this as 'the fundamental discourse of the dutiful citizen', claiming that it ranks among the more 'public' forms of discourse about news. Aside from this, he observes a 'trivial/random personal association' discourse whereby viewers link news stories to their everyday life experiences. Moreover, he observes a discourse that he terms 'media awareness', which is characterised by viewers' considerable knowledge of televisual production elements. Each of these reception modes are, according to Dahlgren, of a more 'private' nature.

If we apply these thoughts to the results of this study, it would seem obvious that the critical, "flawed journalism" view, as well as the "ideological imposition" view of tabloids identified in Chapter 7 represent more 'public' and 'rational' reception modes. They embody readers' responses to the tabloids as news media aiming at informing their audiences. These modes of engagement draw on and contribute to the common public discourse surrounding the social disapproval of tabloids. The evidence suggests that the papers' reputation is, indeed, less than favourable in both Germany and the UK; a conclusion built on the observation that dominantly negative perspectives on tabloid journalism can be identified in academic and professional discourses (cf. Chapters 2 and 4). It is worth re-emphasising that various traces of the papers' low public profile can be identified in audiences' responses to *The Sun* and *Bild*, too. Clearly then, the negative social evaluation of the tabloid media shapes the reading experience crucially. Participants in both countries, for instance, lucidly criticise the papers' reporting styles, debatable truthfulness and trustworthiness, their unethical treatment of people and potential political sway, echoing many of the public reactions towards tabloid formats. Likewise, a majority of readers raised serious concerns about *The Sun* and *Bild*'s impact on audiences, whilst disconnecting themselves from the faceless mass of "others" who were portrayed as more easily manipulated than themselves. Traces of Dahlgren's notion of the 'dutiful citizen' can clearly be observed here, much in line with a classic rational, democratic public sphere point of view. Such findings indicate that a certain "internalised" devaluation of the genre is inscribed in readers' views, which results in a variety of critical, ironic, sceptical, or otherwise detached positions.

In this sense, the research results challenge common stereotypes and myths about the audience of popular newspapers that emanate from the debate in Germany and the UK. It is interesting that despite extensive academic knowledge about 'active' audiences and their complex processes and various contexts of meaning-creation (cf. Chapter 5), most critics of the genre seem to be in danger of stereotyping quite a bit. As Sparks states: 'When we make judgements about tabloids, we are also judging audiences, and we are entering the explosive terrain of social worth.' (2000: 29) Indeed, the audience of the tabloid media is often openly or implicitly depicted as dumb, unreflective, uninterested in (and unaware of) important social and political issues, succumbed to voyeurism and mindless entertainment, and less media literate than other media consumers. Such ideas bear links to common, worryingly negative conceptions of popular and entertaining media formats as brainwashing their consumers and abusing their power, as they are represented in the classic Frankfurt School view of popular culture and its audience. As discussed in Chapter 4, fragments of this view still resonate in many contemporary considerations of the popular press in both countries. Regularly, critics caution that tabloids, or tabloidised reporting, can have potentially harmful effects on the proper workings of democratic society. However, it is worth noting that the evidence presented in this book challenges this view. Tabloid readers are, indeed, experts of the genre, highly knowledgeable about the nature of tabloid reporting and its relationship to other forms of journalism. Refusing to believe everything written in the papers and forming their (political or other) opinions accordingly, most of them claimed to turn to alternative sources of news for more in-depth and trustworthy information.

## Important Crossovers

This feeds into the proposed argument that readers in both countries refuse to take tabloids entirely seriously as news media. Such a claim might be viewed as a confirmation of Sparks' idea that the boundaries between tabloid and serious journalism remain clear, for they embody divergent conceptions of news and journalism (cf. ibid 2000). A similar position has also been taken up by German scholar Klaus Schönbach (2000: 72), who suggests that 'the audience has different expectations for different media'. Indeed, the results of this study, on the one hand, confirm such assumptions, for audiences regularly define *Sun* and *Bild* against "quality" or "serious" journalism, as discussed. Readers make sharp distinctions between "proper" newspapers and tabloids, reflected, for instance, in the terms they use to describe the reading activity (also cf. Chapter 6).

However, the complexity of the tabloid reading experience is only partly reflected in this view, for readers experience mixed emotions when engaging with popular papers. Putting it in Dahlgren's terms, a more 'trivial', 'random' mode of engagement can also be observed, which I have called the "light entertainment" view of popular papers (cf. Chapter 7). A great proportion of readers held the view that the papers are to be taken with a pinch of salt. Reading the genre in a joyous, light and mocking way, they down-played the papers' role as a news media, whilst enjoying the fact that the tabloid press does not seem to accord to common established notions of journalistic quality. Such divergent and contradictory modes of engagement are, essentially, generated by the characteristics of the genre, for audiences clearly respond to the hybrid nature of the popular press. The tabloids portray themselves as news media seeking to inform their audiences, but they employ the narrative strategies and story-types commonly associated with entertainment and fiction (cf. Chapter 2 and 7). This is hugely important to readers' understandings of tabloids. Approaching the papers as the hybrids that they are, audiences continuously challenge clear-cut classifications of media outlets as purely information or purely entertainment-centred. The boundaries between these seemingly opposite dimensions of information and entertainment, reason and emotion, hard news and soft news, and all other dichotomies constructed around the genre thus become blurred. In the process of reading tabloids, one and the same aspect articulates opposite interpretations and value judgements, and readers frequently apply conflicting criteria when engaging with popular papers.

Hence, there are important crossovers and connections between the realms of "information" and "entertainment", the "serious media" and the "tabloid media", the "public" and the "private". Indeed, these must be recognised as equally important to both the production and the consumption of the popular press. These arguments bear links with ideas about popular media texts as connecting such seemingly opposing dimensions (cf., for instance, van Zoonen 2005; Klaus and Lünenborg 2001). As an example in action, this book highlights the relationship between information and entertainment from an audience point of view, demonstrating that tabloids are neither just throw-away commodities, nor taken entirely seriously by their readers. Reading popular papers must be recognised as an important and skilful social and cultural practice of concocting entertainment with mixed messages of information and politics, as well as scornful social and cultural issues. Overall, the readers of popular papers are highly resourceful in dealing with the characteristics of the popular press, for they swiftly negotiate the contradictions embedded in the genre, and confidently distinguish between diverse aspects of tabloids. The power of readers' analyses and assessments are, in this sense, remarkable, for they create an extra filter through which popular papers are read and understood.

## A Friction-filled Experience

Essentially, what this implies is that the reception of tabloid newspapers does not take place in a vacuum. To cite Elisabeth Bird (1992: 1-2), reading tabloids is not an isolated cultural phenomenon, but it is interconnected with other social and cultural contexts and systems. Bird argues that connections between components of a culture are 'not actually neutral' (ibid: 2), explaining that no cultural phenomenon exists in an objective space. She uses the metaphor of a 'hall of mirrors', suggesting that 'everything reflects off everything else in ever-repeating images' (ibid). This idea illuminates the argument that readers and non-readers alike are affected by the social discourses surrounding negative perceptions of the popular media and their audiences. Indeed, there is substantial evidence for the view that readers mirror and reproduce these commonly held values about tabloid journalism in academic and public debates in their own interpretations of *The Sun* and *Bild*. I suggest that the critical discourse about tabloid formats is so ubiquitous in the British and German society that it cannot be ignored by consumers. The analysis of audience responses has indicated that even readers who may think nothing of their consumption of popular papers regularly face judgements and disapproval from their peers. Hence, the widespread scepticism towards the genre that emerges here becomes an integral part of the reading experience, impacting upon audiences' views and shaping their social experiences and relationships. It is also worth highlighting that social class, which has previously been identified as an important category impacting on media understandings, proved to be of less significance than formerly assumed. In terms of the papers' negative social image and the impact this has on the reading experience, a critical discourse about the tabloid media could be identified amongst all audience members taking part in this study, regardless of their socio-economic backgrounds. However, more divided nuances emerged with regard to the ways this was perceived as problematic by different participants (cf. p. 221; and Chapter 9). Hence, the tabloid reception process, overall, emerges as an area of tension and contradiction, a constant struggle. This is due to the fact that the same elements of the popular press attract both favourable and deprecatory value judgements from audiences, depending, as I have demonstrated, on the lens they choose to apply. It is, therefore, fair to argue that the consumption of popular papers involves a balancing act, for readers in both countries juggle a variety of contradicting and ambiguous forces as a result of the social devaluation of the genre which is inscribed in their views and exists alongside (and often congruent with) elements they take pleasure in. As a consequence, the reading of popular newspapers emerges as a friction-filled experience.

## The Tabloids' "Negotiative Space"

If we consider conventional ideas about the core purposes of journalism emerging from liberal theories of the media, the servicing of the economic, political and social system through informing the public is placed at the heart of the media's social charges (cf. Curran 1991; Gripsrud 2000; Sparks 1998). However, the tabloids have often been denied such uses. Yet, I have argued in this book that popular papers create an important "negotiative space" in which readers can indulge, take part and participate. Essentially, the tabloids are able to generate this space though their idiosyncratic writing styles and news values. In accordance with arguments about popular journalism as alternative providers of access to the rational public sphere (e.g. Örnebring and Jönsson 2004; Örnebring 2006; Johansson 2007a), *The Sun* and *Bild* make news and current affairs easy to relate to for many readers. Through their concise, simple, straightforward and everyday kind of writing, the papers grant news access and social participation to large audience sections, which other, more "quality" and "serious" media outlets seem less capable of doing.

However, the social meanings of the popular press are more complex than that. Looking at the results of this study, it is evident that the societal interests vested by tabloid newspapers particularly emanate from their highly engaging potential. Their sociability is remarkable, for they provide an array of issues to talk about, offer a number of opportunities for social interaction both inside and outside the reader community, and provide an excellent basis for collective experiences and social bonding. This is relevant if viewed in relation to some of the media's general functions, particularly their purpose of acting as a kind of social glue; of joining together diverse sections of society through setting the agenda and providing issues to talk about; of representing diverse social groupings; and of communicating culturally shared norms and values. In facilitating and maintaining such significant means of social inclusion, sharing, belonging and identification, the tabloids invite their readers to engage with important social and cultural norms and values.

### Developing a "Vision of the Good and the Bad"

The key to unlocking this potential is in the papers' idiosyncratic content preferences and narrative strategies, which create the "negotiative space". In particular, some of the often strongly criticised elements of tabloids appear to activate and stimulate readers significantly. The focus on personality and the 'melodramatisation' of news and events, for instance, encourages a reception mode characterised by a strong sense of identification and emotional sharing. Echoing ideas about the societal benefits of emotions in media reporting, Dahlgren's notion of the 'vision of the good', which is rooted in passions (2006: 26), has served as a frame from which to approach this particular form of participation facilitated by typical tabloid storytypes. I have argued that emotionalised texts create a sense of 'personal investment' (Hill 2007: 97), showing that readers are inspired to address and discuss 'their view of what the world is and how it should be' (Bird 1997: 102). Thus, the tabloids provide an easily accessible space for meaningful talk about important individual and collective norms and values. A similar pattern emerged with regard to the trivial and entertaining material of tabloids, such as the gossip items. Relating back to Liesbet van Zoonen's arguments about the important crossovers between entertainment and information (2005), an engagement with this type of content can be recognised as one way in which readers are able to develop their conception of right and wrong, their 'vision of the good' to others. Indeed, it is not only a vision of the good, but a "vision of the good and bad" that is at stake here, for both are stimulated by the papers and developed by audiences in response to the text.

At its strongest, the criticism of the tabloid media is channelled towards concerns that the papers 'provide the fuel for dangerous populist flames' (Sparks 2000: 25), as a result of their strong language, unbalanced reporting and biased views. Such arguments are not easily countered; I would, indeed, agree with John Langer (1998) that the 'liberal lament' about tabloid journalism is not entirely misplaced. Yet, the popular media has been recognised as significantly contributing to processes of collective meaning creation within society (Hartley 1996). This study confirms this view. Against the backdrop of audiences' extensive genre knowledge, diversified classification practices, and sceptical attitudes towards the popular press, it is remarkable that, in particular, the tabloids' strong, blatant, and often ideologically charged stances are highly valued by readers for their 'titillating' potential. A large part of the tabloids' appeal relates to their ability to tackle issues and invite discussion. Thematising sensitive matters that seem to oppose the dominant hegemony, the papers address matters and opinions that readers feel are otherwise neglected in society. This stimulates them to consider both minority and majority positions, discuss and negotiate opinions, and develop their "vision of the good and bad". Indeed, audiences work their way through what they conceive of as "right" and "wrong" in response to the tabloids' often-controversial stances. The papers, therefore, can be recognised as inviting readers to consider a range of diverse views, rather than limiting the kinds of reader positions possible. Thus, engaging audience members in the production, negotiation, rehearsal, and re-invention of social and cultural norms and values, the tabloids include audiences in important processes of social and cultural meaning production.

Considering these arguments against the backdrop of declining newspaper readership around the world, and the question of what it is people actually want from newspapers today, the results of this study seem to accord with former *Sun* editor McKenzie's view, highlighted in the BBC Radio 4 broadcast *A farewell to print* (2007). McKenzie claims that due to the wealth of alternative sources of news today, our reading habits have become listening and googling habits. As the Internet has emerged as the primary source for news and information, he argues, newspaper readers are not so much looking for an unbiased reporting of events anymore, instead seeking strong opinions and attitudes, provocation and analysis, which can help them make sense of the world and work through news and events. These comments stress the important role of *The Sun* and *Bild* as organs giving expression to 'un-pc', yet popular voices, a feature which audience members in both countries have praised elaborately.

A chicken-and-egg problem I have touched on a number of times in this book is implied in what has been said so far. The issue at stake relates to a general controversy in media studies about the power of the media versus the power of the audience (cf. Gauntlett 2008; as well as Chapter 4). I have taken the view that each of the antipodal positions of the debate has something to offer to the other, and that the truth, as always, lies in between. Clearly, the challenges of ownership concentration and the mass media's power over the agenda of a country are undeniable and need to be considered when thinking about popular papers' impact on society. However, the readers consulted in this research have demonstrated that there is a limit to the tabloids' influence on their views. They were profoundly critical of the papers' morals and methods, and highly aware of the sensitive relationship between the displayed views and commercial aims. Their often critical and detached positions can, indeed, be interpreted as a response to the tabloids' negative social image, which results in an "internalised" devaluation and widespread scepticism of the genre. I would therefore suggest that, in view of such confident judgement, concerns about the tabloid media's ideological impact on audiences might be overdone.

Yet, reading tabloids involves a careful balancing of notions of ideology, pleasure and, indeed, resistance to what is perceived as the dominant ideology. This is reflected in some of readers' conceptions of *Sun* and *Bild*. Partly in response to the papers' self-portrayal, they are frequently regarded as voice amplifiers and advocates of their readers, seen to take on roles as watchdogs of social justice and equality by expressing what the readers feel and think on their behalf. In a way, such interpretations bear links to the socially significant role of the radical press in nineteenth-century Britain, which marked a strong focal point in the country's development of tabloid journalism. Indeed, important notions of representation and empowerment are implied in readers' regard for tabloids. In accordance with positions advanced by Langer (1998) and Fiske (1992), it is therefore possible to think of popular news as an alternative forum to 'the dominant ideological order established by the serious news' (Sparks 2000: 26). Indeed, a certain feeling of neglect could be observed in participants' talk, reflected in the view that one has to resign to the power of dominant master-codes. *Sun* and *Bild*, however, were regarded as combating such forces through representing the perspective of those not often heard in society, as indicated above. Fiske's notion of community, defined against the 'power-bloc', springs to mind here. His idea of popular pleasure existing in relation to the opposition to power (1989a: 49) implies that some of the essential enjoyments of consuming the popular media derive from the production of such 'oppositional' readings. However, while Fiske maintains that such "resistive" pleasures are essentially subversive and can lead to social change (ibid: 10), I suggest that there are limits to this. Conceiving of *The Sun* and *Bild* as watchdogs of social justice and equality entails addressing social power relations, which can, indeed, be deconstructed symbolically through the text, as I have shown. However, it is questionable whether this leads to actual social change. Following Seaman (1992) and Sparks (1998), I would caution that the sense of empowerment readers derive from this is more likely to sustain existing power relations, rather than foster social action – which is, indeed, highly different from the role of the radical press in nineteenth-century Britain. The idea of readers' resistance to a common dominant ideology through tabloids, then, entails more symbolic forms of empowerment. Such resistive readings differ from actual political resistance, for they predominantly affect the realm of readers' inner feelings and provide reassurance. However, it is disputable whether this leads to substantive societal change. In a way, such concerns are also reflected in audiences' views, for readers appear rather sceptical towards the papers' social consciousness; despite perceiving the tabloids as advocates of their audiences, many participants of this research put forward the belief that the tabloids were more interested in making profit than in advancing readers' welfare.

## Belonging and Becoming

Still, *The Sun* and *Bild* are strongly capable of raising issues relevant to readers' everyday life-worlds; addressing social discourses in ways that speak to a mass audience, and stimulating readers to engaging with these matters. As discussed, the papers, in generating a "negotiative space", provide for the rehearsal and negotiation of important social and cultural norms and values. A crucial theme relating to this concerns the papers' role in promoting a sense of social and territorial belonging and cohesion. Building on existing knowledge about how popular papers might contribute resources to readers' construction of community and identity derived from a few textual analyses, I have explored audience responses to the papers' invitations to constructing national, cultural, and other social belonging (cf. Chapter 9). Benedict Anderson's concept of 'imagined' communities (1991) has provided the basic analytic approach. Anderson foregrounds the social construction of communities by arguing that feelings of belonging are created by the members of a community, who construct it by believing that it exists (cf. Chapter 4). I have also based my considerations on Stuart Hall's ideas about national and other social and cultural identity formations as diverse and contradicting concepts that are constantly reformed through strategies of exclusion and inclusion (1996). *The Sun* and *Bild* have been identified as important resources for readers' construction of social belonging and distinction. They foster social bonding and unity, facilitate forms of territorial loyalty, and provide the ground for diverse modes of identification and detachment from the 'imagined' readership of the papers. Thereby, the tabloids appear particularly capable of providing for the construction of important senses of self and collective identity in contemporary Britain and Germany – two diverse societies in which a multitude of 'imagined' national and other cultural identity formations are possible.

With regard to a sense of territorial attachment and belonging nurtured by the tabloids, the research has drawn attention to the papers' ability to stimulate communication about socially agreed ways in which patriotism and national pride are handled in either country. Linking in with what has been established, this is an example of how the tabloids foster talk and reflection about social and cultural norms and values. Challenging readers through the somewhat 'un-pc' celebration of nationalism, *The Sun* and *Bild* aid the creation and rehearsal of new ways of dealing with such sentiments. Yet, it is important to note that despite various textual offers for the construction of nationhood, national belonging and, indeed, national pride identified in the tabloids' text (cf. Chapter 4; Conboy 2002, 2006; Brookes 1999; Law 2001, 2002), it is not necessarily the nation that readers draw upon when making sense of their territorial belonging. Instead, forms of attachment and pride linked to constructions of local and regional communities have emerged as rather more important than constructions relating to the nation-state. For instance, participants in the UK study responded more positively to patriotic discourses articulated by *The Sun* if these fuelled their sense of 'Englishness', rather than 'Britishness'. German readers, likewise, celebrated *Bild*'s regional editorial section, which reinforced their sense of "local patriotism". These results stress the role of the local and the regional community to feelings of belonging and identification. Significantly, as such smaller territorial scopes provide an untroubled space for sensing unity and commonality, these feelings appear controversial if applied to the national context in each country. The tabloids, therefore, have an important role to play in fostering social bonding, thereby helping people cope with change, globalisation, and the challenges of increasingly diverse and complex societies. Moreover, the research has demonstrated that readers' ideas about what is part of their national and/or regional identity may be amplified by the papers, but the criteria truly determining whether they sense territorial attachment or not appears to lie beyond the media's textual offers. Audiences' senses of belonging to a community have, for that matter, evolved as subjects of negotiation, highlighting the "fragmentariness" and discontinuity in identity formation (cf. Hall 2003).

This idea becomes even more important with regard to the construction of other social identities in relation to tabloids. We know from a number of previous scholarly considerations about the processes of identity formation that ideas of "otherness" and "difference" are highly significant to building a sense of who we are (cf. Hall 2003). Similar can be said of tabloid readers' processes of social identification. In particular, when looking beyond the territorial frame notions of exclusion have proven all the more important to audiences' community constructions. Social inclusion and, indeed, exclusion in relation to tabloids in this study significantly revolved around matters of status, class and taste, which were linked to common stereotypical conceptions of occupational groups and their relation to tabloid newspapers. In many ways, *The Sun* and *Bild* can be used as important symbols to communicate particular social information to others (cf. Chapter 9). The process of identity formation, then, has emerged as a process of deliberate self-positioning within or outside of the 'imagined' community of readers. In contrast to other aspects of the reading experience which largely appeared to be similar between participants of different socio-economic backgrounds (with a few exceptions, as explained in the analysis chapters), the issue of social class plays a highly significant role with regard to the social acceptance of tabloid consumption, both in terms of readers' real social position, as well as the impression they wished to make on others. The more affluent and well-educated the readers of this study, the more socially troublesome the consumption of tabloids appeared to them. In particular, when moving within the realms of what they perceived as social spaces intrinsically occupied by "non-tabloid" readers (such as the arenas of finance and law, for instance), they sensed a strong need to down-play and deny their consumption of tabloid papers. This could be interpreted as a strategic move to raise their profile, avoiding stains on their image that the perceived social stigma of popular papers might have caused. Such findings fit in well with theories about social identity constructions, particularly those advanced by Pierre Bourdieu (1984) and Ervin Goffman (1963), both of whom have stressed the constructed nature of identity through the choices we make and the symbols we use.

Highlighting the relationship between tabloids and notions of social belonging, the study's results also link in with scholarly ideas about the performance of citizenship, and the essential role of "the cultural" to citizenship-identities. As indicated in the review of literature (Chapter 4), the concept of citizenship has been subject to much re-negotiation over the past 50 years or so. Originally, the term referred to membership in a political community, 'imagined' as a nation-state. Articulating notions of nationhood, the condition of citizenship placed strong emphasis on people's civil and political rights and obligations. However, this narrow understanding has been contested, and has undergone significant changes and reinventions in recent years (. van Zoonen 2005: 7 pp.) Citizenship has, as a consequence, been widened to embrace a larger set of types relating to civil, political, social and cultural domains of life.

In particular, ideas about what has been termed 'cultural citizenship' have inspired scholars working in the field of Cultural Studies. Despite the fact that this condition 'has not been well defined' so far (van Zoonen 2005: 8), it is possible to identify some common ground within different approaches. Elisabeth Klaus and Margret Lünenborg suggest the following definition, synthesising ideas from Turner (1994); Hartley (1999) and others:

'Cultural citizenship represents a constitutive part of citizenship in media society. It includes all of those cultural practices that evolve against the backdrop of unequal power relations; providing qualified forms of sharing of the symbolic resources in society. The mass media play a crucial role in these processes; acting as driving forces and protagonists in the construction of individual, collective, social, self- and other-determined identities.' (Klaus and Lünenborg 2004a: 200)

The authors recognise cultural citizenship as the space in which social and cultural meanings are negotiated, established, maintained and re-invented. The concept of cultural citizenship, then, entails important notions of partaking, sharing and participating, which have been addressed extensively in this book. Fitting in with my arguments about the "negotiative space" generated by tabloids, the papers' constitutive role in contemporary cultural and social practices is brought to the fore once more. Indeed, tabloid newspapers, through their idiosyncratic ways of providing links between readers' 'banal' everyday reality and more complex social issues, can be recognised as making resources available to audiences for participating in the processes that constitute cultural citizenship. Klaus and Lünenborg maintain that the particular sense of cultural belonging derived from participating in these cultural processes represents the essential prerequisite to adopting a citizen-identity; thus providing the ground for engaging with the rights and obligations of political and other social kinds of citizenship (ibid: 201). Similarly, Joke Hermes argues that 'the cultural' needs to be recognised as 'entry' to citizenship, 'in the sense of individuals' and social groups' commitment to the common good (or public interest)' (1998: 158). Such reasoning bears links to what has been discussed with regard to the way readers rehearse and negotiate their "vision of the good and bad", in relation to tabloid story-types that are perceived as ill-conforming to commonly agreed norms.

These observations also relate back to conceptions of identity and citizenship as a performance. Van Zoonen asserts: 'Citizenship [...] is something that one has to do, something that requires performance.' (2005: 123; also cf. Dahlgren 2009: 57 pp.) Examining popular fiction dealing with notions of politics, van Zoonen demonstrates that 'the personalization and popularization [...] facilitate people to perform as citizens' (ibid: 124). In many ways, her reflections are echoed by the results of this research, which have, likewise, stressed the activating and stimulating potential of tabloids, and their ways of facilitating means for the performance of identity. Likewise, the performative nature of audiences' social and cultural identity formations has been stressed by this study. In particular readers' management of various notions of belonging and becoming in relation to popular papers emphasises the staged nature of such constructions, thus adding evidence to the idea that identity is, in large parts at least, a performance. Picking up on similar points, Hartley (1999) has argued that citizenship has become an issue of 'do-it-yourself' in relation to the media. He believes that '[...] citizenship is profoundly *mediated* in the modern/postmodern period– we are all 'citizens of media' (Hartley, 1996: Chapter 3) in the sense that participation in public decision-making is primarily conducted through media' (ibid 1999: 157; original Italics). This implies that constructions, such as various kinds of citizenship, closely tie in with media consumption. However, the idea of 'do-it-yourself' citizenship also suggests that the choice of whether or not to adopt a kind of citizen-identity is at least partly made by the audience, rather than being entirely imposed upon them by the media.

Reading the findings of this research in this sense, the important acts of self-positioning in relation to tabloid newspapers highlight both the performative angle of identity, as well as the fact that identity is something people *do*. When drawing attention to the media as resources for processes of identity construction, it seems important to re-emphasise that identities resemble jigsaw puzzles, which most of us construct from an array of intertwined personal, social and cultural resources that we may not even be fully aware of at all times (cf. Gauntlett 2007). Yet, the findings of this study point to a particularly important role of popular papers as providers of stories for readers' to draw on when constructing ideas of self and community. I am entertaining the idea that tabloid newspapers are, indeed, especially suited for a somewhat "strategic" symbolising of notions of identity for two reasons. Firstly, as will have become clear from the extensive discussion of audience responses, the papers' reputation is less than flattering, and this rubs off on their readers. Secondly, tabloids like *The Sun* and *Bild* are omnipresent media outlets, due to their conspicuous layouts and enormous circulations. Hence, the papers, unlike other press outlets, provoke almost anyone to react (often negatively), whether they read the papers or not. As such, the results of this study have demonstrated that reading popular newspapers transports additional social information to almost anyone in contemporary Britain and Germany. Audience members are highly aware of this, and use this knowledge to manage their social identity, deliberately positioning themselves in a community of tabloid readers, or in a community of non-readers.

## SUBTLE DISTINCTIONS: CROSS-NATIONAL DIFFERENCES

I have so far focused on discussing generic aspects of tabloid reading shared by Britain and Germany. However, while both the production and the reception of *The Sun* and *Bild* can, indeed, be recognised as a comparable social practice, this study has also produced evidence of some national variation. Highly insightful, though at times rather subtle, the core issues of variance supplying nationally diverse contexts of meaning-creation shall be summarised and reflected on in this section. Essentially, the differences I found can be linked back to three interrelated contexts. They relate to particular distinctive features of *The Sun* and *Bild*; notable variances in the two countries' media systems; and specific issues relating to the individual socio-cultural contexts and histories of the UK and Germany.

### Accentuating Specific Socio-Cultural Discourses

The most apparent national differences can be traced back to specific socio-cultural discourses accentuated by the front pages of *The Sun* and *Bild* used as media stimuli in this study. Obviously, any media stimulus used in social research invariably refers to specific discourses relevant to the nation or region in which it is published. Thus, it may not seem overly surprising that the front pages of *The Sun* and *Bild* introduced in the focus groups generated nationally diverse discussion themes, for both the papers' stories and readers' processes of meaning-creation, then, always draw on and contribute to the national contexts in which they exist. As such, the study has produced a few highly intriguing findings relating to national particularities. Audience reactions to the British tabloids' headline 'Got the Bastards' and the German paper's 'We are Pope' front page are particularly worth mentioning here, for they most prominently indicated culturally variant contexts of meaning-creation, referring back to events in the individual countries' recent and distant socio-cultural pasts.

In the UK, *The Sun*'s 'Got the Bastards' front page, obviously, inspired participants to discuss the London bomb attacks of 7 July 2005 and related issues. Notably, readers were involved in debating terrorism as a challenge of increasingly diverse cities like London, a discussion which also contemplated issues of migration and integration, 'Britishness', and right and wrong ways of dealing with notions of xenophobia and racial hatred in the UK. Their responses highlight that these issues are truly important themes to modern day Britain. As such, readers' discussions mirrored significant cultural discourses in the UK (at the time of writing). As pointed out, the tabloid served as a resource for discussing, reviewing, and reassessing some of the socially highly-sensitive matters surrounding the London bomb attacks (cf. Chapter 8). In a similar way, *Bild*'s 'We are Pope' headline was subject to intense scrutiny in the German part of this study. Readers demonstrated a range of resistive and oppositional readings, discussing the legacy of Nazi Germany in relation to the tabloid's headline, and contemplating the rules and criteria for approved "Germanness" as a cause of the nation's past. An intriguing yet auxiliary result of this study, then, relates to the observation that Germany's Nazi period still resonates in the nation's everyday life, impacting strongly on people's conceptions of German nationhood and national identity (cf. Chapter 9).

Thus illustrating that *The Sun* and *Bild* frequently address culturally and socially specific discourses and values which readers take up and work through in their reading of the papers, such observations highlight that notions of national identity are intrinsically nation and context-specific, and as such are hardly comparable to that of other countries. This is also reflected in readers' varying responses to patriotic tones addressed by the tabloids. While both national readership groups perceived open displays of patriotism as a social taboo, they differed with regard to their reactions to the tabloids' articulation of these issues. Linking in with the continuing legacy of Nazism, participants in Germany were highly suspicious and resentful of the appropriateness of nationalistic and patriotic meanings in *Bild*. Unlike in Germany, however, most UK participants seemed rather pleased about nationalistic tones addressed by *The Sun*, interpreting these as a welcome change to common "politically correct" approaches. Similarly, the issues around which nationalism evolved in both countries differed somewhat. UK participants particularly drew on notions of national resistance and the idea of people pulling together in times of crisis in their construction of a national sense of self, while German readers were united in their reluctance to sense any German collectiveness. The significance of 'the ways that the preceding regimes, processes and events were remembered, interpreted and assessed' to a nation's collective sense of self is, quite clearly, highlighted here. This has also been discussed by Tiiu Kreegipuu and Epp Lauk (2007: 42 pp.), who emphasise the role of collective memory (particularly of political events) in the construction of nationality and national consciousness. Thus, recognising history and collective memory as central elements to notions of shared identity, the way these are constructed through the media represents an interesting starting point for future academic research (cf. p. 261).

## Treatment of People & Privacy Laws

Aside from accentuating such specific socio-cultural events, the cross-national differences uncovered by this study relate back to diverse features of the two countries' media systems, and reflect distinctive aspects of *The Sun* or *Bild*. Linking in with significant diversities in Britain and Germany's legal conditions for journalism (cf. cf. Chapter 3), the two national audience groups differed in their assessment of the tabloids' treatment of people. While readers in both countries took a "flawed journalism" approach to the papers (cf. Chapter 7), the issues foregrounded by them differed to some extent. UK readers' dismissed *The Sun*'s treatment of people more forcefully, criticising the tabloid's breeching of privacy rights in relation to the idea that the paper's paparazzi were frequently harassing people for their photograph. There is a direct link here to variations between Britain and Germany's press laws. The legal conditions in Britain are considerably less strict, while journalists' occupational rights and privileges are far more extensive in Germany. It has been argued that this results in a more aggressive and partisan British press (Esser 1998: 126; 315). Interestingly, *The Sun*'s 'lawlessness' is, indeed, closely observed and scrutinised by readers, who critically assess the tabloid's reporting, its editors, and its journalists ethically and morally in relation to commonly agreed social norms and values. This, again, is an indication for the view that audiences are aware of the nature of the genre, and knowledgeable about the issues entailed by the tabloid controversy in both countries.

## Politics and Endorsement Traditions

An accompanying theme links in with the national press' diverse endorsement traditions, causing variation in the way audiences conceptualised the tabloids' relationship with their readers and the papers' alleged political power. As discussed in Chapter 2, *The Sun* and *Bild* take rather diverse approaches to stating their political views. The UK press is traditionally partisan, enjoying a diversity of several national daily and Sunday newspapers with differing political stances. *The Sun*, in particular, habitually takes a firm stand on the political views it prefers, telling its readers on a regular basis which party to vote for. The long-standing endorsement tradition of the British press is echoed by UK readers' responses insofar as audience members quite often point out that all of the British papers are biased. Moreover, this was perceived as an integral component of British tabloids (and, indeed, the entire national press) that hardly attracted any criticism – aside from some statements indicating that readers did not necessarily approve of this feature. Importantly, the diversity of political opinions characterising the British press greatly contributed to readers' sense of freedom of choice; by selecting a newspaper that reflects their views, rather than having to put up with a paper's political persuasion, they do not agree with it. What is more, UK participants tended to foreground the belief that political opinion-formation is, in the end, a matter of individuals making up their own mind rather than *The Sun* swaying people's voting intentions. Having said that, the issue of *The Sun*'s political persuasion did attract concern with regard to a faceless mass of "others", and the tabloid's contended impact on political opinion-formation, reflecting the "ideological imposition" approach to popular papers (cf. Chapter7).

Such noticeable confidence emerging from UK readers' responses with regard to their approach to *The Sun*'s alleged political bias was not mirrored by the German part of this study. Unlike the British press, German print outlets have refrained from declaring their liberal or conservative perspective too openly since the end of the Second World War; a measure taken to avoid any resemblance to Nazi propaganda media. Yet, the claim that the tabloid *Bild* is frequently taking a covert political stance despite this general agreement is regularly raised in Germany, and has repeatedly resulted in public criticism and academic scrutiny (cf. Chapters 2 and 4). Indeed, while the idea of a newspaper overtly supporting a particular political party is, indeed, alien to the contemporary German audience, readers recognised a distinct 'indirect', 'concealed' or 'subtle' political bias in the tabloid's reporting. This perception attracted a wealth of criticism, for participants considered such editorial attempts to swaying their political views as extremely hazardous. Generally, while British readers tended to believe that *The Sun* amplifies a belief that already exists in the public domain, the dominant view among German audience members was that *Bild* can originate an opinion, thus truly manipulating readers' opinions. The notion of 'manipulation', indeed, emerged as highly important and distinctive to the German study, for the term pervaded readers' talk, and occurred often, particularly when concerns were voiced that the tabloid might be used as an ideological propaganda instrument to control the masses' opinions. Such cross-nationally divergent conceptualisations of the tabloids' political sway, therefore, connect with the two countries' different journalistic traditions and tabloid marketplaces. However, this also relates back to dissimilar historical developments in Britain and Germany. UK readers' instinctive reaction implying that political opinion formation is a matter of individuals not of newspapers' political bias, it would seem, is rooted in the country's long-standing democratic tradition. Likewise, Germany's social and political history since 1918 evidently still has some impact on audiences' views. With regard to the fear of manipulation, the idea that tabloids deliver political propaganda disguised as news attracted concern among readers in both countries; German participants, however, seemed considerably more distressed by this thought.

## Regional and Local Content

While these aspects predominantly refer to differences in the two countries' media systems, journalistic traditions and historical developments, other diversities more clearly relate to distinctive features of *The Sun* and *Bild* and the papers' diverse histories. Most notably, a specific element of *Bild* is worth re-emphasising here, for it invited particularly favourable judgements from German readers. The issue at stake concerns the tabloid's focus on regional and local news, represented by the several different regional editions of the paper published in Germany every day. Although each copy of *Bild* contains a set of identical back and front pages, the tabloid's various local versions each include individual material on the area in which it is distributed (cf. Chapter 2). While most of the national newspapers in Germany follow a similar model of 'localisation', such regionalised structures are not as common to the British newspaper landscape, which can more clearly be separated into national and local titles (cf. Chapter 3). However, the German readers in this study were rather pleased with the paper's regional focus. Enforcing strong identification, *Bild*'s local section forges strong ties with its audience, and encourages feelings of belonging and community. As discussed, the high level of identification with *Bild*'s local section is, for instance, expressed in a sense of "local patriotism" (cf. Chapter 9) and reflected in the interesting distinction made by readers between the "high quality" of the tabloid's regional pages and the "low quality" of its remaining content (aside from the sports pages; cf. Chapter 7). A variation on the theme evolved around the regular column of *Heiko Brost*, a *Bild* reporter to the tabloid's Hamburg edition. Commenting on banal everyday nuisances occurring in and around the city, Brost's articles were rather well-received by most German participants, who recognised a specific "service" quality in the reporter's writing, and conceived of him as a personified advocate of readers' everyday concerns within their local community.

## Service and Support

Quite similar to such conceptions, a subtle difference between German and British readers' responses concerns variations in their ideas about the impact of *The Sun* and *Bild*'s appeals, campaigns and petitions, as well as assumptions about whom these may benefit. Linking in with what has been detailed about the "social value" view of popular papers (cf. Chapter 7), UK audience members voiced the belief that *The Sun* can make a positive impact on the national community as a whole. The tabloid was, for instance, seen to maintain social safety through initiatives such as the paper's long-running 'naming and shaming' paedophiles campaign. Such notions bear resemblances to the British tabloids' social inheritance. Stemming from the investigative journalism of the 'New Journalism' period between 1880 and 1914, traces of this particular kind of journalistic fact-finding and critical scrutiny can, indeed, be identified in *The Sun*'s editorial stance of today. Recognising such important social functions, readers view the tabloid as an institution serving to disclose, draw attention to and tackle issues of interest to a wider social public. Similar ideas could be observed among *Bild*'s readers; the German audience, however, was generally more likely to think of the tabloid as a rather personal saviour, attending to individual's needs rather than those of larger social groupings. A strong indication for the highly personal, yet banal everyday life significance readers perceive surrounding the tabloid's potential support, the theme of "going to the paper for help" marked a particularly important discussion topic in Germany. Albeit both national readership groups left no doubt that they believed the tabloids only publish stories that would sell well, the idea of the paper as an individual supporter in the minor and major challenges of readers' everyday lives did not seem to be limited by these considerations in German readers' views. This could be seen as a reflection of *Bild*'s self-evoked image, advanced, for instance, by the paper's long-standing '*Bild* crusades for you' campaigns, which have been hugely successful commercially.

**Humour and Joking**

A last distinctive theme worth mentioning reflects a further diverse characteristic of the two newspapers. As discussed, *The Sun* and *Bild* can be recognised as similar phenomena in general; some aspects, however, are not shared as much as others. Aside from dissimilar approaches to stating their political opinion, the tabloids differ particularly in their emphasis on notions of humour and joking. While *The Sun* has been singled out for specialising in funny word plays, puns and humorous descriptions, such notions are less overtly recognisable in the German tabloid's reporting. *Bild* appears rather more serious in tone, placing more emphasis on summing up the gist of things rather than featuring mocking puns, accentuating jokes and striving to raise a laugh (cf. Chapter 2). Such diverse foci in the papers' style are echoed in the responses of the two national readership groups. In line with the "light entertainment" approach to popular papers (cf. Chapter 7), the British part of this study was characterised by a dominantly "fun"-centred view of *The Sun*, which proved very popular amongst the majority of participants, regardless of their socio-economic status. UK readers often praised the paper's comical style, funny headlines and puns, interpreting *The Sun* as a fun, comic-like, light read. Audience members in Germany also showed some ironic detachment from the genre; however, strongly "fun"-centred approaches and ironic views of *Bild* only occurred to a marginal extent. Moreover, they emerged as somewhat privileged perspectives, for such positions were more likely to be addressed by the affluent and well-educated readers of this study, rather than by audience members from poorer groups.

These cross-national differences reflect the papers' divergent reporting styles, but they may also be a consequence of diverse characteristics of the two national tabloid marketplaces. The variety of national tabloids in the UK, presumably, leads to a much stronger competition than in Germany, raising the need for individual newspapers to stand out from the range of available print outlets. Hence, *The Sun* might have specialised in witty nerve and cheeky humour in order to become more distinguishable, differentiating itself from the *Daily Mirror*, for instance (cf. Chapter 5; Johansson 2007a). In comparison, the German *Bild*, being the country's only national tabloid, enjoys a more advantaged position on the market. However, it also represents the central focal point for criticism, attracting accumulated disapproval and concern from opponents of the genre (cf. Chapter 4). It is interesting that these diverse settings are, likewise, reflected in readers' talk. As a consequence of several of the issues mentioned, somewhat dissimilar discussion patterns could be observed in the focus groups in either country. As mentioned, readers in the UK were more likely to approach *The Sun* as "light entertainment"; hence, the discussion often followed a critical-light movement. In Germany, "flawed journalism" and "ideological imposition" views tended to be more dominant, for readers' talk was marked by a critical-concerned manner of argumentation, and participants were more likely to foreground concerns relating to *Bild*'s presumed manipulative powers on other audience members (cf. Chapter 7). Such differences, however, also point to possibly divergent communication styles in the UK and Germany. For instance, a 'sense of humour' has long been recognised a quintessential element of 'Britishness' and 'Englishness' (cf. Priestley 1976), and the art of pleasing through making jokes is still regarded a desirable social skill in the UK. It would seem that the dominant discussion patterns found by this study, amongst other things, pointed to diverse socio-cultural practices. Likewise, German readers' repeatedly occurring fear of 'manipulation' shows that the impact of a nation's specific tradition and history is, indeed, truly important to media understandings.

## LOOKING AHEAD: FUTURE PERSPECTIVES

Participants' continuously sceptical and critical positions towards genre have struck me as remarkable throughout the research, and the question of where the dominantly dismissive attitude towards the entertainment media stems from deserves some further scholarly attention. Several perspectives can be imagined here, including a study seeking to explore if tabloid readers are, indeed, more critically aware than readers of broadsheets. Focusing on a greater variety of media outlets, such a project might shed a more nuanced light on the notion of 'critical audiences' by generating further knowledge about audiences' trust in the media, and the media's true impact on audiences' opinion-formation. A comparison between tabloid and "serious" media outlets might also produce fascinating insights into whether or not people tend to believe in the serious media more easily, perhaps because they are less scrutinised in the public domain and less devalued socially. Moreover, the relationship between the development of media literacy skills and the social (d)evaluation of individual media outlets might be explored by such an approach.

In terms of extending knowledge regarding tabloid newspaper audiences, there is a case to be made for a detailed investigation of further sections of the readership. It would be highly interesting to explore if the "untypical" readers; i.e. the more affluent and well-educated readership sections, demonstrate reception practices that differ from those established by this study. My results have indicated the existence of such differences to some extent. For instance, the study has shown that ironic reading positions are particularly attributable to readers from privileged social backgrounds – at least with regard to the German audience. Future research could also ask whether there is something like a "professional" reading mode by focusing on journalists and their engagement with tabloids. Albeit many journalists read tabloids, they have not yet been considered a tabloid readership group worthy of scholarly attention. However, they represent the media outlets that regularly refer to stories in popular papers, and can be considered as opinion leaders with regard to the social evaluation of tabloids. A research project investigating their interpretations of the popular press could also be combined with an examination of professional role conceptions.

Similarly, comparing the reception of online and offline editions of both popular and serious newspapers would make a valuable future research topic, particularly against the backdrop of rapidly changing media landscapes and the still burning question of whether the printed newspaper has a future. Likewise, it would be interesting to ask about the value of online and offline forms of editorial participation which many newspapers offer today (for instance, *Bild*'s 'reader reporters'; cf. Chapter 2), and the way this kind of citizen-generated material is perceived by audiences, with particular regard to notions of quality in reporting and issues of trustworthiness.

Furthermore, ideas relating to readers' social identity constructions could be expanded some more. Aside from the socio-cultural frame by which national and other social identity formations have been analysed in this book, the individual psychic processes involved in the construction and maintenance of identity and difference have not been addressed in so much detail. Moreover, it might be interesting to compare the construction of social identities in relation to tabloids with similar processes in relation to other media outlets. For instance, my concluding hypothesis about tabloids as particularly useful artefacts for signalling a certain kind of social identity to others remains to be tested. A further topic for future research in this field concerns the relationship between history, collective memory and the construction of nationality and national consciousness, as well as the role of the media in these processes. These notions might also be examined with regard to the origins of the discomfort triggered by tabloids. For instance, it is worth asking if there is something like collective social memory, which leads us to despise the tabloid media and related formats.

Last not least, having studied two different cultures, the relationship between Britain and Germany seems a fascinating topic for future academic endeavours. Some traces of this were found by this study, but they could not be developed to their full potential for obvious reasons. Hence, studying the image of the one in the eyes of the other, and the media's role in this, might generate highly interesting results of interest to many British and German perspectives both within the academy and beyond.

# Bibliography

ABC (2010) *The Sun: Standard Certificate of Circulation for August 2010*, Berkhamsted: ABC.
Abell, J., Condor, S., Lowe, R.D., Gibson, S. & Stevenson, C. (2007) 'Who ate all the Pride? Patriotic Sentiment and English National Footbal Support', *Nations and Nationalism*, 13(1): 97-116.
Adorno, T. & Horkheimer, M. (1972, originally published in German 1947) 'The Culture Industry', in *Dialectic of Enlightenment*, London: Verso Editions.
*A Farewell to Print*. Can Newspapers Survive? (2007). BBC Radio 4. Sunday, 11 November 2007.
Alabarces, P., Tomlinson, A. & Young, C. (2001) 'Argentina versus England at the France '98 World Cup: Narratives of Nation and the Mythologizing of the Popular', *Media, Culture and Society*, 23: 547-66.
Alberts, J. (1972) *Massenpresse als Ideologiefabrik. Am Beispiel 'BILD'*, Frankfurt am Main: Athenäum-Verlag.
Albrecht, R. (1982) 'Bild-Wirkung – Annäherung an die Wirksamkeit einer Institution', *Neue Politische Literatur*, Jg. 27(3): 351-74.
— (1986) 'BILD-Wirkung (II): Neue Ansichten einer alten Einrichtung', *Neue Politische Literatur*, 31(2): 274-86.
Anderson, B. (1991) *Imagined Communities*, London: Verso.
Ang, I. (1985, originally published in Dutch 1983) *Watching Dallas: Soap Opera and the Melodramatic Imagination*, London: Routledge.
— (1990) 'Culture and Communication: towards an Ethnographic Critique of Media Consumption in the Transnational Media System', *European Journal of Communication*, 5(2-3): 239-60.
— (1996) *Living Room Wars: Rethinking Media Audiences for a Postmodern World*, London: Routledge.
Arendt, F. (2009) 'Explizite und implizite kultivierende Wirkung der Kronen Zeitung', *M&K Median & Kommunikationswissensschaft*, 57(2): 217-37.
Arens, K. (1971) *Manipulation: Kommunikations-psychologische Untersuchung mit Beispielen aus Zeitungen des Springer-Konzerns*, Berlin: Spiess.

Axel Springer AG (ed) (2000) *Ein Bild von BILD: Käuferanalyse*, Hamburg: Axel Springer AG.

Badalori, C. (2003) 'European Citizens and the Media. National Reports: Public Opinion in the European Union, Executive Summary', available at http://europa.eu.int/comm/public_opinion/archives/eb/ebs_158_media.pdf (accessed 25 June 2005).

Baggini, J. (2007) 'How racist is Britain?' *The Guardian*, 23 January 2007.

Baldwin, C. (2008) *Broadcasting Britishness? Identity, Diversity and the Role of the National Media. Conference Report*, Oxford: Said Business School, University of Oxford.

Bar-Tal, D. & Staub, E. (1997) 'Introduction: Patriotism: Its Scope and Meaning', in D. Bar-Tal & E. Staub (eds) *Patriotism in the Lives of Individuals and Nations*, Chicago: Nelson-Hall Publishers, pp. 1-19.

Barbour, R.S. & Kitzinger, J. (eds) (1999) *Developing Focus Group Research: Politics, Theory and Practice*, London: Sage.

Barnett, S. (1998) 'Dumbing Down or Reaching Out', in J. Seaton (ed) *Politics and the Media: Harlots and Prerogatives at the Turn of the Millennium*, London: Blackwell, pp. 75-90.

Baudrillard, J. (1996, originally published in French 1968) *The System of Objects*, London: Verso.

Baum, A. (2001) 'Ein Tiefpunkt', *Message*, (2): 103-105.

BBC NEWS (2000) '"Crisis? What crisis?"', available at http://news.bbc.co.uk/2/hi/uk_news/politics/921524.stm (accessed 25 January 2010).

— (2003) '"Lawless" tabloid days over – Morgan', available at http://news.bbc.co.uk/2/hi/uk_news/politics/2840145.stm (accessed 2 November 2004).

— (2004) 'How did the Sun reporter do it?' available at http://news.bbc.co.uk/2/hi/uk_news/politics/3665420.stm (accessed 25 January 2010).

Bebber, H. (1997) 'Seitenwechsel', *Journalist*, (5): 83-85.

Bechdolf, U. (1999) *Puzzling Gender: Re- und De-Konstruktionen von Geschlechterverhältnissen im und beim Musikfernsehen*, Weinheim: Dt. Studien-Verlag.

Bechmann, R., Bischoff, J., Malander, K. & Loop, L. (1979) *BILD – Ideologie als Ware. Inhaltsanalyse der BILD-Zeitung*, Hamburg: VSA-Verlag.

Becker, C. (1996) 'Ideen statt Schreibe: Der "British way" stellt seine eigenen Anforderungen an Journalisten', *Medium Magazin*, 11(6): 44-46.

Beeston, R. & Theodoulou, M. (2005) 'Saddam "to sue for $1m" over photos taken in prison cell', *The Times*, 21 May 2005: p. 4.

Bek, M.G. (2004) 'Research Note: Tabloidization of News Media. An Analysis of Television News in Turkey', *European Journal of Communication*, 19(3): 371-386.

Berger, F. & Nied, P. (eds) (1984) *Wenn BILD lügt – kämpft dagegen. Neue Untersuchungen, Fallbeispiele und Gegenaktionen*, Essen: Klartext-Verlag.

Billig, M. (1995) *Banal Nationalism*, London: Sage.

Bird, S.E. (1992) *For Enquiring Minds: A Cultural Study of Supermarket Tabloids*, Knoxville: University of Tennessee Press.
— (1997) 'What a Story! Understanding the Audience for Scandal', in J. Lull & S. Hinerman (eds) *Media Scandals: Morality and Desire in the Popular Culture Marketplace*, Cambridge: Polity Press, pp. 99-121.
Bird, S.E. & Dardenne, R. W. (1997) 'Myth, Chronicle and Story: Exploring the Narrative Qualities of News', in D. Berkowitz (ed) *Social Meanings of News?* Thousand Oaks: Sage: 333-50.
Bishop, H. & Jaworski, A. (2003) '"We beat 'em'": Nationalism and the Hegemony of Homogeneity in the British Press Reportage of Germany versus England during Euro 2000', *Discourse and Society*, 14(3): 243-71.
Black, I. (2002) 'How the Sun cast a two-faced shadow on the eurozone', *The Guardian*, 8 January, p. 5.
Blackbourn, D. & Eley, G. (1984) *The Peculiarities of German History*, New York: Oxford University Press.
Blain, N., Boyle, R. & O'Donnell, H. (1993) *Sport and National Identity in the European Media*, Leicester: Leicester University Press.
Blöbaum, B. (1992) 'Die Unerreichten und die Unerreichbaren. Ansätze zu einer Typologie der Nichtleser', in G. Rager & P. Werner (eds) *Die tägliche Neu-Erscheinung: Untersuchungen zur Zukunft der Zeitung*, Münster: Lit Verlag, pp. 45-64.
Blumler, J.G. (1999) 'Political Communication Systems all Change: a Response to Kees Brants', *European Journal of Communication*, 14(2): 241-49.
Blumler, J.G. & Gurevitch, M. (1995) *The Crisis of Public Communication*, London: Routledge.
Blumler, J.G., McLeod, J.M. & Rosengren, K.E. (eds) (1992) *Comparatively Speaking: Communication and Culture across Space and Time*, Newbury Park, CA: Sage.
Bocock, R. (1993) *Consumption*, London: Routledge.
Bohnsack, R. (2000) *Rekonstruktive Sozialforschung: Einführung in die Methodologie und Praxis qualitativer Forschung*, Opladen: Leske & Budrich.
Böll, H. (1974) *Die verlorene Ehre der Katharina Blum oder: Wie Gewalt entstehen und wohin sie führen kann*, Köln: Kiepenheuer & Witsch.
— (1984) *Bild – Bonn – Boenisch*, Bornheim-Merten: Lamuv.
Bond, R. (2006) 'Belonging and Becoming: National Identity and Exclusion', *Sociology*, 40(4): 609-26.
Bordieu, P. (1984, originally published in French 1979) *Distinction: A Social Critique of the Judgement of Taste*, London: Routledge.
Brants, K. (1998) 'Who's Afraid of Infotainment?' *European Journal of Communication*, 14(2): 315-35.
Brants, K., Hermes, J. & Zoonen, L. v. (eds) (1998) *The Media in Question: Popular Cultures and Public Interests*, London: Sage.

Brettschneider, F. & Wagner, B. (2008) '"And the winner should be" Explizite und implizite Wahlempfehlungen in der Bild-Zeitung und der Sun', in B. Pfetsch & S. Adam (eds) *Massenmedien als politische Akteure: Konzepte und Analysen*, Wiesbaden: VS Verlag für Sozialwissenschaften / GWV Fachverlage, pp. 225-44.

Brichta, M.K. (2002) 'Die BILD-Zeitung aus der Sicht ihrer Leserinnen und Leser: Eine qualitative Rezeptionsstudie', unpublished Master thesis, Universität Hamburg, Germany.

— (2010) 'Zwischen Popularität und Abwertung: Zur Bedeutung der "Bild-Zeitung" im Alltag ihres Publikums', in J. Röser, T. Thomas & C. Peil (eds) *Alltag in den Medien – Medien im Alltag*, Wiesbaden: VS Verlag für Sozialwissenschaften, pp. 202-19.

Bromley, M. (1998) 'The "Tabloidising" of Britain: "Quality" Newspapers in the 1990s', in M. Bromley & H. Stephenson (eds) *Sex, Lies and Democracy. The Press and the Public*, New York: Addison Wesley Longman, pp. 25-38.

Bromley, M. & Tumber, H. (1997) 'From Fleet Street to Cyberspace: The British "Popular" Press in the Late Twentieth Century', *Communications*, 22(3): 365-78.

Bromley, R., Göttlich, U. & Winter, C. (eds) (1999) *Cultural Studies: Grundlagentexte zur Einführung*, Lüneburg: zu Klampen.

Brookes, R. (1999) 'Newspapers and National Identity: The BSE/CJD Crisis and the British Press', *Media, Culture & Society*, 21(2): 247-63.

Brooks, P. (1984) *The Melodramatic Imagination?* Columbia University Press.

Brown, L. (1992) 'The British Press, 1800-1860', in D. Griffiths (ed) *The Encyclopedia of the British Press 1422-1992*, Basingstoke: Macmillan Press, pp. 24-32.

Bruck, P.A. & Stocker, G. (1996) *Die ganz normale Vielfältigkeit des Lesens. Zur Rezeption von Boulevardzeitungen*, Münster: Lit Verlag.

Brumm, D. (1980) 'Sprachrohr der Volksseele? Die BILD-Zeitung', in M.W. Thomas (ed) *Porträts der deutschen Presse*, Berlin: Spiess, pp. 127-143.

Buckingham, D. (2000) *The Making of Citizens: Young People, News and Politics*, London: Routledge.

Büscher, H. (1996) *Emotionalität in Schlagzeilen der Boulevardpresse. Theoretische und empirische Studien zum emotionalen Wirkungspotential von Schlagzeilen der BILD-Zeitung im Assoziationsbereich "Tod"*, Frankfurt am Main: Lang.

Carey, M.A. (1994) 'The Group Effect in Focus Groups: Planning, Implementing, and Interpreting Focus Group Research', in J.M. Morse (ed) *Critical Issues in Qualitative Research Methods*, London: Sage, pp. 225-41.

Certeau, M.D. (1984) *The Practice of Everyday Life*, Berkley: University of California Press.

Chippindale, P. & Horrie, C. (1999) *Stick it up your Punter! The Uncut Story of the Sun Newspaper*, London: Simon & Schuster.

Chong, L. (2005) 'Lawyers give split opinions on the strength of lawsuit', *The Times*, 21 May, p. 4.

Chrisholm, L. (1995) 'European Youth Research: Tour de Force or Turmbau zu Babel?' in L. Chrisholm, P. Buchner, H.-H. Kruger & M. Bois-Reymond (eds) *Growing Up in Europe: Contemporary Horizons in Childhood and Youth Studies*, Berlin: deGruyter, pp. 21-32.

Coliver, S. (1993) 'Comparative Analysis of Press Law in European and other Democracies', in Article 19 (ed) *Press Law and Practice. A Comparative Study of Press Freedom in European and other Democracies*, London: International Centre Against Censorship, pp. 255-90.

Colley, L. (1992) *Britons: Forging the Nation 1707-1837*, New Haven, Conn.; London: Yale University Press.

Conboy, M. (2002) *The Press and Popular Culture*, London: Sage.

— (2006) *Tabloid Britain: Constructing a Community through Language*, London: Routledge.

Condor, S. (2000) 'Pride and Prejudice: Identity Management in English People's Talk about "this country"', *Discourse and Society*, 11(2): 175-205.

Connell, I. (1991) 'Tales of Tellyland: The Popular Press and Television in the UK', in P. Dahlgren & C. Sparks (eds) *Communication and Citizenship: Journalism and the Public Sphere*, London: Routledge, pp. 237-54.

— (1992) 'Personalities in the Popular Media', in P. Dahlgren & C. Sparks (eds) *Journalism and Popular Culture*, London: Sage, pp. 64-83.

— (1998) 'Mistaken Identities: Tabloid and Broadsheet News Discourse', *Javnost/The Public: Tablodization and the Media*, 5(3): 11-31.

Corinth, E. (2005) 'Das ist der Wahnsinn! Bild macht uns alle zum Papst!' available at http://www.heise.de/tp/r4/artikel/19/19931/1.html (accessed 9 February 2010).

Corner, J. (1998) *Studying Media: Problems of Theory and Method*, Edinburgh: Edinburgh University Press.

Corner, J. & Pels, D. (eds) (2003) *Media and the Restyling of Politics: Consumerism, Celebrity and Cynicism*, London: Sage.

Corrigan, P. (1997) *The Sociology of Consumption: an Introduction*, London: Sage.

Curran, J. (1991) 'Rethinking the Media as a Public Sphere', in P. Dahlgren & C. Sparks (eds) *Communication and Citizenship: Journalism and the Public Sphere*, London/New York: Routledge, pp. 27-56.

— (2003) 'Press History', in J. Curran & J. Seaton (eds) *Power without Responsibility: the Press and Broadcasting in Britain*, London: Routledge, pp. 1-106.

Curran, J., Douglas, A. & Whannel, G. (1980) 'The Political Economy of the Human Interest Story', in A. Smith (ed) *Newspapers and Democracy: International Essays on a Changing Medium*, Cambridge: MIT Press, pp. 288-316.

Curran, J. & Seaton, J. (2003, sixth edition) *Power without Responsibility: the Press and Broadcasting in Britain*, London: Routledge.

Curran, J. & Sparks, C. (1991) 'Press and Popular Culture', *Media Culture & Society*, 13(2): 215-37.

Curtice, J. (1999) 'Was it The Sun that won it again? The Influence of newspapers in the 1997 election campaign', *CREST Centre for Research into Elections and Social Trends, Working Papers,* 75, available at http://www.crest.ox.ac.uk/papers/p75.pdf. (accessed 3 September 2005).

Custer, U. (1997) 'Tränen, Tiere und Tore: Wechselwirkungen der zunehmenden Boulevardisierung von TV und Presse', *Media Spectrum,* (2-3): 42-44.

Dahlgren, P. (1988) 'What's the meaning of this? Viewers plural sense-making of TV news', *Media Culture & Society,* 10: 285-301.

— (1991) 'Introduction', in P. Dahlgren & C. Sparks (eds) *Communication and Citizenship: Journalism and the Public Sphere,* London/New York: Routledge, pp. 1-24.

— (1992) 'Introduction', in P. Dahlgren & C. Sparks (eds) *Journalism and Popular Culture,* London: Routledge, pp. 1-23.

— (2006) 'Civic Participation and Practices: Beyond "Deliberative Democracy"', in N. Carpentier, P. Pruulmann-Vengerfeldt, K. Nordenstreng, M. Hartmann, P. Vihalemm & B. Cammaerts (eds) *Researching Media, Democracy and Participation: The intellectual Work of the 2006 European Media and Communication Doctoral Summer School,* Tartu: Tartu University Press, pp. 23-33.

— (2009) *Media and Political Engagement: Citizens, Communication and Democracy,* Cambridge: Cambridge University Press.

Dahlgren, P. & Sparks, C. (eds) (1992) *Journalism and Popular Culture,* London: Sage.

Davies, N. (2000) *The Isles: a History,* London: Papermac.

Davis, S. (1993) 'How Bad is the Nine O'Clock News?' *Independent on Sunday,* 28 November, p. 4.

Davison, W.P. (1983) 'The Third-Person Effect in Communication', *Public Opinion Quarterly,* 47(1): 1-15.

Delano, A. & Henningham, J. (1995) *The News Breed: British Journalists in the 1990s. Report of the School of Media of the London College of Printing,* London: London Institute.

Delmer, S. (1963) *Die Deutschen und ich,* Hamburg: Nannen Verlag.

Dernbach, B. & Roth, J. (2007) 'Literalität des Alltags: Von Scannern, Gehern und Direkteinsteigern – Eine Typologie von Verhaltensmustern beim Zeitunglesen', *Medien & Kommunikationswissenschaft,* 55(1): 24-42.

Der Spiegel (1992) 'Pest und Cholera', *Der Spiegel,* 46(28): 46-47.

Dewall, G.v. (1997) *Press Ethics: Regulation and Editorial Practice,* Düsseldorf: The European Institute for the Media.

Donsbach, W. (1991) *Medienwirkung trotz Selektion. Einflussfaktoren auf die Zuwendung von Zeitungsinhalten,* Köln/Weimar: Böhlau.

Donsbach, W. & Büttner, K. (2005) 'Boulevardisierungstrend in deutschen Fernsehnachrichten: Darstellungsmerkmale der Politikberichterstattung vor den Bundestagswahlen 1983, 1990 und 1998', *Publizistik,* 50(1): 21-38.

Donsbach, W. & Klett, B. (1993) 'Subjective Objectivity: How Journalists in Four Countries define a Key Term of their Profession', *Gazette*, 51: 53-83.

Dörner, A. (2000) *Politische Kultur und Medienunterhaltung: Zur Inszenierung politischer Identitäten in der amerikanischen Film- und Fernsehwelt*, Konstanz: UVK.

Douglas, T. (2004) 'Forty Years of The Sun', available at http://news.bbc.co.uk/2/hi/uk_news/magazine/3654446.stm (accessed 2 November 2004).

— (2005) 'Could it be the Sun wot wins it again?' available at http://news.bbc.co.uk/2/hi/uk_news/politics/vote_2005/frontpage/4470557.stm (accessed 26 January 2010).

Döveling, K. (2005) *Emotionen – Medien – Gemeinschaft: Eine kommunikationssoziologische Analyse*, Wiesbaden: VS Verlag für Sozialwissenschaften.

Dovifat, E. (1927) *Der amerikanische Journalismus: Mit einer Darstellung der journalistischen Berufsbildung*, Stuttgart: Deutsche Verlagsanstalt.

— (1930) *Auswüchse der Sensations-Berichterstattung*, Stuttgart: Tagblatt-Buchdruckerei.

Droege, F. (1968) 'Konzept einer empirischen Stereotypenforschung. Methodische Überlegungen zu einer Aussagenanalyse der "Bild"-Zeitung', *Publizistik*, (13): 340-347.

Dulinski, U. (2003) *Sensationsjournalismus in Deutschland*, Konstanz: UKV.

Edelstein, A.S. (1982) *Comparative Communication Research*, Beverly Hills, CA: Sage.

Eliasoph, N. (1998) *Avoiding Politics: How Americans Produce Apathy in Everyday Life*, Cambridge: Cambridge University Press.

Engel, M. (1996) *Tickle the Public: One Hundred Years of the Popular Press*, London: Indigo.

Engelman, J. (ed) (1999) *Die kleinen Unterschiede: der Cultural Studies Reader*, Frankfurt am Main: Campus.

Enzensberger, H.M. (1983) 'Der Triumph der BILD-Zeitung oder Die Katastrophe der Pressefreiheit', *Merkur*, (420): 651-662.

Esser, F. (1997) 'Journalistische Kultur in Großbritannien und Deutschland: Eine Analyse aus vergleichender Perspektive', in M. Machill (ed) *Journalistische Kultur: Rahmenbedingungen im internationalen Vergleich*, Opladen: Westdeutscher Verlag, pp. 11-136.

— (1998) *Die Kräfte hinter den Schlagzeilen: Englischer und deutscher Journalismus im Vergleich*, Freiburg/München: Verlag Karl Alber.

— (1999) '"Tabloidization" of News: A Comparative Analysis of Anglo-American and German Press Journalism', *European Journal of Communication*, 14(3): 291-324.

FAZ.NET (2005) 'Wellenreiter: Wir sind Papst. Was nun?' available at http://www.faz.net/s/RubCC21B04EE95145B3AC877C874FB1B611/Doc~E6F0

A5E92B32944288EFEECCC4391B6EC~ATpl~Ecommon~Scontent.html (accessed 9 February 2010).

Fern, E.F. (2001) *Advanced Focus Group Research,* London: Sage.

Feshbach, S. & Singer, R.D. (1971) *Television and Aggression: An Experimental Field Study,* San Francisco, Calif.: Jossey-Bass.

Fischer, H.-D. (1978) *Reeducations- und Pressepolitik unter britischem Besatzungsstatus: Die Zonenzeitung "Die Welt" 1946-1959. Konzeption, Artikulation und Rezeption,* Düsseldorf: Droste Verlag.

Fiske, J. (1987a) *Television Culture,* London: Methuen.

— (1987b) 'TV: Re-Situating the Popular in the People', *Continuum: The Australian Journal of Media & Culture,* 1(2): Film, TV and the Popular.

— (1989a) *Reading the Popular,* London: Unwin Hyman.

— (1989b) *Understanding Popular Culture,* London: Unwin Hyman.

— (1992) 'Popularity and the Politics of Information', in P. Dahlgren & C. Sparks (eds) *Journalism and Popular Culture,* London: Routledge, pp. 45-63.

Fiske, J. & Hartley, J. (2003) *Reading Television,* London: Methuen.

F&S Medienservice GmbH & Schäfer Marktforschung GmbH (2005) *Vertrauen in Medien und Politik: Was die Deutschen von ihren Medien halten. Online-Umfrage März 2005,* Hamburg: F&S Medienservice GmbH.

Franklin, B. (1997) *Newzak and News Media,* London: Arnold.

Fraser, N. (1992) 'Rethinking the Public Sphere: A Contribution to the Critique of Actually Existing Democracy', in F. Barker, P. Hulme & M. Iverson (eds) *Postmodernism and the Reading of Modernity,* Manchester: Manchester University Press, pp. 197-231.

Garnham, N. (1990) *Capitalism and Communication: Global Culture and the Economics of Information,* London: Sage.

— (1997) 'Political Economy and the Practice of Cultural Studies', in M. Ferguson & P. Golding (eds) *Cultural Studies in Question,* London: Sage, pp. 56-73.

Gauntlett, D. (2007) *Creative Explorations: New Approaches to Identities and Audiences,* London: Routledge.

— (2008, second edition) *Media, Gender and Identity: An Introduction,* London: Routledge.

Gauntlett, D. & Hill, A. (1999) *TV Living,* London: Routledge.

Gavrilos, D. (2003) 'Editor's Introduction: Communicating the "New Patriotism": What Does It Mean to Be a Citizen in a Global Context?' *Journal of Communication Inquiry,* (27): 333-336.

Gehrs, O. (2006) 'Achtung, Fritz! Die englische Boulevardpresse hat die Macht, Wahlen zu entscheiden – andererseits tut man gut daran, sie nicht zu ernst zu nehmen', *Frankfurter Rundschau,* 15 August, p. 13.

Geisel, K. (1995) *"Die Schöne und das Biest"- wie die Tagespresse über Vergewaltigung berichtet,* Münster, Hamburg: Lit Verlag.

Gellner, E. (1983) *Nations and Nationalism,* Oxford: Blackwell.

Gibbs, A. (1997) 'Focus Groups', *Social Research Update*, 19, available at http://www.soc.surrey.ac.uk/sru/SRU19.html (accessed 3 May 2006).
Giddens, A. (1991) *Modernity and Self-Identity: Self and Society in the Late Modern Age*, Cambridge: Polity Press.
Gitlin, T. (1997) 'The Anti-political Populism of Cultural Studies', in M. Ferguson & P. Golding (eds) *Cultural Studies in Question*, London: Sage, pp. 25-38.
Glaser, B.G. & Strauss, A.L. (1967) *The Discovery of Grounded Theory. Strategies for Qualitative Research*, New York: Aldine.
— (1978) *Theoretical Sensitivity. Advances in the Methodology of Grounded Theory*, Mill Valley, Calif.: Sociology Press.
Glover, S. (2005) 'Will *The Sun* cast a shadow over Tony's tilt at third term?' *The Independent*, 11 April, p. 9.
Goffman, E. (1963) *Stigma: Notes on the Management of Spoiled Identity*, Englewood Cliffs: Prentice Hall.
Goldbeck, K. (2004) *Gute Unterhaltung, schlechte Unterhaltung: Die Fernsehkritik und das Populäre*, Bielefeld: Transcript.
Göttlich, U. (1997) 'Kontexte der Mediennutzung: Probleme einer handlungstheoretischen Modellierung der Medienrezeption', *monatage/av*, 6(1): 105-13.
Göttlich, U. & Winter, C. (1999) 'Wessen Cultural Studies? Die Rezeption der Cultural Studies im deutschsprachigen Raum', in R. Bromley, U. Göttlich & C. Winter (eds) *Cultural Studies: Grundlagentexte zur Einführung*, Lüneburg: zu Klampen, pp. 25-39.
Graber, D. (2003) 'The Media and Democracy: Beyond Myths and Sterotypes', *Annual Review of Political Science*, (6): 139-60.
Graf-Szczuka, K. (2006) 'Typisch Leser! Wie man die Leserschaft durch Typologien beschreibt', in G. Rager, K. Graf-Szczuka, G. Hassemer & S. Süper (eds) *Zeitungsjournalismus. Empirische Leserschaftsforschung*, Konstanz: UVK, pp. 270-80.
— (2007) *Der kleine Unterschied: Eine Typologie jugendlicher Zeitungsleser und -nichtleser*, Hamburg: Verlag Dr. Kovac.
— (2008) 'Die Persönlichkeit der Zeitungsleser: Neue Erkenntnisse zur Mediennutzung von Jugendlichen', *Journalistik Journal*, 31 March 2008, available at http://journalistik-journal.lookingintomedia.com/?p=104 (accessed 2 Dec 2009).
Greenbaum, T.L. (1998) *The Handbook for Focus Group Research*, London: Sage.
Greenslade, R. (2009) 'Hillsborough: how the Sunday Times – and the Sun – reported on the tragedy', available at http://www.guardian.co.uk/media/greenslade/2009/apr/15/hillsborough-disaster-sundaytimes (accessed 26 January 2010).
Griffith, P. & Leonard, M. (eds) (2002) *Reclaiming Britishness*, London: Foreign Policy Centre.
Griffiths, D. (ed) (1992) *The Encyclopedia of the British Press 1422-1992*, Basingstoke: Macmillan Press.
— (2006) *Fleet Street. Five Hundred Years of the Press*, London: British Library.

Grimberg, S. (2002) 'The News Corporation Ltd.' in L. Hachmeister & G. Rager (eds) *Wer beherrscht die Medien? Die 50 größten Medienkonzerne der Welt. Jahrbuch 2003*, München: C.H. Beck, pp. 118-27.

Gripsrud, J. (2000) 'Tabloidization, Popular Journalism, and Democracy', in C. Sparks & J. Tulloch (eds) *Tabloid Tales: Global Debates over Media Standards*, Oxford: Roman & Littlefield Publishers, pp. 285-300.

Guardian on Saturday (2009) 'Hillsborough: 20 years on, Liverpool has still not forgiven the newspaper it calls "the Scum"', *The Guardian on Saturday*, 18 April, p. 10.

Habermas, J. (1989, originally published in German 1962) *The Structural Transformation of the Public Sphere: an Inquiry into a Category of Bourgeois Society*, Cambridge: Polity Press.

— (1996; originally published in German 1992) *Between Facts and Norms: Contributions to a Discourse Theory of Law and Democracy*, Cambridge, Mass.: MIT Press.

Habicht, D. (2004) 'Nutzungsmotive von Lesern der BILD-Zeitung: Eine qualitative Studie', unpublished Master thesis, Ludwig-Maximilians-Universität München, Germany.

— (2006) '"Die sprechen den Leuten aus der Seele". Motive für die Nutzung der BILD-ZEITUNG', in N. Huber & M. Meyen (eds) *Medien im Alltag. Qualitative Studien zu Nutzungsmotiven und zur Bedeutung von Medienangeboten*, Münster: Lit Verlag, pp. 151-67.

Hachmeister, L. & Rager, G. (2005) *Wer beherrscht die Medien? Die 50 größten Medienkonzerne der Welt. Jahrbuch 2005*, München: C.H. Beck.

Hall, S. (1973) *Encoding and Decoding in the Television Discourse*, Birmingham: The University of Birmingham.

— (1980) 'Encoding/Decoding', in S. Hall, D. Hobson, A. Lowe & P. Willis (eds) *Culture, Media, Language: Working Papers in Cultural Studies 1972-79*, London: Hutchinson, in association with the Centre for Contemporary Cultural Studies, University of Brimingham, pp. 128-38.

— (1983) 'The Great Moving Right Show', in S. Hall & M. Jacques (eds) *The Politics of Thatcherism*, London: Lawrence and Wishart, pp. 19-39.

— (1996) 'Introduction: Who Needs "Identity"?' in S. Hall & P.D. Gay (eds) *Questions of Cultural Identity*, London: Sage, pp. 1-17.

— (2003) 'Cultural Identity and Diaspora', in J.E. Braziel & A. Mannur (eds) *Theorizing Diaspora: A Reader*, Malden, Mass.; Oxford: Blackwell Publishers, pp. 223-46.

Haller, M. (1995) 'Boulevard in der Krise? Journalisten auf der Suche nach der wahren Empfindung', *Sage & Schreibe*, (3): 8-9.

— (2001) '"Da wird viel geheuchelt". Michael Haller im Gespräch mit Günther Barth', *Message*, (1): 10-11.

Hallin, D.C. & Mancini, P. (1997) 'Drei Modelle von Medien, Journalismus und politischer Kultur in Europa: Grundlegende Überlegungen zu einer komparativen europäischen Journalismusforschung', in G.G. Kopper & P. Mancini (eds) *Kulturen des Journalismus und politische Systeme: Probleme internationaler Vergleichbarkeit des Journalismus in Europa – verbunden mit Fallstudien zu Großbritannien, Frankreich, Italien und Deutschland*, Berlin: VISTAS Verlag GmbH, pp. 11-28.

— (2004) *Comparing Media Systems: Three Models of Media and Politics*, Cambridge: Cambridge University Press.

Hanfeld, M. (2005) '"Bild"-Chef Kai Diekmann: Wir sind die gedruckte Barrikade der Straße', *Frankfurter Allgemeine Zeitung*, 15 September, p. 42.

Hansen, A., Cottle, S., Negrine, R. & Newbold, C. (1998) *Mass Communication Research Methods*, London: MacMillan.

Hartley, J. (1982) *Understanding News*, London: Routledge.

— (1996) *Popular Reality – Journalism, Modernity, Popular Culture*, London: Arnold.

— (1999) *Uses of Television*, London: Routledge.

Hartmann, F. (1995) 'Die Bild-Zeitung. Mit gebemstem Schaum', *Sage & Schreibe*, (3): 10-12.

Hasebrink, U. (2006) 'The Audiences' Perspective on Global Media Landscapes', in W. Uricchio & S. Kinnebrock (eds) *Media Cultures*, Heidelberg: Universitätsverlag Winter, pp. 49-60.

Hepp, A. (1999) *Cultural Studies und Medienanalyse*, Opladen/Wiesbaden: Westdeutscher Verlag.

Hepp, A. & Winter, R. (eds) (2006, third edition) *Kultur – Medien – Macht. Cultural Studies und Medienanalyse*, Wiesbaden: VS Verlag für Sozialwissenschaften.

Herd, H. (1952) *The March of Journalism: The Story of the British Press from 1622 to the Present Day*, London: George Allen & Unwin.

Hermes, J. (1995) *Reading Women's Magazines*, Cambridge: Polity Press.

— (1998) 'Cultural Citizenship and Popular Fiction', in K. Brants, J. Hermes & L. van Zoonen (eds) *The Media in Question: Popular Cultures and Public Interests*, London: Sage, pp. 157-68.

— (2005) *Re-reading Popular Culture*, Oxford: Blackwell.

Higgins, M. (2004) 'Putting the Nation in the News: the Role of Location Formulation in a selection of Scottish Newspapers', *Discourse and Society*, 15(5): 633-48.

Hill, A. (2005) *Reality TV: Audiences and Popular Factual Television*, London: Routledge.

— (2007) *Restyling Factual TV*, London: Routledge.

Hobsbawm, E.J. (1990) *Nations and Nationalism since 1780: Programme, Myth, Reality*, Cambridge: Cambridge University Press.

Hobson, D. (1982) *Crossroads: the Drama of a Soap Opera*, London: Methuen.

Hoggart, R. (1957) *The Uses of Literacy*, London: Chatto and Windus.

Hohlfeld, R. (1999) 'Konvergenz und Konkurrenz: Programmprofile im dualen System', in W. Hömberg (ed) *Rundfunk-Kultur und Kultur-Rundfunk*, München: Katholische Universität Eichstätt, pp. 57-78.
Höke, S. (2004) 'Die tagesaktuelle Boulevardpresse in Großbritannien und Deutschland: Ein internationaler Vergleich am Beispiel der inhaltlichen Struktur und Ansprechhaltung von *The Sun* und *Bild*', unpublished Master thesis, Universität Leipzig, Germany.
— (2005) 'Der alltägliche "Wow"-Effekt', *message*, (2): 80-83.
Hooper, J. (2003) 'German chancellor sees red in privacy battle with British tabloid newspaper', available at http://www.guardian.co.uk/media/2003/jan/20/mailonsunday.pressandpublishing (accessed 14 June 2005).
Humphreys, P. (1997) 'Politisches System, Massenmedien und Journalismus in Großbritannien: Ein analytischer Aufriss', in G.G. Kopper & P. Mancini (eds) *Kulturen des Journalismus und politische Systeme: Probleme internationaler Vergleichbarkeit des Journalismus in Europa – verbunden mit Fallstudien zu Großbritannien, Frankreich, Italien und Deutschland*, Berlin: VISTAS Verlag GmbH, pp. 29-60.
— (1996) *Mass Media and Media Policy in Western Europe*, New York/Manchester: Manchester University Press.
Hurwitz, H. (1972) *Die Stunde Null der deutschen Presse: Die amerikanische Pressepolitik in Deutschland 1945-1949*, Köln: Verlag Wissenschaft und Politik.
Ionescu, A. (1996) 'Kriminalberichterstattung in der Tagespresse. Eine empirische Untersuchung der Tageszeitungen BILD, Nürnberger Nachrichten und Süddeutsche Zeitung im Zeitraum Januar und Juni 1989', unpublished Ph.D. thesis, Universität Nürnberg, Germany.
Iyengar, S. & Morin, R. (2006) 'Red media, Blue Media: Evidence for a Political Litmus Test in Online News Readership', *The Washington Post*, 3 May.
IVW Informationsgemeinschaft zur Feststellung der Verbreitung von Werbeträgern e.V. (2010) *Quartalsauflagen Tageszeitungen 3/2010*, Berlin: IVW.
Jäckel, M. & Peter, J. (1997) 'Cultural Studies aus kommunikationswissenschaftlicher Perspektive: Grundlagen und grundlegende Probleme', *Rundfunk und Fernsehen*, 44(1): 46-68.
Jackson, P., Stevenson, N. & Brooks, K. (2001) *Making Sense of Men's Magazines*, Cambridge: Polity Press.
Jäger, S. (1993) *Der Groß-Regulator. Analyse der BILD-Berichterstattung über den rassistisch motivierten Terror und die Fahndung nach der RAF im Sommer 1993*, Duisburg: Duisburger Institut für Sprach- und Sozialforschung.
Jensen, K.B. (1991) 'Chapter 7: Media Audiences. Reception Analysis: Mass Communication as the Social Production of Meaning', in K.B. Jensen & N.W. Jankowski (eds) *A Handbook of Qualitative Methodologies for Mass Communication Research*, London; New York: Routledge, pp. 135-62.

— (1999) 'Knowledge as Received: a Project on Audience Uses of Television News in World Countries', in J. Gripsrud (ed) *Television and Common Knowledge*, London; New York: Routledge, pp. 125-35.

— (2002a) 'Media Effects: Quantitative Traditions', in K.B. Jensen (ed) *A Handbook of Media and Communication Research: Qualitative and Quantitative Methodologies*, London: Routledge, pp. 138-55.

— (2002b) 'Media Reception: Qualitative Traditions', in K. B. Jensen (ed) *A Handbook of Media and Communication Research: Qualitative and Quantitative Methodologies*, London: Routledge, pp. 156-70.

Jensen, K.B. & Rosengren, K.E. (1990) 'Five Traditions in Search of the Audience', *European Journal of Communication*, 5: 207-38.

Jogschies, R. (2001) *Emotainment – Journalismus am Scheideweg: Der Fall Sebnitz und die Folgen*, Münster: Lit Verlag.

Johansson, S. (2006) '"Sometimes you wanna hate Celebrities":Tabloid Readers and Celebrity Coverage', in S. Holmes & S. Redmonds (eds) *Framing Celebrity: New Directions in Celebrity Culture*, London: Routledge, pp. 343-58.

— (2007a) *Reading Tabloids: Tabloid Newspapers and Their Readers*, Huddinge: Södertörn Academic Studies.

— (2007b) '"They Just Make Sense": Tabloid Newspapers as an Alternative Public Sphere', in R. Butsch (ed) *Media and Public Spheres*, Basingstoke: Palgrave Macmillan, pp. 83-95.

Journalism Studies (2008) *Special Issue: The Future of Newspapers*: Routledge, 9 (5).

Jung, E. (2007) 'Das reportende Rasen', available at http://www.sueddeutsche.de /kultur/artikel/849/127645/print.html (accessed 24 August 2007).

Kamps, K. (ed) (1998) *Fernsehnachrichten: Prozesse, Strukturen, Funktionen*, Opladen: Westdeutscher Verlag.

Kellner, D. (1997) 'The Frankfurt School and British Cultural Studies: The Missed Articulation', in J. McGuigan (ed) *Cultural Methodologies*, London: Sage, pp. 12-41.

Kepplinger, H.M. (1998) *Die Demontage der Politik in der Informationsgesellschaft*, Freiburg: Alber.

Kitzinger, J. & Barbour, R.S. (1999) 'Introduction: The Challenge and Promise of Focus Groups', in R.S. Barbour & J. Kitzinger (eds) *Developing Focus Group Research: Politics, Theory and Practice*, London: Sage, pp. 1-20.

Klaus, E. (1996) 'Der Gegensatz von Information ist Desinformation, der Gegensatz von Unterhaltung ist Langeweile', *Rundfunk und Fernsehen*, 44(3): 402-17.

— (1998) 'Genre und Geschlecht: Die Soap-Opera Diskussion', in E. Klaus *Kommunikationswissenschaftliche Geschlechterforschung: Zur Bedeutung der Frauen in den Massenmedien und im Journalismus*, Opladen/ Wiesbaden, pp. 321-73.

Klaus, E. & Lünenborg, M. (2001) 'Journalismus: Fakten, die unterhalten – Fiktionen, die Wirklichkeit schaffen', in A. Baum & S. J. Schmidt (eds) *Fakten und Fiktionen. Über den Umgang mit Medienwirklichkeiten*, Konstanz: UVK, pp. 152-64.

— (2004a) 'Cultural Citizenship: Ein kommunikationswissenschaftliches Konzept zur Bestimmung kultureller Teilhabe in der Mediengesellschaft', *Medien und Kommunikationswissenschaft*, 52(2): 193-213.

— (2004b) 'Medienhandeln als Alltagshandeln: Über die Konstituierung gesellschaftlicher Identität durch cultural citizenship in der Mediengesellschaft', in H. Bonfadelli & O. Jarren (eds) *Mediengesellschaft: Strukturen, Merkmale, Entwicklungsdynamiken*, Wiesbaden: VS Verlag für Sozialwissenschaften, pp. 100-13.

— (2005) 'Die Bedeutung kommunikativer Grundrechte in der globalen Gesellschaft', in P. Rössler & F. Krotz (eds) *Mythen der Mediengesellschaft – The Media Society and its Myths*, Konstanz: UVK, pp. 415-29.

Klaus, E. & O'Connor, B. (2000) 'The Meaning of Pleasure and the Pleasure of Meaning. Towards a definition of Pleasure in "Reception Analysis"', in H.-B. Brosius (ed) *Kommunikation über Grenzen und Kulturen. Berichtsband der Jahrestagung der Deutschen Gesellschaft für Publizistik- und Kommunikaitonswissenschaft (DGPPuK) vom 12. bis 14. Mai 1999 in Utrecht zum Thema Kommunikation über Grenzen und Kulturen*, Konstanz: UVK, pp. 411-428.

Klaus, E. & Röser, J. (2005) 'Keeping an Eye on Society: Gender Studies and Communication Studies in Germany', Paper presented at the First European Communication Conference, Amsterdam, Netherlands, 24-26 November 2005.

Klein, J. (1997) 'Boulevardisierung in TV-Kulturmagazinen?' in W. Holly & B. U. Biere (eds) *Medien im Wandel*, Opladen: Westdeutscher Verlag, pp. 103-12.

Klein, M.-L. & Pfister, G. (1985) *Goldmädel, Rennmiezen und Turnküken. Die Frau in der Sportberichterstattung der BILD-Zeitung*, Berlin: Bartels & Wernitz.

Klingemann, H.D. & Klingemann, U. (1983) '"Bild" im Urteil der Bevölkerung: Materialien zu einer vernachlässigten Perspektive', *Publizistik*, 28: 239-59.

Knodel, J. (1993) 'The Design and Analysis of Focus Group Studies: A Practical Approach', in D.L. Morgan (ed) *Successful Focus Groups: Advancing the State of the Art*, Newbury Park, CA: Sage, pp. 35-50.

Köcher, R. (1985) 'Spürhund und Missionar: Eine vergleichende Untersuchung über Berufsethik und Aufgabenverständnis britischer und deutscher Journalisten', Ph.D. thesis, Universität München, Germany.

— (1986) 'Bloodhounds or Missionries: Role Definitions of German and British Journalists', *European Journal of Communication*, 1: 43-64.

Kohn, M.L. (ed) (1989) *Cross-National Research in Sociology*, Newbury Park, CA: Sage.

Kopper, G.G. & Mancini, P. (eds) (2003) *Kulturen des Journalismus und politische Systeme: Probleme internationaler Vergleichbarkeit des Journalismus in Europa, verbunden mit Fallstudien zu Grossbritannien, Frankreich, Italien und Deutschland*, Berlin: Vistas Verlag.

Koschnick, W.J. (1998) 'Abkehr vom Boulevard', *Journalist*, (11): 12-22.

Koszyk, K. (1966) *Deutsche Presse im 19. Jahrhundert: Geschichte der deutschen Presse, Teil 2*, Berlin: Colloquium-Verlag.

— (1972) *Deutsche Presse 1914-1945: Geschichte der deutschen Presse, Teil 3*, Berlin: Colloquium-Verlag.

— (1986) *Pressepolitik für Deutsche 1945-1949: Geschichte der deutschen Presse, Teil 4*, Berlin: Colloquium-Verlag.

Krotz, F. (1993) 'Fernsehen fühlen: Auf der Suche nach einem handlungstheoretischen Konzept für das emotionale Erleben des Fernsehens', *Rundfunk und Fernsehen – Forum der Medienwissenschaft und Medienpraxis*, 41: 477-96.

Krüger, R.A. (1983) 'Gruppendiskussionen: Überlegungen zur Rekonstruktion sozialer Wirklichkeit aus der Sicht der Betroffenen', *Soziale Welt*, 34(1): 90-109.

Krüger, U.M. (1996) 'Boulevardisierung der Information im Privatfernsehen: Nichttagesaktuelle Informations- und Infotainmentsendungen bei ARD, ZDF, RTL, SAT.1 und Pro Sieben 1995', *Media Perspektiven*, (7): 362-74.

— (1998) 'Zum Stand der Konvergenzforschung im dualen Rundfunksystem', in W. Klingler, G. Roters & O. Zöllner (eds) *Fernsehforschung in Deutschland: Themen, Akteure, Methoden, Teilband 1.1*, Baden-Baden: Nomos, pp. 151-84.

Kubitza, M. (2006) 'Verlorene Generation? Was Jugendliche von Jugendseiten erwarten', in G. Rager, K. Graf-Szczuka, G. Hassemer & S. Süper (eds) *Zeitungsjournalismus. Empirische Leserschaftsforschung*, Konstanz: UVK, pp. 252-60.

Küchenhoff, E. & Keppler, G. (1972) *Bildverfälschungen. Analyse der Berichterstattung der BILD-Zeitung über Arbeitskämpfe, Gewerkschaftspolitik, Mieten, Sozialpolitik. Bd. 1 (Analyse) und 2 (Belege)*, Frankfurt am Main: Europ. Verl.-Anst.

Kumar, K. (2003) *The Making of English National Identity*, Cambridge: Cambridge University Press.

Kurtz, H. (1993) *Media Circus – The Trouble with America's Newspapers*, New York: Random House.

LAE – Leseranalyse Entscheidungsträger e.V. (2009) *Leseranalyse Entscheidungsträger in Wirtschaft und Verwaltung*, Frankfurt am Main: LAE – Leseranalyse Entscheidungsträger e.V.

Lamnek, S. (1989) *Qualitative Sozialforschung. Band 2: Methoden und Techniken*, München: Psychologie Verlags Union.

— (1995, third edition) *Qualitative Sozialforschung. Band 1: Methodologie*, Weinheim: Psychologie Verlags Union.

— (1998) *Gruppendiskussionen: Theorie und Praxis*, Weinheim: Psychologie Verlags Union.

Langer, J. (1998) *Tabloid Television: Popular Journalism and the 'Other News'*, London: Routledge.

Law, A. (2001) 'Near and Far: Banal National Identity and the Press in Scotland', *Media, Culture & Society*, 23(3): 299-317.

— (2002) 'Tabloid Nation: The Front Pages of the Daily Record', *Media Education Journal*, (31): 4-8.

Liebes, T. (1984) 'Ethnocriticism: Israelis of Moroccan Ethnicity negotiate the Meaning of *Dallas*', *Studies in Visual Communication*, 10(3): 46-72.

— (1988) 'Cultural Differences in the Retelling of Television Fiction', *Critical Studies in Mass Communication,* 5(4): 277-92.

Liebes, T. & Katz, E. (1985) 'Mutual Aid in the Decoding of *Dallas*: Preliminary Notes from a Cross-Cultural Study', in P. Drummond & R. Patterson (eds) *Television in Transition,* London: British Film Institute, pp. 187-98.

— (1986) 'Patterns of Involvement in Television Fiction: A Comparative Analysis', *European Journal of Communication,* 1(2): 151-71.

— (1990) *The Export of Meaning: Cross-Cultural Readings of "Dallas",* New York: Oxford University Press.

Lindemann, M. (1969) *Deutsche Presse bis 1815: Geschichte der deutschen Presse, Teil 1,* Berlin: Colloquium-Verlag.

Link, J. (1986) 'Elementare narrative Schemata in der Boulevardpresse', in R.M. KLOEPFER, Karl-Dietmar (ed) *Narrativität in den Medien,* Münster: MAkS-Publ., pp. 209-30.

Linton, M. (1995) *Was it the Sun Wot Won it?* Oxford: Nuffield College Press.

Livingstone, S. (2003) 'On the Challenges of Cross-National Comparative Media Research', *European Journal of Communication,* 18(4): 477-500.

Livingstone, S. & Bovill, M. (eds) (2001) *Children and their Changing Media Environment: a European Comparative Study,* Mahwah, NJ: Lawrence Erlbaum.

Lohmeyer, H. (1992) *Springer: Ein deutsches Imperium. Geschichte und Geschichten,* Berlin: Edition q.

Loos, P. & Schäffer, B. (2001) *Das Gruppendiskussionsverfahren: Theoretische Grundlagen und empirische Anwendung,* Opladen: Leske & Budrich.

Lull, J. (1980) 'The Social Uses of Television', *Human Communication Research,* 6(3): 197-209.

— (1988a) 'How Families Select Television Programmes: A Mass Observational Study', *Journal of Broadcasting and Electronic Media,* 26(4): 801-11.

— (1988b) *World Families Watch Television,* London: Sage.

— (1990) *Inside Family Viewing: Ethnographic Research on Television's Audiences,* London: Routledge.

Lünenborg, M. (2005) *Journalismus als kultureller Prozess: Zur Bedeutung von Journalismus in der Mediengesellschaft. Ein Entwurf,* Wiesbaden: VS Verlag für Sozialwissenschaften.

MacDonald, M. (2000) 'Rethinking Personalization in Current Affairs Journalism', in C. Sparks & J. Tulloch (eds) *Tabloid Tales: Global Debates over Media Standards,* Oxford: Roman & Littlefield Publishers, pp. 251-66.

Machill, M. (1997a) 'Journalistische Kultur: Identifikationsmuster für nationale Besonderheiten im Journalismus', in M. Machill (ed) *Journalistische Kultur: Rahmenbedingungen im internationalen Vergleich,* Opladen: Westdeutscher Verlag, pp. 11-22.

— (ed) (1997b) *Journalistische Kultur: Rahmenbedingungen im internationalen Vergleich,* Opladen: Westdeutscher Verlag.

Mackay, H. (1997) *Consumption and Everyday Life*, London: Sage.
Maguire, J., Poulton, E. & Possamai, C. (1999) 'The War of the Worlds? Identity Politics in Anglo-German Press Coverage of EURO 96', *European Journal of Communication*, 14(1): 61-89.
Marlow, J. (2002) 'Some Thoughts on the Poetics of the Order of Mediatized Political Discourse: Facts, Fun and Fulmination in the Tabloids', *Contemporary Politics*, 8(4): 335-42.
May, T. (2001) *Social Research: Issues, Methods and Process*, Buckingham: Open University Press.
Mayring, P. (2003, eighth edition) *Qualitative Inhaltsanalyse: Grundlagen und Techniken*, Weinheim: Beltz Verlag.
McCroone, D. (1997) 'Unmasking Britannia: the Rise and Fall of British National Identity', *Nations and Nationalism*, 3(4): 579-96.
McGuigan, J. (1992) *Cultural Populism*, London: Routledge.
— (1997) 'Cultural Populism Revisited', in M. Ferguson & P. Golding (eds) *Cultural Studies in Question*, London: Sage, pp. 138-53.
McLachlan, S. & Golding, P. (2000) 'Tabloidization in the British Press: A Quantitative Investigation into Changes in British Newspapers 1952-1997', in C. Sparks & J. Tulloch (eds) *Tabloid Tales: Global Debates over Media Standards*, Oxford: Roman & Littlefield Publishers, pp. 75-90.
McNair, B. (1995) *An Introduction to Political Communication*, London/New York: Routledge.
— (2003, fourth edition) *News and Journalism in the UK: A Textbook*, London: Routledge.
Media-Micro-Census GmbH (2010) *Media-Analyse für Publikumszeitschriften, Supplements, Tageszeitungen, Kongress, Lesezirkel, Kino, Hörfunk, Fernsehen*, Frankfurt am Main: Arbeitsgemeinschaft Media-Analyse e.V. (ag.ma).
Meyen, M. (2004, second edition) *Mediennutzung. Mediaforschung, Medienfunktionen, Nutzungsmuster*, Konstanz: UVK.
Michaels, E. (1985) 'Ask a Foolish Question: On the Methodologies of Cross Cultural Media Research', *Australian Journal of Cultural Studies*, 3(2): 45-59.
Mikos, L. (2006) 'Cultural Studies im deutschsprachigen Raum', in R. Winter & A. Hepp (eds) *Kultur-Medien-Macht: Cultural Studies und Medienanalyse*, Wiesbaden: VS Verlag für Sozialwissenschaften, pp. 177-92.
— (2009) 'John Fiske: Populäre Texte und Diskurs', in A. Hepp, F. Krotz & T. Thomas (eds) *Schlüsselwerke der Cultural Studies*, Wiesbaden: VS Verlag für Sozialwissenschaften, pp. 156-64.
Minzberg, M. (1999) *BILD-Zeitung und Persönlichkeitsschutz. Vor Gericht und Presserat: Eine Bestandsaufnahme mit neuen Fällen aus den 90er Jahren*, Baden-Baden: Nomos Verlag.
Moores, S. (1993) *Interpreting Audiences: the Ethnography of Media Consumption*, London: Sage.

— (2000) *Media and Everyday Life in Modern Society*, Edinburgh: Edinburgh University Press.
— (2005) *Media/Theory. Thinking about Media and Communications*, London: Routledge.
Morgan, D.L. (1997) *Focus Groups as Qualitative Research*, London: Sage.
Morley, D. (1980) *The "Nationwide" Audience: Structure and Decoding*, London: BFI.
— (1981) '"The Nationwide Audience" – A Critical Postscript', *Screen Education*, 39: 3-14.
— (1983) 'Cultural Transformations: The Politics of Resistance', in H. Davis & P. Walton (eds) *Language, Image, Media*, Oxford: Basil Blackwell, pp. 104-17.
— (1992) *Television, Audiences & Cultural Studies*, London: Routledge.
— (1999) 'Finding out about the World from Television News: Some Difficulties', in J. Gripsrud (ed) *Television and Common Knowledge*, London; New York: Routledge, pp. 136-58.
Mortimore, R., Atkinson, S. & Skinner, G. (2000) 'What the Papers say: Do Readers believe what the Editors want them to?' Paper presented at the EPOP Conference, University of Edinburgh, Scotland, 8-10 September 2000.
MRS Market Research Society (2005) 'MRS Social Grade Approximation for the 2001 Census', available at http://www.mrs.org.uk/networking/egg/eggsocialgrade.htm (accessed 26 July 2006).
Muckenhaupt, M. (1997) 'Boulevardisierung in der TV-Nachrichtenberichterstattung', in W. Holly & B. U. Biere (eds) *Medien im Wandel*, Opladen: Westdeutscher Verlag, pp. 113-34.
Müller, E. (1993) '"Pleasure and Resistance". John Fiskes Beitrag zur Populärkulturtheorie', *Montage/av*, 2(1): 52-66.
Müller, H.D. (1968) *Der Springer-Konzern. Eine kritische Studie*, München: Piper.
Müller, K.F. (2010) *Frauenzeitschriften aus der Sicht ihrer Leserinnen. Die Rezeption von Brigitte im Kontext von Biografie, Alltag und Doing Gender*, Bielefeld: Transcript.
Naeher, G. (1991) *Axel Springer: Mensch, Macht, Mythos*, Erlangen: Straube.
Nairn, T. (1981) *The Break-Up of Britain: Crisis and Neo-Nationalism*, London: Verso Editions.
National Readership Surveys Ltd (2010) 'NRS Readership Estimates – Newspapers and Supplements: July 2009 – June 2010', available at http://www.nrs.co.uk/toplinereadership.html (accessed 26 November 2010).
Negt, O. & Kluge, A. (1993) *Public Sphere and Experience*, Minneapolis: University of Minnesota Press.
Neverla, I. (1992) *Fernseh-Zeit. Zuschauer zwischen Zeitkalkül und Zeitvertreib*, München: Ölschläger.

Nowak, S. (1976) 'Meaning and Measurement in Comparative Studies', in S. Nowak (ed) *Understanding and Prediction: Essays in the Methodology of Social and Behavioral Theories*, Dordrecht (Holland): Reidel, pp. 104-32.

Nusser, P. (1991) *Trivialliteratur*, Stuttgart: Metzler.

O'Donnell, H. (1994) 'Mapping the Mythical: a Geopolitics of National Sporting Stereotypes', *Discourse and Society*, 5(3): 345-80.

O'Malley, T. & Soley, C. (2000) *Regulating the Press*, London: Pluto Press.

Örnebring, H. (2006) 'The Maiden Tribute and the Naming of Monsters: Two Case Studies of Tabloid Journalism as Alternative Public Sphere', *Journalism Studies*, 7(6): 851-68.

Örnebring, H. & Jönsson, A.M. (2004) 'Tabloid Journalism and the Public Sphere: a historical perspective on tabloid journalism', *Journalism Studies*, 5(3): 283-95.

Øyen, E. (ed) (1990a) *Comparative Methodology: Theory and Practice in International Social Research*, London: Sage.

— (1990b) 'The Imperfection of Comparisons', in E. Øyen (ed) *Comparative Methodology: Theory and Practice in International Social Research*, London: Sage, pp. 1-18.

Park, A., Curtice, J., Thomson, K., Phillips, M., Johnson, M.C. & Clery, E. (2008) *British Social Attitudes: The 24th Report*, London: Sage.

Pasquay, A. (2010) *Die deutsche Zeitungslandschaft – Entwicklungen und Perspektiven*, Berlin: Bundesverband Deutscher Zeitungsverleger e. V. (BDZV).

Patterson, T.E. & Donsbach, W. (1996) 'News Decisions: Journalists as Partisan Actors', *Political Communication*, 13(4): 455-468.

Pohlmann, S. (2007) 'Vorsicht, Paparazzi! Mit den Foto-Handys kamen die Leserreporter. Bilanz einer umstrittenen Medienpraxis' available at http://www.tagesspiegel.de/medien-news/Paparazzi-Leserreporter;art15532,2365883 (accessed 9 February 2010).

Postman, N. (1985) *Amusing Ourselves to Death: Public Discourse in the Age of Show Business*, New York: Viking.

Press Complaints Commission and Axis Communications (2008) 'Press Complaints Commission 08: The Review', available at http://www.pcc.org.uk/assets/111/PCC_Ann_Rep_08.pdf (accessed 15 May 2010).

Preston, P. (2004) 'Tabloids: Only the Beginning', *British Journalism Review*, 15(1): 50-55.

Pursehouse, M. (1991) 'Looking at the Sun: into the 90s with a Tabloid and its Readers', *Cultural Studies from Birmingham*, (1): 88-133.

Radway, J. (1984) *Reading the Romance*, Chapel Hill: University of North Carolina Press.

Rager, G. (2003) 'Jugendliche als Zeitungsleser: Lesehürden und Lösungsansätze', *Media Perspektiven*, (4): 180-86.

Rager, G., Graf-Szczuka, K., Bodin, M. & Thiele, M. (2004) 'Wer liest Zeitung? Einflussfaktoren auf die Zeitungsnutzung Jugendlicher', *Zeitschrift für Medienpsychologie*, 16(1-2): 2-16.

Rager, G., Rinsforf, L. & Werner, P. (2002) 'Empirisches Beispiel: Wenn Jugendliche Zeitung lesen. Nutzungsmuster und Rezeptionsinteressen von jungen Zeitungslesern und –nichtlesern', in N. Groeben & B. Hurrelmann (eds) *Lesekompetenz. Bedingungen, Dimensionen, Funktionen*, Weinheim/München: Juventa, pp. 174-85.

Rager, G. & Werner, P. (2002) 'Dahinter steckt immer ein kluger Kopf. Acht Thesen zum Nutzen der Tageszeitung', in N. Groeben & B. Hurrelmann (eds) *Medienkompetenz. Voraussetzungen, Dimensionen, Funktionen*, Weinheim/München: Juventa, pp. 268-81.

Reinemann, C. (2008) '"Guter Boulevard ist immer auch außerparlamentarische Opposition" – Das Handeln von *Bild* am Beispiel der Berichterstattung über Hartz IV', in B. Pfetsch & S. Adam (eds) *Massenmedien als politische Akteure: Konzepte und Analysen*, Wiesbaden: VS Verlag für Sozialwissenschaften / GWV Fachverlage, pp. 196-224.

Renger, R. (1997) 'Spaß an "Information". Journalismus als Populärkultur', *Medien Journal*, (4): 23-38.

— (2000) 'Journalismus als kultureller Diskurs: Cultural Studies als Herausforderung für die Journalismustheorie', in M. Löffelholz (ed) *Theorien des Journalismus. Ein diskursives Handbuch*, Wiesbaden: Westdeutscher Verlag, pp. 467-81.

— (2002) 'Populäre Printprodukte transkulturell', in A. Hepp & M. Löffelholz (eds) *Grundlagentexte zur transkulturellen Kommunikation*, Konstanz: UVK, pp. 474-99.

— (2006) 'Populärer Journalismus', in A. Hepp & R. Winter (eds) *Kultur – Medien – Macht: Cultural Studies und Medienanalyse*, Wiesbaden: VS Verlag für Sozialwissenschaften, pp. 269-84.

Requate, J. (1995) *Journalismus als Beruf: Entstehung und Entwicklung des Journalistenberufs im 19. Jahrhundert. Deutschland im internationalen Vergleich*, Göttingen: Vandenhoeck & Ruprecht.

Riedmiller, T. (1988) *Arbeitslosigkeit als Thema der BILD-Zeitung*, Tübingen: Tübinger Vereinigung für Volkskunde.

Robbins, K. (1998) *Great Britain: Identities, Institutions and the Idea of Britishness*, London: Longman.

Robertson, G. & Nicol, A. (1992, third edition) *Media Law*, Harmondsworth: Penguin.

Rogge, J.-U. (1988) 'Gefühl, Verunsicherung und sinnliche Erfahrung: Zur Aneignung von populären Medien im Prozess der Zivilisation', *Publizistik*, (2-3): 243-63.

Roll, E. (1999) 'Vorschreiben, was die Leute denken', *Süddeutsche Zeitung*, 16 June, p. 3.

Rooney, D. (1998) 'Dynamics of the British Tabloid Press', *Javnost/The Public*, 5(3): 95-107.
— (2000) 'Thirty Years of Competition in the British Tabloid Press: The Mirror and the Sun 1968-1998', in C. Sparks & J. Tulloch (eds) *Tabloid Tales: Global Debates over Media Standards*, Oxford: Roman & Littlefield Publishers, pp. 91-110.
Rose, S. O. (2003) *Which People's War? National Identity and Citizenship in Britain, 1939-1945*, Oxford: Oxford University Press.
Röser, J. (1998) 'Methoden und Befunde der Medienforschung kritisch betrachtet. Probleme und Potentiale bei der Analyse weiblicher Fernsehinteressen', in P.C. Hall (ed) *Weibsbilder und TeleVisionen. 30. Mainzer Tage der Fernsehkritik des ZDF*, Mainz, pp. 119-26.
— (2000) *Fernsehgewalt im gesellschaftlichen Kontext: Eine Cultural Studies-Analyse über Medienaneignung in Dominanzverhältnissen*, Wiesbaden: Westdeutscher Verlag.
Rössler, P. (2002) 'Viele Programme, dieselben Themen? Vielfalt und Fragmentierung: Konvergenz und Divergenz in der aktuellen Berichterstattung. Eine Inhaltsanalyse internationaler TV-Nachrichten auf der Mikroebene', in K. Imhof, O. Jarren & R. Blum (eds) *Integration und Medien*, Wiesbaden: Westdeutscher Verlag, pp. 148-67.
Rowe, D. (2000) 'On Going Tabloid. A Preliminary Analysis', *Metro*, (121/122): 78-85.
Rust, H. (1984) *Die Zukunft der Mediengesellschaft. Ein ethnologischer Essay über Öffentlichkeit und Kommunikation*, Berlin: Spiess.
Sampson, A. (1996) 'The Crisis at the Heart of our Media', *British Journalism Review*, 7(3): 42-51.
Sandig, B. (1972) 'Bildzeitungstexte. Zur sprachlichen Gestaltung', in A. Rücktäschel (ed) *Sprache und Gesellschaft*, München: UTB, pp. 69-80.
Saxer, U., Bonfadelli, H., Hättenschwiler, W. & Schanne, M. (1979) *20 Jahre Blick: Analyse einer schweizerischen Boulevardzeitung*, Zürich: Seminar für Publizistikwissenschaft (SfP).
Schäfer, H. (1968) 'Die BILD-Zeitung, eine Ordnungsmacht im Spätkapitalismus', in H. Grossmann & O. Negt (eds) *Die Auferstehung der Gewalt: Springerblockade und politische Reaktion in der Bundesrepublik*, Frankfurt/ Main: Europ. Verl.-Anst., pp. 19-31.
Schiller, D. (1981) *Objectivity and the News. The Public and the Rise of Commercial Journalism*, Philadelphia: University of Pennsylvania Press.
Schirmer, S. (2001) *Die Titelseiten-Aufmacher der BILD-Zeitung im Wandel. Eine Inhaltsanalyse unter Berücksichtigung von Merkmalen journalistischer Qualität*, München: Verlag Reinhard Fischer.
Schlesinger, P. (1991) *Media, State and Nation: Political Violence and Collective Identities*, London: Sage.
Schneider, W. & Raue, P.-J. (1998) *Handbuch des Journalismus*, Hamburg: Rowohlt.

Schnell, R., Hill, P.B. & Esser, E. (1993, fourth edition) *Methoden der empirischen Sozialforschung*, München: Oldenbourg.

Schönbach, K. (1997) 'Tageszeitungen auf dem Prüfstand', *Sage & Schreibe*, (7&8): 48-51.

— (2000) 'Does Tabloidization Make German Local Newspapers Successful?' in C. Sparks & J. Tulloch (eds) *Tabloid Tales: Global Debates over Media Standards*, Oxford: Roman & Littlefield Publishers, pp. 63-74.

— (2004) 'A Balance Between Imitation and Contrast: What Makes Newspapers Successful? A Summary of Internationally Comparative Research', *Journal of Media Economics*, 17(3): 219-28.

Schönbach, K. & Peiser, W. (1997) 'Was wird aus dem Zeitunglesen?' *Zeitungen in den Neunzigern: Faktoren ihres Erfolges*, Bonn: ZV Zeitungs-Verlag Service, pp. 9-22.

Schönbach, K., Stürzebecher, D. & Schneider, B. (1994) 'Oberlehrer und Missionare? Das Selbstverständnis deutscher Journalisten', in F. Neidhardt (ed) *Öffentlichkeit, öffentliche Meinung, soziale Bewegungen*, Opladen: Westdeutscher Verlag, pp. 139-61.

Schuler, T. (1998) 'Lebenslänglich Kisch-Preisträger', *Berliner Zeitung*, 26 November.

Schütte, W. (1996) 'Mündlichkeit und Schriftlichkeit im Fernsehen', in B.U. Biere (ed) Tübingen: Narr Verlag, pp. 101-34.

Schwacke, B. (1983) *Kriminalitätsdarstellung in der Presse*, Frankfurt am Main: Lang.

Seaman, R. (1992) 'Active Audience Theory: Pointless Populism', *Media, Culture & Society*, (11): 301-11.

Seymour-Ure, C. (1994) 'The Media in Postwar British Politics', *Parliamentary Affairs*, 47: 530-47.

— (2001, second edition) *The British Press and Broadcasting since 1945*, Oxford: Blackwell Publishers.

Smith, A. (1979) *The Newspaper. An International History*, London: Thames & Hudson.

Smith, A. & Porter, D. (eds) (2004) *Sport and National Identity in the Post-War World*, London: Routledge.

Smith, M. (1994) *Paper Lions: The Scottish Press and National Identity*, Edinburgh: Polygon.

Snoddy, R. (1992) *The Good, the Bad and the Unacceptable: The Hard News about the British Press*, London: Faber & Faber.

Sontheimer, M. (1995) 'Ein hartes Blatt. Journalismus an der Grenze der Geschmacklosigkeit', *Spiegel Special*, (1): 38-43.

Sparks, C. (1998) 'Introduction', *Javnost/The Public: Tablodization and the Media*, 5(3): 5-31.

— (1999) 'The Press', in J. Stokes & A. Reading (eds) *The Media in Britain: Current Debates and Developments*, Basingstoke/New York: Palgrave, pp. 41-60.

— (2000) 'Introduction: The Panic over Tabloid News', in C. Sparks & J. Tulloch (eds) *Tabloid Tales: Global Debates over Media Standards*, Oxford: Roman & Littlefield Publishers, pp. 1-40.

Sparrow, A. & Stratton, A. (2009) 'Tory "contract" with the Sun threatens to cloud BBC's judgement, warns Mandelson', *The Guardian*, 12 November, 8.

Spiegel Online (2006a) '"Bild"-Fehler: Korrektur von ihrer schönsten Saite', available at http://www.spiegel.de/kultur/gesellschaft/0,1518,426712,00.html (accessed 24 August 2007).

— (2006b) 'Germany's Patriotism Problem: Just Don't Fly the Flag', available at http://www.spiegel.de/international/0,1518,411948,00.html (accessed 21 November 2009).

— (2006c) 'It's Okay to be German Again', available at http://www.spiegel.de/international/a-420558.html (accessed 21 November 2009).

Steel, M. (2009) 'You almost have to feel sorry for Gordon Brown', *The Independent*, 11 November, 31.

Stevens, R. (1998) 'For "Dumbing Down" Read "Accessible"', *British Journalism Review*, 9(4): 32-35.

Storey, J. (1993) *An Introductory Guide to Cultural Theory and Popular Culture*, Athens, Georgia: University of Georgia Press.

Straubhaar, J.D. (1991) 'Beyond Media Imperialism: Asymmetrical Interdependence and Cultural Proximity', *Critical Studies in Mass Communication*, (8): 39-59.

Strinati, D. (2004) *An Introduction to Theories of Popular Culture*, London: Routledge.

Stumberger, R. (2007) 'Die neue Zerhackstückelung der Welt – Der Bürger-Journalismus als Farce der Partizipation', available at http://www.heise.de/tp/r4/artikel/24/24364/1.html (accessed 9 February 2010).

Sundermeyer, O. (2006) 'Leser-Reporter: Werden wir jetzt alle Paparazzi? *Frankfurter Allgemeine Zeitung*, 25 July, p. 36.

Tamir, Y. (1997) 'Reflections on Patriotism', in D. Bar-Tal & E. Staub (eds) *Patriotism in the Lives of Individuals and Nations*, Chicago: Nelson-Hall Publishers, pp. 23-41.

Taylor, S.J. (1992) *Shock! Horror! The Tabloids in Action*, London: Black Swan.

Telegraph, T. (2009) 'Hillsborough Timeline. It is twenty years since 96 Liverpool fans lost their lives at Hillsborough', available at http://www.telegraph.co.uk/sport/football/leagues/premierleague/liverpool/5150076/Hillsborough-timeline.html (accessed 27 January 2010).

Thomas, T. (2003) *Deutsch-Stunden: Zur Konstruktion nationaler Identität im Fernsehtalk*, Frankfurt/Main: Campus Verlag.

Thomaß, B. (1998) *Journalistische Ethik: Ein Vergleich der Diskurse in Frankreich, Grossbritannien und Deutschland*, Opladen: Westdt. Verlag.

Thompson, E.P. (1963) *The Making of the English Working Class*, London: Victor Gollancz.

Thompson, J.B. (1993) 'The Theory of the Public Sphere', *Theory, Culture and Society*, 10(3): 179-87.

Thull, M. (2005a) 'Ein Medienstar – bis zuletzt: Das Sterben von Papst Johannes Paul II über Tage das Fernsehthema', *Funkkorrespondenz*, (14): 3-6.

— (2005b) '"Papa Ratzi": Der neue Papst und die Medien', *Funkkorrespondenz*, (16): 3-4.

Triandis, H.C. (1995) *Individualism & Collectivism*, Boulder/Oxford: Westview Press.

Tunstall, J. (1996) *Newspaper Power: The New National Press in Britain*, Oxford: Clarendon Press.

Turner, B. S. (1994) 'Postmodern Culture/Modern Citizens', in B. v. Steenbergen (ed) *The Condition of Citizenship*, London: Sage, pp. 153-68.

Turner, G. (1999) 'Tabloidization, Journalism and the Possibility of Critique', *International Journal of Cultural Studies*, 2(1): 59-76.

Turner, G. (2003, third edition) *British Cultural Studies: An Introduction*, London: Routledge.

Tzortzis, A. (2006) 'Amateurs Get in on the Paparazzi Beat', available at http://www.nytimes.com/2006/08/14/technology/14pix.html?_r=1 (accessed 9 February 2010).

Uribe, R. & Gunter, B. (2004) 'Research Note: The Tabloidization of British Tabloids', *European Journal of Communication*, 19(3): 387-402.

Victor, P. (1994) '"News at Ten" Takes a Turn Towards the Tabloids', *Independent on Sunday*, 22 May, p. 2.

Virchow, F. (2008) '"Fordern und fördern" – Zum Gratifikations-, Sanktions- und Gerechtigkeitsdiskurs in der BILD-Zeitung', in U. Wischermann & T. Thomas (eds) *Medien – Diversität – Ungleichheit: Zur medialen Konstruktion sozialer Differenz*, Wiesbaden: VS Verlag für Sozialwissenschaften, pp. 254-62.

Viroli, M. (1997) *For Love of Country: An Essay on Patriotism and Nationalism*, Oxford: Oxford University Press.

Vogtel, R. (1986) 'Die Gefühle der Bild-Zeitung', *Psychologie und Gesellschaftskritik*, Jg. 10(1): 41 pp.

Voss, C. (1999) *Textgestaltung und Verfahren der Emotionalisierung in der BILD-Zeitung*, Frankfurt am Main: Lang.

Wagner, B. (2007) '"Bild – unabhängig – überparteilich"? Die Wahlberichterstattung der erfolgreichsten Boulevardzeitung Deutschlands', in B. Weßels, F. Brettschneider & O. Niedermayer (eds) *Die Bundestagswahl 2005: Analysen des Wahlkampfes und der Wahlergebnisse*, Wiesbaden: VS Verlag für Sozialwissenschaften, pp. 145-70.

Wallraff, G. (1977) *Der Aufmacher. Der Mann, der bei Bild Hans Esser war*, Köln: Kiepenheuer & Witsch.

— (1979) *Zeugen der Anklage. Die 'Bild'-beschreibung wird fortgesetzt,* Köln: Kiepenheuer & Witsch.
— (1981) *Das BILD-Handbuch bis zum Bildausfall,* Hamburg: Konkret Literatur Verlag.
— (1985) *Bild-Störung: Ein Handbuch,* Köln: Kiepenheuer & Witsch.
Waugh, P. (2009) 'Howzat, Murdoch! Brown takes his revenge', *Evening Standard,* 12 November, pp. 1; 8-9.
Weber, K. (1978) *Die Sprache der Sexualität in der BILD-Zeitung. Ein interdisziplinärer Versuch über formal-synthetische Literatur,* Berlin: Guhl.
Weight, R. (2002) *Patriots: National Identity in Britain 1940-2000,* Basingstoke; Oxford: Macmillan.
Weischenberg, S., Löffelholz, M. & Scholl, A. (1994) 'Merkmale und Einstellungen von Journalisten', *Media Perspektiven,* (4): 154-67.
Wende, D. (1990) *Über die medizinische Berichterstattung von Krebs in Tageszeitungen und deren kritische Bewertung. Dargestellt am Beispiel der "Frankfurter Allgemeinen Zeitung" und der "Bild-Zeitung" in den Jahren 1974, 1976 und 1978. Dissertation an der Universität Bochum,* Bochum: Brockmeyer.
Wiggershaus, R. (1994) *The Frankfurt School: Its History, Theories and Political Significance. Translated by Michael Robertson,* Cambridge: Polity Press.
Wilke, J. (2000) *Grundzüge der Medien- und Kommunikationsgeschichte: Von den Anfängen bis ins 20. Jahrhundert,* Köln/Weimar/Wien: Böhlau Verlag.
Williams, R. (1961) *The Long Revolution,* London: Chatto & Windus.
Willmann, H. (1974) *Geschichte der Arbeiter-Illustrierten Zeitung: 1921-1938,* Berlin: deb Verlag Das Europ. Buch/Dietz-Verlag.
Worcester, R.M. (1998) 'Demographics and Values: What the British Public Reads and What it Thinks About its Newspapers', in M. Bromley & H. Stephenson (eds) *Sex, Lies and Democracy: The Press and the Public,* London/New York: Longman, pp. 39-48.
World Association of Newspapers and News Publishers (2009) *World Press Trends 2009,* Paris: World Association of Newspapers and News Publishers.
Zaller, J. (2003) 'A New Standard of News Quality: Burglar Alarms for the Monitorial Citizen', *Political Communication,* 20(2): 109-30.
Zeit Online (2006) 'Magie der Heiterkeit', available at http://www.zeit.de/2006/25/01_leit_2_25 (accessed 24 August 2007).
Zillmann, D. (1988) 'Mood Management Through Communication Choices', *American Behavioral Scientist,* 31(3): 327-40.
van Zoonen, L. (2005) *Entertaining the citizen: When Politics and Popular Culture Converge,* Lanham, MD: Rowman & Littlefield.

# Appendix

## FOCUS GROUP GUIDE (ENGLISH VERSION)

Inspirational to the design of this guide were the ones devised by Hill (2005: appendix), Liebes and Katz (1990: 159 pp.) as well as Bruck and Stocker (1996: 58 pp.) to whom I owe acknowledgements.

### Introduction

- Welcome;
- This is for a research project we're doing about newspapers;
- *The Sun* = Britain's most popular newspaper;
- We'd like to know what readers think about it, your views;
- What we're doing over the next weeks is asking people to get together in small groups like this and talk to us about their opinion on *The Sun;*
- What we're interested in is to learn what you like and what you hate about *The Sun;*
- No right and wrong answers; important to me to hear your opinion, also opposing views;
- We also have a few back issues here to show you and talk about that you might have seen before;
- No market research, no work for *The Sun*, but for my own Ph.D. research;
- We have to record this discussion so for the purpose of the recording please try not to talk all at once;
- Feel free to talk to each other rather than me (supposed to be a group discussion rather than interview);
- Like to start with a short introduction: Names, and when and where you normally read *The Sun.*

## Part 1: Likes & Dislikes

### What are *The Sun*'s strengths and weaknesses in your opinion?
(refer to last question in the questionnaire)

Probe:
- Gossip stories (also in sports section);
- Page three girls/page three lads
- Easy read;
- Headlines;
- Telling how it is
- Service/advice;
- Investigative journalism;
- Made-up stories and lies.


## Part 2: Specific Themes

### Patriotism/National Pride/National Identity
(media stimulus 'Got the Bastards')

**What do you think about the way *The Sun* handled this issue?**

Probe:
- Headline;
- Patriotism in general;
- Role of sports reporting (example past scenario: British Lions winning Rugby World Cup; example future scenario: England winning Football World Cup).

### Politics & politics
(media stimulus 'Red smoke for Labour')

**What role does *The Sun* play in Politics?**

Probe:
- Do you think *The Sun* could win an election campaign for a particular party?
- What about other issues; can *The Sun* influence other things?

## Scandal/Treatment of People

(media stimulus 'Kate's £200 a day cocaine habit')

**How does *The Sun* treat people?**

Probe:
- Right and wrong ways (example controversial case: paedophile mix-up in 2003)
- Ordinary people v. celebrities.


## Part 3: Image of *The Sun*

**Is there anything that makes the paper particularly special in your opinion, perhaps compared to other newspapers?**

Probe:
- Difference between reading *The Sun* and reading other papers.

**How would you describe a typical *Sun* reader?**

Probe:
- What distinguishes you from a typical *Sun* reader?
- Who else reads *The Sun*?/Who does not read *The Sun*?

**How do people react to you reading *The Sun*?**

Probe:
- Friends & family
- Strangers (reading it on the bus/in a café)


## Sum up and questions

**Is there anything else that you would like to discuss?**